In *The Limits of American Literary Ideology in Pound and Emerson*, Cary Wolfe analyzes the dynamics of radical individualism and the sort of cultural critique it generates in Ralph Waldo Emerson and Ezra Pound. The book aims to demonstrate that any form of individualism modeled on the logic and structure of private property will always reproduce the very contradictions and alienations that it set out to criticize and remedy. Part of what makes this study unique and important is that it employs a critique of the ideology of individualism – an ideology still powerful and seductive in contemporary America – to build a bridge between major figures from two literary periods (modernism and American romanticism) often viewed in stark opposition. In doing so, this study is nearly alone in extending the critical paradigms and techniques of one of the most exciting new fields of cultural critique (the so-called New Americanist criticism) to examine a period (modernism) and a type of writing (poetry) that it has largely ignored.

CAMBRIDGE STUDIES IN AMERICAN LITERATURE AND CULTURE

The Limits of American Literary Ideology in Pound and Emerson

Cambridge Studies in American Literature and Culture

Editor
Eric Sundquist, Vanderbilt University

Founding editor
Albert Gelpi, Stanford University

Advisory Board
Nina Baym, University of Illinois, Champaign-Urbana
Sacvan Bercovitch, Harvard University
Albert Gelpi, Stanford University
Myra Jehlen, University of Pennsylvania
Carolyn Porter, University of California, Berkeley
Robert Stepto, Yale University
Tony Tanner, King's College, Cambridge University

Continued on pages following the Index

The Limits of
American Literary Ideology
in Pound and Emerson

CARY WOLFE
Indiana University, Bloomington

CAMBRIDGE
UNIVERSITY PRESS

Published by the Press Syndicate of the University of Cambridge
The Pitt Building, Trumpington Street, Cambridge CB2 IRP
40 West 20th Street, New York, NY 10011–4211, USA
10 Stamford Road, Oakleigh, Melbourne 3166, Australia

First published 1993

Printed in the United States of America

Library of Congress Cataloging-in-Publication Data
Wolfe, Cary
The limits of American literary ideology in Pound and Emerson / Cary
Wolfe.
 p. cm. – (Cambridge studies in American literature and culture ; 69)
Includes bibliographical references and index.
ISBN 0–521–44555–8
1. American literature – History and criticism. 2. Individualism
in literature. 3. Emerson, Ralph Waldo, 1803–1882 – Political and
social views. 4. Pound, Ezra, 1885–1972 – Political and social
views. 5. Politics and literature – United States. 6. Literature
and society – United States. I. Title. II. Series.
PS169.I53W65   1993
810.9′ 358 – dc20   93–18475
                                                        CIP

A catalog record for this book is available from the British Library.

ISBN 0–521–44555–8 hardback

Permissions

The last section of Chapter 5 originally appeared, in slightly different
form, in *American Literature*, which has graciously granted permission
to reprint.

Quotations from the works of Ezra Pound are used by permission
of New Directions Publishing Corporation:

Ezra Pound: *Selected Prose 1909–1965*. Copyright © 1963 by The Estate
of Ezra Pound.
Ezra Pound: *Selected Letters of Ezra Pound 1907–1941*. Copyright © 1950
by Ezra Pound.
Ezra Pound: *Pavannes and Divagations*. Copyright © 1958 by Ezra Pound.
Ezra Pound: *Literary Essays of Ezra Pound*. Copyright © 1935 by Ezra
Pound.
Ezra Pound: *Personae*. Copyright © 1926 by Ezra Pound.

Contents

Acknowledgments

Writing literary criticism is at once a very solitary *and* cooperative kind of undertaking, and because of this one incurs two very different kinds of debts in working through a project of this sort. As for the second type of debt, the communal one, it is hard to know where they begin and end – what is owed and to whom for specific critical engagements, for broader theoretical insights that proved formative for the course of one's own work, or just for the more daily intellectual kinship and encouragement that make all of this possible and rewarding in the first place. Let me try then, at least, to manage my debts by expressing my gratitude here to those friends and colleagues who had a particularly direct hand in the conception and completion of this project. As for the others, you will recognize yourselves, I hope, in these pages.

Townsend Ludington's graduate seminar in American studies at Chapel Hill years ago provided the generous latitude I needed for the initial, uncertain explorations that eventually resulted in this study. From Eric Sundquist and the readers at Cambridge University Press, from Cathy Davidson and Fredric Jameson at Duke University, and from my colleagues Patrick Brantlinger and Mary Favret at Indiana, I received invaluable critical advice whenever I asked for it and encouragement when I needed it. Eric Wolfe's help with manuscript preparation kept the process on schedule, and funding from the office of Research and the University Graduate School at Indiana University, Bloomington, helped bring the project to completion. Before, during, and after this project, for all sorts of things, I owe a special debt of gratitude to Frank Lentricchia – friend, teacher, instigator.

As for the first kind of debt, the kind having to do with the solitary nature of our work, I know exactly who deserves credit, even if I can never know how much: Woody, for his unblinking company, and most of all Luccia, for the many modes of her understanding and support.

Bloomington, Indiana
July 1993

ix

Introduction

When I first began work on this study, I was fortunate enough to have at my disposal two superb research libraries, one at Duke and one at Chapel Hill. But neither collection, I soon discovered, included a hard copy of Ezra Pound's *Jefferson and/or Mussolini* – an eclectic and disturbing text that was central to Pound, crucial to my understanding of him, but little known outside Poundian circles and often marginalized within them. Eventually, as dumb luck would have it, I stumbled upon a copy in the political science section of a local used-book store whose main holdings, it seemed, were in gardening and science fiction. It would be easy, of course, to overread the politics of this curious little episode, but let me suggest that the eventual conclusions we might reach about its significance would likely reproduce one of the two dominant modes of Pound criticism in the past forty years: the conspiracy theory, which imagines that the traditional Pound industry has engaged in a more or less conscious suppression of the embarrassingly political Pound (who is distilled in texts like *Jefferson and/or Mussolini*), the better to defend the supposedly autonomous work of the poet; and the autonomy-of-art theory of those who would so conspire.

My characterization of the situation is obviously schematic, but it serves to illustrate my larger point: that critics who would engage Pound's work find themselves framed from the outset by a kind of critical cold war, one that forces them into something resembling the role of Marc Antony at the funeral in *Julius Caesar*. Over the years, Pound critics have come too often to *either* bury *or* praise him, to constitute him by turns either as a Fascist and anti-Semite in his very fiber and genesis or as a literary genius whose "true" self (the self that produced the stalwart poetry of high modernism) can somehow be separated from the disturbing and sometimes revolting political and racial proclamations of the sort we find in Pound's later prose and in his Rome Radio speeches.[1]

If I have just glanced synoptically at the theoretical oversimplification

1

of this all-too-habitual condition of Pound studies, then let me be a bit clearer about its critically disabling consequences. A politically engaged criticism of Pound would, by definition, need to move beyond this displacement of broad economic, social, and ideological problems onto Pound, the unique – and therefore romanticized – subject of admiration or revulsion. It is here, at this juncture and against this pressing critical necessity, that the either-orist imperative so often at work in Pound studies exerts its institutionally powerful and politically disabling force. If we want to come to terms with the ideological character of Pound's cultural project, then we need to explore precisely what is ideological about it: its internally contradictory, fractured, and self-conflicted nature,[2] its capacity to appeal in some respects even as it repels in others.

In practical terms, the central contradiction that a political reading of Pound needs to engage is that his palpable attractions – his early defense of individual and cultural difference in the face of economic Taylorization and cultural commodification, and his recognition that problems of aesthetics are at once fully social and even, finally, economic – are inextricably wedded to his reprehensible obsessions. And to do justice to that complexity we must work, in turn, to avoid making one of those dimensions of Pound a mere epiphenomenon, a mere negative moment, of the other. Only then can we provide an adequate picture of Pound's literary ideology in its full range and power, instead of a caricature of it. And only then can we begin to dispel the critically facile and politically naive impression that once we have unmasked Pound's ideological failures or declared them beside the aesthetic point, we have once again made the world safe for literary democracy. For my purposes here, we need to recognize that Ezra Pound's literary ideology has at least as much in common with Ralph Waldo Emerson's brand of American individualism as it does with Benito Mussolini's Italian fascism, and we need to realize at the same time that this is not necessarily good news. Pound's liberationist Emersonian side cannot be separated from his authoritarian fascist side: That, it seems to me, is the disturbing and instructive political point that the polarization of Pound studies so often mitigates against.

As I have already suggested, it is not my intention here to replace that polarization – or the differences kept too neatly separate by it – with my own totalizing structure. Instead, I want to reframe those differences (between the "good" and "bad" Pound, a "bad" Pound and a "good" Emerson, and even, indirectly, between American romanticism and modernism) within a larger literary ideology inscribed in Emerson's work and reproduced in striking detail, but with important differences, in the cultural project of Ezra Pound. This is not to suggest, of course, that there is some sort of monolithic American literary ideology that is immune in its totalizing grandeur to the concrete determinations of class, race, gender, ethnicity, and other historical contingencies. Such a reading would describe not the truth of the literary ideology at work here (not, in other words, the historical and material conditions that make it possible to think that ideology in the first place) but rather the unchanging, imaginary content which that ideology would have us believe. It *is* to suggest, however, that in both bodies of writing we find a powerful ideological structure that can accommodate and indeed make use of historical, cultural, and individual differences, if only to politically recontain and disarm then by reconstituting them in light of some overarching principle (Emerson's "Reason" or "Oversoul," say, or Pound's Confucian "way") by which the *value* of those differences is determined.

My point, then, is not that Emerson is an important and unrecognized "influence" on Pound.[3] Nor am I arguing that Pound's unexpected linkage with Emerson diminishes his relations to the many different figures in American history and culture with whom he felt common cause (Thomas Jefferson, the Adamses, Andrew Jackson, Martin Van Buren, Walt Whitman, and Henry James are the most storied examples). The Pound/Emerson connection does not compete with these other prominent and important influences, because, in a fundamental sense, it encompasses and comprehends them.

What I mean by this may be clarified by reference to a recent representative reading of Pound's relationship with two of his more illustrious American forebears: Thomas Jefferson and John Adams. Those relations changed, of course, and as Reed Way Dasenbrock had recently argued, Pound's shift in focus and admiration from Jefferson to Adams in the 1930s is politically symptomatic of his deepening infatuation with Italian fascism, and specifically with Benito Mussolini.[4] According to Dasenbrock, when Jefferson appears in the middle cantos, he is admired as representative of *virtù*, of the ethical fortitude, intellectual energy, and pragmatic innovation that must be embodied in the man of state if the republic is to fend off the corruption that always accompanies commerce.[5] Adams, on the other hand, comes to supplant Jefferson in Pound's political concerns more and more as the decade of the thirties wears on – chiefly, Dasenbrock argues, because Pound becomes more interested during this period in the techniques, mechanisms, and pragmatics of government. Increasingly, Pound found not Jefferson's ethical example but Adams's constitutional theorization (and specifically his insistence on the strong, single leader) a more promising means of ensuring that the state would not succumb to the debasements of oligarchy.[6]

But the more fundamental point here, it seems to me, is that Pound's interest in both strategies is driven by his dedication above all else to the sanctity of the individual, whom such principles and techniques are meant to serve in the first place and who constitutes their raison d'être. Pound's abiding concern with the individual, in other words, is what the Russian formalists would call "the motivation of the device" for his interest in Jefferson and Adams. After all, Jeffersonian innovation is not a good in and of itself – indeed, it might well be a recipe for anarchy – nor is the political machinery of Adams, which constitutes for Pound just so much legalistic scaffolding if not erected for ethically defensible purposes. The strategies of both Jefferson and Adams, in other words, are just that – strategies. They are secondary phenomena built atop a more fundamental commitment to an ideologically prior form of individualism that it is their duty to support and help realize.[7]

So I am not so much questioning the importance in Pound's work of acknowledged American influences such as Jefferson's agrarian ideal or Adams's more aristocratic concern with political stability as I am reframing them. And in any case, it is important to remind ourselves in the course of that reframing that whatever Pound himself may have thought about his inheritance of those principles and ideals, it is only a part of the story, and in many ways the least dependable part. It is perfectly possible, in other words, that Pound is an indifferent critic of Pound. The same might be said, too, of our other subject, Ralph Waldo Emerson. Emerson felt little affinity for Jacksonianism. Indeed, some of his most bitter criticism is reserved for what he called "this rank, rabble party, this Jacksonism of the country."[8] But, as Michael T. Gilmore has shown, his social critique is nevertheless thoroughly enmeshed in Jacksonianism's most fundamental ideological characteristic: Both "wanted to preserve the virtues of a simple agrarian republic without sacrificing the rewards and conveniences of modern capitalism."[9]

My central point, then, is that Pound's connection with Emerson must be viewed not as a relationship of conscious affinity, admiration, or influence but as one of *ideological* kinship in a broad cultural logic whose operations extend far beyond the ability of the individual to master them by personal fiat or disarm them by soul-searching and self-reflection. It is in this sense that Pound's relation to Emerson encompasses and comprehends his relations to Adams, Jeffferson, and other freely acknowledged sources. And it is from this vantage that we can see how Pound's more familiar political and cultural inheritances were motivated from the very outset of his career by an individualism whose radical, all-or-nothing character is quintessentially Emersonian.

Part of what marks Pound's individualism as Emersonian is its sheer intensity, but it is also something more, something built into its very structure. In both writers, those overarching principles ensuring the sanctity of individual difference have nothing to do, it turns out, with the individual; indeed, they are utterly *other than* the self, and their power resides in the fact that they are not contingent upon all of those things (gender, race, regional upbringing, and so on) that we usually associate with distinctive selfhood. For Emerson and for Pound, the paradoxical fact about individual difference – the very engine of their social critique and the origin and end of their cultural politics – is that the individual can ascend to the pinnacle of selfhood only by disappearing at the very moment of its attainment.

In Emerson's corpus this strange and powerful form of individualism finds its supreme expression in what is probably its most famous appearance (or disappearance) in American literature, in the "transparent eyeball" passage in *Nature*, where Emerson imagines it with maximum compression: "I am nothing; I see all." In Pound, it finds a different, more restrained voice in his invocation, in Canto XIII, of the Confucian shibboleth "each in his nature." Here, as in Emerson, the self achieves true selfhood only by becoming transparent to – subject to – the enduring laws and rhythms of a larger natural and ethical totality. What separates Emerson's fully realized self from the monomania of, say, Melville's Ahab is that the Emersonian self has become "part or parcel of God." In the same way, what prevents Pound's Confucian imperative from serving as carte blanche for rampant egoism and anarchy is that the subject can have his nature only if nature has him. "His nature," it turns out, is not "his" at all. We can all possess different things (our natures, our selves) only if we all possess – or more precisely are *possessed by* – the same thing: Emerson's God or Spirit, Pound's Confucian "way."

If all of this sounds familiar, it should, for it describes nothing other than the central organizing structure of the economic and ideological totality of Pound's and Emerson's America: private property. It is this structure that provides the conditions of possibility – the social "logic of content," to borrow Fredric Jameson's phrase – for the radical individualism of Pound's and Emerson's "American literary ideology." I have given it that name in my title because that ideological structure seems to me so remarkably pervasive in American culture that it is nearly invisible. Although I cannot pursue that argument in any convincing way here, it is worth noting that many of our most exciting and persuasive critics have found the structuring force of the logic of property at work in many different registers in American culture: Wai-chee Dimock in Herman Melville's "poetics of individualism"; Walter Benn Michaels in "the logic of naturalism"; Carolyn Porter in "the plight of the participant observer" in Emerson, Henry James, and others; Michael T. Gilmore in the canonical works of American romanticism; and Houston A. Baker, Jr., in what he calls the "fundamental, 'subtextual' dimension of Afro-American discourse," that is, the "fully *commercial* view" found in the slave narratives of Frederick Douglass and many others, where the structure of oppression at work in the logic of property is unmasked when the self, ironically and tragically, tries to wrest *private* ownership of itself away from another.[10]

My argument, then, is that the radical individualism of both Pound and Emerson reproduces the structure and contradictions of private property in conceiving self-realization in terms of the logic of self-possession, that is, in essentially, if sometimes obliquely, Lockean terms. What makes their cultural projects distinctively and, as it were, normatively American, however, is how relentlessly they push the structure of Lockean self-ownership to its conceptual and ideological limits. In their emphatic insistence upon the central value of the autonomous, inalienable property of self, Pound and Emerson map, as few others have, the ideological attractions and dangers of radical individualism. They articulate what we might well think of as the idealistic and dangerous American perfection of Lockean liberalism.[11]

We can sharpen our sense of the specificity of this kind of individualism in Pound and Emerson by briefly contrasting it with another famous literary expression of American individualism, namely, Walt Whitman's. Even though Whitman's democratic impulses (if not his rather more proletarian ones) are shared by Pound and Emerson, the Whitmanian self is, structurally speaking, a *decentered* subjectivity fundamentally at odds with the self-possession of Emersonian self-reliance and Poundian *virtù*. The "Myself" of Whitman's *Song*, Larzer Ziff writes, is "clearly close kin to Emerson's Me," but for Whitman "the same all-dominant individual is far more social. His kingdom includes nature but it is finally a kingdom peopled with fellow men," a "swarming collectivity."[12] The Whitmanian self is partner to what Donald Pease has called a "mass logic" in which "the masses free or 'untie' the individual from bondage to his own person," so that he "both completes himself, hence knows perfect liberty, and experiences himself completed by everything else, hence knows democratic equality."[13]

The Whitmanian self, in other words, is clearly *other*-reliant in a way that is intrinsically antithetical to the individualism of Emerson and Pound. In this connection we need only contrast Whitman's "man-en-masse" and "body electric" with Emerson's many proverbial characterizations of self-reliance (and with the biting critiques of the Jacksonian crowd which that doctrine generated). And as for Pound, he may have acknowledged his bonds to Whitman when he allowed in 1909 that "the vital part of my message, taken from the sap and fibre of America, is the same as his." But he nevertheless found Whitman "an exceedingly nauseating pill" whose "crudity is an exceeding [*sic*] great stench"[14] because his poetry was driven too much by "his time and his people" and too little by the *virtù*, the centered individuality, which might organize that social and historical content into the sort of poetry that Pound himself wanted to write, poetry of precision and discrimination.

Whitman's "mass logic," then, throws into relief the structural specificity and ideological kinship of Pound and Emerson's individualism. But to identify that kinship as "ideological" is not by any means to say that the critiques generated by their version of individualism were not rhetorically powerful, socially volatile, and potentially dangerous to the status quo. It is to say, however, that the Lockean individualist basis of those social critiques operates as an ideological "strategy of containment"[15] serving to disarm and delimit their full economic and political implications by recasting what are properly issues of fundamental economic and political structure into problems of ethics and personal conduct.[16] Thus, both writers reproduce on the level of the subject the basic economic structure (in this case, private property) that organizes the kind of society against which their social critiques rebelled in the first place. And this is how ideology performs its political work, by providing a safe staging ground for democratic debate and pluralist critique, while at the same time siphoning off potentially revolutionary discontent and discord.[17]

Within that space of containment, though, the ideology of radical individualism in Pound and Emerson ranged freely and often tempestuously between the polar extremes of democracy and elitism, libertarianism and authoritarianism. From beginning to end, both explored, plumbed, but never abandoned those extremes, and in neither one do we find a clearly sustained and coherent development away from a democratic position and toward a more consolidated elitist one (or vice versa). We should not be surprised, I think, to discover this sort of instability in the individualism of Pound and Emerson; indeed, the fundamental point here *is* that very instability. A subject that is conceived on the Lockean model (the internal contradictions of which are only intensified by what I have called its American extension and perfection) is bound to be extremely unstable, as unstable, in fact, as private property itself, that strange entity which is riven by, indeed *constituted* by, contradiction, because it is both a concrete object with a use value and yet merely a vehicle for the abstract exchange value it bears. Like private property under capitalism, the Emersonian or Poundian self is sovereign and inalienable and yet is threatened at every moment with alienation and effacement. After all, as Frank Lentricchia points out, private property "is property only if it *is* alienable."[18]

It is in this sense, then – and not in their overt beliefs, attitudes, or preferences – that Pound and Emerson are genealogically bound by a shared ideology. At the same time, however, it is important to remember that ideological structures predispose and delimit, but do not wholly determine in advance, their effects in practice. The same ideological formation may produce (to use Kenneth Burke's appropriately inelegant formulation) very different "unintended by-products," and we must pay attention to "how the particular choice of materials and methods in which to embody the ideal gives rise to conditions somewhat at variance with the spirit of the ideal."[19] This is surely the case with Pound's growing endorsement of fascist state power in the thirties, which is nevertheless driven by an intense Jeffersonian desire to protect the individual against rampant corruption and exploitation by the powers of international finance.[20] And it is just as surely wrong, as one recent critic has reminded us, to conflate "Emerson's commitment to the appropriation of nature with its future applications by corporate trusts or land-grabbing expansionists."[21]

For my purposes here, this means that we need not feel compelled to argue *either* that Pound and Emerson are both fascists *or* that neither is simply because they both reproduce the ideology I will be investigating in the following pages. As even casual readers of Pound and Emerson will know, that ideology leads to very different (and sometimes very real) political consequences in these two writers. It does so in large part for a reason that is fully on the surface of both bodies of work yet is easy to overlook: Pound and Emerson, as we shall see, adhere to conceptions of praxis and the value of action that could not be more different. What Pound called the "volitionist" imperative of his later ethics and economics led him to actualize the disturbing possibilities for practice contained in the ideology of Emerson but held in check by the latter's fiercely idealist impatience with social and political programs of any kind. We must not only allow that difference between Pound and Emerson, I think, but invite it, because only by doing so can we begin to understand the possibilities and dangers of practice contained in our cultural hopes and aesthetic ideals. Only by doing so can we begin to trace the full range of those very different orbits that unexpectedly encircle the same ideological firmament, expansive and yet familiar.

In the first four chapters, I focus primarily on Pound's career through the period 1917–1918, when he sought to establish his vision of a culture that would respect "the peripheries of the individual" and would enable the self to maintain what Emerson, in an apocalyptic moment for American culture, had called "an original relation to the universe." Pound found the defense of individual difference put into exemplary cultural practice not in Emerson, however, but in the stylistic rigor of Henry James, whom Pound praised for his hatred of oppression and his "continuing labor for individual freedom." Interestingly enough though,

James traced *his* own sense of individual difference back to Emerson, whose visits to the James household Henry vividly remembered, and whose "independent and original way" was to find even more forceful expression in the later, pragmatist career of Henry's brother, William. The Jameses, then, serve as a bridge spanning the years and stylistic differences between Pound and Emerson, and they serve for my purposes to locate Pound not as a modernist so much as the inheritor of a very American lineage of individualist cultural practice. It was that lineage which would be maintained in Pound's reviews of Robert Frost, another writer of difference whom Pound in London vigorously "boomed," as he put it, despite his own most deeply ingrained tastes and preferences. In doing so, Pound made good on his central claim for the role of "The Serious Artist": that he always works toward "a recognition of differences, of the right of differences to exist, of interest in finding things different."

Like Emerson both early and late, who recognized that "the machine unmans the user" by turning "the whole man" into a mere appendage of his productive means (or the American Scholar into a "bookworm"), Pound's early social critique was in open revolt against capitalist modernity's tendency to view the self as a spectral abstraction, as a merely economic agent – as "a unit," Pound wrote in "Provincialism the Enemy," "a piece of the machine." We tend to forget that Pound was born only three years after Emerson's death; it is just as easy to overlook how much continuity exists between Emerson's economic moment and Pound's own. Because of the extremely rapid and unimpeded development of assembly-line capitalism in mid-nineteenth-century New England, Emerson was able to glimpse, before the fact as it were, the alienating productive matrix of modernism that Pound would later confront in its fully developed form. For the early Pound, as for Marx before him and Antonio Gramsci after him, the Taylorization and commodification of capitalist society threatened the very vitality and potency of the individual and aimed to turn the self into a desexualized deformation, a "gelded ant." Against the materialism of Marx and Gramsci, however, and in tandem with the idealism of his ideological ancestor Emerson, Pound believed that the answer to those structures of oppression and alienation lay not in collective economic transformation but rather within the individual who could somehow escape his or her economic determinations by holding fast to the vital realm of culture, the realm of freedom.

From the very outset of his career, however, Pound would encounter a system of *literary* production that seemed a frighteningly direct expression of this imperious economic base and that tempered his humanist idealism with the unmistakably material constraints he confronted every

day in his attempt to establish himself as a poet and critic. Extending
Emerson's incisive critique of conformity in "The American Scholar,"
and voicing what Emerson had called "the disgust which the principles
on which business is managed inspire," Pound identified in the big
American magazines (*Harper's*, the *Atlantic*) and in anthologies like
Palgrave's *Golden Treasury* a "system of publishing control" that promoted conformity in the writer and the writer's products and economically enforced that conformity in the literary marketplace. What Pound
called "the style of 1880" may have been good for the magazine business, but it was an anathema to a culture of individual difference and
social change.

In these terms, Pound's Imagist project must be viewed as an intervention, indirectly but fully political, against the deadening abstraction
of capitalist economy and its cultural expressions. Like his modernist
ideological counterpart Theodor Adorno (who sought to reaffirm "the
preponderance of the object" in the face of abstract exchange value and
the "identity principle," which was its privileged conceptual form), Pound
in his Imagism wanted to free the self by restoring the world of concrete
objects to a kind of complexity that defied cultural formulas and automated convention. In essays like "Vorticism" and "The New Sculpture," Pound made it clear that the fully liberated individual could be an
individual only by letting the other be other.

But true to his ideological inheritance (which would become clear in
his fitful attempts to reconcile Imagism's premium on "objectivity" with
the primary freedom of the artist), Pound believed that the power to
renovate and restore the world of the object, and so liberate individual
vision, finally lay with the self's power to rise above, if only it would,
those very forces of the literary market whose constraining power Pound
had analyzed so compellingly in his early prose. "Emotion," he maintained, is the "organizer of form" and could by sheer internal pressure
liberate the world of things. And when we ask of him, as we must, what
organizes emotion? his answer – it is wholly Emersonian in structure
and impulse – can only be: the self and only the self, lest its generative
political promise, its destructuring "*whim*" (as Emerson called it in "Self-
Reliance"), be lost.

Finally, however, this ethical idealism – and its politically disabling
refusal to subject the self to collective structures and alliances of any kind
– may be seen as an ideological expression of a more properly political
problem: the tendency, in Emerson, Pound, William James, and many
another, to figure the self in terms that reproduce the language, structure, and contradictions of private property. From the very outset of his
career, in "I gather the Limbs of Osiris," "Patria Mia," and "The Serious
Artist," Pound would argue that the "donative" artist can give to his

culture the "permanent property" of art, but only if he has first come
into the self-possession of his own *virtù*. In so conceiving the inalienable
individual, Pound not only reproduced the logic of property but also
reenacted the basic transaction of Emersonian self-reliance and its
investment in culture: "There is a property in the horizon," Emerson
famously wrote, "which no man has but he whose eye can integrate all
the parts, that is, the poet."

It is in the logic of property that we can locate the source of the central
ideological effect that we will examine in these pages: that strange dissociation of ethics, economics, and politics which enables both Pound
and Emerson to present the energetic entrepreneur, for instance, as a
model of self-reliance and *virtù,* while at the same time attacking the
stultifying force of the economic structure that makes possible and is
reproduced by entrepreneurship itself. For Pound, in early essays like
"Patria Mia" and "Osiris," problems of determinate, historically specific
economic structures are time and again rewritten as historically untethered
problems of ethics and human nature. And consequently, a potentially
coherent and potent materialist critique is recast by the heat of idealism,
which holds that the fundamental problem is not particular economic
and social structures but rather how they are used (or abused) by selves
who freely choose – in which case, one must ask, why worry about
those structures, as Pound so often does, in the first place?

Like Pound, Emerson worried about those structures and institutions
a great deal, and in his journals and essays like "Self-Reliance" and "The
American Scholar" he wanted to situate himself between the Jacksonian
mass on the one hand and the abuses of money and property that
constituted for him "the want of self-reliance" on the other. Because
of his commitment to individual and not collective power, however,
Emerson was forced to conclude that whereas the mass is an unqualified
evil, property is merely a "mischief." Jacksonianism attacks the self at
its very seat of power by making it mob-reliant. But property, at least,
is private, and it may even become the very sign of self-reliance, may
become what Emerson calls, in an altogether stunning phrase, "living
property," which "perpetually renews itself wherever the man breathes."
From this vantage, Emerson's well-known later conservatism may be
seen as the inevitable and logical conclusion of an ideological position
already staked out, for all the apparent differences, in his earlier work.
And from this vantage, Pound's metaphor of choice (in his important
early poem "A Pact") for his relationship to Whitman – and, beyond
that, to the American poetic tradition – is as ideologically symptomatic
as it is unexpected for this famous enemy of usury: "Let there be,"
Pound offers, "commerce between us."

It is no news to the contemporary reader – and it was not news to

Emerson and Pound (or to Hawthorne and Melville, for that matter) – that the enterprising, inventive self is, in the gender codes of American culture, a thoroughly masculine being. Like Emerson before him, who in "Self-Reliance" attacked the "feminine rage" of "the cultivated classes," Pound in "Patria Mia" saw poetry in America becoming, under the genteel cultural establishment, "a sort of embroidery for dilettantes and women." And like William James before him, who thought that the "refined" and "tepid" "middle-class paradise" of early modern culture needed an injection of "the sterner stuff of manly virtue," Pound sought recourse to the adventure and experience of poet-heroes like Bertran de Born. It is important to understand, though, that when Pound took up his early critique of what he called the genteel "gynocracy," his purpose, like Emerson's and James's, was not to mount a misogynist attack on women-as-such (as if there were such a thing as women-as-such) but rather to engage in a class-specific critique of those genteel cultural institutions that attempted to universalize middle-class mores. That much would become clear in his attacks on manly "red-blood" poets like Bliss Carmen and Richard Hovey and in the cultural and class specificity of poems like *Hugh Selwyn Mauberley*, "L'Homme Moyen Sensuel," "Portrait d'une Femme," and much of the *Lustra* volume of 1916, where gender codes combine with the power of property in complex and often unexpected ways.

But if the famous female figure of "Portrait d'une Femme" is the very antithesis of Poundian *virtù*, then so too, it seems, is Pound's beloved Bertran de Born in "Near Perigord," that ambitious and complicated prelude to the *Cantos*, where we find Pound's poet-hero beheaded, symbolically castrated, and in a real sense poetically impotent in the face of his desire. What are we to make of this rather shocking characterization of one of Pound's privileged figures of poetic *virtù*, whose feminization seems only doubly assured in light of the phallocentric theory of gender that Pound develops in his writings on Remy de Gourmont? And as if that were not enough, how are we to account for early poems such as "On His Own Face in a Glass" and "Histrion," which quite unexpectedly suggest that *Pound himself* lacks precisely that kind of manly originality and *virtù* which he located in Cavalcanti, Villon, and his other early models of poetic individuality? This is a startling self-critique, perhaps, but it is less so when we remind ourselves that here again Pound had Emersonian precedent. For Emerson, we should remember, self-reliance is finally self-surrender, and the fundamental precondition for achieving phallic poetic originality is that one must first become a feminized empty space so that "the currents of Universal Being circulate through me."

What we find in these striking early poems of Pound is (to use Kaja

Silverman's term)[22] a curiously "*male* lack," an absence or loss (or, in more Freudian terms, a fear of castration), that lies at the very center of the phallic poetic ideal and that, in poems like "Near Perigord," is projected onto the feminine, the better to be disavowed. In the end, then, what is most ideologically significant in Pound's politics of gender (and before that, by implication, in Emerson's) is not so much his positioning of himself in particular poems as either masculine or feminine but rather his reproduction of the gender system itself, which structures, organizes, and contains those positions and sustains the mechanism of patriarchal power even where it seems most disowned.

I begin the second part of this study by examining the nature of economy and the economy of nature in Pound's later work. Early in his career, Pound had criticized the lyric ideal embodied in texts like Palgrave's *Golden Treasury*, which imagined a realm of permanent aesthetic value "more golden than gold" that transcended the economy of the marketplace. In Pound's own corpus, however, that ideal of value is challenged only to be reproduced in an unbroken chain of texts extending from a whole host of poems in *A Lume Spento* and the early San Trovaso Notebook, through the "Envoi" to *Mauberley*, and on into many, many passages in the *Cantos*, where we find Pound marking his supreme standard of cultural and poetic value with the privileged signifier of gold, which radiates from Malatesta's Tempio and adorns gods and goddesses. Even though Pound in his prose after 1918 would reject the gold standard of value in the realm of economics, the structure and contradictions of that system of value survive and are reproduced in the signifying economy of the *Cantos*. Like Emerson, who in *Nature* set the "bullion" of authentic poetic language against the "paper currency" of debased words, Pound wanted to separate the "gold" or "permanent property" of art and poetic vision from that fallen realm where real money changes hands. In doing so, however, he only succeeded in "capitalizing" – as Emerson had in essays like "Compensation" – a realm of aesthesis that, he believed, should transcend all economies.

More than any other figure in the *Cantos*, perhaps, Sigismundo Malatesta – that "entire man" as Pound called him – makes it clear that history, politics, and economics must be redeemed by a realm of aesthetic value that is not, or should not be, subject to the debasements of the marketplace. We do indeed admire the difficulty of Malatesta's struggle, as Pound intends us to, but only, in the end, the better to admire the Tempio constructed out of it. Malatesta's Tempio endures under the sign of gold, which, in Pound's words, "gathers the light about it." By Pound's intentions, the Tempio is the antithesis of all commodities; but by the logic of the broader economy structuring those intentions, it is the *ultimate* of all commodities, the "permanent property" ceded to history by artistic vision. As Pound's long poem unfolds, the *Cantos'* store of gold, like the golden light of the Tempio, becomes more and more dematerialized and ideal, the better to serve as a more and more pliable and versatile arbiter of that poetic value which is dispensed by the poet with absolute authority.

At the end of Chapter 5, we look back briefly to the very beginnings of Pound's career and find the contradictions that trouble Pound's conjugations of the relationship between poetic and real economies already at work in his early proposals for patronage. Here too, Pound aims to free the poetic self from capitalist economy, but he only succeeds in reproducing its logic and necessity. The artist, Pound argues, should be relieved of *his* status as a commodity subject to the market. But he can be so freed, it turns out, only by relying on the munificence of an aristocracy of capital dependent upon the perpetuation of that very economic system that makes patronage necessary in the first place.

I begin Chapter 6 with a brief reprise of Emerson's vision of the relationship between economics and nature (a vision discussed in Chapters 2, 3, and 5) and then move away from him for the remainder of the chapter to show that in time Pound, too, would find in the excesses of the market not only a sin against the artist but also, as Canto XLV tells us, a "sin against nature." And so it is that Pound will spend a good deal of his later career – in *Guide to Kulchur*, in the economic prose and money pamphlets, and even in the *Cantos* – contemplating how the gap between nature and economic value might be closed, how economics might, like the authentic poetic word, be an extension, not a negation, of the natural totality. Pound's *"rivoluzione continua,"* it turns out, is a revolution *backward* toward a precapitalist, and distinctly populist, past where the organic whole of nature, economics, politics, and art needs – and tolerates – no mediation. Nowhere is that vision staged with more power and ceremony than at the very heart of Pound's long poem in Cantos XLV–LII, and especially in Canto XLIX (the so-called Seven Lakes Canto), whose ideological motivations may be focused in light of Pound's prose of the same period and in his handling of his Chinese sources.

Because of Pound's overt materials and models in these poems (the Confucian *Li Ki*, Hesiod's *Works and Days*), it is difficult to see that the totality of nature, economics, and political power that is unfolded at the very center of the *Cantos* may be read as a late but quite consonant chapter in the ideology of American populism and its vision of what one historian calls a "lost agrarian Eden." As we see in essays of the thirties such as "Mang Tsze," Pound, by way of his Chinese sources, radicalized fundamental elements of the populist vision – most significantly, its tendency to reconstitute problems of economics as issues of ethics and personal conduct – into a more properly authoritarian and totalitarian position. The overtly ideological character of that position is unmasked (by the hand of history, as it were) in *The Pisan Cantos*, the most-discussed sequence of Pound's long poem. In these cantos, written while Pound was imprisoned by the Allies and was suffering psychological collapse, the epistemological machinery that throughout the poem had read nature as the transparent sign of a larger ideological coherence suddenly breaks down. And it is in that dysfunction – in the freeing of nature from ideological work into newly discovered moments and microscapes, "When the mind swings by a grass-blade" – that the poem reveals, as no personal confession could, its fully ideological character.

In the final section and last chapter of this study, I attempt to map the formal coordinates of Pound's literary ideology on the micro- and macrolevels of poetic sign and genre. Like Pound's later economics, his ideogrammic theory of the sign as he developed it in the thirties (against Frege, Saussure, Peirce, and modernist sign theory in general) wants a language motivated by that which it represents, which might heal the prototypically modernist rift between what Frege called "sense," "reference," and "idea" (or value). The price of such signifying confidence, however, might by now be guessed; if interpretation is the investigation of discord and disagreement, then clearly this is a language beyond interpretation – and therefore beyond the individual and social differences that interpretation stages and in whose name Pound struggled early in his career. Here again, though, Pound had strong American precedent in Emerson, who in "The Poet" warned us not to "miswrite" the poem that is already there in nature, awaiting our transcription. In this sense, then, "The Chinese Written Character as a Medium for Poetry" is perhaps the most Emersonian document in the Pound corpus and finds Emerson's desire for language's "re-attachment" to nature alive and well at the heart of the modernist era.[23]

Pound's radicalization of his ideogrammic ideal for the poetic sign during the thirties developed hand in hand with his growing didactic mission in both poetry and prose, and helped to underwrite an increasingly authoritarian and antidemocratic poetics that sought to reduce, not plumb, interpretive discord and textual difference. And this increasingly totalitarian myth of language finds its perfect generic form in the epic, which (to oversimplify for a moment) stands in relation to its social totality as the ideogram does to the natural coherence it signifies. It should be clear by now, however, that to read the *Cantos* as an epic is to recapitulate, rather than solve, the poem's formal and ideological contradictions, because it is to presuppose social conditions of possibility for that form which clearly no longer exist. In this sense, Pound's poem, insofar as we read it as epic, is a massive, but ideologically symptomatic, contradiction; it simultaneously assumes and attempts to bring into being the social and natural totality whereby it might be possible to read the poem as the epic that it finally fails to be.

In fact, once we realize that the coherence of the *Cantos* and its universe is not substantial but rather ideological, it makes a good deal more sense to read the poem as a kind of dialectic of epic and Menippean satire, where moments of visionary permanence alternate with the anatomy and castigation of historical failure and social vice. But with *The Pisan Cantos*, it is clear that Pound can no longer situate himself outside that realm of failure on some putatively natural, unassailable ground. With *The Pisan Cantos*, something happens that cannot happen in the universe of the epic, and that is simply historical change itself. And with *The Pisan Cantos*, an authentic character, his violent past productive of an uncertain end, emerges from a battle of epic and Menippean types to provide a portent of what the poem will in time declare about itself: "I cannot make it cohere." In that admission of defeat, however, resides a kind of success, a candor that ideology fears, a truth it loathes and is doomed to confess.

PART I

PART 1

1

A Politics of Difference

If what we now call postmodernism is any indication, we have yet to come to terms with the risks, matched only by the atavistic hankering, involved in asking the question, what does it mean to be American? Even the form of the question itself seems somehow quintessentially American: a sign, perhaps, of its essentialist allure and ahistorical dangers, and not only for Americans. As Régis Debray's famous quip about the post-1968 Left in France testifies – they set sail for Maoist China and landed in California – and as Jean Baudrillard's recent forays into the Epcot Center of the American Mind indicate,[1] it seems as if the whole world (or at least that part of it which can afford to) is asking itself that same question. In fact, Fredric Jameson has argued that recent Continental theories of the postmodern self are "secretly North American in their content, if not their form."[2] And Jameson's suspicion is seconded by Stuart Hall, who reminds us that postmodernism is really about "how the world dreams itself to be American."[3]

America, in other words, seems to be an idea whose time has come. What is curious, however, is that this appears to have *always* been the case. For nearly two centuries, European thinkers have seen in America (for better or for worse, depending on their ideological positions) the "end of history" and the egalitarian, antiauthoritarian, and democratic society identified (with a similar range of ideological response) by present-day theorists of the postmodern. As Alexandre Kojève observed in 1948 in a now-famous passage, "the Hegelian–Marxist end of History was not yet to come, but was already a present, here and now . . . in the North American extensions of Europe. One can even say that, from a certain point of view, the United States has already attained the final stage of Marxist 'communism.'"[4] Indeed, Kojève's interpretation of the American way of life as "the type of life specific to the posthistorical period"[5] would be sustained forty years later in Baudrillard's beloved symbol of the great desert of the American West, which literalizes, as it were, Kojève's Hegelian assertion that "Nature survives Time."[6] In *America*, Baudrillard would find what another famous French traveler saw in this new and strange land a century and a half earlier, thereby initiating an ongoing romance between European intellectuals and the peculiar promise of what would come to be known, before Baudrillard's time, as American exceptionalism.[7]

What tends to get lost in these accounts (and what gets left out in Stuart Hall's characterization) is the most curious and significant fact of all: that American culture dreams *itself* to be American, regularly indulging a habit as durable, apparently, as it is immaterial. This relentless fantasy of self-definition becomes something of a national pastime, of course, during American political campaigns. The 1988 presidential bid of George Bush gave us Kojève's neo-Hegelianism in reverse with its slogan "Let's make America America again"; and Ronald Reagan's campaign four years earlier likewise told us that Americanness was, paradoxically, both the origin and end of our resolve to "stay the course."

Four years before that, Reagan's 1980 campaign crafted one of the more remarkable little pieces of American culture in recent memory in that famous state-of-the-art television spot which began its own compressed social history of the United States with the words, spoken by the impeccable male voice of the Gallo wine commercials, "It's morning in America." As the daily paper arrives and the primevally suburban mist gently disperses the rising sun to hold in soft focus the manicured lawns, the freshly painted houses, and the white kids on the latest model of mountain bike, we hear once more the story told by Ralph Waldo Emerson when he wrote in "The Poet" that "America is a poem in our eyes; its ample geography dazzles the imagination." We hear one more time the promise named by Ezra Pound when he imagined, at the dawn of modernism, an "American Risorgimento," the awakening or resurgence that was latent, he hoped, in a moribund homeland.

To declare "morning in America," in other words, is to seize upon the founding *obvious* of American life, this absence of history by which all days are magically the same day, each defined by the waking promise of something about to happen, each a call for renewed faith – no other word will serve – in America as a land of pure potential where anything is and should be possible, where the nightmare of history has run its course before the film starts rolling. With the collapse of the temporal continuity whereby tomorrow might be seen as, say, the living out of the consequences of yesterday's actions, the paradoxical American business of beginning again can commence. If all this sounds familiar, in other words, that is precisely the point, the source of this protonarrative's power and the sign of its severe limits as well. American culture from the beginning has told such a story repeatedly and – this is most revealing

– from the full range of political positions. This story, it seems, is democratic; it admits Martin Luther King, Jr., as well as William Jennings Bryan, Eugene Debs as well as Richard Nixon.[8]

In 1836, Ralph Waldo Emerson sounded a similar note, maybe *the* rendition, in the essay *Nature*: "Why should not we also enjoy an original relation to the universe?" "Why should we grope among the dry bones of the past, or put the living generation into masquerade out of its faded wardrobe? The sun shines to-day also. There is more wool and flax in the fields. There are new lands, new men, new thoughts."[9] For Emerson, the endless harvest that is America ("more wool and flax") stood as both origin and end, promise and fulfillment, as both incentive for spiritual renovation and a sign that the birth of the new man had already taken place – not "there will be more" but "there *is* more."[10] "Our day of dependence, our long apprenticeship to the learning of other lands, draws to a close," Emerson wrote in "The American Scholar." "Events, actions arise, that must be sung, that will sing themselves."[11] To hasten that process along, however, Emerson called upon us – nowhere more forcefully than at the opening of that lecture in 1837 – to throw off the crushing weight of those institutions of class, church, and convention whose name was "England." For Emerson, history was properly the unfolding of Spirit in the traits and actions of "universal man."[12] But when the workings of "the active soul" became ossified and sedimented in dead traditions and institutions – when they became "congealed" in what Jean-Paul Sartre would later call the "practico-inert"[13] – "Man Thinking" threatened to turn into "the book-worm" and the self-sufficient "system" of the new man into a mere "satellite" of the old.[14] "Tradition," Michel Foucault has shrewdly observed, "makes it possible to rethink the dispersion of history in the form of the same";[15] for Emerson, it threatened to freeze and fix the active soul into something less than active, and in so doing to make the original relation and the new self a good deal less than original and new.

As Emerson complained in "The American Scholar," the active power of creation, of origination, was constantly being threatened by its objective manifestations. "Yet hence arises a grave mischief," he wrote. "The sacredness which attaches to the act of creation, the act of thought, is transferred to the record. . . . The writer was a just and wise spirit: henceforward it is settled the book is perfect."[16] For Emerson, material-ism always harbors this threat: The creative and original man creates that which inhibits creativity and originality, and the dynamic principle of the "new man" is betrayed when it is captured and reified by the by-products of the active self. "Society is a wave," Emerson writes in "Self-Reliance." "The wave moves onward, but the water of which it is composed does not. The same particle does not rise from the valley to the ridge. Its unity is only phenomenal."[17] The form – whether book or social institution – may change, society may "progress," but the substance that creates it does not. So it is that Emerson enjoins us to break free – every day, every moment – from objects and institutions, which we must leave in our wake. Thus, Emerson's inaugural vision of the American self is bent on radical *rupture*, not liberal revision. In the fiery polemical form of the early essays, the truth of the Emersonian man is not subject to liberal tinkering – it is all or nothing.

It is clear, then, that the Emersonian break with history – and with those objects that embody its threat to make the American self a repetition of that history – constitutes the primal scene of the American individual not as a narrative moment but as a *lyric* one. Narrative depends upon something retained from the past that undergoes transformation in time, but this is precisely what is forbidden to the truth of Emersonian Spirit and the self that it drives. Lyric, on the other hand, establishes its radical difference from all other moments; it carries no teleology or continuum, lest it be lost to a coherence not of its own making. Like the Emersonian self, the lyric moment at its extreme is a genre all unto itself.[18] Not surprisingly, then, Emerson's concept of language assimilates the past to the promise of the present. In the "Language" section of *Nature*, it is above all *immediacy* that characterizes right language. We need to realize that "words are signs of natural facts" because "every natural fact is a symbol of some spiritual fact."[19] Linguistic forms should close, not open, the temporal gap between language, nature, spirit; and it is Emerson's desire that the communication of spirit's truth take place in an instant, rather than being strung out in time in a signifying chain.[20] Or again, in "The Poet," it is the "flowing or metamorphosis" of the imagination, its fluid ever-changingness, that constitutes the truth of language and that enables the self to experience its own truth in moments of lyric ecstasy: "And now my chains are to be broken," Emerson writes. "I shall mount above these clouds and opaque airs in which I live . . . and from the heaven of truth I shall see and comprehend my relations."[21] To speak of a generative American narrative, then, is to constitute the very oxymoron that Emerson was writing against. It is to reinstate those conditions of possibility for narrative that for Emerson threatened the promise of the new, original, and lyric self.

In constructing and projecting an essentially lyric stance toward temporality and the possibility of history, does the founding vision of the American self therefore realize, before the fact, the "end of ideology" we have heard so much about since Daniel Bell coined the phrase more than two decades ago?[22] Perhaps it does, if you conceive ideology in the bad old 1930s sense of the word, as something like a public political position replete with alliances, platforms, and Manichean polemics – if you conceive it, in other words, in terms Emerson would have rejected (and indeed did reject in writings like the essay "Politics"). But in terms of more recent concepts of ideology, nothing could be farther from the truth. As Gerald Graff has drawn the contrast, the ethos of this new ideology

> is no longer one of fixed, absolute principles but rather one of adapting to changing times. . . . For it is only by a systematic destruction of the past that the need for new markets and stepped-up consumption can be satisfied. This consumerist pluralism doesn't mean "the end of ideology" – pluralism itself being an ideology – but neither does it resemble the imperious ruling-class ideology posited by traditional radical theory.[23]

If the past has been destroyed, however, in what sense can we say that times are "changing" (or that society, for that matter, is "progressing")? Emerson himself knew that to be original and new is to be, on strictest principle, unrepeatable. Therefore "new" in the American myth of origin is not new at all – or rather, it is perpetually (and therefore paradoxically) new because that past in relation to which the new might be perceived *as* new has been, as Graff reminds us, obliterated. For consumer capitalism as well as for the Emersonian self, it seems, "new words" and new products may signify but must not contain the movement of originality. We might know the presence, but not the essence, of the whole self by the objects it produces, including objects like social and political structures. For consumers of commodities as well as for the Emersonian self, it is finally not *how* the self is made new that is crucial but rather *that* the self is so remade.

Nowhere is this clearer, for Emerson's part, than at the end of the essay "Experience" (1844), written shortly after the death of his son, an event that must have further galvanized his reluctance to measure the self by its objects and practice:

> Also that hankering after an overt or practical effect seems to me an apostasy. In good earnest I am willing to spare this most unnecessary deal of doing. Life wears to me a visionary face. Hardest roughest action is visionary also. It is but a choice between soft and turbulent dreams.[24]

For Emerson, the "unnecessary deal of doing," practice in and upon the object world, is the long way, and finally the *wrong* way, to self-reliance. If "the overt or practical effect" (such as his opposition to the Fugitive Slave Law) emerges in the process, then so be it; but self-reliance must always return to it subject.

We must remember that Emerson figured America's social and political rupture with the Old World as a phenomenological rupture as well, a freedom from encrusted convention that enabled a new lived relation to the world of things, a freshness of perception of both natural and social forms. Emerson makes the point with particular vigor in the small, powerful essay "Circles": "Permanence is but a word of degrees," he assures us. "Our culture is the predominance of an idea which draws after it this train of cities and institutions. Let us rise into another idea; they will disappear."[25] In his invectives against what the formalists would later call "prosaic" or "automated" perception, Emerson imagined that things might not only be seen new but also be seen *through*. The phenomenological transparency of the famous "transparent eyeball" passage in *Nature* is but a paradigm for the process whereby the object world is dissolved into what Emerson calls, in a moment of charged political ambivalence, the "uncontained" beauty for which it is but a sign.[26] "In nature every moment is new," he reminds us in "Circles," "the past is always swallowed and forgotten; the coming only is sacred."[27] By Emerson's logic, then, the object world appears under the aegis of its own disappearance and serves to both signal and generate a desire for perceptual originality which that world itself cannot – and should not, by Emerson's lights – fulfill.

As Emerson never tired of saying, "The world is nothing, the man is all."[28] To realize that truth, the Emersonian self had to be emptied and cleansed of history and its institutions by what one critic has called an "enabling amnesia,"[29] which would ready this newly and voraciously empty self for the "currents of Universal Being," which Emerson hoped would fill it. But given the enormity of this quintessentially American desire, produced by the absence of history at its very center, is it any wonder that this self might be receptive to a very different kind of exhilarating immediacy, one that would likewise elevate spiritual refreshment, in the name of originality and freedom, above the "overt or practical effect"?

After all, the romance of the commodity, too, generates a limitless desire for the perceptually new, and for the new self, which cannot be fulfilled on the material ground of capitalism. As Frank Lentricchia has conjugated this primary contradiction:

> The perpetual production of the "new" commodity ensures, of course, that commodity-utopia will not be achieved, that desire is unappeasable, which is what consumer capitalism is all about: turning the potentially revolutionary force of desire produced on capitalist terrain toward the work of conserving and perpetuating consumer capitalism.[30]

The commodity, too – to borrow Emerson's phrase – makes life "a series of surprises"; the commodity too "admits us to a new scene."[31]

For consumer capitalism as well, the object world is always on the way to obsolescence, always in need of renovation. And for the American self constituted by historical rupture and bent on the experiential newness which aims to keep it that way, that is as it should be.

It is a little easier to see the structure of Emersonian desire at work in the late capitalist, postmodern subject of desire when we remind ourselves that a recent television commercial uses Emerson to say in every aspect of its representation that Reebok footware lets "U. B. U." – the very logo itself a graphic rupture with that representational convention called spelling.[32] Meanwhile, in the voice-over, a male narrator, self-consciously embodying the voice of cultural authority (how ironic for Emerson), recites line after line from "Self-Reliance," as we cut, in rapid succession, from one image of sneaker-induced originality to another: "insist on yourself, never imitate"; "to be great is to be misunderstood"; and (the unkindest cut of all) "whoso would be a man, must be a nonconformist."[33] Whereas the Emerson of "Self-Reliance" provides the spoken text for Reebok, the Emerson of "Experience," who eschewed "this most unnecessary deal of doing," serves as the oblique subtext in a series of roughly contemporaneous Nike ads. While suitably grainy black-and-white montage cuts quickly from John McEnroe in a fist-pumping tantrum to scenes of street life that have little in common except Nike sneakers, the Beatles' droll and practice-weary "Revolution" plays in the background: "Don't you know it's gonna be (shooby-do) all right?" Need it be said that the revolution has come indoors, where Emerson had always said it was, the new self with new eyes its origin and end?[34]

Nike's most recent commercial allows us to close out our trilogy of postmodern Emersonian ads in grand style. This spot uses that latter-day Emersonian "representative man" John Lennon (in his post-Beatle phase) to make radical celebration – even by Nike's standards – of the democratization of commodity culture. Here, Emerson's text does not appear at all but is so pervasive that it is invisible. And we look right through the welling encouragement of "Self-Reliance" to Lennon's "Instant Karma," which refers us, in turn, back to the end of *Nature*. There, Emerson's orphic poet reminds us that we are all incarnations, however diminished, of that originary self who, in Emerson's myth of creation, "filled nature with his over-flowing currents. Out from him sprang the sun and moon; from man the sun, from woman the moon. The laws of his mind, the periods of his actions externized themselves into day and night, into the year and seasons."[35] That self appears to be alive and well in Nike's reading of John Lennon, and its karma can be affirmed in an instant simply by stopping by the nearest shoe store and purchasing the latest model of sneaker, which will help us bring out the god (or the

Michael Jordan) in all of us. Any Emersonian will already know the answer to Lennon's question:

> Who in the world do you think you are?
> A superstar? Well right you are.
> Well we all shine on
> Like the moon, and the stars, and the sun.
> Well we all shine on.
> On and on and on and on and on.

The point is not to defend Emerson, that most fluid and ductile of thinkers, as a sort of monument (the kind for which he himself had no use) against such appropriations. The point is that we make our own "Emerson" in putting his texts and his authority to use. And in the above cases, "we" is not only or even mainly professional scholars and critics. In its way, Reebok's Emerson is faithful to its source in confirming that originality is not only the sign, but the very condition, of American selfhood. In the absence of Emerson's faith in the law of Nature and Spirit, "Trust thyself" becomes a matter of style, and that potentially explosive desire for a world in which "U." can "B." "U." is parcelized and displaced by an endless procession of the signs of difference that money can buy. Emerson could not have imagined it, but in another sense no one could have imagined it more fully.

EMERSON, POUND, AND THE JAMESES

In "Self-Reliance," Emerson laid down the first principle of his cultural politics: "You take the way from man, not to man."[36] It is an ideology shared, in surprising detail and with similar ambivalence, by Ezra Pound in the period up to 1918, and its conceptual contradictions and formal problems in part determine, but also set into sharp contrast, the later Pound and his long shadow. That Emerson's first principle might serve as the ideological backbone of Pound's early social critique is difficult to see for all sorts of reasons. First, as Pound himself admitted in his essay "What I feel about Walt Whitman" (written in 1909 but not published until 1955), it was his habit to "conceal my relationship to my spiritual father" (in this case, Whitman) "and brag about my more congenial ancestry – Dante, Shakespeare, Theocritus, Villon."[37] Nevertheless, he countered, "the vital part of my message, taken from the sap and fibre of America, is the same as his."[38] And that sap flowed from "pioneer" roots throughout the family tree of Pound's more literal ancestry (or so he fancied). As he put it in a letter to William Carlos Williams, written from London in 1917:

> And America! What the hell do you a bloomin' foreigner know about the place? Your pere only penetrated the edge, and you've never been west of the Upper Darby, or the Maunchunk switchback. . . .

> My dear boy, you have never felt the whoop of the PEEraries. You have never seen the projecting and protuberant Mts. of the Sierra Nevada. WOT can you know of the counthry?
>
> You have the naive credulity of a Co. Clair immigrant. But I (der grosse Ich) have the virus, the bacillus of the land in my blood, for nearly three bleating centuries.[39]

No wonder, then, that Pound once quipped that he could produce a social history of the United States from his family annals; that pioneer "bacillus" which was America had, after all, produced him: a modernist who thought himself not partially but quintessentially American.[40]

Pound's invocation of the considerably more proletarian Whitman, in those circumstances in which he was wont to consider his "ancestry," points to another issue that has made his Emersonian roots hard to see: How are we to interpret the central political thrust of Pound's early critique? It is a project on behalf of the democratic individual's resistance to modernity's imperial impositions of system and structure? Or is it rather, as Kathryne V. Lindberg has recently suggested, an essentially elitist (and well-nigh proverbial) plaint of the disenfranchised artist?[41] The very desire to put the question in that form, however – *either* the democratic masses *or* the writer – is, as we shall see, one of the central targets of Pound's early project. It is true that in his early work the model for the healthy, unalienated individual is usually (sometimes implicitly) the artisan. But that is a long way indeed from saying that Pound's early critique is elitist (as the storied history of the artisan figure in the annals of Marxist criticism ought to make clear).

In fact, Pound's early position is often, if not always, radically democratic, and nowhere is that impulse clearer than in a set of essays written between 1910 and 1918, where Pound stakes out a position whose libertarian thrust extends well beyond the confines of the literati: "Those things are right which give the greatest freedom, the greatest opportunity for individual development to the individual, of whatever age or sex or condition."[42] This particular passage is taken from what seems to me the central document of his early career: the essay "Patria Mia," written in the winter of 1910–1911 though published serially and in book form a year later. Pound would reiterate the point, in both principle and effect, in a number of other early essays as well, whether the subject under discussion was modern techniques of production, the system of magazine publishing in America, or the creation of literary character. Across all these contexts, and with an intention far from purely aesthetic, Pound would take the Emersonian way from man, though *to* where, at this early juncture, he could not guess.

If Pound hardly ever mentions Emerson, we may say that he did not need Emerson because he had Henry James – and because what he admired in technical precision in the latter he found lacking (to put it mildly) in the former. In a fascinating letter written at age twenty, what is of primary interest is what Pound does *not* see in Emerson and what James would provide later, in spades, for the young poet in London. Pound's mother had written him to register her approval of a rhetorical analysis of "Self-Reliance" he had recently undertaken. And Pound's response, which already shows signs of his jaunty epistolary style, provides an index for the aesthetic values that were soon to become political ones as well, all of which he found wanting in the "Easterner" Emerson:

> Also madam you shouldn't begin to crow just because I happen to hear a little emmerson. He and all that bunch of moralists, what have they done? Why, all that is in their writings that's good is from the bible & the rest is rot. They have diluted holy writ. They have twisted it awry. They have it is true weakened it sufficiently for the slack minded & given vogue to the dilutation. The chief benefit of reading them is this. You can't trust a word they say & the exhilaration produced by this watchfulness for sophistries is the only benefit.[43]

For this twenty-year-old student of comparative literature, what Emerson apparently lacks is the quality giving authority to that world of Cavalcanti (or the Bible or Dante) "where one thought cuts through another with clean edge."[44] Emerson was no friend of that precision and demarcation which resists the boiling down of radiant gists to "unbounded undistinguished abstraction"[45] – "undistinguished" as philosophy because the particulars of which it is composed are themselves "undistinguished" in another sense, their differences not respected but obliterated.

But Pound's distrust of abstraction and "dilutation" in Emerson points the way to all that he admired in Henry James, whose writing stood as an indictment and painstaking anatomy of "all the sordid petty personal crushing oppression, the domination of modern life" – James, the "hater of tyranny," the author of "book after early book against oppression."[46] What Pound respects in James is not only the "emotional greatness" of his fight against tyranny but most of all his technical ability to render the struggle of the modern self in precise, atomic terms – terms that Emerson, apparently, had not mastered.[47] Even though Pound found Emerson's technique an affront to his aesthetic values, the same cannot be said of their shared political intent. How else to explain the unmistakable echo in Pound's essay on James of what Emerson himself had articulated so eloquently seventy years earlier in the essay "Politics"? There, he had written, "Whenever I find my dominion over myself not sufficient for me, and I undertake the direction of [my neighbor] also, I overstep the truth, and come into false relations to him. . . . This is the history of governments, – one man does something which is to bind another."[48] And what Pound writes of James may well have been written of Emerson – or, for that matter, *by* Emerson: "What he fights is 'influence,' the impinging of one personality on another; all of them in the highest degree damn'd, loathsome and detestable."[49] But the phrase that follows these lines may serve to point up what was lacking in Emerson, and what James possessed in abundance: Above all, James's writing is a monument to "respect for the peripheries of the individual."[50]

It is the particularity of the phrasing here – "the *peripheries* of the individual" – which seems to indicate that precise shading of individual differences so abundant in James and so lacking in Emerson "the moralist." James possessed that will toward particularity and precision which would form the political text not only of Imagism writ large but also of the judiciously cadenced portraits of *Hugh Selwyn Mauberley*, Pound's self-professed attempt to condense the James novel. Conversely, we can almost sense that for Pound the Emersonian self was simply *too* much; it was everywhere, all over the place, and therefore maybe no place. In its yawning proportions, it lost on the way to idealism whatever "peripheries" it might possess, and lost consequently that particularity and precision which Pound thought the only true medium for a hater of tyranny. In "Patria Mia" this important distinction, and James's way with distinction, are particularly clear; what makes James's "continuing labor for individual freedom" effective is that he "delineates these things to perfection."[51] Or again, six years later in "Provincialism the Enemy," it is James's "sense of differences . . . the slight difference in tone"[52] that makes the struggle for liberty in James not a diluted moralism but rather a truly viable political aesthetic.

It is ironic then, to say the least, that Henry James, remembering Emerson's visits to his childhood home at 58 West Fourteenth Street, would recall later that *Emerson's* true genius was "for seeing character as a real and supreme thing."[53] Emerson impressed upon the young James the value of individuality, its precise shadings and nuances so crucial to its proper aesthetic.[54] Henry recalled listening to the illustrious visitor:

> Just then and there for me in the sweetness of the voice and the finish of the speech – this latter through a sort of attenuated emphasis which at the same time made sounds more important, more interesting in themselves, than by any revelation yet vouchsafed us. Was not this my first glimmer of a sense that the human tone *could*, in that independent and original way, be interesting? It had given me there in the firelight an absolutely abiding measure.[55]

And by another turn of the literary/historical screw, what Pound saw in Henry James (and what Henry himself saw in Emerson) *and* what Pound saw but did not like in Emerson (his misty meditative side) emerge as two sides of Emerson himself in *William* James's account. In Frank Lentricchia's words:

> There was, William said (and in this he prefigures by several years brother Henry's memory), the *real* Emerson, who was "so squarely and simply himself" – this Emerson's "hottest side" was his non-conformist, even antinomian conviction of the unsurpassable value of the individual. Alongside this Emerson, William placed the transcendental idealist whose favored element was the "tasteless water of souls."[56]

Two Emersons, then, the latter of which, the soul taster, was taken by Pound to be the whole. We may trace Pound's Emersonian lineage in this way: What Pound admired above all in Henry James, Henry James himself traced back to Ralph Waldo Emerson's "independent and original way."

But there is more: The defense of the inviolable "peripheries of the individual" that Pound found so eloquently represented in the textures of James's prose would find its most pointedly antiimperialist formulation not in Henry but in his brother, William, who like Pound thought "abstraction" to be a far from purely theoretical matter. As Patricia Rae has recently argued, Pound's theories of the image and vortex rejected symbolist transcendence for the same reasons that James's empirical psychology rejected the claims of philosophical Idea: Neither tradition could do justice to the self's heterogeneous experience of a complex world composed of "innumerable unforetold particulars."[57] And as Walter Sutton points out, James's vision of a "pluralistic universe," of what he called a "strung-out" world composed of finite particulars (in contrast to the "block" universe and unifying "All" of monistic idealism), finds a striking parallel in both the formal procedures of the *Cantos* and the insistence on the "intellectual and emotional *complex*" of Pound's Imagist doctrine.[58]

The political stakes of this strand of American modernism are probably sketched most compellingly by Frank Lentricchia in his penetrating and politically engaged reassessment of William James, where he suggests that the cultural politics of American modernism may be traced from the second Emerson that James remembered – the antinomian Emerson of molecular political force – to the antiimperialism that came on late but strong in the career of William James, and nowhere more forcefully than in the lectures delivered in 1906 and 1907 and collected in the book *Pragmatism*.[59] For James as for Pound, modernity threatened the individual with unprecedented forces of coercion, assimilation, and purification, which they both took to be the pernicious manifestations of a *conceptual* imperialism, whose coded term, for both, was "abstraction." And this was far from innocent academic business. As Kenneth Burke would point out roughly thirty years after James's *Pragmatism*, in similar terms and with shared political intent, abstraction is perforce *order*, and "the more closely you scrutinize the conditions required by order, the surer you are to discover that order is impossible without *hierarchy*." And hierarchy, in turn (here the move intent on creating political pause), is a principle, Burke reminds us, that governs the distribution of *authority*.[60]

James came at this problem from a number of directions, some of them more or less overtly political, others more locally engaged in his specific intellectual context. On the terrain of "academic philosophy," he offered a cranky diagnosis of philosophical abstraction's desire to eradicate the messy heterogeneity of local and historical texture – an imperialism of thought that, as Lentricchia argues, is the shadowy and insidious twin of its less subtle political counterpart.[61] As James put it:

> The world of concrete personal experience to which the street belongs is multitudinous beyond imagination, tangled, muddy, painful, and perplexed. The world to which your philosophy professor introduces you is simple, clean, and noble. The contradictions of real life are absent from it. . . . Purity and dignity are what it most expresses.[62]

In Lentricchia's reading, it is the last sentence here that ups the stakes considerably for the pragmatic philosopher: Academic philosophy does not *create* "purity and dignity," it *expresses* them.[63] Absolutist philosophy, in other words, is only one particular manifestation of a more pervasive and insidious desire to clean house in the world, and rationalist abstraction is but one example of what Lentricchia calls the "*will to refine*" that would make the world safe for (our) order.[64] (And James well knew, in the thick of our imperialist ventures in Cuba and the Philippines, who "we" were.)

For James, imperialism in all its forms meant the forcible eradication not only of cultural heterogeneity but even, at times, of life itself:

> Your typical ultra-abstractionist fairly shudders at concreteness: other things equal, he positively prefers the pale and spectral. If the two universes were offered, he would always choose the skinny outline rather than the rich thicket of reality. It is so much purer, clearer, nobler.[65]

That the practice known as "imperialism" might find organic expression in the theory James dubbed "ultra-abstraction" is clear in James not only in political effect but also in philosophical principle. James's pragmatic method, his politically tuned variant of Charles Sanders Peirce, takes as its point of departure the realization that "there can *be* no difference anywhere that doesn't *make* a difference elsewhere – no difference in abstract truth that doesn't express itself in a difference in concrete fact and in conduct consequent upon that fact, imposed on somebody, somehow, somewhere, and somewhen."[66] From the Jamesian perspective, theoretical difference is not only a theoretical matter: Its consequences are lived out at the business end of practice. James realized the contemporary truism that theory produces history. But he also realized that it produces it not only for theoreticians.

Not surprisingly, then, James's intellectual activism posits a powerful kind of antiontology to match his antiphilosophy; it refuses to specify once and for all the theoretical essence of the human subject, so that the concrete, historical subject may be better protected: "The world we live in," as James writes in a phrase central to Lentricchia's critique, "exists diffused and distributed, in the form of an infinitely numerous lot of *eaches*."[67] That Jamesian impulse toward plurality will be ardently sustained, as Patricia Rae reminds us, in the early Pound's continual insistence on how "manmade and provisional" our truths must be to take account of, and not to fudge, the untidy multiplicity of the self's manifold "direct experience."[68]

If James's project is Emersonian in one obvious sense, it is un- (even anti-) Emersonian in precisely its link with Pound's critique. The exercise of activist volition that for James, and, increasingly, for Pound, constituted the *obligation* of pragmatism to match the freedom it maintains was for Emerson, as he made clear in "Politics," only an indulgence of the very imperialism of will that all three thinkers sought to combat.[69] For all three, the paramount value of individual difference was a given; but Pound and James knew, better than Emerson, how easily and quickly that difference could be taken away.

"ROBERT FROST (TWO REVIEWS)"

If his Herculean endeavors on behalf of writers like Eliot and Joyce are any indication, Ezra Pound was well aware that cultural activism on behalf of individual difference depended on the nitty-gritty, everyday duties of the local intellectual, the embedded cultural worker. In his untiring agency for a host of struggling poets and prose writers, Pound demonstrated in word and deed that he had a keen sense of the material and institutional sites on which such a struggle would have to be waged.

A case in point is Pound's early efforts on behalf of Robert Frost, whom Pound met in London in January 1913 through F. S. Flint.[70] After receiving from the publisher a copy of Frost's first book, *A Boy's Will* (the title itself was a very un-Poundian homage to Longfellow), Pound worked quickly to convince Harriet Monroe to publish him in *Poetry* magazine and told his father, Homer, in June that he could not send him a copy of Frost's book just yet because "I'm using mine at present to boom him and get his name stuck about."[71] Curiously, though, it is quite clear from the early correspondence that Pound had reservations about this rustic nativist, and nothing resembling a wholesale endorsement – nothing approaching, say, his early reaction to Eliot's poetry – can be found.[72] This is significant, I think, because it indicates that his efforts on Frost's behalf were conducted not because Frost's work held up a mirror to his own proclivities but rather because this worn American had achieved an individuality of voice and production as far as could be from Pound's own, one that needed not only to be respected but to be actively promoted because of, not in spite of, its difference.

Pound took up Frost's case not only in letters to Monroe and others but also, more publicly, in reviews of *A Boy's Will* and *North of Boston* – the first in the *New Freewoman* (shortly to become the *Egoist*) in September 1913, the second in Monroe's *Poetry* for December 1914.[73] It is the lack of aesthetic common ground between the two men that makes these two short pieces particularly revealing in the context of Pound's early project. What little common ground there is, however, emerges early on in the first review, in a moment of sober praise by no means shouted from the rooftops: "This man has the good sense to speak naturally and to paint the thing, the thing as he sees it."[74]

By the time he wrote his review, Pound was primed for the keen, spartan diction of Frost's early work, in part because he had already learned his own lesson in an early comeuppance unrivaled in his whole long career. In 1911 he had visited Ford Madox Ford (then Hueffer) in Giessen, Germany, with a copy of his recently published *Canzoni* in tow to present (proudly, no doubt) to the established novelist. When Hueffer read the things, a kind of athletic epiphany took place, known now in Pound circles simply as "Ford's roll." As Pound recounted it nearly thirty years later, Hueffer

> felt the errors of contemporary style to the point of rolling (physically, and if you look at it as a mere superficial snob, ridiculously) on the floor . . . when my third volume displayed me trapped, fly-papered, gummed and strapped down in a jejeune provincial effort to learn, *mehercule*, the stilted language that then passed for "good English" . . . that roll saved me at least two years, perhaps more. It sent me back to my own proper effort, namely toward using the living tongue.[75]

If Pound's diction here is any index, Ford's critique could not have been more pointed. By the time of Pound's retelling, "provincial" had long since been a most serious term of political reproach in Pound's critical lexicon, connoting not only narrow-mindedness but also the support, implicit or explicit, of a system of repressive norms and abstract formulas that threatened to turn the individual into "the 'unit,'" as Pound put it, "the piece of the machine."[76] In effect, Pound had accused himself of being, up to this point in his poetic career, not part of the solution but part of the problem.

If Ford's roll helped propel Pound into the twentieth century by forcing him to "make it new" in poetic voice and diction (he would shortly declare, "No good poetry is written in a manner twenty years old"),[77] Robert Frost had been moving in the same direction for some time. And Frost had found his mentor in prose as well – specifically, in the American realist tradition of Howells. Under the pressure of the realist novel, both writers, despite their many differences, were coming to understand the necessity of "a language absolutely unliterary," and Frost declared his own "war on clichés" even as Pound was waging his battle against "good English."[78] For both writers, freedom *from* predigested lyric abstraction meant freedom *to* engage a world seen new because the textuality which made that world available could be remade – crisp, delineated, and sharp. As Frost put it in echo of Pound, but without the bravura of the avant-garde sloganeer, in poetry the word must be "moved from its old place, heightened, made new."[79]

For Pound, the move away from stilted diction and toward "the living tongue" (figured, appropriately, in participial form) carried with it a second aesthetic imperative, one hinted at in his admiration of Frost's ability to paint "the thing as he sees it." Pound's other major debt to Ford (acknowledged early, late, and often) was the realization that "poetry should be written at least at well as prose,"[80] that it should consist not of abstract bombast and slack expression (Ford's term was "rhetoric") but of images and impressions rendered with "clarity and precision."[81] In 1915 Pound would make it clear that his emergent modernism shared more than a little with Frost's conviction that a return from abstract "literary" diction to words made new meant most of all a return to life, to the dramatic textures of human beings in situation, to what William James had called, nearly a decade earlier, "the rich thicket of reality." What Pound wrote to Harriet Monroe in that year was being written by Frost, in both poems and letters, a literary world away. Pound insisted on

> objectivity and again objectivity, and expression: no hindside-beforeness, no straddled adjectives (as "addled mosses dank"), no Tennysonianness of speech; nothing – nothing that you couldn't, in some circumstance, in the stress of some emotion, actually say.[82]

For Pound, Frost's aesthetic, like that of Henry James, worked to render that difference in the bearing of voice and texture which captures the unique bent of the self in social context. Therein lay its modernism and its liberating value. Writing now of *A Boy's Will*, he observes, "One reads the book for the 'tone,' which is homely, by intent, and pleasing, never doubting that it comes direct from his own life, and that no two lives are the same."[83] How curious it is that Frost's "homely" tone might be "pleasing" to the expatriate who had declared, in 1911, his aim of creating a "curial" voice more "dignified" than "daily speech."[84] But Pound had changed in the two years since, and despite their differences in training, poetic production, and almost everything else, he was ready to hear Frost's clearly defined difference and its political corollary: the *fact* that "no two lives are the same." So it is that Pound is quick to praise Frost's treatment of his rustic subject: "He has never turned aside to make fun of it. He has taken their tragedy as tragedy, their stubbornness as stubbornness."[85] Frost treats his subjects, in other words, with the respect for individual difference and locale with which Pound here treats Frost. Herein lay a most unlikely modernist solidarity of difference. "Mr. Frost's people are distinctly real," Pound now realizes. "I don't want much to meet them, but I know that they exist, and what is more, that they exist as he has portrayed them."[86] Pound would not have been disturbed in the least to hear that Frost's people would not have wanted much to meet him either.

IN DEFENSE OF "WHIM"

The reviews of Frost are only a conspicuous, because (as it turns out) canonical, example of the early Pound's literary ideology at work. Four years later, his essay on Henry James would flesh out their implications: "Peace comes of communication," and art is nothing if not "a struggle for communication."[87] But what art communicates, and what peace consists of, is the kind of individual and social difference Pound had encouraged in booming Frost: "This communication is not a levelling," he writes, "it is not an elimination of differences. It is a recognition of differences, of the right of differences to exist, of interest in finding things different."[88] In another early essay ("The Serious Artist" of 1913), Pound's concept of individual difference would be pushed to its most radical and utopian implications, and art's social utility would be seen to consist in a kind of continual guerilla warfare against those habits of mind and social convention that would too readily assimilate the "peripheries of the individual" to the fixed center of society's ruling interests.

In "The Serious Artist," Pound takes quite seriously what Emerson told us in "Self-Reliance": "Society everywhere is in conspiracy against the manhood of every one of its members."[89] For Pound more than for Emerson, this meant that the activist intellectual should work – in poetic word and editorial deed – to unsettle any society that would take modern relations of production as a model for human relations in general, a conviction only underscored by Pound's historical training in comparative literature. But more important – and easier to miss – Pound's figure in "The Serious Artist" for the individual as the very antithesis of the capitalist machine reaches back to the red-hot Emerson that William James admired, to that inaugural vision of American individualism in its most unwrapped form. "From the arts," Pound writes in echo of the famous passage in "Self-Reliance," "we learn that man is *whimsical*, that one man differs from another. . . . That they do not resemble each other as do buttons cut by machine."[90]

In the name of that unanalyzable, ever-changing (and more than a little cocksure) thing called "whim," Pound was declaring, in so many words, solidarity with the vision of inviolable individualism that everywhere drives the early critique of Emerson himself. In the original passage in "Self-Reliance," Emerson went so far as to reject even the pigeonholing structures of the bourgeois family: "I shun father and mother and wife and brother when my genius calls me. I would write on the lintels of the door-post, *Whim*." And, Emerson adds – giving antinomian edge to his democratic goodness – "Expect me not to show cause why I seek or why I exclude company."[91] In "The Serious Artist," Pound registered his agreement: "It is not the artist's place to ask you to learn, or to defend his particular works of art, or to insist on your reading his books. Any artist who wants your particular admiration is, by just so much, the less artist."[92] For Pound as for Emerson, the call for the rights of individual difference is matched by a refusal of imperial impositions of any kind – of economic production, of familial piety, and even, perhaps especially, of aesthetic preference.

In neither case, however, did this necessarily mean a refusal of liberating political vision, for the world of difference envisioned and promoted by the serious artist resembles nothing so much as the world after capital presented by Marx and Engels, in a rare glimpse, in *The German Ideology*. The right to *whim* that joins Pound and Emerson joins them both to the utopian political affirmation of what Marx and Engels called "the total life of the individual."[93] It is in that individual's name that Emerson will reject the structuring force of family in rather uncanny anticipation of the moment in *The German Ideology* where Marx and Engels argue that the first form of divided labor that attacks self-development is to be found in the nuclear family.[94] And despite their political differences, Emerson would have readily agreed with Marx and Engels that the "one-sided" and "crippled" development of the self under the division of labor[95] – the self subjected, as a commodity, to a market in which his or her labor is bought and sold – needed to be replaced by a world that "makes it possible for me to do one thing today and another tomorrow, to hunt in the morning, fish in the afternoon, rear cattle in the evening, criticise after dinner, just as I have a mind, without ever becoming hunter, fisherman, shepherd or critic."[96]

At this juncture in his career, Ezra Pound's utopian vision was strikingly similar in both impulse and contour. Pound, like the early, "romantic" Marx, imagined a world in which the whole self might be at home, in which "you can admire, you can sit in the shade, you can pick bananas, you can cut firewood, you can do as you jolly well please."[97] Like Marx, and like Emerson, Pound thought the total life of the individual more various than the current economic and political structures that bound it. But the means of making that vision a concrete reality would take in Pound's career a shape unlike anything Marx or Emerson had imagined.

2

Critiques of Capitalist (Literary) Production

What clinches the Pound/Emerson connection is not only that both writers worked squarely within the ideology of individualism – Emerson its premier exponent in American literary history, Pound its not-so-obvious modernist inheritor – but mainly that the ideology they shared generated in both largely the same conclusions about those social institutions and cultural conventions that bore down upon the active center of their politics. Pound's storied career as magazine editor, advisor, and all-around promoter and guru testifies to the fact that, for him, the problem of ideology was a good deal more complex than simply endorsing or rejecting a given "world view." Indeed, the target of Pound's critique of literary production is not so much "false consciousness" as it is *enforced* consciousness shaped and reproduced by material institutions and practices. In this respect, Pound's modernism can be sharply distinguished from Emerson's romantic side, the Emerson for whom it would be overly simple, but not wrong, to say that something very much like false consciousness prevents the liberation of the self-reliant individual.

But there was another Emerson, of course, and that one sounded very much like Pound the shrewd modernist when he zeroed in on the relationship between economic production and ideological reproduction. *That* Emerson was dismayed to find that the increasing division of labor and the insidious logic of specialization in capitalist production had found their way into cultural and scholarly practice as well. And it was that Emerson – polemical strategist par excellence – who took no prisoners at the opening of "The American Scholar":

> Man is not a farmer, or a professor, or an engineer, but he is all. Man is priest, and scholar, and statesman, and producer, and soldier. In the *divided* or social state these functions are parcelled out to individuals. . . . Man is thus metamorphosed into a thing, into many things. . . . The priest becomes a form; the attorney a statute-book; the mechanic a machine; the sailor a rope of the ship.[1]

38

From 1837 (when Emerson delivered this address to the Harvard Phi Beta Kappans) to 1843, Emerson's critique of capitalism was sometimes wily, sometimes strident, but always sustained. And for that Emerson, the "sinister side" of American "freedom of intellection" was a lot like the sinister side of American freedom of enterprise, which sacrificed the producers to the product, self-reliance to self-interest. "There is nothing more important in the culture of man," he insisted, "than to resist the dangers of commerce."[2] And this was so, as Michael Gilmore puts it, because Emerson saw the deadening conformity promoted by the market "as a problem not of Society in the abstract but of the particular social environment emerging under capitalism."[3]

Emerson's fears were to be realized, even in those sectors of capitalist society seemingly most free from the pressures of the marketplace. Years later, in *English Traits*, he reminded us that "universities are of course hostile to geniuses, which, seeing and using ways of their own, discredit the routine."[4] As Emerson had told us twenty years earlier in the opening sentence of *Nature* – where he compared that depressing catalog of "biographies, histories, and criticism" to building "the sepulchres of the fathers"[5] – discrediting the routine was very much the avocation, if not the vocation, of the intellectual. Twenty years before *English Traits*, at the opening of his career, Emerson asked in his journals a question that he made it his mission to keep before his listening and reading public: "Why should we write dramas, & epics, & sonnets, & novels in two volumes? Why not write as variously as we dress & think?"[6]

The provincialism and fealty to tradition that Emerson defines here Pound himself would declare "the Enemy" in 1917. And the "drilled and scholastic," as Emerson called them, those hapless workers on the intellectual assembly line, would make their appearance in Pound's critique as well. Pound too saw that the university – that sphere of human activity which conservative critics keep telling us is most free of political taint – treated "the student as the bondslave of his subject, the gelded ant, the compiler of data." And Pound recognized, as Emerson had, that what was happening in the sphere of culture was only "the symptom of the disease" created by the capitalist dream of production. As Pound put it, in terms that everywhere echo Emerson's call for intellectual independence, "It is all one with the idea that the man is the slave of the State, the 'unit,' the piece of the machine."[7]

Neither Pound's "gelded ant" nor Emerson's "bookworm" can achieve any transference of power between what Emerson called "the active soul" and the cultural work that should make *other* souls active, because those economic and cultural structures within which the self operates require a divided, not a whole, self. For Emerson, the political implications were chilling; how could the dynamic whole man, "Man Thinking," be empowered when his social context asked him to become "a mere thinker, or still worse, the parrot of other men's thinking"?[8] Emerson's conception of the liberating poet makes it clear just how rhetorical this question is; instead of giving us "not metres, but a metre-making argument,"[9] the "mere thinker" is a mindless repeater who mimes the cultural formulas and literary conventions that are themselves apt expressions of the repetitive machinery of commerce and production.

It is in part that machinery in its specifically American form which made it possible for Emerson to anticipate – sometimes in spirit, sometimes in the very letter – the modernist social critique of Ezra Pound. Aside from the brute but startling fact that Pound was born only three years after Emerson's death, we need to remember that there is greater continuity than one might think between Emerson's economic context and Pound's own. As Carolyn Porter has argued, we find in Emerson's economic moment "a set of geographical, social, and political conditions which were to foster a relatively, even uniquely, unimpeded capitalist expansion." These distinctly American conditions, Porter argues, rapidly accelerated the process of atomization and alienation in America before the European, and modernist, fact.[10] For Porter, in short, the standard features usually associated with modernism (anomie, subjectivism, and so on) are anticipated in the literature of the antebellum American Northeast because the economic conditions of modernity are anticipated there as well.

From this vantage, it is important to underscore the uneven regional development of the American economy, even though the period saw the development of canal and railroad transportation create for the first time a truly national market and with it a soaring need for labor (whether native or immigrant).[11] Between 1800 and 1860, population increased from five to thirty-one million, and urban numbers swelled from 5 to 20 percent of the national total as the major cities grew almost tenfold.[12] Swift as the changes were, they came even earlier and more rapidly to Emerson's region. The so-called American System of manufacturing had been introduced in Connecticut in 1799, and the assembly-line methods, interchangeable parts, and division of labor that were its hallmarks would hold the future for American labor and industry.[13] As late as 1850, only 15 percent of the American labor force was employed in manufacturing (compared to *60* percent in England).[14] But national statistics can be misleading, for in 1820, although only 350,000 people worked in factories or mills nationwide, in Emerson's New England fully 100,000 workers were already employed in textile mills alone by 1815.[15]

Emerson himself was well acquainted with the pioneer of the New

England textile industry, Francis Cabot Lowell. They had entered college together, and after Emerson's house burned in 1872, Lowell himself made a "munificent donation," as Emerson put it, to help him rebuild.[16] Lowell, of Boston Brahmin stock, created the Boston Manufacturing Company in 1813, and the famed "Lowell System" quickly became legendary in American industry.[17] Lowell was determined, as one economic historian puts it, to instill in his workers "a spirit of earnestness, moral uplift, and financial self-improvement" and to distance his American project from the "looseness and moral depravity" that plagued the English factories.[18] But the reality, which would become clear when Lowell's female work force went on strike in 1831, was that the "Lowell girls" worked six 12-hour days a week and paid half their weekly wage to the company for room and board.[19] And while textile worker productivity, under the increasing pressure of automation and specialization, doubled between 1830 and 1850, real wages (at Lowell and elsewhere) fell or stood still.[20]

Such was the economic transformation and the human toll it levied taking place in Emerson's backyard in his formative years. Emerson was well acquainted with the changes and with the alienation they bred: "If the wishes of the lowest class that suffer in these long streets should execute themselves," he recorded in his journal in 1834, "who can doubt that the city would topple in ruins."[21] Indeed, as Maurice Gonnaud has suggested, it is in part the unmistakable menace of what unchecked capitalist development had wrought that drove Emerson to move from Boston to Concord in 1835.[22] Emerson would exact a kind of revenge, however, during the economic crisis of 1837, when the assumption that man must mold himself to the dictates of economic and historical law would be shaken to its very foundations.

By the time Emerson delivered his lecture on the American scholar to the Harvard Phi Beta Kappa Society in August of 1837, America had already undergone in the preceding months the worst year in its economic history. Thousands had rioted in New York, protesting inflated prices for food, and had raided the city's flour warehouses; cotton had fallen in price by one-half; and public-land sales in the West had decreased by 82 percent.[23] In April, not even the cruelest month of 1837, he surveyed the economic wasteland of the panic: "Cold April; hard times; men breaking who ought not to break; banks bullied into the bolstering of desperate speculators; all the newspapers a chorus of owls. . . . Loud cracks in the social edifice."[24] Still, the depression left Massachusetts and the Boston banks (which held Emerson's deposits) relatively unscathed, which allowed him to coolly investigate the meaning of the panic from a safe economic distance.[25] For Emerson, the ridiculous fiction of a society governed by rational economic law was now exposed for the delusion be always knew it to be, and he took no small satisfaction in the revelation.

A little over a month later, in another journal entry, he could meditate on the metaphysical lesson the country was already learning from its misplaced faith in the rule of commerce: "The black times have a great scientific value. It is an epoch so critical a philosopher would not miss. . . . What was, ever since my memory, solid continent, now yawns apart and discloses its composition and genesis. I learn geology the morning after an earthquake. . . . The Artificial is rent from the eternal."[26] If the market system had up to this point made self-reliance and self-interest difficult to distinguish, the sham of the latter and the urgency of the former must have now been unmistakable to the Harvard audience listening to "The American Scholar." As one critic has noted, Americans were now ready to hear the message of the "founder-member of the only party that had won ground in the panic – the idealists."[27]

By 1910, when Ezra Pound was in New York taking notes for the essay that would be published serially the next year as "Patria Mia," it had become a little more difficult for idealists to gain ground. For one thing, Emerson's economic context was struggling to establish what Pound's early economic moment took wholly for granted: namely, the monumental rationalization and systematization of economic and social life.[28] Emerson had seen in the marketplace a parodic inversion of self-reliance: "We eat and drink and wear perjury and fraud in a hundred commodities," he wrote, thinking of the self-made man pursuing self-interest only to find himself wholly dependent upon the machinery that broke down in 1837.[29] But what Pound saw in capitalist modernity was the threat not of the false self but of no self at all. It was not market but corporate, monopoly capitalism, whose beginnings, with the so-called Second Industrial Revolution, roughly coincided with Pound's birth in 1885. And that economic structure was rapidly systematizing previously uncolonized corners of American life, in ways unimaginable to Emerson, when Pound took up the critique of his country, in self-imposed exile, in 1910.[30]

That social logic, whose beginnings Emerson was barely able to glimpse but which Pound confronted as the very engine of modernity in his early critique, finds something like a privileged figure in the method of production known as Taylorization, modern capitalism's extreme division of labor into discrete, repetitive, and totally controlled tasks.[31] In fact, Frederick Taylor's *Principles of Scientific Management* was published in the same year as "Patria Mia" (though Taylorization derived from experiments that had been under way since the 1880s).

Taylorization, as Emerson's critique more than suggests, was something that, in the logic and development of capitalism, had been waiting to happen. Again, statistics are revealing but only partly so. Between 1865 and 1929, the percentage of the population employed in industrial and manufacturing jobs increased from 18 percent to only 22.5 percent.[32] At the same time, however, the ratio of capital investment to manufacturing output steadily increased from the 1860s until 1919, largely to take advantage of burgeoning developments in industrial technology.[33] As James Knapp argues in *Literary Modernism and the Transformation of Work*, the factory system of Emerson's era began an irrevocable process in which technological developments were bound to outstrip the capability of the worker to realize the full productive capacity of the technologies. By the end of the nineteenth century, Knapp argues,

> it was widely believed that the advance of industry would not be able to continue at its past rate unless future improvements in the tools of work were accompanied by appropriate – and planned – changes in the workers themselves. Predictable uniformity was one of the changes most earnestly sought.[34]

The results, as predictable as they are well known, are recorded in depressing detail in studies such as Harry Braverman's magisterial *Labor and Monopoly Capital: The Degradation of Work in the Twentieth Century*: the diminution of artisanal and skilled labor on the one hand and, on the other, the intensification of physical and psychological demands on workers, who, under a relentless division of labor, were becoming as faceless and interchangeable as the dulling, repetitive tasks they performed.[35]

No American modernist had a keener sense of that fact and the normalized culture it promised than Ezra Pound, who felt that the urge to treat the self as merely a "unit," a "piece of the machine," was but one symptom of a more pervasive "desire to control the acts of other people" – a compulsion (particularly American, if we believe Tocqueville) motivated by "a lust after uniformity."[36] More than half a century before Michel Foucault's meditation on the dystopian political unconscious of modernity in *Discipline and Punish*, Pound identified the imperial forces of normalization and control at work in the realm not only of economic production but also of cultural reproduction.[37] The abstraction-factory of the university, Pound tells us, is chiefly in the business of "hammering the student into a piece of mechanism for the accretion of details, and of habituating men to consider themselves as bits of mechanism for one use or another."[38] The economic powerhouse of modern capitalism needs a new kind of subject, and with the help of the educational system it produces one in its own image: as mechanism, as object.

Here again, Pound's emphasis on the objectifying power of the university anticipates, in a rather uncanny way, Foucault's anatomy of the examination as the means by which individuals are made objects of knowledge, the better to be controlled. "The examination," Foucault writes,

> is the technique by which power, instead of emitting the signs of its potency, instead of imposing its mark on its subjects, holds them in a mechanism of objectification. In this space of domination, disciplinary power manifests its potency, essentially by arranging objects. The examination is, as it were, the ceremony of this objectification.[39]

Although these critiques – one modern, the other postmodern – share a diagnosis of modernity's structures of cultural oppression, they are separated by a signal and in fact periodizing difference: What Pound is out to protect from such a system – namely, what he called "man's right to preserve the outlines of his personality"[40] – can no longer be said to exist in Foucault's postmodernism. For Foucault, the notion of "the individual" is *itself* part of that structure of domination, a "fictitious atom of an ideological representation of society," which power may now exploit and put to reproductive use.[41]

Thrown into relief by the harsh light of Foucault, Pound's early social criticism is now easier to situate along a spectrum of more or less romantic critiques ("romantic," at least, in Foucault's terms) of capitalism's colonization of the individual. Indeed, the insistence on the problem and priority of the individual that separates Pound from Foucault is precisely what joins him to Emerson's fellow romantic, the early Marx of the *Economic and Philosophical Manuscripts*. As Peter Nicholls points out in his discussion of Pound's economics, there are, of course, many obvious and crucial differences between Pound and Marx; for example, Social Credit economics, which Pound turned to after 1918, tended to focus too intently upon the problems of distribution and inadequate purchasing power, while ignoring the central problem of private property and the *relations* of production – the implications of the fact that one person's labor can be owned by another.[42] Still, the early Pound shares more with the early Marx than critics (of whatever political bent) have recognized, an oversight, but an understandable one exacerbated not only by Pound's later politics but also by his quarrels with Marx's concept of value and his insistence on the primacy of class, which Pound always found an anathema to his individualist project.

As in Pound's early social critique, the conceptual linchpin of Marx's early critique of alienated labor is the process of abstraction, whereby labor becomes "*external* to the worker" and "does not belong to his essential being." Marx's worker, like Pound's "unit," "does not confirm himself in his work, but denies himself, feels miserable and not happy, does not develop free mental and physical energy, but mortifies his flesh and ruins his mind."[43] When concrete labor power under capital is made *abstract* – is made, that is, a commodity subject to a system of exchange value – then the objects of production return to their producers as alien and other, as a loss, not an expression, of the self. And the result – one explored with considerably more precision and subtlety in chapter 1 of *Capital*'s first volume – is that "the *devaluation* of the human world grows in direct proportion to the *increase in value* of the world of things."[44] Abstraction in Marx, then, names a double dynamic of both subject and object. Abstract labor "not only produces commodities; it also produces itself and the workers as a commodity."[45] And this diagnosis too is shared by the early Pound. In capitalist modernity, subject and object trade places, as it were; it is not simply a matter of mass-produced rubbish but of the "outlines of personality" being hammered into an object. As James Knapp points out, Marxist thinkers like Georg Lukács would in the 1920s continue to focus upon the human as well as economic implications of abstraction by insisting, in Lukács's words, that "fragmentation of the object of production necessarily entails the fragmentation of its subject."[46] But Pound, in a set of essays written between 1911 and 1917, even before his discovery of Social Credit economics, had already reached those same conclusions: "To this end," Pound wrote in 1917 echoing Marx's critique of mortification, "you are to sacrifice your mind and vitality."[47]

When Pound writes "vitality" here, we may conjecture that he has in mind something quite specific – namely, sexual vitality, that presumably last unconquered enclave of the modern subject. We need only remember the Osiris of his early essay, his fascination with the cult of Eleusis, or his interest in Remy de Gourmont to remind ourselves that sexual, artistic, and productive vitality for Pound are closely wedded (and often with phallic infatuation).[48] What is compressed, then, in Pound's early figure of the modern intellectual worker as a "gelded ant" (a double reduction, not only an insect but a *castrated* one) is capitalist modernity's annihilation of the sexual self, which would be played out in grand style ten years later in Eliot's *The Waste Land*. In this light, what Pound called the preternatural "lust" after conformity emerges as a cruelly appropriate figure indeed for the power and depth of those forces threatening the self's creativity and even procreativity.

It is a theme that would find a shrewd and critical anatomist in the Antonio Gramsci of the *Prison Notebooks*, and the bitter historical irony of mentioning Pound and Gramsci in the same breath does not go unnoticed here.[49] For Gramsci, Taylorization (or what he calls "Fordism," Henry Ford having adopted Taylor's method with particular zeal) not only attacks the worker's body and time but also seeks to turn him into a "trained gorilla" (Taylor's own deformation) by breaking up "the old psycho-social nexus of qualified professional work, which demands a certain active participation of intelligence, fantasy and initiative on the part of the worker."[50] For Gramsci, the "puritanical initiative" of a Ford was the all-too-logical educative expression of Taylor's mechanical techniques; it aimed at nothing less than the mechanizing and obliteration of the creative, undisciplined self.

But Ford was only the latest and most technically relentless agent of capitalism's pious dream of production. In the 1870s and 1880s, apologists like Unitarian minister Jonathan Baxter Harrison helped define the climate in which Taylor's experiments in time and motion efficiency were just getting under way. Harrison instructed the American public in *Certain Dangerous Tendencies in American Life* (1880) that workers should have "little leisure for vicious thoughts, for nourishing mischievous and profligate desires." Recasting the individual in terms of his or her work (by lengthening the workday or intensifying the pace and repetition of labor) meant holding the line against "the animal nature and passions," which threatened to subvert discipline, production, and (if we believe Harrison) life as we know it.[51]

In a parodic way, then, capitalism too sought to "make it new," except here "it" was the modern worker, who was to be remade into a psychosexual gelding incapable, as Gramsci puts it, of that "productive creation" in which "the worker's personality [is] reflected whole in the object created."[52] So Taylor's "trained gorilla," it turns out, is a phrase too disingenuous and overly modest. As Gramsci realized, "the truth is that the new type of man demanded by the rationalisation of production and work cannot be developed until the sexual instinct has been suitably regulated and until it too has been rationalised."[53] In this light, if Pound's artisanal model of production seems nostalgic (and it cannot but seem so from our vantage) it is, as in Marx and Gramsci, an enabling nostalgia, a defiant figure for the associated sensibility of the whole self, which capitalism would divide and conquer.[54]

Pound's critique of modern capitalist production shares much with the phenomenology of alienation described by Marxism's romantic side, but it has even more in common with the American romanticism deriving from Emerson. What binds Pound to the line of Emerson is precisely what separates him from his European counterparts. His strident defense of the individual is accompanied by a peculiarly American absence of any structural concept of class. For Pound as for Emerson, to affirm individuals as members of a given class was not to affirm them at all but to actively efface the individual differences that made them worth saving to begin with. And consequently, the antidotes to alienation for both cannot be class-based but can be initiated only by the particular self whom reform is by and for.

While in England in 1847, Emerson saw the same industrial conditions, in largely the same areas, that led Marx and Engels to the very philosophical antithesis of idealism.[55] Emerson's account of those conditions in *English Traits* (1856) shares much with the early Marx's feeling for the human toll of England's industrial might:

> [It] is found that the machine unmans the user. What he gains in making cloth, he loses in general power. . . . The incessant repetition of the same hand-work dwarfs the man, robs him of his strength, wit and versatility, to make a pin-polisher, a buckle-maker, or any other specialty.[56]

Emerson's critique is also aware of the economic structure, which produced phenomenological disenchantment as surely as it produced commodities. Having observed the symptoms in human terms, he then turned to lay bare the disease: "Then society is admonished of the mischief of the division of labor, and that the best political economy is care and culture of men. . . . In true England all is false and forged. This too is the reaction of machinery, but of the larger machinery of commerce."[57]

Like Marx's critique, Emerson's implicates not only the technical means of production but the *mode* of production – the more pervasive economic and social logic – as well.[58] And like Pound's anatomy of objectification and alienation, of the self being "hammered" into an object, Emerson's critique recognizes that the truth of capitalist production may be read in its "false and forged" impress on its subjects. Emerson knew, as Pound would later put it, that "the man who makes steel rails in order that steel rails shall be made is little better than the mechanism be works with."[59] But what precedes and follows this moment in Pound's critique serves, most of all, to sharply differentiate his own position from that of Marx and at the same time to bind him to his Emersonian roots.

For alienation in Marx is fundamentally not a phenomenological but an economic category; it is not a matter of volition, self-transformation, or having a good attitude but is instead a built-in feature of the relations of production in which one person's labor may be abstracted and owned, as a commodity, by another. In Pound and in Emerson, however, the phenomenology and economic structure of alienation are strangely dissociated, almost as if to point up their particularly American faith in the power of the individual on the one hand and, on the other, to mark the political limitations of a position that refuses to subject the unique self to collective action. What precedes the foregoing quotation from Pound is this: "Civilization means the enrichment of life and the abolition of violence: the man with this before him can indubitably make steel rails, and, in doing so, be alive."[60] And what comes after points not so much to the potential, just now invoked, of the self to transcend its immediate material and economic conditions but rather to the bitter response that can and did follow when the idealist's hand is forced by the individual's failure of self-realization: "He is no safeguard against Kaiserism," Pound admonishes; "he is as dangerous and as impotent as a chemical. He is as much a sink of prejudice as of energy, he is a breeding ground of provincialism."[61]

Having read our Emerson closely,[62] we should not be surprised to come upon this passage in Pound, with its move from buoyant faith in the potential of the individual to sinking disgust when such potential remains unfulfilled. Emerson himself was to give full expression to both extremes, the former usually in his essays, the latter almost always reserved for his journals. At the end of "The American Scholar," hard on the heels of the 1837 panic, Emerson makes the first, critical move we saw a moment ago in Pound:

> The mind of this country, taught to aim at low objects, eats upon itself. There is no work for any but the decorous and the complaisant. Young men of the fairest promise . . . are hindered from action by the disgust which the principles on which business is managed inspire, and turn drudges, or die of disgust, some of them suicides.[63]

And when Emerson asks himself and his audience, "What is the remedy?" the answer he provides resembles nothing so much as Pound's advice to the happy maker of steel rails: "If the single man plant himself on his instincts, and there abide, the huge world will come round to him."[64] But when Emerson discovered, like Pound, that such a model for social transformation was not so easily actualized by those selves upon whom change depended, he too could turn on those same individuals, whose complacency was the only obstacle between this world and a better one. As for those unreliable because un-self-reliant selves, they were, as Emerson wrote of the Jacksonian mob, "the emblem of unreason; mere muscular & nervous motion, no thought, no spark of spiritual life"[65] – very much, we are forced to say, like those whose conditions Pound and Emerson set themselves to unmasking in the first place.

DEATH BY REPRODUCTION: POUND'S CRITIQUE OF THE LITERARY MARKET

When Pound turned, however, to examine the dominant institutions of American literary publishing and circulation just after the turn of the century, he was much more the shrewd modernist who refused to accept what most romantics, in a spasm of worldly revulsion and self-definition, like to claim: that the material conditions of literary production are ephemeral, beside the point. Again, Foucault is a useful touchstone here, because what Pound knew about American literary production was what Foucault would punningly diagnose later in his speculations on the twin phenomena of authorship and authority: that one can speak, or (a little less dramatically) one can make a living as an author, only if one's writing is "authorized" by the order of discourse that makes possible its appearance.[66]

But in other ways, Pound out-Foucaults Foucault by naming the names, in poetry, prose, and letters, of the responsible parties who profit directly or indirectly from the institutions and systems that enforce the discursive formation.[67] What Foucault surrenders in his archeological project of "pure" description (his phrase)[68] is precisely the unsettling recognition of the active merger of individual agency and social structure that gives Pound's critique such local, polemical power. Foucault, in a gesture entirely characteristic of his postmodernism, all but refuses to specify the particular powers and interests that materially sustain, and are sustained by, discursive norms and structures. And he is even more reluctant to trace these local forces of coercion – powerful *because* immediate, local – to the mode of production in general.[69]

Pound, however, is more than ready to do both, and nowhere more pointedly than at two key moments in his early career: The first, recalled in 1929 in "How to Read," represents something like a definitive encounter, in 1917, with the commodification of the literary object under modern capitalism; the second, at the heart of "Patria Mia," investigates the effect of that commodification on the literary subject, who must work within the forms and practices determined by the literary marketplace.

The particular commodity in question in the 1917 episode was Francis Palgrave's *Golden Treasury of the Best Songs and Lyrical Poems in the English Language*, a sort of greatest hits collection of recycled lyrics in the mode of Tennyson (not surprisingly), the dominant poetry anthology in America from roughly 1860 to 1920 (a little more surprisingly), and also (very surprisingly indeed) a best-seller. As Frank Lentricchia has pointed out, Palgrave's conception of the lyric, stated in his preface and bodied forth in the selections, reads like a catalog of all that poetic modernism would work to combat: The lyric must include no narrative, no personal or local color, no blank verse, and therefore no colloquial or dramatic rhythms of speech – nothing that smacks of the workaday world, for which lyric provides the pause that refreshes.[70] In Palgrave's words, he hoped that his *Golden Treasury* would provide "a storehouse of delight to labor and to Poverty" by filling the worker's "scanty hours" for "self-improvement " with the directives of "higher and healthier ways than the world."[71]

It is not so much that Palgrave's lyric rejects the realist textures of Howells and Dreiser that is central here – this is, I think, but a symptom. After all, a similar, antirealist generic bent may, as in Shelley's poetry or Adorno's aesthetics, betoken a very different kind of politics.[72] What lies at the heart of Palgrave's unwitting and unconscious trivialization of lyric is above all its conception of culture as *therapeutic*. And in this Palgrave's anthology simply embodied, in that particularly distilled and rarified form called lyric, a pervasive concept of culture endemic to all spheres of American life at the turn of the century, which defined themselves against the rationalized world of business and labor, whether in the Arts and Crafts movement, the simple-lifers, the various forms of theosophy, or official high culture itself. Most significantly (as Jackson Lears has noted in his extensive cultural history of the period) the therapeutic world view served to legitimize modern capitalist society because its very logic "involved a denial of the conflicts in modern capitalist society, an affirmation of continuing harmony and progress."[73]

Palgrave's conception of lyric, however, does not exactly "deny" conflicts – it recognizes "poverty" and the "scanty hours" left to those who endure it – so much as it defines itself against them. (After all, if the realist discourses of that world do not matter, then there is no reason to disallow them.) Consequently, Palgrave's lyric is if anything more complicit with the existing order than mere "denial" might suggest. By Palgrave's logic, lyric would do its cultural work of legitimation by being other-worldly in direct proportion to the failure of the real world to provide "higher and healthier" delights. Palgrave's lyric culture is a kind of automatically self-regulating mechanism of cultural compensation and symbolic legitimation. To paraphrase Mae West's famous line, when the real world is good, lyric is very good; but when the real world is bad, lyric is better.

Still, we have to ask what made Palgrave's concept of lyric culture not only possible but in fact hegemonic? Pound's answer in "How to Read" directs our attention, characteristically, not to the literary mores of the day but to the broader economic system in which they circulated; not to the text, but to everything outside it. As Pound tells it, he had in late 1916 an idea for an anthology that could provide a history of poetry to stand next to the history of painting which then existed at the National Gallery in London. He presented an outline of the project to an agent, who, duly impressed (or so we are told) with Pound's on-the-spot production of a three-hundred-item list, whisked it off to a "long-established publishing house." Two days later Pound received an urgent summons from the agent, who, in his haste, had not noticed that a central intention stated in the proposal was this: "It is time we had something to replace that doddard Palgrave."[74] The source of the agent's horror was not so much Pound's slap at the venerable editor but rather that the slap had been forwarded to Palgrave's publisher, Macmillan and Co. "But don't you know," the agent cried, "that the whole fortune of X & Co. is founded on Palgrave's *Golden Treasury?*" As Pound suddenly realized, meditating later on the rather unmediated way in which taste and literary production are determined by the profit motive, "I perceived that there were thousands of pounds sterling in electro-plate, and the least change in the public taste, let alone swift, catastrophic changes, would depreciate the value of those electors."[75] In that moment, Pound realized that what determined the meaning and value of poetry – in this case, an anthology – was itself but a directly determined effect of the price of silver and the desire to make an investment in it pay rich returns. What Pound realized, in short, was that poetry was not only a commodity but was, in fact, a by-product of *another* commodity.

Even well before the Palgrave episode, in 1914, Pound had already made it clear how deeply he understood the forces that made lyric poetry, despite all appearances, very much a thing of this world. In the previous months, Amy Lowell's publishers had been promoting one of her books by advertising her in American papers and magazines as "the foremost member of the 'Imagists' – a group that includes William Butler Yeats, Ezra Pound, and Ford Madox Hueffer." In response to this "arrant charlatanism," as Pound called it, he shot back to Lowell in a letter: "I don't suppose anyone will sue you for libel; it is too expensive. If your publishers 'of good standing' tried to advertise cement or soap in this manner, they would certainly be sued."[76] The irresponsible abstraction that Pound had attacked from the very beginning was here, in the form of false advertising, having far from abstract consequences. Poetry, Pound already knew, was not just any commodity, like cement, say, or soap; it was a particularly degraded one because the stakes, in purely economic terms (the terms privileged by modern capitalist society), were so low.

More than that, though, Pound realized during the exchange something else that will lead us into the next definitive moment of his early career. Speaking now of Lowell's publishers, Pound ended his letter:

> However we salute their venality. Blessed are they who have enterprise, for theirs is the magazine public. P.S. I notice that the canny ——n in his ad refrains from giving a leg up to any of the less well known members of the school who might have received a slight benefit from it.[77]

But this fact about commodity culture, of course, cuts both ways: The reason Lowell's publishers were more than happy to use the names of Yeats, Pound, et al. was that those famous names *sell*. So in the present economic and cultural context, it is not only the literary artifact that is a commodity but also the literary *self*: "Yeats, Pound, Hueffer," just so many products in the line of goods now peddled under the brand name "Imagism." "I don't suppose anyone will sue you for libel": Pound's charge was not a veiled threat but in fact a massive understatement, a confession of the powerlessness of the real, concrete individual who has no control over his commodified cultural persona.

What Pound learned in these moments was just how direct the relationship between capitalism and literary culture could be. The enemy of change, of "invention," of making it new, was not only or even primarily the literati, he discovered, but rather the corporate giants like X & Co. who, by controlling the material means of literary production, simultaneously controlled the public's taste and perception of what poetry and indeed culture should be. To put it bluntly, what Pound learned, early and decisively, was that the struggle for modernism, for heterogeneity and invention, for literary change and the desire for social change it expressed, was unavoidably a struggle with everything *other than* the text.

That Pound knew this from the very beginning – and that his storied interest in economics is a direct result of it – is clear from that second moment already mentioned, the critique of literary production presented in "Patria Mia." There, Pound unpacks much of what is epigrammatically condensed in his letter to Lowell, and he makes it clear as well that the poet may be a visionary, a revolutionary, or any number of other things, but he is also and above all a *producer*.[78] In contrast to his later obsession with distribution, Pound's focus here is how the mode of production coerces, channels, and even determines the producer's possible modes of self-expression in his product.

And what could be a better site for an investigation of these matters than the dominant American magazines of the day and the entrenched genteel writers who controlled them – those means of literary production that, more than the anthologies, exerted considerable power over the day-to-day life of the would-be writer? What Pound in his letters called "the *Century–Harper's* ginger-bread, stucco, paste-board ideal"[79] was, despite the metaphors, far from purely a matter of taste. Indeed, for most young American writers, it was a matter of survival. Pound never tired of attacking the genteel establishment, and he did so nowhere with greater gusto than in "L'Homme Moyen Sensuel," an uproarious satire written in 1915 and modeled on Byron's *English Bards and Scotch Reviewers*. Like the Byron who expressed his rowdier moods in ingenious rhymes, Pound took no prisoners in his incisive anatomy of the literary world ruled by "that infant tick / Who's now the editor of *The Atlantic*" and by "Henry Van Dyke, who thinks to charm the Muse you pack her in / A sort of stinking deliquescent saccharine."[80] As these lines more than suggest, the genteels represented for Pound nothing less than a systematic assault (albeit clothed in starched shirt and manners) on the very possibility of literary individuality and invention. As he put it in four-square bad taste later in the same poem, the genteels were the expression of

> that invidious
> Lurking, serpentine, amphibious and insidious
> Power that compels 'em
> To be so much alike that every dog that smells 'em
> Thinks one identity is
> Smear'd o'er the lot in equal quantities.[81]

Pound knew how to put his Byron (and many another writer) to good use, and here he captures the first principle of genteel culture in a compound rhyme that recalls nothing so much as the temper of Byron's great "intellectual / hen-pecked you all" in the "Dedication" to *Don Juan*. In the commodified culture of the genteels, Pound reminds us, "identity is / quantities."

Of course, he arrived at his diagnosis of American "magazitis" not by way of Marx but rather under the spur of his individualist inheritance and the artisanal model of production it valorized.[82] Nevertheless, his focus on the conditions of production enabled him to see in capitalism precisely what was unmistakable to Antonio Gramsci. And it led him to conclusions that were stridently anticapitalist but not exactly either Marxist or rank-and-file populist (much less fascist). At this juncture (he was twenty-six) he had been radicalized but not yet, in any coherent sense, politicized.

In "Patria Mia," Pound provides us with a sketch of modern magazine production that is immediately striking in its account of how thoroughly the Taylorization of commodity production had been absorbed into the literary process, which Palgrave told us transcended it. As Pound put it, with the weariness (already) of the literary journeyman:

> As the factory owner wants one man to make screws and one man to make wheels and each man in his employ to do some one mechanical thing he can do almost without the expenditure of thought, so the magazine producer wants one man to provide one element, let us say one sort of story and another articles on Italian cities and above all, nothing personal.[83]

The editor wants, in other words, a writerly version of Taylor's "trained gorilla," since the "expenditure of thought" cannot help but be a troubling expenditure of self – the introduction, let us say, of a very unwanted kind of currency into the editorial economy. And from the perspective of not the producer but the product, life on the literary assembly line is an assault on the kind of literary production that the investment of the whole self makes possible. In a passage that prefigures both *Mauberley*, its two gross of broken statues, and the defense of the artisan against usury in Cantos XLV and LI, Pound writes: "In 'San Zeno' at Verona, one finds columns with the artisan's signature at the bases. Thus: '*Me Mateus fecit.*' That is what we have not and can not have where columns are ordered by the gross. And this is a matter of 'industrial conditions.' "[84]

In modern America the literary self subject to the market (and what literary self was not?) faced what seemed to Pound an unavoidable double bind, one built into what he matter-of-factly called the "system of publishing control."[85] The aspiring writer in America in 1910 faced either self-annihilation or self-annihilation: Either give up the difference of self that makes a poetic difference to produce the extruded, anonymous product that sells, or buck the system of write-to-fit and starve in the name of experiment. As Pound characterized it:

> The serious artist does not play up to the law of supply and demand. He is like the chemist experimenting, forty results are useless, his time is spent without payment, the forty-first or the four hundredth and first combination of elements produces the marvel, for posterity as likely as not. The tradesman must either cease from experiment, from discovery and confine himself to producing that for which there is a demand, or else he must sell his botches, and either of these courses is as fatal to the artist as it would be to the man of science.[86]

Artists, since they must make their living by payment for piecework, will be prosperous only insofar as they translate that payment into a good per-hour rate. Pound's early encounters with the literary market told him that the way to do that was to imbue the literary object not with the signature of the self one finds on the columns at San Zeno but with what Karl Mannheim calls, in a wonderfully apt figure, the "anonymity of money."[87] The effects of this system of control and dehumanization on literature's critical and subversive potential were obvious to the young Pound, who knew firsthand that those prosperous writers whose success freed them to experiment were precisely the ones who had no demonstrated interest – and no real motive – in doing so. If Pound seemed to suggest in other places that the writer might stand free of the system of production and exchange, there is no hint of it here: "This," he knows, "is unescapable."[88]

The full ideological force of American magazine culture is not really felt, however, until we recognize that it constitutes, both in its standards and in its system of production, a stance toward history as well – or, more precisely, toward the possibility of history. As Fredric Jameson points out, the structure of both commodification in the economic sphere and the reification it produces in social relations is fundamentally one of *repetition*. And the various modernisms have nothing in common so much as the felt pressure to break the economic (but not only economic) compulsion, not to produce, but merely to *reproduce*.[89] Nowhere is this fact about modernism registered earlier or with more acumen and verve than in Pound's early critique, which anticipates corollary changes in his poetic practice (begun in earnest in *Ripostes* of 1912) by some two years.

But the linkage between the economic structure of commodification and the ideological representation of history exposed by Pound is not clear until we articulate what Pound's Palgrave anecdote only hints at in positing *change* as the primary enemy of X & Co. In their fetishism for the utterly finished literary commodity, the American magazines pushed the dynamic social processes of reading and writing into fixed forms and then economically enforced *that* demand by forcing writers to define themselves in terms of the static, anonymous items they produced.[90] All of which (as Roland Barthes's seminal essay "Myth Today" makes clear) is to make historical change quite literally unthinkable, because historical change is, after all, nothing other than difference across time. And all of which, moreover, is to transmogrify historically contingent social forms into the opposite of history, into what Barthes calls "the enormous mass of the undifferentiated, of the insignificant, in short, of Nature."[91] What Barthes calls the "anonymity of the bourgeoisie" – the expression on the level of class, as it were, of Mannheim's "anonymity of money" – derives from the fact that the bourgeois ideology

> transforms the reality of the world into an image of the world, History into Nature. And this image has a remarkable feature: it is upside down. The status of the bourgeoisie is particular, historical: man as represented by it is universal, eternal.[92]

To return, then, to Pound, we are now in a better position to appreciate the full scope and power of what we can now call the literary ideology of the magazines, which not only alienates writers in their work and promotes uniformity in the literary product but also, and just as important, enforces a vision of society and culture that holds that the world of today is the world of forever, that the poetry of today is a poetry for all ages, that the situation of the poet in 1910 is not a matter of economic compulsion and cultural politics but a natural fact. We can now more fully appreciate not only the humor but also the political point of Pound's satire in "Patria Mia":

> It is well known that in the year of Grace 1870 Jehovah appeared to Messrs Harper and Co. and to the editors of "The Century," "The Atlantic," and certain others, and spoke thus: "The style of 1870 is

the final and divine revelation. Keep things always just as they are now." . . . And if you do not believe me, open a number of "Harper's" for 1888 and one for 1908. And I defy you to find any difference, save on the page where the date is.[93]

Later, in "Provincialism the Enemy," Pound would make it clear that this sort of literary ideology was not only antihistoricist but anti-democratic as well:

Popularization in its decent and respectable sense means simply that the scholar's ultimate end is to put the greatest amount of the best literature (i.e. if that is his subject) within the easiest reach of the public; free literature, as a whole, from the stultifying taste of a particular genera-tion. This usually means, from the taste of the generation which has just preceded him, and which is always engaged in warping the mass humanity of Welt literature into the peculiar modality of its own needs or preferences. . . . He is, or should be, engaged in an attack on provin-cialism of time, as the realist author is engaged in an attack on provin-cialism of place.[94]

A "provincialism of time" – a particularly Poundian figure for what he had identified, without fully knowing it, as the self-interested and elitist cultural offspring of capitalism's economic democracy. But Pound knew that writers and readers in such a situation are free only as producers and consumers of commodities are free. At this juncture, Pound wanted not another kind of elitist culture but another kind of freedom. As he put it years later, "I do not believe mass culture makes any such specific and tenacious attack on good art as that which has been maintained during the last forty years of 'capitalist, or whatever you call it' ci – or whatever you call it – vilization."[95]

IMAGISM

Pound's critique of literary production provides the terms by which the full political force of Imagism may be best understood: Imagism not as the latest, new and improved literary commodity (exactly what he attacked in the appropriation by Amy Lowell's publisher) but as the intended antithesis of commodification; as intervention, on behalf of the literary subject and artifact, at a specific moment in the literary history of capital. If anything is to be learned from Imagism, we must recognize that its impulse and its doctrine were generated in a historical situation, against a quite specific kind of culture and society. If, in Pound's terms, the struggle for literary modernism was a struggle with everything *outside* the text, how could it be otherwise?

Strictly speaking, Pound did not "invent" Imagism, nor was he its most long-standing practitioner. As early as 1908–1909, T. E. Hulme's

Poet's Club, which included the young Pound in its membership, had been exploring Bergson-inspired ideas that had much in common with the later versions of Imagism; and Amy Lowell continued to publish Imagist anthologies up through 1917, long after Pound had abandoned the movement.[96] But what Pound did was to provide the central critical manifesto for Imagism, and in doing so he gave the counterpoetics of early modernism a strategic coherence it badly needed in both Edwardian London and genteel America. Not that this was Pound's initial intention, if we believe his version of events. As he recalled in 1915, voicing the same impulse that drove the reviews of Frost, "the whole affair was started not very seriously chiefly to get H. D.'s five poems a hearing."[97] That accomplished, Imagism and its accompanying critical declarations became a landmark of modernist poetics.

In Pound's own corpus, the doctrine of the Image is prefigured in the "Osiris" essay by what he called "the method of Luminous Detail," the modernist agon of the "method of sentiment and generalisation" so fashionable in fin-de-siècle culture and its inheritors.[98] Like the Image, which gives "that sudden sense of freedom from time limits and space limits,"[99] the luminous detail provides "sudden insight into circumjacent conditions, into their causes, their effects, into sequence, and law."[100] And "Osiris" provides a glimpse as well of the negative, critical force Pound marshalled in Imagism's list of "don'ts." Before the Imagist fact (talking his cue from Ford Madox Hueffer's early doctrine), Pound admonished: "The artist seeks out the luminous detail and presents it. He does not comment."[101]

Already, the complex contradictions of Imagist doctrine are coming into view. On the one hand, luminosity of detail liberates the concrete percept, and thereby furnishes a poetic vehicle to free the self from the prison of prepackaged abstraction. "The truth is the individual," Pound writes in "Osiris," and he means it in both these senses (individual percept, particular self) and in every sense.[102] On the other hand – and this must jump off the page for the contemporary reader – to promote an aesthetics that might free us from space and time and transport us into a realm of final causes and "law" is to supplant the sham (reified) permanence of "the style of 1880" with a literary ideology equally debilitated by its ahistorical idealism.

But as much could be said, of course, of any number of modernist aesthetic doctrines, and in fact it *was* being said by the earlier Yeats, whose romantic mysticism Pound found, for all his admiration, a bit out of touch with the times.[103] What Yeats called "The Symbolism of Poetry" would reveal, in his words, "the laws of art, which are the hidden laws of the world"; the symbol would "give a body to something that moves beyond the senses."[104] As James Longenbach argues in his study of

Pound's relationship with Yeats, Pound wanted to retain the value of what he called "'symbolism' in its profounder sense," which he found in Yeats's work, but hoped at the same time to sharpen the difference between Imagism and what symbolism tended to degenerate into: "mushy technique" and merely "literwary" conventional meaning.[105] If the first part of Yeats's doctrine sounds like it would be right at home in Pound's "Osiris" essay, the second half, however, quite conspicuously separates Yeats's symbolism from what looks at first glance like its Imagist soul mate.

Two points here will help clarify the difference. For Yeats, the way to make contact with that thing which moves beyond the senses is to utilize "the element of evocation, of suggestion." Consequently, poetry for Yeats must be the Manichean opposite of "the scientific movement . . . which [is] always tending to lose itself in externalities of all kinds."[106] Pound, however, repeatedly insists that Imagism's method is not suggestion but "direct treatment of the 'thing'"[107] – that its very vehicle, in other words, is "externalities." As Pound put it, in sharp (and premeditated) opposition to the Yeats/Symons line: "I believe that the proper and perfect symbol is the natural object . . . so that a sense, and the poetic quality of the passage, is not lost to those who do not understand the symbol as such, to whom, for instance, a hawk is a hawk."[108] Not surprisingly, then, Pound's early project will not attempt to gain any metaphysical mileage by defining itself against the boogeyman of science. If anything, Pound seeks solidarity with it in the struggle against sentiment and generalization. Time and again in Pound's early prose, the poet is figured as a "steam-gauge" or "voltameter," as "a good seismograph" – as one, in other words, whose business is anything but the dreamy unknowable.[109] Imagist "freedom," it appears, is one thing, and symbolist transcendence, quite another. As Patricia Rae points out, "the Image, however much it might resemble the inspiring Idea of the *Symbolistes*, is in fact an entity firmly situated in that experiential realm approved by empirical psychology."[110]

In Pound's work, the difference between Imagism and symbolism is seldom rendered in more detail than in the essay "Vorticism":[111]

> Imagism is not a symbolism. The symbolists dealt in "association," that is, in a sort of allusion, almost of allegory. They degraded the symbol to the status of a word. They made it a form of metonymy. One can be grossly "symbolic," for example, by using the term "cross" to mean "trial." The symbolists' symbols have a fixed value, like numbers in arithmetic, like 1, 2, and 7. The imagists' images have a variable significance, like the signs a, b, and x in algebra.[112]

But this must seem puzzling since Pound, in the previous passage, was at pains to preserve "a sense" for the poetic word. So what can it mean to attack the "fixed value" of the symbol on behalf of the "variable significance" of the image? Pound's diction here provides a clue, I think, by making (none too clearly) a subtle but important distinction between the terms "value" and "significance." The value of the symbol is fixed, as Pound conjugates it, "almost" as allegorical meaning is fixed, and the symbol is therefore "degraded" because it is reduced to a univocal meaning by formulaic conventions that determine, before the poetic fact, the structure of meaning to which the symbol refers for its value. In which case, from Pound's point of view, who needs poetry or the image? The image, on the other hand, as Pound famously formulated it, "presents an intellectual and emotional complex in an instant of time."[113] The image is of "variable significance" not only because it is a *complex* – polyvalent, heterogeneous, not one but many meanings – but also because it occurs in a lyric moment, a moment of rupture, not complicity, with poetic and perceptual convention. To put it another way, the image takes place not by virtue of the conventions that reduce polyvalent history to univocal tradition but rather in a present whose value is yet to be determined. In this sense, we may say that the significance of the image is variable because the meaning of the present is.

But if this is the case, then Pound may be eliminating historicity altogether in his attempt to free us from deadening convention.[114] If the symbol is for Pound suffocatingly overdetermined by literary convention, the image may seem to us, on the other hand, to have no determinations at all. As we will see, however, Pound went to great lengths to make it clear, not that the image was wholly free, but only that it should be free from the paralyzing forces that made "cross" equal "trial." In turning away from the world of *Harper's* and Edwardian London, Pound turned toward a poetics that would bring the self into fresh contact with a world of things whose significance was complex beyond anything imaginable to the culture of capitalism, which had gotten used to ordering columns, and poems, by the gross.

As counterstatement against the commodification of culture, Pound's Imagism has, oddly enough, much in common with Theodor Adorno's later attempts to restore what he called "the preponderance of the object."[115] Pound and Adorno, polar opposites though they seem, find modernist solidarity in a common enemy; they both share a modernist horror of the cultural and political effects of what Adorno called the "identity principle," or what Pound excoriated under the name "abstraction." To look at Pound through the lens of Adorno is to remember that Pound's early project was finally, if not solely, a critique of the tyranny of abstract exchange value over qualitative heterogeneity and difference.

If, to use Adorno's famous phrase, "all reification is a forgetting," then what modernity had forgotten, in Pound's view, was not only the heterogeneity of present things and selves but also the fact that the value of the poetic lay in that concrete world of difference which was the repressed nightmare of commodity culture. What Martin Jay has called Adorno's Nietzschean concept of reification stressed as well the loathesome suppression of the heterogeneous object world in the gray sameness of abstract equivalence.[116] For Adorno, reification was not simply a problem of the subject – as if, having secured our tyranny over the world of things, all that remained was to make proper use of that tyranny. What Adorno called the identity principle had roots in the principle of abstract exchange, and he even suggested that all forms of abstract thought could be traced to it as well. For Adorno as for Pound, to see things in terms of an identity principle, in terms of that hollow unity which was possible only in abstraction, was not to see them at all.

If for Adorno the source of reification was exchange and if all reification was "a forgetting," solving it, however, did not mean restoring an original wholeness in which all differences would be abolished. On the contrary, it would mean the restored tension and fruitful interchange of subject and object, self and other[117] – a renewed premium, as Pound wrote in the essay on James, on "the right of differences to exist, of interest in finding things different."[118] Adorno's phrase "the preponderance of the object" thus emerges (from another part of the field, as it were) as a particularly apt expression of the modernist desire crystallized in Pound's Imagism. It was Adorno's wager, in so many words, that the Self could be a Self only by letting the Other be Other.

This is the sense, I think, of Pound's position in "The New Sculpture" (1914), where he argues, in a rich and complex figure:

> The old-fashioned artist was like a gardener who should wish to turn all his garden into trees. The modern artist wishes dung to stay dung, earth to stay earth, and out of this he wishes to grow one or two flowers, which shall be something emphatically not dung, not earth.[119]

It is significant, particularly in light of Adorno's subversion of the subject/object dichotomy, that Pound's constellation here combines three terms – "trees," "earth/dung," "not earth/dung" – and not only two. The new artist's aim is not simply to replace one sort of identity principle ("trees") with another but rather to subvert altogether the possibility of identity: not to create "trees" (or, what amounts to the same sin of identity, "not-trees") but rather to perpetuate differences in the plural (not dung and not earth).

The new art would thus be one of greater rigor and fidelity: rigor, because one had to present an intellectual and emotional complex with maximum economy (Pound's list of "don'ts" included forty-odd strictures against abstraction, ornament, the iamb, description); and fidelity, because Imagism was "direct treatment of the 'thing'" in all its complexity, freed from crushing allegorical precedence and reduction. As Pound put it, the new poetry was an echo of Flaubert, a "constatation of fact."[120]

To raise the name of Flaubert, however, is to recognize that another fact – namely, Ford Madox Hueffer's influence on the early Pound – is curious indeed. If "Ford's roll" led Pound to renovate his diction as only a speechless criticism could, the novelist's actually verbalized strictures for the art of prose and poetry would find their way into Pound's early aesthetic in all sorts of places: in his writings on impressionism, in his admiration of Joyce's "realism," and most fundamentally in the doctrine of Imagism. What is curious about this literary relationship is how diametrically opposed Pound and Ford were when it came to the political character of culture. Consider, for instance, that what Ford admired in Henry James was not his hatred of tyranny, not his defense of the individual (not, in other words, what Pound admired), but rather his refusal of any "public aims" for his art. For Ford, what makes James a master is the fact that he "has bestowed his sympathies upon no human being and upon no cause, has remained an observor, passionless and pitiless."[121] In short, the uses to which Pound and Ford put Henry James could not be more different, and to come to terms with the politics of Imagism, we must come to terms with the Ford in Pound.

As Pound recalled in 1939 in his obituary for the novelist, in the years preceding the young American's arrival in London no one but Ford "held that French clarity and simplicity in the writing of English verse and prose were of immense importance as in contrast to the use of a stilted traditional dialect, a 'language of verse' unused in the actual talk of the people . . . for the expression of reality and emotion."[122] Pound would acknowledge this debt early and often, and he traced what he would later call "the prose tradition in verse" to Ford's "insistence upon clarity and precision . . . in brief, upon efficient writing."[123] It was Ford who provided much of the technical machinery,[124] if not the liberating impulse, for the literary ideology Pound would later bring to bear on the cultural establishment.[125]

Given those principles, which were to become the famous watchwords of the Imagist poetic, it is significant that what Pound also admires in Ford is "his power to render an impression,"[126] for "impressions" are not easily reconciled with the well-known Imagist dicta of precision, objectivity, and hardness. And it is even more curious, as one recent critic points out, that in the period 1912–1914 Pound was espousing these (apparently Ford-inspired) principles at the same time he was engaged in a frontal assault on impressionism, most vehemently in the pages of Blast.[127]

This would pose no problem, except for the fact that impressionism was Ford's avowed aesthetic. So how, then, do we reconcile all of this? To praise the ability to render an impression is to appeal to the active work of subjective consciousness, but to promote objectivity and precision is to call for a writing whose rigor consists in the fact that it makes no such appeal. Imagism seemed to want it both ways: to liberate individual difference in literary production, only to challenge that very priority of the subject with calls for objectivity and precision. What was it that should get expressed in art anyway, the self or the objective world purged of subjective finesse?

This persistent contradiction was addressed but never really solved by Ford. On the one hand, he was quite insistent in arguing that impressionism was a *realism*, and he praised Pound and the Imagists for their "rendering of the material facts of life, without comment and in exact language."[128] But what then of the qualitative differences between selves and their creations? Ford was not willing to surrender that either (few modernists were), and he argued (on the other and irreconcilable hand) that impressionism was also "a frank expression of personality." "The measure of its success," he wrote, "will be just the measure of its suitability for rendering the personality of the artist."[129] Apparently untroubled by the contradiction, Ford hoped that the impressionist could have his objectivity and eat it too.

But he could do so, it turns out, only in solipsistic isolation. As Michael Levenson has characterized it, Ford eventually came to the conclusion that impressionism "is entitled, even obliged, to be personal in the presentation of reality, since there must be no pretense of a neutral body of knowledge. To render reality then *is* to manifest individuality. Since they are necessarily personal, perceptions of the real are expressions of the self."[130] But of course this solves nothing, as Levenson well realizes. Ford is simply responding to the subject/object problem posed by his aesthetic by evicting (through the back door in the dark, as it were) any pretension to objectivity altogether. Or more precisely, the object is now made a mere moment, a mere epiphenomenon, in the movement of an essentially closed subjectivity.

But this is not all. Ford's final move – and here the desire for formal autonomy plays its last card – is toward an impressionism so pure, so much of the moment, that it should not be corrupted by what we normally associate with the historical, concrete self. The immediacy of the impression must now be rendered free of the contaminants of individual will, belief, opinion, and attitude. Impressionism remains self-expression – because it is the finite self that receives the impress of objects – but only because the self has been reduced to something close to the status of an object, a passive machine for recording impressions and events.

Impressionism is now, in Levenson's phrase, "a subjectivity in which the subject has disappeared."[131]

These problems lay as well at the heart of the Imagist aesthetic, waiting to free but also to challenge the priority of individual difference. What will become clear in Pound's reworking of Ford, however, is that Imagism will call for the disappearance not of subjectivity in toto but rather of a certain *kind* of subjectivity. And that call is made possible only by virtue of the fact that Pound was willing to embed in social situation the self that Ford wanted to keep pure and free of social taint. Imagism's stress on objectivity contains a political imperative that Ford's doctrine never entertained: It is a coded plea for freedom from the kind of imperial abstraction that made subjects not central but epiphenomenal, not active but passive.

To understand the politics that emerges in this difference between Pound and Ford is to abandon any quasi-scientific reading of Imagism (despite Pound's many scientific metaphors). It is to give up the ghost of reconciling what are already this doctrine's obvious antinomies. Indeed, these contractions *cannot* be solved in their own terms, on the formal level at which we find them. At this juncture, in other words, we are forced to see Imagism as a historically specific intervention seeking to show, as in relief, that the real danger to the individual lay not in the Imagist call for precision and objectivity but precisely in those conventions that would seem to endorse "subjectivity" in the form of received opinion, belief, and practice. Imagism's objectivist imperative must now, in other words, be recontextualized so that its contradictions may propel us into a realm where it may be grasped as a moment in a field of ideological discourse and contest.

From this perspective, Imagism may now be seen to express a full-throttled individualism that is fully in the American grain of Pound's literary ideology. As Patricia Rae points out, Pound's Imagist and Vorticist insistence on the concrete, experiential contingencies of individual difference links him directly with William James's pragmatism.[132] And beyond that, we should add, for Imagism as for Emerson an "original relation" with the object world was a figure for a self so ferocious in its insistence on the right to individual and social difference that it could never really be challenged – as Ford's fragile, socially untethered individualism was challenged – by any objectivist bias. Pound may have in part inherited from Ford the principles that would usher in a new era in poetry, but the imperative of those principles in Pound's hands left Ford slumbering in a fin-de-siècle political twilight. Pound's individualist inheritance created in him a readiness, wholly absent from Ford, to join matters of culture and aesthetics with a larger critique of the societies they perpetuated and underwrote.

We remember that the first of Imagism's famed principles calls for "direct treatment of the 'thing,'" but it is a thing, significantly, either "subjective or objective."[133] Just what this "subjective" thing might look like, and how it might be distinguished from an objective thing, Pound spells out with a little more precision in the section of the essay "Affirmations" (1915) entitled "As for Imagisme." Here, Pound (now in his Vorticist phase) clarifies what appeared aphoristically obscure in the earlier doctrine. What creates the image, it turns out, and what in fact creates all form, is "*emotion*."[134] The image can therefore be of two kinds. As for the first: "It can arise within the mind. It is then 'subjective.' External causes play upon the mind, perhaps; if so, they are drawn into the mind, fused, transmitted, and emerge in an Image unlike themselves."[135] The subjective Imagist "fuses" data from the external world and quite literally produces a new piece of reality (*not* dung, *not* earth), which exists only by virtue of individual emotion. On the other hand, "the Image can be objective," Pound counters. "Emotion seizing up some external scene or action carries it intact into the mind; and that vortex purges it of all save the essential or dominant or dramatic qualities, and it emerges like the external original."[136] The objective Imagist, in this reading, does not so much create as restore heterogeneity in the object world by purging it of everything *but* its essential difference.

In either case, though, it is emotion, the mind, the vortex of the self, that makes possible the Imagist difference. And because Pound's fundamental assumption is that objective heterogeneity is a given (that assumption is the rationale of the Imagist's project), his appeal that the particularity of things should be so recognized is, in the end, an appeal to the individual, to consciousness. It is finally "emotion" that is the "organiser of form."[137] It is "emotion" that makes all of this – either subjective or objective Imagism – possible. So it is that Pound argues again and again, against the later Ford, that the artist must not be thought of "as wholly passive, as a mere receiver of impressions."[138] And so it is that Pound would attack cubism, that apparent co-conspirator of Vorticism, for its passivity, its suppression of personality.[139]

If, as Pound argued in 1912, "poetry is identical with the other arts in this main purpose, that is, of liberation," and if its function is "to strengthen the perceptive faculties and set them free from . . . such encumbrances, for instance, as set moods, set ideas, conventions,"[140] then it is clear, by Pound's own logic, that the artist's work can so liberate its readers only *after* the individual artist has undertaken a project of self-renovation. In this sense, then, what Imagism requires is first and foremost a rigor of *self*. Or as Pound put it, with maximum compression, "I believe in technique as the test of a man's sincerity."[141] Clarity and precision, then, are *ethical* imperatives squarely in line with the signed column of "Patria Mia": a call, against long odds indeed, for the creative self to somehow surmount a socioeconomic context that systematically enforces a way of seeing that is also a way of *not* seeing.

But at this point, we must ask: If emotion organizes form, then what organizes emotion? For Pound – and for the ideology of radical individualism motivating his early project – the answer can only be, on strictest principle, "the self and only the self." For Pound as for Emerson and his other inheritors, if anything else organizes it, then all is lost. As Pound noted with approval in "Vorticism," a Russian correspondent who once thought him a symbolist had now recognized that Imagism was, in our terms (and in the correspondent's echo of "Nature"), Emersonian in intent: "I see," he now realized, "you wish to give people new eyes, not to make them see some new particular thing."[142]

So to move into the epistemologically renovated universe of the image was to enter a world where not only things but selves as well had been set free. Imagism called, in short, for a modernist cultural self-reliance. From this vantage, we can now see that Pound's talk about "freedom from time limits and space limits" – his apparent symbolist hangover – might have proposed lyric escape, but not exactly escape to another, transcendent world. Instead, Imagism presented the possibility of escape into a new and (a redundancy) Emersonian sort of self, one that could realize itself not in symbol or allegory but only by becoming, as it were, a genre unto itself.

The Imagist self, however, needed the object world to keep its lyricism honest, to provide a stay against the symbolist dissolution of subject and object and the threat to difference it embodied. In this sense, Pound's modern self was lyric, not in spite of, but because of the unimaginably complex topography in which it moved, one that created for the poet "needs beyond the existing categories of language."[143] The Imagist self was lyric, then, not only because it was out of time but also because it was *not* out of this world. By confronting an object world that has its own being, its own difference, the self can discover its own. "Poetic language," Pound maintains, "is the language of exploration."[144]

So this modern self, like the American self Emerson envisioned, is fully lyric only by virtue of the fact that its identity is uncertain. Like Emerson, Pound was quite acute and detailed in itemizing the rigor required to make it new. But although Pound tells us that Imagism creates freedom *from*, he has nothing to say about what it allows freedom *to* do. Once liberated from history's allegorical reductions, we enter into a self that is free only because it is undefined and undefinable. Pound's Imagism – in its quintessentially Emersonian refusal to indulge in its own conceptual imperialism, and in its Jamesian dedication to the concrete world of contingency and difference – also refuses to flesh out the contours of a lyric self so pure that no economic or political structure can accompany it.

3

Economies of Individualism

Pound's early critique on behalf of personal and social difference stakes out an individualist position of enormous attraction, and not only for Americans. Jean-Paul Sartre, a modernist of very different ideological investment and Pound's opposite in almost every respect, devoted considerable critical attention to the priority of the subject as well, and nowhere with more dexterity than in *Search for a Method*: "Valéry is a petit bourgeois intellectual, no doubt about it," Sartre wrote. And with a compression Pound would have admired, he added, "But not every petit bourgeois intellectual is Valéry."[1] For Sartre, that recognition called for renewed attention to biography, and it gestured toward a larger theoretical point as well: To deny the fact that individuals differ insofar as the manifold determinations of their situations differ – to dissolve the subject, in other words, by making it a mere epiphenomenon of vast social and ideological structures – is to indulge a self-serving idealism, if not a full-blown metaphysics.[2] But Pound's early individualism, just because it is so radical, refuses (unlike Sartre's) to subject the self to class and collective structures. Consequently, it is severely limited not so much in fact but in the politics which that fact determines, because it establishes an unbridgeable gulf between the individual difference he valued and any collective means whereby such a fact might be constitutive of social relations in general. In its assiduous protection of "the peripheries of the individual," Pound's individualism, despite its liberationist impulse and rationale, threatens to leave us in a stalemate between the private sphere of difference and the social, material sphere of all those features of modernity that promise to devour it.

This dilemma haunts the very heart of American individualist ideology as well, and the central figure in that tradition provides the most dramatic example of its attractions and limits. For Emerson, as perhaps for no other, to will social change through pragmatic action is to indulge the imperial overstepping of personal boundaries that is, in the essay

"Politics," of a piece with the oppressive history of governments. Emerson's political mission for the self is the very antithesis of struggle, and particularly of class struggle in its Manichean, classical Marxist form. "When we discern justice, when we discern truth," Emerson writes in "Self-Reliance," "We do nothing of ourselves, but allow a passage to its beams."[3] It was Emerson's wager that self-reliance and the "influence of private character" would supersede the "proxy" of political practice, would work their way from person to person and override "all cities, nations, kings" without need of "army, fort, or navy."[4] To define the self in terms of its class solidarity was to enable not self-reliance but instead that collective heresy of other-reliance, which drains the reservoir of self-trust. Emerson's political agency, at once transcendental and intensely private, could not and should not be legislated by collective alliances. This was not Emerson's greatest wager for social change; it was, in essence, his *only* wager.

Indeed, as several recent critics have noticed, the very structure of authentic Emersonian action contains an injunction against mistaking mere deeds for the truth, which can be neither produced nor contained by them. As Myra Jehlen puts it, Emerson's "necessary actor"

> is a paradoxical being whose willful intervention either to hasten the future's advent or, worse still, to redefine it, can only distort the perfect order that already exists implicitly and thus delay its explicit realization. Not only are deeds and revolutions not needed, they are forbidden.[5]

The Emersonian self must instead concern itself with the *conditions and principles*, not the pragmatics, of action.[6] And when the individual understands what makes authentic actions and actors possible (Spirit, Reason, the Oversoul), he also, at the same time, realizes that those forces, because they cannot be resisted or altered, make particular actions and interventions spurious. It is by this logic – and only this logic – that Emerson's "political" applications of his philosophical idealism make sense: "Wherever a man comes, there comes revolution."[7]

If the final determinant of the self's value and efficacy is that same self, however, then how are we to decide whether this ideology promotes a democratic defense of individual difference or rather an undemocratic excuse for unbridled egoism? Here, Pound's modernism helps to shed light on just how troubled Emerson's concept of agent and act could be when forced beyond the historical moment it outlasted. Emerson, having recourse to the ready-made cultural rhetoric of religious or spiritual transcendence, could acknowledge that individual difference sometimes meant inequality. But this unhappy fact was so, he could argue, only because some selves had failed to achieve self-reliance, had failed to recognize, in other words, precisely that oneness in Spirit or Universal Being in which (sooner or later) we are all equal. That machinery of transcendence in large part allowed what might have been an authoritarian egoism in Emerson (as in his friend Carlyle) to dissolve so often into exactly the opposite. Personal authority was indeed more than merely personal, but it could not be enforced or produced by concrete actions.

For the modernist, however, the appeal to spiritual transcendence and the equality it guarantees is largely foreclosed (or at least quite problematic), and it becomes much more difficult to argue that the kind of individual difference known as egotism, elitism, or inequality is only apparent because "only" material and historical. And if that is the case, then practice in and on the object world assumes an importance it never had in Emerson. This fact is borne out, of course, by Pound's later interest in economic programs and reform; but it is also exemplified by Pound's later willingness to espouse authoritarian enforcement of economic and political practices, which a renewed premium on concrete action makes possible and in some sense even requires. In short, if modernists want to believe that some selves are not only different from but also better than others, they must do so without recourse to that spiritual supplement that would reclaim inequality in this world for equality in the next. Consequently, the price of retaining one's individualism is the constant danger of elitist egoism and the authoritarian politics it breeds.

Pound's own individualism was fully fraught with the ambivalence and instability of Emerson's own, shuttling fitfully as Emerson's had between elitism and populism, aristocracy and democracy. One recent critic has suggested, in fact, that something like an abrupt change in Pound's position took place between the writing of "The Serious Artist" in the fall of 1913 and the publication of his essay "The New Sculpture" in February of 1914. Michael Levenson has argued that Pound's essentially humanist position in "The Serious Artist" is transformed in "The New Sculpture" into a "radical egoism."[8] Pound, like his fellow *Blaster* Wyndham Lewis, now presents the artist as the enemy of society, and he espouses a vehemently antidemocratic cultural politics. As the first issue of *Blast* would put it six months later in unambiguous puce and black, he now appeals "TO THE INDIVIDUAL" but has "nothing to do with 'The People.'"[9]

Levenson attributes this sudden shift in Pound's position in large part to the influence of Allen Upward's philosophy of radical egoism on what had been up to this point in Pound's career only an inchoate tendency. By the time of his essay on Upward in the *New Age* for April 1914, Pound had come to admire Upward's emphasis on "the special faculties of the individual," faculties that justified, in Pound's words, "a syndicat of intelligence"[10] remote from (and in fact opposed to) the democratic masses. Levenson suggests that Pound learned from Upward the lesson not so much of difference as of *inequality*. And that new understanding led Pound to declare in "The New Sculpture" that the artist "has dabbled in democracy and he is now done with that folly."[11]

Levenson's argument is perfectly correct as far as it goes, but it does not go far enough. The egoistic position, which Levenson treats locally, must, I think, be traced back to the contradictions of Pound's ideological inheritance, which are unique neither to Pound nor to modernism. Nowhere are those conflicts more evident than in Emerson himself, who usually reserved for his journals the desire to have it all, both untouchable self-reliance and the kind of culture that seemed to require, as its social ferment, something other than radical democracy. For the early Emerson, this fitful coexistence was endemic not only to America but to the very relationship between society and culture. At age twenty-one, while working as a reluctant schoolmaster and facing daily the growing threat of proletarianization, Emerson gave voice in his journal to the social discrimination that cultural discrimination seemed to require. "Aristocracy is a good sign," he wrote.

> Aristocracy has been the hue & cry in every community where there has been anything good, any society worth associating with, since men met in cities. It must be every where. 'Twere the greatest calamity to have it abolished. . . . Robinson Crusoe's island would be better than a city if men were obliged to mix together indiscriminately heads & points with all the world.[12]

As we have already seen, the young Pound himself could have easily written these lines,[13] and to view Pound's conflicted individualism through the window of Emerson's own is to recognize that Pound saw in Allen Upward largely what he was prepared – I mean, in a sense, *set up* – to see. Not surprisingly, then, in Pound's early career as in Emerson's, we can locate nothing like an abrupt, once-and-for-all adoption of elitist egoism and a concomitant rejection of the more democratic position.

We will remember that "Patria Mia" (written in 1910–1911) stages its critique on behalf of the individual "of whatever age or sex or condition." And throughout his career (almost as if in reaction to his *Blast*ian pronouncements) Pound would insist that his individualism was radically democratic, not for artists only. In "Murder by Capital," written in 1933, he looked back, a little embarrassed, to his early avant-garde elitism and provided his own riposte to set the record straight: "If there was (and I admit that there was) a time when I thought this problem [of art's commodification] could be solved without regard to the common man, humanity in general, the man in the street, the average citizen, etc., I retract, I sing palinode, I apologise."[14] And in one of his last interviews, conducted early in 1960, he located the value of art in its affirmation of the "heteroclite" nature of individual difference and concrete context. In a statement that must remind us of his early critique of literary production, Pound characterized the good modernist fight as "the struggle to keep the value of a local and particular character, of a particular culture in this awful maelstrom, this awful avalanche toward uniformity." The terms here could not be closer to those of the early essay on James: "The whole fight," he persists, "is for the conservation of the individual soul."[15] There is no break, then – as even this brief survey makes clear – but rather the uneasy and sometimes violent co-existence of two different, and finally opposed, political vectors that the ideology of individualism might follow.

In one of his earliest essays, "I gather the Limbs of Osiris" (published in late 1911 and early 1912), Pound provided evidence of just how deeply inscribed these contradictions were in his literary ideology. There, his central figure for the uniqueness of the literary individual is fiendishly difficult to define, and as we will see, this is his political, if not rhetorical, intent. Still, what Pound calls the *virtù* of the unique poetic self reaches across a range of historical and literary contexts, which may help us to clarify Pound's agenda for individualism in his "Osiris" essay. The concept of *virtù* has its origins in the Italian Renaissance, where it is, according to J. G. A. Pocock, a figure for the ethical fortitude, intellectual activity, and openness to innovation that ensure the health of democracy against decadence and corruption.[16] As Reed Way Dasenbrock has pointed out, this political context has especially direct relevance to Pound's later work. But more compellingly pertinent to the period of Pound's "Osiris" and "Patria Mia" is the immediate literary context from which he seemed to have derived his use of the term. Though he saw it wonderfully exemplified in Guido Cavalcanti and, before that, in Homer, his immediate source for the concept is Walter Pater's preface to *The Renaissance* (where Pater models the concept, in turn, on a passage from book 12 of Wordsworth's *The Prelude*).[17] There, Pater had written that *virtù* (or "virtue") is "the property each [thing] has of affecting one with a special, a unique impression of pleasure. . . . And the function of the aesthetic critic is to distinguish, to analyse and separate its adjuncts. . . . His end is reached when he has disengaged that virtue."[18]

Pound's extension of Paterian *virtù* (and here its anticipation of Imagist doctrine is clear)[19] underscores the active, transformative power of the poetic *self* required to bring out the *quidditas* of things in themselves. Poundian *virtù* is, in James Longenbach's words, a name for "the essence of individuality."[20] On this point, Pound has plenty to say (again in anticipation of Imagist doctrine and its list of "don'ts") about what *virtù* is not: It is not, he tells us, "a 'point of view,' nor an 'attitude toward life,' nor is it the mental calibre of 'a way of thinking,' but something more substantial which influences all these."[21] Even if *virtù* is "substantial," it is not, for all that, really a substance. *Virtù* is rather that more elusive thing: a principle of differentiation by which selves may be kept separate – the difference, we might say, of difference. As Pound characterizes it:

> The soul of each man is compounded of all the elements of the cosmos of souls, but in each soul there is some one element which predominates, which is in some particular and intense way the quality of *virtù* of the individual; in no two souls is this the same. It is by reason of this *virtù* that a given work persists. It is by reason of this *virtù* that we have one Catullus, one Villon.[22]

But just as soon as we learn that *virtù* is an element, Pound tells us in a difficult figure from Dante that it is a formal relation, "the centre of a circle which possesseth all parts of its circumference equally."[23] And as both element and relation, Pound's *virtù* both is and is not like the romantic psychology of genius that its rhetoric tells us it is. He seems to impart a particular kind of substantial being to all literary genius by attributing to it an intensified element that is one with "the cosmos of souls." However, his figure from Dante seems to withdraw that very possibility: different circles, different centers, their only similarity anything *but* substantial.[24] What Pound wants, it seems, is nothing short of a paradox: a principle of identity on behalf of difference, one that might keep these particular individualities apart and delineated, unconfused with one another.

This seems to be precisely the desire that motivates his further development of the concept, where he is at pains to make differences respectful of each others' centers. "Having discovered his own *virtù*," Pound writes, "the artist will be more likely to discern and allow for a peculiar *virtù* in others."[25] For Pound, the centeredness of self that *virtù* marks is anything but imperial; it enables mutual recognition, differences in the plural.[26] It is, to borrow Dilthey's characterization of understanding, "a rediscovery of the I in the thou."[27] It is a sort of realization in the flesh of Pound's poetic principle "Dichten = condensare,"[28] and its transmission into durable poetic form will take place (as the example of Pound's Henry James reminds us) by "virtue of precision,"[29] the particular self's proper stylistic mode.

At the same time, however, it is clear that Pound wants to make *virtù* not merely a negative principle of individual difference in general but also a positive assertion of qualitative and hierarchical differences *between* individuals. Nowhere is this clearer than in his distinction between what he calls the "symptomatic" and the "donative "author: between the writer who is merely reflective of his time, who will, as Pound puts it, "mirror obvious and apparent thought movements"; and that other type, whose value resides in his ability to surmount the constraints of social context.[30] The donative author, because he has found and focused his *virtù*, "seems to draw down into the art something which was not in the art of his predecessors." His work is "interpretive" in the broadest sense; it brings to light "things present but unnoticed."[31] It is this ability that enables the donative author to be quite literally *avant-garde*, at the leading critical edge of society. "He discovers," Pound writes, "or better, 'he discriminates.'"[32] It is the donative author that Pound had in mind when he penned his famous modernist slogan "Artists are the race's antennae."[33]

Through the concepts of *virtù* and the donative author, Pound aims to show us what aesthetic difference an individual difference makes. But in doing so, he constructs a kind of trickle-down theory of art's social utility, one very much intact, as we shall see, in his later belief that the effects of social and economic ills show first in the arts.[34] This belief, which cuts squarely against materialist theory, is of even greater ideological moment when we realize that what enables the donative author's perception, and therefore art's social utility, is not only his ability to make new connections among material drawn from the historical moment but, more important, his capacity to *transcend* history. For if the writer does not affect such transcendence, he becomes that other thing less rare, the "symptomatic" author. In Pound as in Pater, *virtù* names "a genius which overtops its age" and makes contact with "the universal and re-usable elements of the craft."[35] *Virtù*, as Poundians Longenbach and Korn point out, names the intersection of individual difference and "a transhistorical spiritual world"[36] in which "all literature is a-historically significant,"[37] one in which, as Pound famously put it, "all ages are contemporaneous."

The transhistorical claim that underwrites the crucial distinction between the donative and the symptomatic author is quite clear in Pound's discussions of Whitman, who stands as the supreme example of the symptomatic writer, the type who is all too bound by his social milieu: "Whitman, 'The Reflex,'" as Pound calls him "who left us a human document, for you cannot call a man an artist until he shows himself capable of reticence and of restraint, until he shows himself in some degree master of the forces which beat upon him."[38] Whitman, we might say, gives us the poetry of the social and historical self, but he does not give of his *virtù*, because finally he does not possess it. The case of Whitman – that expansive self who claimed, "He who touches this book touches a man" – makes it clear that the virtuous author gives to society not so much himself (Whitman, after all, had done plenty of that) but rather the ability to *think beyond history*, which transforms historical material into the enduring, transhistorical stuff of art.[39]

From this perspective, we can say that even though Pound's immediate source for the concept of *virtù* may have been Pater, the kind of individualism Pound has in mind when he uses the term may have had its origins in the Renaissance but finds its maximal expression in the American and Emersonian vision of the self whose promise resides in its capacity to stand outside history, the better to put history's materials and lessons to use. And from this perspective, too, we are now better equipped to understand the full ideological significance of the language of economy in Pound's rhetoric of *virtù*.

It is, we remember, a center that "possesseth" the parts of its circumference equally, which means, I take it, bringeth into "orderly arrangement," and thus transcendeth, in Pound's terms, the historical forces that beat upon it. The transhistorical aesthetic economy only hinted at here becomes quite explicit in "The Serious Artist," where Pound describes not its supply side, as it were, in the artist of *virtù* but rather its demand side in the artifact produced; not what the donative artist possesses but rather what he gives:

> The permanent property, the property given to the race at large is precisely these data of the serious scientist and the serious artist; of the scientist as touching the relations of abstract numbers, of molecular energy, of the composition of matter, etc.; of the serious artist, as touching the nature of man, of individuals.[40]

The rhetorical linchpin of "permanent property" that opens this passage fully specifies what the economy of *virtù* had only suggested: There is a kind of knowledge, immune to historical change and decay and registered in certain works of art, to which the currency, as it were, of historical forms of knowledge must appeal for full meaning. "Permanent property," in other words, names a conceptual economy of aesthetics and knowledge that not only transcends but also redeems economies of the more utilitarian and pedestrian sort.

It would be a mistake, though, to consign Pound too rapidly to the antiutilitarian camp of high humanism (even though this aesthetic is beginning to look right at home there). Pound often goes to great pains to make it clear that art's social utility is often very direct and quite untranscendental. He will argue, for instance, that "the true artist is the champion of free speech"[41] and that "the *mot juste* is of public utility" because "we are governed by words, the laws are graven in words, and literature is the sole means of keeping these words living and accurate."[42] Most directly of all, he also recognized what he called "the cash value of art," its production and circulation in an economy that was far from transcendental:

> The net value of good art to its place of residence has been computed in logarithms; I shall not go into the decimals. When there was talk of selling Holbein's *Duchess of Milan* to an American, England bought the picture for three hundred and fifty thousand dollars. They figured that people came to London to see the picture, that the receipts of the community were worth more per annum than the interest on the money. . . . Mr. F. M. Hueffer has said that the difference between London and other places is that "No one lives in London merely for the sake of making money enough to live somewhere else."[43]

Although it is true, as Barbara Herrnstein Smith has recently argued, that antiutilitarian critiques often employ the language of economics in their attempts to transcend *all* economies,[44] in Pound's case a crucial distinction needs to be made. As the passages we just examined indicate, his aesthetic attempts not so much to transcend economy as to transcend *history*.

To put it another way, Pound's transhistorical aesthetic economy is not primarily thematic (as in the garden-variety humanist appeal) but is instead essentially ideological; that is, it does not claim or take as its central topic the transcendental privilege of art so much as it builds the necessity of that claim into its very conceptual structure. From this vantage, it is clear that Pound's discourse reproduces the ideology of that worldly economy from which his rhetoric draws its figures. Capitalism, too, wants to be the economy of economies, and it too represents its own historical relations of production as transhistorical and natural.[45] So when Pound declared that property might be "permanent," he may have attempted to speak beyond history, but he could do so only by speaking, in another sense, squarely within it.

Pound was not by any means the first American writer, or the only one, whose work confronted this ideology and its infrastructural economic logic only to reproduce them. As Michael T. Gilmore has argued, in the nineteenth century "traits of romantic art that arise out of an antagonism toward the market system prove upon closer inspection to replicate the very conditions against which they protest."[46] Gilmore is right, I think, but not because Emerson and his contemporaries (or Pound and his) were gullible dupes of capitalism – far from it. For Emerson (and for many others), being American meant being unencumbered by the binding structures of class, church, and all the sheer weight of those European institutions that circumscribed the self's social, economic, familial, and cultural relations. But those institutional determinations were also an inheritance, a fact pointedly symbolized in

Emerson's own struggle to find a proper vocation – for himself and, symbolically, for the American intellectual. By Emerson's time, no longer could Americans intent on attaining cultural and social power assume that it would be guaranteed them simply because they entered the ministry or the law.[47] In fact, by the time Emerson took up the ministry, he had *already* experienced the bitter discrepancy between his creeping proletarianization as a schoolteacher and the status and power of the Boston upper class, which he often defended and to which he felt entitled to belong.[48]

In short, those social structures that Americans felt bound to reject nevertheless empowered the individual by informing and backing him with the accumulated force of history and its practices. The question, then, was this: How was the American to reproduce that powerful cultural subject without reproducing the social structures that had traditionally ballasted it? Needing some common sign of their respective standing as social beings, but rejecting the traditional structures of social election, Americans were, as Quentin Anderson puts it, "forever filling the leaky vessel of self-esteem with possessions."[49] Americans, Tocqueville and others told us, sought the trappings of social standing and power (much to Emerson's dismay) in what Emerson excoriated in many, many places as "the base estimate of the market."[50]

There were, however, other possibilities for the American individual. It might define itself not by the dictates of mediating social structures but rather in terms of either an absolute object (the new continent, the virgin land) *or* an absolute subject (God, or a god within). As Jehlen notes, however, these are in fact coterminous in the hegemonic vision of American selfhood, and nowhere is that clearer than in Emerson himself, for whom the convertibility of Nature and Spirit, object and subject, is the first among many first principles telling us that "the whole of nature is a metaphor of the human mind."[51]

As Gilmore and others have made clear, however, this newly defined self did not escape the logic and mediation of the market against which it rebelled – in fact, quite the reverse. Wai-chee Dimock has suggested (taking her cue, quite appropriately, from Emerson's own use of the language of economy) that the Emersonian self is fundamentally a space of "experiential scarcity," which is the very sign of the American individual's liberation from the sedimented forms of the past. Instead of being a lack or deficiency to be overcome, that scarcity lying at the absent center of the American self is instead a "native birthright" underwriting the American self's radical freedom and autonomy.[52] Paradoxically, that scarcity is, according to Dimock, the very property American individuals must possess to assume their full, distinctive identities. As Emerson puts it toward the end of "Experience" (in an important and complex passage that locates for us the very conditions of possibility for this voracious and expansive individualism): "We must hold hard to this poverty, however scandalous, and by more vigorous self-recoveries, after the sallies of action, possess our axis more firmly."[53]

It should come as no surprise, then, that the fundamental mode of the Emersonian self, as several recent critics have pointed out, is not production (as it is for Marx) but rather *acquisition*.[54] "It is the nature of the soul," Emerson writes in "Compensation," "to appropriate all things."[55] And why not? If selfhood, Nature, and the "scarcity" and "poverty" of history are coterminous in Emerson, then self-possession and the freedom it makes possible must manifest themselves in possession of the object world, in spirit and structure if not in pragmatic deed. Thus, Emerson's *Nature* at one and the same time puns upon and reproduces the Lockean notion of property. Men may hold the deeds to their farms, Emerson tells us, but "none of them owns the landscape." "There is a property in the horizon," Emerson writes, "which no man has but he whose eye can integrate all the parts, that is, the poet."[56] Emerson's poet enables us to gain critical distance on the false, merely historical title and deed of market possession. And once we have achieved that distance, we can hear the full resonance of Emerson's imperative: "Know then that the world exists for you."[57]

Emerson's poet, then, also confers upon property and possession a new and unexpected authenticity. This doubleness of critique and reinscription is, as we shall see, entirely characteristic of Emerson's work. In "Compensation," for instance, his scorn for the debased marketplace does not keep him from finding, as Gilmore puts it, "economic categories applicable to the operations of the Soul."[58] In short, if Emerson participates quite often in the surgical exposure of capitalism's evils and excesses, he also (particularly in his later career) participates in what Gilmore dubs "the commercialization of all things."[59] On the one hand, Emerson insists, as forcefully as any American writer ever has, that "the reliance on Property, including the reliance on governments which protect it, is the want of self-reliance."[60] On the other hand, from the very beginning of his career, he also reminds us, as in *Nature*, that property "is a preceptor whose lessons cannot be foregone," that its logic is not accidental and capricious but rather "is the surface action of internal machinery, like the index on the face of a clock," and that our relationship to it, for better or for worse, reflects our "experience in profounder laws."[61]

After Emerson and before Pound – between a modernism incipient and one fully arrived – William James attempted as well to turn the heavily freighted rhetoric of capitalism to advantage. In *The Principles of Psychology*, he tried to figure individual difference in a language that might resist modernity's systematic assaults on the self. In a passage that recalls Pound's Dantesque figure for *virtù*, James characterized the true self as the "innermost center within the circle." Like Pound's "Dichten = condensare" made flesh, it is the "*self of all the other selves*," the place of what Emerson and Pound called "whim" – the seat, in James's words, of "the fiats of the will."[62] But like Emerson's, James's unanalyzable self is an acquisitive one as well; in fact, this self is not composed of the "transient external possessions" of house and bank account but is rather *itself* a more permanent, inalienable, and extremely private kind of property. As Lentricchia puts it, "James finds (or thinks he finds) truly inalienable private property located at (and *as*) the core of selfhood."[63] Or in James's words: "It seems as if the elementary psychic fact were not *thought* but *my thought*, every thought being *owned*."[64]

Those fleeting forms of ownership like bank deed and paper title should not be mistaken, James tells us, for the elementary fact of selfhood – not because they are ownership, but because they are not ownership *enough*. In James, authentic possession constitutes a double relation: The self that does the owning is also the self that is owned. As Walter Benn Michaels has argued, the past thoughts that make up the Jamesian self are indeed owned by the present self, but that present self, its thoughts, will in turn be owned by the future self. And so for James, selfhood is, as Michaels puts it, nothing less than "the constant transformation of owner into owned."[65] It is not too much to say, with Lentricchia and Michaels, that ownership in James is not the effect of selfhood but rather its very condition.

If, as James puts it, "the worst a psychology can do is so to interpret the nature of these selves as to rob them of their worth,"[66] then his rhetoric may well realize his own worst fears, because it makes selfhood coterminous with the most fundamental alienation of all, one generated by the central contradiction at the core of capitalism. As Lentricchia points out, "property under capitalism can be property only if it *is* alienable"[67] – only if it can be, in James's words, "robbed."

Rather than challenging the fundamental institution of a mode of production whose effects they abhorred, James and, as we shall see, Pound and Emerson wanted to make the logic and structure of private property safe for the individual. In reaction against the narrow modern sense of property as material possession – the house and bank account that James wanted to keep at arm's length, the farmer's deed and title that Emerson rhetorically worked over in *Nature*, or the cement and soap of Pound's letter to Amy Lowell – these American defenders of the self radicalized the relationship between property and selfhood by making it *more* intimate, not less. For all three, selfhood is essentially a Lockean proposition, wherein the self is in essence, as C. B. McPherson writes, "the proprietor of his own person or capacities . . . an owner of himself."[68] But if this most private kind of property seems to present a vision strong for the self's freedom, it also contains its own negation.

What McPherson writes of Locke could be written as well of Emerson, Pound, and James: "Not only has the individual a property in his own person and capacities, a property in the sense of a right to enjoy and use them and to exclude others from them; what is more, it is this property, this exclusion of others, that makes a man human."[69] To see the individual as property, in other words, is to see it as alienated from others, foundationally so and by definition. As Marx characterized it, in the critique that stands behind McPherson's own, this type of individual will see in others "not the *realization* but the *limitation* of his own freedom," because freedom for such a self means the right "to enjoy and dispose of one's resources as one wills."[70] All of which is to say that insofar as the self is conceived as a kind of private property, I will alienate and threaten your freedom insofar as I realize my own, and vice versa.

Thus, James, Emerson, and Pound, in figuring the individual within the logic of private property, also figure it, against their intentions, as the very enemy of all those other selves they deeply wanted to be equally autonomous as well. And what is more, in doing so they declare, in the same moment and against their strongest impulses, the permanence of that alienation and the structures generating it. By stressing in their critiques not capitalism as an implacable logic but rather modernity as a moment when that logic went awry, Pound and James say in so many words that capitalist relations – and, by extension, the alienation they produce – are not historical and changeable but permanent and given. They are the fundamental facts of life because they are the fundamental facts of selfhood. Pound thought of freedom this way: "to do that which harms not another."[71] But given this economy of American individualism, how could the self allow freedom for others and yet maintain its own?

"LIVING PROPERTY": EMERSON, ENTREPRENEURS, AND THE JACKSONIAN "MOB"

In taking the self as the seat of power and social change, the critiques of Emerson, Pound, and James centered, finally, not upon the logic and structure of capitalist relations but rather upon the uses to which that structure was put in the conduct of atomistic individuals. Their critiques, in other words, were essentially, if not solely, ethical. After all, if the self's efficacy lay in the degree of its own self-possession, then how could anything other than the self freely choose how that personal property should be disposed? Pound and James well realized that in capitalist modernity the right to individual and social difference was being threatened. But for them, as for Emerson, the means to overcome that threat could rest only with the individual actions of discrete selves.

Emerson, of course, was wary about (but not immune to) defining the self as property, *virtù*, or anything else for that matter. But Emerson's critique – fully, unsurpassably ethical – was wholly embattled by the contradictions that Marx identified in his critique of the property basis of personal rights, contradictions that made reconciling supreme selfhood with the social and collective Other a troubling and often stormy prospect. To borrow Wai-chee Dimock's phrase, intersubjectivity in Emerson is the "seamy side" of his model of the self, because the individual who is rooted in self-ownership owns "property that is infinitely alienable, perhaps already alienated because the Other is always there, always eager as rival and usurper."[72] In Emerson, this contradiction, and the bitter skepticism it breeds, gets expressed in any number of ways: in his reflections on aristocracy and culture, in his war against history and convention, but most of all in his ethical distinction between the self-reliant individual and the Jacksonian "mob," which obscures the truth of the self.

This is not to say that Emerson, who was capable of almost Olympian distance from emotional identification, was wholly unsympathetic to the Jacksonian masses. His sharp sense of the human toll of capitalism, the market, and nascent industrialism – a pang of recognition that is unmistakable not only early on in "The American Scholar" and "Self-Reliance" but also much later in texts such as *English Traits* – often led him to direct his critical ire not toward the "mob" itself but at the powers that created and sustained it. Emerson's awareness that the blame for the downtrodden condition of the Jacksonian masses lay not mainly with them but with the propertied and monied interests that produced them is recorded with particular forthrightness in his journals:

> It seems to every meeting of readers and writers as if it were intolerable that Broad street paddies and barroom politicians, the sots and loafers & all manner of ragged & unclean and foul mouthed persons without a dollar in their pocket should control the property of this country. . . . But is that any more than their share whilst you hold property selfishly? They are opposed to you: yes, but first you are opposed to them.[73]

It is not surprising that Emerson set down this particular entry in 1841, because, as Sacvan Bercovitch has recently argued, in that same period the critique of the powers of property, which had been brewing and sometimes bubbling ever since *Nature*, reached full boil in Emerson's journals and letters, in essays like "Man the Reformer," and in talks like "Lecture on the Times." In the vigorous social critique of 1840–1841, Emerson "may be said to have come *to the edge* of class analysis," to have moved "*almost* beyond the bounds of liberalism."[74] In those texts, Emerson reminds us that "the State must consider the poor man, and all voices must speak for him. . . . Let the amelioration in our laws of property proceed from the concession of the rich, not from the grasping of the poor." His hope is that "new modes of thinking" "shall destroy the value of many kinds of property and replace all property within the dominion of reason and equity."[75]

As Bercovitch points out, Emerson's critique of property would shortly take a very different tack, and in the years 1842 to 1850 we find increasingly what Bercovitch terms Emerson's "unabashed endorsements . . . of what can only be called free enterprise ideology."[76] In a way, this divergence could have been predicted all along, but if Jacksonianism set the interests of the people against the power of property,[77] Emerson would counterpoise self-reliance against both. The whole of "The American Scholar" is informed in part by precisely this struggle to drive home the realization that property and political mass movement are false alternatives in a false dialectic:

> Men, such as they are, very naturally seek money or power; and power because it is as good as money, – the "spoils," so-called, "of office." And why not? for they aspire to the highest, and this, in their sleepwalking, they dream is highest. Wake them and they shall quit the false good and leap to the true, and leave governments to clerks and desks. This revolution is to be wrought by the gradual domestication of the idea of Culture. . . . The private life of one man shall be a more illustrious monarchy, more formidable to its enemy, more sweet and serene in its influence to its friend, than any kingdom in history.[78]

The money power and the Jacksonian revolution, which promised to challenge it, are not, Emerson tells us, polar forces between which the self must choose: hence Emerson's backhanded reference to the Jacksonian spoils system; and hence, too, the ironic force of the word "power" in the above passage, a loaded term in Emerson's lexicon, but here, "as good as money" (which is to say, no good at all). For the self asleep, the self not yet fully in possession of its faculties, it is quite "natural" (again the irony is unmistakable) that property interests and political movements exert considerable attraction. It is not the "naturalness" of the logical progression that is assailable here, in other words, but the self-annihilating premise from which that logic proceeds. In taking the way not from man but to man, property and mass politics create a world that makes perfect – and perfectly ephemeral – sense.

By Emerson's logic, then, both political collectives and property interests are equally "false," since they are both equally – which is to say
completely – beside the point of selfhood. But if that is the case, then
how are we to account for the extreme discrepancy of tone we often find
between Emerson's revulsion toward the Jacksonian mass and his rather
more gentle handling of the "dreams" of property? In the most schematic terms, our answer, I think, is that property, at least, is private.
Mass movement, on the other hand, is that particularly pernicious form
of falsehood that depends upon the dissolution of individual distinction.
Where property substitutes "false" ends for the "true" ends of selfhood,
mass movement attacks its very raison d'être.

So it is that Emerson can continue to lament in his journal for 1844,
"The masses – ah if you could read the biographies of those who com-
pose them!"[79] even as he continues to reserve for "this rank rabble party,
this Jacksonism of the country"[80] some of his most viscerally acid
criticism:

> If I were in love with life & as afraid of dying as you seem to insinuate
> I would go to a Jackson Caucus or to the Julien Hall & I doubt not the
> unmixed malignity, the withering selfishness, the impudent vulgarity
> that mark those meetings would speedily cure me of my appetite for
> longevity.[81]

It is worth repeating that assessments like this one, written in 1834, were
driven not by Emerson's desire to revel in his own superiority but rather
by his will to liberate individuals from political hypocrisy of whatever
stripe and into a new self-trust, wherein the only genuine politics lay.[82]
As he confessed in his journal, again in 1844, "My Genius loudly calls
me to stay where I am, even with the degradation of owning bankstock
and seeing poor men suffer whilst the Universal Genius apprises me of
this disgrace & beckons me to the martyr's & redeemer's office."[83]

We can get an even firmer grasp on the tonal discrepancy in Emerson's
handling of the masses and property by remembering that the centerpiece of the passage from "The American Scholar" examined earlier is
the "Culture" Emerson had in mind when he wrote that "the best political economy is care and culture of men."[84] For Emerson, that culture
was precisely what was missing in Jacksonianism, which is "heedless of
English," Emerson writes in a complex figure, "& of all literature – a
stone cut out of the ground without hands."[85] If the first fundamental
flaw of Jacksonianism is that it attacks the self at the very seat of its
power, the second is that it is the very enemy of Emersonian Culture,
and of the revolutionary political economy that depended upon it.
Jacksonianism, in Emerson's figuration, is an almost geological kind of
phenomenon, its mass a "blind mechanical force" that eradicates any

trace of individual quality.[86] It is featureless, a blockish parody of the fluid workings of Spirit. For all Emersonian purposes, it is dead.

So it is not elitist spite but rather a matter of principle that outstrips his individual sympathies for human suffering and oppression and motivates Emerson when he writes (in one of his less charitable moods) that the worst aspect of charity is that

> the lives you are asked to preserve are not worth preserving. The calamity is the masses. I do not wish any masses at all, but honest men only, facultied men only, lovely & sweet & accomplished women only; and no shovel-handed Irish, & no Five-Points, or Saint Gileses, or drunken crew, or mob, or stockingers, or 2 millions of paupers receiving relief, miserable factory population, or lazzaroni, at all.[87]

For Emerson, charity could only confirm the *lazzaroni* in their indolence, could only further entrench the masses in their pauperism. Emerson was not blind or insensitive to the plight of the masses; his empathy and even outrage are present throughout his work, early and late. But it was his deep conviction that to give in to the masses and the history that created them was to give up the possibility of the only victory that mattered: the atomistic renovation of individual selves. To engage in charity for the masses was to confirm, not alleviate, all that made them "not worth preserving."[88]

"Self-Reliance" gave this harsh fact of individual affirmation an even harsher corollary:

> Then again, do not tell me, as a good man did to-day, of my obligation to put all poor men in good situations. Are they *my* poor? I tell thee, thou foolish philanthropist, that I grudge the dollar, the dime, the cent I give to such men as do not belong to me and to whom I do not belong.[89]

But the right kind of selves, once fully self-reliant, *could* belong to each other, could in fact own each others' individual properties without threat of alienation or misuse. Emerson imagined that personal properties and potentials, once wholly owned by their proprietors, could be exchanged in a spiritual economy that would not violate them. And as for those selves, Emerson declared, "There is a class of persons to whom by all spiritual affinity I am bought and sold; for them I will go to prison if need be."[90] This is a startling moment in Emerson, not because of its idealism but because of the supercharged Lockean individualism through which Emerson transmits it. What Emerson attempts here is nothing less than what Pound and James would later attempt: a rescue, conscious or unconscious, of the institution of private property from its alienations and contradictions, a rewriting not of the form and structure, but only of the ethical content, of capitalism's central institution.

That rewriting might be a revolutionary move were it not for the fact that the capitalist exchange value upon which property is based *has* no content of the sort that Emerson here seeks to subvert.[91] Abstract exchange has no truck with concrete, qualitative, or individual difference; quite the reverse, it is purely quantitative. Its form, in this sense, *is* its content, and that form is reinscribed and reproduced in Emerson's attempt to redeem it for an authenticity that its logic will not permit. In short, Emerson may have poised self-reliance against both property interests and the Jacksonian mass, but the "political unconscious" of his rhetoric (to borrow Fredric Jameson's phrase) tells us that he has cast his lot with property.

This is a little less surprising when we remember that for Emerson it was finally not *how* the self was realized but rather *that* it was so realized which was of supreme importance. From this vantage, if property and profit were only epiphenomenal, could they not, when held in perspective, signal as well as anything else – books, poems, or heroic deeds – the active soul at work? "The harvest," Emerson admitted,

> will be better preserved & go farther laid up in private bins, in each farmer's corn barn, & each woman's basket, than if it were kept in national granaries. . . . Take away from me the feeling that I must depend on myself. . . . & instantly I relax my diligence & obey the first impulse of generosity that is to cost me nothing, and a certain slackness will creep over all my conduct of my affairs.[92]

Might not the structure of private property provide, moreover, a jump-start for that self-realization which Emerson hoped would be spontaneous in a better America?

For Emerson, apparently, it did indeed, because he saw in the enterprising entrepreneur the spirit of self-development that was lacking in mobs of whatever kind.[93] Emerson's answer to the rise of commerce, industry, and the teetering edifice of debt and credit that accompanied it was not to reject capitalism but to simplify and reinvigorate it by restoring a more direct relationship between individual industry and economic prosperity.[94] A more rigorous economy of selfhood that might anchor the larger dealings of commerce became one of the objects of Emerson's preacherly tone and rousing parallelism:

> The true way of beginning is by austere humility and lowness. Leave far off the borrowed capital, and raise an estate from the seed. Begin with the hands, and earn one cent; then two, then a dollar; then stock a basket; then a barrow; then a booth; then a shop; then a warehouse, and not on this dangerous balloon of a credit make his first structure.[95]

And when he turned his attention toward "the question of socialism,"[96] Emerson suggested in his journals that the relationship between self-reliance and self-interest was a good deal more direct than he would elsewhere allow: "You shall not so arrange property as to remove the motive to industry. If you refuse rent & interest, you make all men idle & immoral." And, he continues, in a phrase that sounds a lot more like the new Right than the old Left, "As to the poor a vast proportion have made themselves so."[97]

But again we are forced to ask: How can Emerson actively defend private property when it is, by the logic of his idealism, strictly epiphenomenal? And if it is epiphenomenal, then why should he care to take any position on it whatsoever? The answer to this question, at once the most general and the most fundamental, lies, I think, in the ethical nature of Emerson's critique.[98] The ethical critic – of which Emerson is the supreme American example – is concerned not with the determining force of property as a social structure but rather with the uses to which that property is put by selves who must, on principle, freely choose.[99] Emerson would not dismantle agencies of alienation like "rent and interest" but rather would turn them to didactic advantage to teach the self that its freedom is not dependent upon them. For the fully realized self, property holds no threat of mystification, no "false good," and so poses no danger and needs to remedy. But for the individual who is not yet fully self-reliant, the structure of property might force him to realize the truth that transcends all economy: You make it on your own, or not at all. That was – above and beyond Emerson's changing sympathies and antipathies for the Jacksonian masses and the innovative entrepreneurs – the structuring conviction of his social critique.

At a key moment in "Self-Reliance," Emerson strains to speak beyond the language of property, beyond the coveting of it, which is a sign, in his words, of "the want of self-reliance." "A cultivated man," Emerson writes,

> becomes ashamed of his property out of new respect for his nature. Especially he hates what he has if he see that it is accidental, – came to him by inheritance, or gift, or crime; then he feels that it is not having; it does not belong to him. . . . But that which a man is, does always by necessity acquire; and what the man acquires is living property, which . . . perpetually renews itself wherever the man breathes.[100]

For the subject of that Emersonian "Culture" which promised a revolutionary American political economy, acquisition is his natural mode and property his fitting expression. If "living property" is coterminous with "that which a man is," if it is not renewed but "renews itself" wherever man breathes, then we are forced to say that, for Emerson, you shall know a man by what he can call his – or better yet, by what he has *made* his. This is particularly true of the later Emerson of essays like "Wealth," the Emerson who believed that "property rushes from the idle and imbecile to the industrious, brave, and persevering."[101] For that Emerson, "living property" is the very sign of active self-realization – where it comes, there comes self-reliant man, there comes revolution.[102]

Emerson has his concept of dead property as well, of that which comes by "accident," by "donation or inheritance to those who do not create it."[103] So for Emerson, whether property is alive or dead depends upon the status of the owner. He writes in "Wealth," "There is always a reason, *in the man,* for his good or bad fortune, and so in making money."[104] And by Emerson's logic, if there is such a thing as living property, then there must also be such a thing as technically living people who are, for all Emersonian purposes, dead. These people, of course, are none other than Emerson's "mob," that thing of "mere muscular & nervous motion, no thought, no spark of life in it."[105] Emerson wanted instead a political economy with a human, even poetic face, one based upon *Nature*'s understanding that property is "the surface action of internal machinery," that "it is hiving, in the foresight of the spirit, experience in profounder laws."[106] And he found that economy symbolized in the good capitalist, the man of energy who could not be farther from the blockish mass. "A judge and a banker," he writes,

> must drive their craft poetically as well as a dancer or a scribe. That is, they must exert that higher vision which causes the object to become fluid and plastic. . . . Economy must be poetical, inventive, alive: that is its essence, and therein it is distinguished from mere parsimony, which is a poor, dead, base thing.[107]

From our present vantage, Emerson could not have known how right he was, how modern capitalism would provide one testament after another to the wonders of a "fluid and plastic" economy driven by a fierce, unabashed self-reliance.

"THE TRUTH IS THE INDIVIDUAL": POUND, ENTREPRENEURS, AND THE LIMITS OF "EXPERIENCE"

The problematic dissociation of ethics, economics, and politics that lay at the structural center of Emerson's literary ideology allowed Ezra Pound as well to offer as a model of democratic self-reliance not only the renovative scholar, or even the virtuous poet, but also the enterprising entrepreneur – the man who would, as Emerson put it, drive his craft in the name of a "higher vision."[108] Pound opens his own account of the entrepreneur in "Patria Mia" by drawing a sharp contrast, as Emerson had, between this inventive, energetic self and the clutching, materialistic businessman who had already become well-nigh proverbial in American culture, and who would be submitted later by Pound, in the Hell Cantos, to all sorts of degradations. The figure Pound sketches here will reappear under many names later in his career; it is an early prototype, on native ground, of Odysseus, Jefferson, and Malatesta. "The type of man who built railways, cleared the forest, planned irrigation," Pound writes,

> is different from the type of man who can hold onto the profits of subsequent industry. Whereas the first man was a man of dreams, in a time when dreams paid, a man of adventure, careless – this latter is a close person, acquisitive, rapacious, tenacious. The first man had personality. . . . The present type is primarily a mask, his ideal is the nickel-plated cash register, and toward the virtues thereof he doth continual strive and tend.
>
> The first man dealt with men, the latter deals with paper.[109]

This passage provides in miniature a kind of barometer for Pound's later attitudes toward democracy and the individual's place in it, and it also highlights, as if in echo, how closely wedded those attitudes were to the ideology of Emerson. In anticipation of Pound's concluding metaphor above and the vision it carries, Emerson had written in "Compensation" that

> the real price of labor is knowledge and virtue, whereof wealth and credit are signs. These signs, like paper money, may be counterfeited or stolen, but that which they represent, namely, knowledge and virtue, cannot be counterfeited or stolen.[110]

Like Pound's, Emerson's vision of authentic personal economy was not managerial or professional but essentially entrepreneurial, insisting as it did on a tight causal relationship between the self's ethical fortitude (its persistence, skill and energy) and the economic benefits such a self deserved and usually enjoyed.[111] Moreover, the oblique reference in Pound's passage above to his grandfather Thaddeus ("built railways, cleared the forest") reminds us just how centrally he felt himself an inheritor of the American democratic promise embodied in his grandfather's entrepreneurial vigor.[112]

That democratic spirit could be embodied in poets too, of course, and if we pay attention to those qualities Pound highlights – a love for adventure, a full-throttled carelessness – then it must come as no surprise that Whitman, both in spite and because of his roughness, stands as "the American keynote" of our literature. In him, Pound writes, "I find this same sort of thing. . . . It is, as nearly as I can define it, a certain generosity, a certain carelessness or looseness, if you will. . . . A desire for largeness, a willingness to stand exposed."[113] Whitman is the *literary* "man of dreams," a poetic "man of adventure, careless," a literary "man of personality," the poetic figure in the carpet of "Patria Mia."

In his early correspondence Pound confided that he thought of himself, too, as a poet for that democratic spirit he inherited from his grandfather. He himself (or so his rhetoric suggests) was something of a young Whitman, landing not in Brooklyn but on the beachhead of Edwardian London, ready to inject the "bacillus" of democratic adventure into the stultifying literary capital of the English-speaking world. Not long after "Patria Mia," he wrote to Harriet Monroe of his intrepid adventures in "deah old London": "For one man I strike there are ten to strike back at me. I stand exposed. It hits me in my dinner invitations, in my weekends, in reviews of my own work. Nevertheless, " he added with a hint of relish, "it's a good fight."[114]

Given the adventurous "exposure" that Pound attributes to Whitman and to himself, and by way of his martial metaphor, we can join our poets in democratic solidarity to Pound's entrepreneur friends, both of whom, we learn, had "fought in battles and sailed before the mast" – both of whom had been exposed, in other words, in far-from-literary contexts that called for a quite direct and unflinching kind of self-expression. But as much might be said, after all, of any mercenary or drunken sailor. And in fact it *was* being said by the likes of Bliss Carmen and Richard Hovey, poets of what Pound mockingly called "the 'school of virility,' of 'red blood,'" popular singers (very popular) of a sort of neomedieval martial ideal.[115]

Our concerns, however, are quickly met when Pound moves to qualify his swashbuckling praise of Whitman, not because Whitman is not democratic enough, but because he is not artist enough. "Here is a spirit," Pound writes, that is largely "hostile to the arts."[116] It seems, in other words, that those very qualities making Whitman the preeminent "symptomatic" writer of American literature are precisely those preventing him from assimilating other times and cultures, the better to rise above his social context as befits a properly "donative" poet. If, as Pound put it, technique is the test of a man's sincerity, then Whitman has all the sincerity of the great writer but none of the technique to match it. In Whitman, "the artist is ready to endure personally a strain which his craftsmanship would scarcely endure."[117]

What we must have, then, is not only experience but experience and a wide-ranging mastery of cultures in vital combination.[118] Pound, ranging across epochs and literatures, would give voice to that rare combination in 1911 in "The Seafarer" and later, most famously, in the Odysseus and epic poet of the *Cantos*. He found that same combination alive in the flesh in 1910, however, not in literary magazines and universities but in his entrepreneur friends, who were, like Odysseus and his own seafarer, far from your common sailors before the mast. One of them, Pound notes approvingly, is a master of "reading between

Shakespeare and Rabelais," and the other pilots "a vocabulary and a racy, painted speech that would do no shame to an Elizabethan."[119] Like Whitman, these men are fully engaged with and open to their age; but unlike Whitman, the meaning of their experience is not bound by it.

Of the many notable aspects of Pound's entrepreneur anecdote, most notable is its remarkable reversal of one of modernism's stock oppositions: It asks us to set not art against the marketplace but rather one sort of self – energetic, innovative, experienced – of whatever chosen pursuit, against another. As in Emerson, it is motivated by its emphasis on the nature of the individual, not on the accompanying social structures that might determine or mediate selfhood. And as in Emerson, too, the type of individual who determines an authentic economy is at once transhistorical *and* particularly American: transhistorical in the sense that that sort of self may be found in ancient Greece, Renaissance Florence, and 1910 New York, but particularly American in that that sort of individualism was the central founding principle for the country that imagined itself the land of individualism's perfection. True, Pound had contrasted Whitman's "American keynote" with the seafarer poet's "English keynote": the one, an adventurous openness; the other, a rigorous reticence.[120] But the ethical fortitude that bound them together in the struggle against provincialism and cultural myopia -- what made them both keynotes, as it were - was stronger than what gave them their different textures. The seafarer poet, as Pound puts it, was "the man ready for his deed, eager for it, eager for the glory of it, ready to pay the price." And in Whitman, Pound saw "the same sort of thing," a self who would "undertake nothing in its art for which it will not be in person responsible."[121]

It was obviously Pound's intention to imbue with that same kind of fortitude the rough-and-ready characters found everywhere in his early personae and translations. In the martial worldliness of early poems like "Sestina: Altaforte," in the "daring ado" of "The Seafarer," and in the *polumetis* ("many-mindedness") of Odysseus in the early *Cantos*, Pound recorded the enduring value of the self willing to take chances, the adventurous individual who was willing to pay the price levied by experience, the better to restore the inventive and subversive force of literature by injecting it with what that self had learned. In his edition of Cavalcanti, for instance, Pound wanted to reignite "traces of a tone of thought no longer considered dangerous, but that may have appeared about as soothing to the Florentine of A.D. 1290 as conversation about Tom Paine, Marx, Lenin and Bucharin would be to-day in a Methodist bankers' board meeting in Memphis, Tenn."[122]

Because Pound located the *virtù* of individualism in many past epochs and cultures, it is difficult to see that his modernist project of creating and restoring a literature for change was, by his own reasoning, one for which the American character was particularly well equipped. Pound's early social critique makes it clear that America, in its loosening of social and cultural convention and in its openness to change and innovation, was the land of virtuous individualism's greatest promise. From Pound's perspective, an American modernism was something that was just waiting to happen – and sooner rather than later – because America was the point of convergence between the very subversive vitality of literature and the type of self whose mode, too, was invention and risk. Pound meant to be taken more seriously than we might imagine when he maintained that the "American Risorgimento" would "make the Italian Renaissance look like a tempest in a teapot!"[123]

More and more, Pound came to view the constructive individual and its productions not only as the essence of modernism's promise, and America's as well, but also as the very engine and value of history itself. It is energy and volition – and precious little else – that will unite key figures in the *Cantos* who otherwise have precious little in common. What the cultural provincialism of the landlocked present needs, from Pound's perspective, is not exactly history but rather the *experience* of the energetic self that makes history vital and valuable. Pound's individualism, it turns out, has in mind not just any individual but a very special kind of individual. And not just any history but a certain kind of history.

What these contradictions indicate, I think, is that Pound's appeal to experience, and to the individuals who possess it, is itself, to use Fredric Jameson's phrase, an "ideological supplement" whereby the contingent world of history can be used as an antidote to the fallen present and yet can be ideologically contained.[124] To put it another way, the contingencies of history ("fought in battles, sailed before the mast") must be acknowledged as real and significant if that heroic surmounting and mastery of them called experience is to take place and be heroic. Experience is the process whereby the historical world becomes mere material for the self that can transcend it and can thereby be something *other than* a repetition of those other selves (the genteels, say) that it criticizes. In short, experience names not the fact but the *value* of history, a value that cannot help but be, by definition, transhistorical. Indeed, by any other definition, the self – any self – could not *not* have experience, and the whole distinction between those who "have" it and those who do not would be called into question. The category of experience, then, names not the immersion of all selves in contingency but rather the ability of some selves to step outside it.

What the category of experience in Pound reveals is that his critique, like Emerson's, is essentially, if not purely, an ethical one. And, appropriately enough for Pound's and Emerson's ideology, the ethical frame of interpretation is ultimately a privatizing, individualizing mode of thought, one that readily assimilates the binding determinations of history to the supposedly changeless features of human experience, the better to assimilate *that*, in turn, to an equally transhistorical conception of "human nature."[125] In "Patria Mia," the political consequences of the ethical critique are not hard to find, for to cite the self-reliant entrepreneur as a positive example of experience and volition is to assume that the economic and social structures sustained and reproduced in entrepreneurship bear no structurally necessary relation to the capitalist economy and culture, whose effects Pound almost always deplores because, by Pound's own logic, they work to prevent self-realization and cultural vitality. For Pound, it is finally not a question of the determinate economic and social structures which make possible entrepreneurial activity itself (and which that activity, in turn, makes possible). It is rather a matter of making a wholly ethical distinction between "good" (read: energetic and adventurous) entrepreneurs and "bad."

Nor is this the only example of the early Pound's assimilation of historically specific economic and political structures to the timeless categories of ethics. Even before "Patria Mia," he had expressed in the "Osiris" essay his admiration for one Frank ("Baldy") Bacon, who, it is recorded in Canto XII, "bought all the little copper pennies in Cuba":

> Every man who does his own job really well has a latent respect for every other man who does *his* own job really well; . . . whether it be a matter of buying up all the little brass farthings in Cuba and selling them at a quarter percent, advance, or of delivering steam-engines to King Menelek across three rivers and one hundred and four ravines . . . the man who really does the thing well, if he be pleased to talk about it, gets always his auditors' attention; he gets his audience the moment he says something so intimate that it proves him the expert; he does not, as a rule, sling generalities; he gives the particular case for what it is worth; the truth is the individual.[126]

What is symptomatic about Pound's praise of Bacon – and a little shocking when viewed within the context of Pound's storied interest in economics – is that in this passage the primacy of the economic, to put it bluntly, runs up against the primacy of the ethical, and the ethical wins.

The treatment of Bacon in Canto XII is usually read by Kenner, Cookson, and other Poundians as a parable against the sins of usury, but as Peter Nicholls has persuasively argued, Pound's Bacon seems to call for a quite different interpretation.[127] Bacon, true, engages in the sort of economic activity attacked throughout the *Cantos* – he is a usurer, he corners currency and sells it at interest – but this is precisely what makes Pound's treatment of him problematic. He is not admonished but admired (in "Osiris" and in the *Cantos*) on ethical grounds that readily dissociate his expertise and volition from their accompanying economic structure. The intimate knowledge and experience of the particular case that make a man an "expert," that disclose the "truth of the individual," are explicitly invoked in "Osiris" on Bacon's behalf. In Canto XII, for example, Pound praises his particularized knowledge about "which shipping companies were most careless; where a man was most likely / To lose a leg in bad hoisting machinery."[128]

Bacon, like the entrepreneurs of "Patria Mia," has experience, and that experience exempts him from the judgment Pound readily passed on the economic structure that depended on agents like Bacon himself. Pound wanted to keep Bacon the economic man and Bacon the ethical man separate; or more precisely, he wanted to subsume the former under the latter. Therefore, Pound's ethical critique, like Emerson's, forces us to say that the problem is not entrepreneurship but particular entrepreneurs; not capitalism as a structure with an intractable logic but particular capitalists.

"A PACT"

In "What I feel about Walt Whitman," Pound made it clear how much the literature of modernity needed the sort of American character he had been exploring since his earliest prose. The encrusted Victorian culture in which he found himself needed an injection, as he put it, of the "sap and fibre of America," the "bacillus" of democratic openness, which, Pound told William Carlos Williams, was the lifeblood of his family tree. To make a place for adventure and change in the inert literary establishment of London, "I should like," he wrote, "to drive Whitman into the old world. I sledge, he drill."[129] But years later, he would look back, in the *Cantos*, with a colder eye to that native ground which seemed not so much open as vacant, which had "no classics, / no American history / no centre, no general root."[130] His country, it seemed, had all the promise of a great culture but none of the conditions that might enable its flowering.

In a way, those lines in the *Cantos* register one of Pound's most quintessentially American moments. Emerson himself had expressed the same ambivalence toward an American culture whose promise and failure both stemmed from its lack of a common root. As for the promise, Emerson saw the American self as a molecular and dispersed force; like Pound's "bacillus," it was the living image of an equally wild American nature whose very essence was growth and change. For the Emerson of "The American Scholar," nature seemed "without center, without circumference." But that fact had to lead the self to realize what Emerson would explain later in his essay: The individual seeking culture, suddenly in the dizzying historical open, had to look not to the law of history and its enclosing structures but to the law of nature. It had to find "roots running under ground whereby contrary and remote things cohere and flower out from one stem." Once fixed on self-reliance, with no history in its field of vision, the American thinker and writer might realize that self and nature "proceed from one root; one is leaf and one is flower; relation, sympathy, stirring in every vein." Against history and tradition, Emerson placed his hopes in a coherence of nature and Spirit that, he believed, made selves and societies possible: "And what is that root? Is not that the soul of his soul?"[131]

In a different mood, however, Emerson knew that this coherence, and the culture it promised to make possible, were not so easily realized. And in those moments (they became, it seems, more and more frequent), he lamented that the "contrary and remote things" of American culture did not express multeity in unity but instead constantly threatened to become anarchy rather than democracy, a chaos of energies in which no culture worth having seemed possible. For that Emerson – the Emerson who admired aristocratic culture but not its social base – it seemed that America "all runs to leaves, to suckers, to tendrils, to miscellany." American culture threatened to become something "profuse, procumbent . . . out of which no cedar, no oak will rear up a mast to the clouds!"[132] Emerson's native country was as frustrating as it was promising because there were precious few selves who had taken up the ethical transformation that might reveal to them the soul of their soul, and in so doing enable them to both cultivate and be the new poetic wood, the cedar and oak, of American culture.

But Emerson would have found just what he was looking for in the early Ezra Pound, who, in a little poem called "A Pact," declared common ground with the project Emerson had called for eighty years earlier. In this poem, though, Pound comes not to Emerson but to Whitman as "a grown child" to "a pig-headed father" – he is "old enough now to make friends." Our modernist now realizes that Whitman is the type of democratic man who brought American writing into the clearing and pointed the way for those who would follow: "It was you that broke the new wood," Pound tells him. "Now is a time for carving."

How, exactly, is this project to be carried out? As if in answer to that question, Pound's poem takes an unmistakably Emersonian turn. The next line reminds us that what must be "carved" is not only the wood of American culture but in fact the selves with whom the American promise rests: "We have one sap and one root." The new wood of America, and of a particularly American poetry, depends, as Emerson said it did, upon the selves who must sustain and shape it. This fashioning is a *self*-fashioning, and this carving, a self-carving: They themselves are "sap" and "root." The project of American democracy and culture is now revealed to be what Emerson had always said it was: an ethical project incumbent upon the family tree of those energetic and constructive individuals who, like Pound's grandfather and like the enterprising spirits of "Patria Mia," break new wood by making themselves new.

By the light of Emerson, we can now make sense of what has always seemed a crucial but puzzling moment in Pound's early career. The final line of the poem is a seemingly incomprehensible figure for this modernist enemy of the bourgeoisie: "Let there be," Pound concludes in affirmation, "*commerce* between us."[133] It is only by the logic of ethics and the Emersonian self that Pound can move quite easily from the ambiguity of the opening "pact" – a blood oath between metaphorical father and son or a trade agreement? – to the relatively more "natural" relations of patrilineage, and then from there, by way of the mediating figure of the family tree, to the organicism of the "new wood," of democratic self and American promise.

It is that self which redeems the socioeconomic dimension that resurfaces at the end of the poem in the form, now, not of a "pact" but of "commerce." We can, after all, have that economic structure which Pound's early critique everywhere taught us to fear, so long as it is filtered, so to speak, through the right kind of self, through the family tree that would make it new. This pact turns out indeed to be a trade agreement, but one with the force of nature behind it. And this commerce could be, as Emerson himself said, poetic: an authentic, because ethical, transaction, one whose innocence could be guaranteed, against all odds, by virtue of the participants.

4

"Gynocracy" and "Red Blood": Pound and the Politics of Feminization

By virtue of his manly rhetoric of *virtù*, Pound compels us to situate his critique of American culture within an economy of gender as well. As an antidote to the evils of abstraction, conformity, and what a later critical vocabulary would call reification, Pound seems to offer us an exclusively male world of experience, of rough-and-tumble, bone and sinew, which constantly threatens to evaporate into the clichés of macho, rugged individualism. As we shall see, however, Pound's critique is a good deal more complex than that. When he set the *virtù* of the "entire man" over against what he called the "gynocracy" of genteel writers and editors like Edmund Clarence Stedman, Richard Watson Gilder, and Robert Underwood Johnson,[1] he engaged himself not so much in some misogynist battle of the sexes as in yet another effort in a long line of American endeavors by male writers to move literature from the drawing-room margins it occupied at the turn of the century into the public sphere, where it might be taken seriously as a liberating force for social critique and change.[2]

The rhetoric of gender and feminization in Pound's cultural critique is particularly complex to assess for a whole host of reasons, not the least of which is that in Pound's work the figure of gender – like that of economics – can never be read in isolation or taken, as it were, at face value. It is almost always, and overtly so, articulated in tandem with the other major concerns of class, economics, and cultural production in Pound's ambitious and totalizing critique. It is certainly true (as we shall see in our discussion of his work on Remy de Gourmont) that Pound's relation to the figure of woman and "the feminine" is sometimes both essentialist and misogynist, and indeed there is probably no more famous "phallocrat" among the modernists (though D. H. Lawrence and Wyndham Lewis are certainly strong contenders) than Pound himself.[3]

But because gender, overtly or not, is always articulated in conjunction with ideology, and because concepts of the subject are always crossed by structures of property and class, Pound's sexist sentiments are only where we must *begin* in assessing the politics of gender in his work. Though we need to pay full attention to Pound's phallocratic posturing, that does little to help us understand other apparently paradoxical and quite conspicuous facts in the Pound file, which we will address below: his strong *support* for women writers like Marianne Moore and Mina Loy; his bitterly pointed *critique* of masculinist, "red-blood" writers like Bliss Carmen and Richard Hovey; and, most important of all, his surprising representation of *himself* – both in early poems and, later, in the *Cantos* – as a writer not of phallic power and authority but of transitive emptiness and absence, an empty space coded feminine and waiting to be filled by authorial voices of the past.

These are more than anomalies in the Poundian text, and to make sense of them we must go beyond the surface of Pound's sexist attitudes (and certainly beyond any essentialist notion of gender)[4] to explore his relationship to *the gender system itself.* To put it another way, what is most important here is Pound's reproduction of a structure of gender built upon an unequal, hierarchical dichotomy, *regardless* of which side of that dichotomy Pound may align himself with at any given moment. Although it must be noted that the use of the gender system, by Pound and by others, has real material effects on women, we must limit ourselves here to disclosing the "political unconscious" of Pound's relationship to gender by examining not only his professed attitudes about gender but, more important, the system and structure that organize and reproduce those attitudes.[5]

Before we do so, however, we need to understand that there is an immediate historical context that is crucial in coming to grips with the problem of gender in Pound's cultural critique. That his attempt to combat the privatization of literature would time and again invoke the discourse of patriarchy was less a matter of intended malice on Pound's part (though sometimes it was just that) than of the structuring force of a pervasive cultural logic confronted by all would-be modern American poets. Frank Lentricchia has shown in his recent study of Wallace Stevens that the situation of the modern male poet in America was a structurally schizophrenic one in which the poet must confront that impulse in himself to engage in an activity so thoroughly coded as feminine (because presumed to be contemplative and passive, not productive and active) that it cannot be reconciled with its opposite, the economically productive, masculine public sphere. As Lentricchia has drawn the contrast, how could lyric poetry be a serious pursuit for an American male, whose culture told him that authentic self-realization had to be achieved in the realm of "econo-machismo," where to know yourself is "to know yourself as economic man, fit for the hurly-burly of the marketplace where the big boys slug it out."[6]

In Lentricchia's reading, it was this logic that led Stevens to think of his verse writing, with maximum guilt, as "positively lady-like."[7] It was also this logic that led him, on the other (masculine) hand, to a tremendously successful career at Hartford Accident and Indemnity. That Stevens could not resist the force of American modernity's perfect – and perfectly schizophrenic – couple of masculine economic utility and feminine lyricism testifies to the coercive power of this cultural paradigm. Indeed, as Lentricchia has demonstrated, Stevens's inability to resist it is one of the turbulent sources of his poignant lyric desire to escape and make new – escape *by* making new – a world in which the whole self could never feel at home.

Pound's response to what Ann Douglas has called (in a book of the same title) "the feminization of American culture" could not, by all appearances, be more unlike Stevens's. The fact, or perception, that poetry in America, under the sway of the genteels, had become "lady-like" was apparently not a source of guilt for Pound; in fact, it was often exhibit A in his critique of contemporary culture. Pound seemed to have no doubts about his ability to stack up to what Stevens called, in a phrase of some longing, "your man poets." The rigorous historical and comparative training that would shortly produce *The Spirit of Romance* and the early poetry that draws upon the same sources gave Pound a purchase on the contemporary scene that is wholly absent, characteristically so, in Stevens. If lyric culture in America is feminized, Stevens felt at the deepest level, then so much the worse for my desire to write lyric. But for Pound, if art in America had become "frilled paper decoration," then from his vantage that reflected not upon him but instead upon the sad state of affairs that required his renovating *virtù* and the cultural critique that would accompany it.

When Pound in "Patria Mia" diagnosed the effects of leaving American literature to the likes of Henry Van Dyke and R. U. Johnson (those masters of what Pound derisively tagged "the style of 1880"), he found it no surprise that Americans "cannot be expected to take it seriously."[8] And not being taken seriously meant, in genteel New York or Edwardian London, being "left to the care of ladies' societies, and of 'current events clubs'"[9] – which was fine, Pound thought, if you saw literature as the moral equivalent of bingo, but was not if you had sailed before the mast or taken your Shakespeare to heart or submitted poetry and criticism to the test of something other than the dictates of *Harper's* and the *Century*. To perpetuate the idea that poetry was merely cultural decoration and social window dressing, "a sort of embroidery for dilettantes and women," was not only to perpetuate the insidious Palgravian ideal of lyric as therapeutic – which is to say not as socially central but as a palliative for that which is – but also to ensure that "serious people, intently alive [will] consider poetry as balderdash."[10]

Looking back even further, beyond the moment of modernism, we can see that Pound's critique of the cultural "gynocracy" was only the latest in a long line of American male invectives against the feminization of literature: from Hawthorne's infamous complaint, in a letter of 1855, about "the damn'd mob of scribbling women"[11] to the polemics of many a late-nineteenth-century proponent of realism against what one of them called (in an altogether typical phrase of *ressentiment* and economic envy) "this paradise of women."[12] In short, these oppositions (masculine/feminine, serious/nonserious), as Ann Douglas has shown, may be vintage Pound, but they are also vintage American cultural ideology from the mid-1800s on.[13] By engaging the discourse of feminization in the services of his critique, in other words, Pound was activating a cultural paradigm whose force had been almost irresistible for nearly a century. Emerson himself, despite the fact that souls presumably had no gender – as they had (according to William James) no taste – could not resist its logic. In fact, Douglas has suggested that Emerson left the clergy precisely because it had become so "feminized." Eric Cheyfitz points out, however, that the vocation of authorship he took up in reaction was itself so culturally coded as feminine by Emerson's day that his change of career amounted to jumping out of the frying pan only to land in the fire.[14]

The decade of the 1850s was a veritable *economic* "paradise of women": Susan Warner's *The Wide, Wide World*, Harriet Beecher Stowe's *Uncle Tom's Cabin*, and Maria Cummins's *The Lamplighter* reached unprecedented sales. Nevertheless, in "Self-Reliance," Emerson assured us that of all the pressures threatening the nonconformist, the "feminine rage" of the cultural establishment should be the least of his worries. As he put it in that athletically polemical essay, in anticipation of Pound's early writings on the value of experience: "It is easy enough for a firm man who knows the world to brook the rage of the cultivated classes. Their rage is decorous and prudent, for they are timid, as being very vulnerable themselves."[15] Experience made the man "firm" and potent and gave him a readiness for change and a taste for adventure that made him invulnerable to the frilly decorum that, Pound told us, was as insubstantial as paper.

In "The American Scholar," well before the 1850s, Emerson did not deny the validity of patriarchy's logic but instead was troubled by the accuracy of its claims against feminized American culture:

> The so-called "practical men" sneer at speculative men, as if, because they speculate or *see*, they could do nothing. I have heard it said that

the clergy, – who are always, more universally than any other class, the scholars of their day, – are addressed as women; that the rough, spontaneous conversation of men they do not hear, but only a mincing and diluted speech. . . . As far as this is true of the studious classes, it is not just and wise. Action is with the scholar subordinate, but it is essential. Without it he is not yet man.[16]

If the clergy are called "women," Emerson says, then let them be less womanly by taking action and living fully in the "rough, spontaneous" world where culture comes not at the expense of life. If the speculative self is wholly private, then it deserves the name of "woman" and deserves as well the scorn of those men who deem utility and action in the world the measure of manliness. With the discourse of patriarchy behind him, Emerson, in so many words, says to the American scholar: Take action, not contemplation, and you will be man enough; be man enough, and you will be scholar enough.

In a later journal entry, though, Emerson's discourse complicates the patriarchal logic he had readily put to didactic use in his lecture to the Harvard Phi Beta Kappans. There, he never questioned the terms of patriarchy; it is not "unjust," he told us, that the term of "woman" should be so used but that the contemplative man should be deserving of it. In this journal entry, however, he strategically qualifies and reframes the gendered terms of his earlier critique:

> In America out of doors all seems a market; indoors, an air-tight stove of conventionalism. Every body who comes into the house savors of these precious habits, the men, of the market; the women, of the custom. In every woman's conversation & total influence mild or acid lurks the *conventional devil*.[17]

In an important sense, Emerson's quarry here is *other* than gender, because "habit" and "convention" know no gender (or, more precisely, know *both* genders). Habit and convention (whether of the market or of the domestic space) are the real enemies of experience and change, and not the genders sustaining them.

Looking back, then, we can see that the resentment driving Emerson in "The American Scholar" to defend the life of contemplation is not, despite appearances, directed exactly toward women but rather toward those who trivialize the work of intellect by making its raison d'être the denial of the social, the world of experience. The "injustice" is not that so-called practical men (only half-selves themselves) deem the speculative life feminine; the injustice is to treat the life of contemplation as if it were *only* that. However, that is only the manifest content of Emerson's critique here, and it should not obscure the fact that even as Emerson attempts to complicate the gendered terms of his critique by crossing them with the apparently gender-neutral acquiescence to social conventions, his underlying rhetoric reminds us that "habit" and "convention" are – historically and in the dominant cultural code – more well acquainted with one gender than the other.

Roughly sixty years after "The American Scholar," William James would engage in the same sort of critique but would complicate matters considerably (and in this he anticipates Pound by a decade) by crossing the rhetoric of the feminization of American culture with an emphasis on its class basis. In an essay of 1899, James lamented that the "middle-class paradise" of American culture was too "tame," "refined," "tepid," and "harmless" because it allowed for none of the risk-taking adventure and experimental openness that Pound would later make synonymous with the American self.[18] James's terms could not be closer to Pound's: "Bourgeoisie and mediocrity, church sociables and teachers' conventions," had supplanted "human life in its wild intensity."[19] And James's response to this "wretched culture" would be right at home in Pound's early prose as well: "Let me take my chances again in the big outside worldly wilderness with all its sins and sufferings."[20]

But just as James's rhetoric seems poised to position cultural vitality out of reach in a chivalric past, he suddenly realizes that the sort of heroism and experience that genteel culture has made him crave lies close to hand "in the daily lives of the laboring classes," in the "strength and strenuousness" of their work.[21] James tells us that we need not look down the ages but rather across the class lines of 1890s America to infuse this middle-class culture of "sentimentalists and dreamers" with the "sterner stuff of manly virtue."[22] In James's hands, then, masculine and feminine become strategic, because class-specific, terms used to subvert the culture of the dominant class that produced them. Like Emerson, James wants a culture not so much of manhood, it seems, as of selfhood and posits as Emerson does in "Compensation" an ideal self that needs both genders, as it were, to be complete – a "marriage of two different parents," as James puts it, of the ideals and sensibility of culture with the "courage and endurance" of labor.[23] But like Emerson's figuration too, James's reproduction of the gender system is revealed not in his overt desire for an apparently androgynous ideal of selfhood but rather in his more fundamental use of the rhetoric of feminization in the first place. Which is simply to say that James, like Emerson, however well intentioned, cannot control, by rhetorical strategy or fiat of will, the discourse of gender that speaks through his own figures and cuts against his bid for equality with its own historically constituted asymmetry, its own unequal weighting of a dichotomy that only looks equal.

We find the same sort of desire and contradiction in Pound's early critique of feminized culture. For Pound, too, those who saw the literary or scholarly life as one of escape from James's "worldly wilderness" perpetuated a situation in which the would-be writer or scholar could be only half a self insofar as he pursued his literary ambitions. Like James and Emerson, when Pound proposed for his anti-Palgravian anthology that each poem be chosen "not merely because it was a nice poem or a poem Aunt Hepsy liked,"[24] he had in mind a figure not of womanhood as such but rather of something like its provincial, parodic Other. Consequently, Aunt Hepsy is Pound's figure not for the denial of manhood so much as the denial of *self* hood; she is the suffocating antithesis not only of Bertran de Born but also of the women Pound greatly admired: his Sappho, his "Francesca," his woman of Cavalcanti's *Donna mi priegha* in Canto XXXVI, his Roman matron Marozia. For Pound, the culture of Aunt Hepsy, in other words, was not the culture of women since time immemorial but rather of *this* America, which saw literature as "embroidery" and "decoration," as something that demanded about as much investment of self as the clubby status-mongering of "ladies' societies."

It is important to note what is easily missed in Pound's last figure here: It is class-inflected as well. (After all, working-class women in 1910 were neither "ladies" nor members of "societies.") This aspect was present from the earliest days of Pound's social critique in "Patria Mia," where he acknowledged: "It has been well said of the 'lady in society' that art criticism is one of her functions. She babbles of it as of 'the play,' or of hockey, or of 'town topics.' She believes in catholicity of taste, in admiring no one thing more than anything else."[25] She believes, in other words, that culture is one of those many things – like going to the Christmas ball, perhaps – that well-off people make sure to do, one of those forms of recreation and amusement that requires no discrimination and even less commitment. William James had called the hand of genteel culture by revealing the other kinds of class experience systematically repressed in its universalization of middle-class mores. Pound's critiques of feminized culture likewise are almost always directed at specific targets, which, more often than not, are backed by that economic power and potency which patriarchy almost always figures as masculine.

This complex and often surprising crossing of gender and class is particularly pronounced in, for example, *Hugh Selwyn Mauberley*, in which Lady Valentine and Mr. Nixon must be seen, by patriarchy's logic, as coded figures who are quite masculine indeed where it matters most – in the economic sphere. It is the modernist *poet* who awaits the lady's commands in "the stuffed–satin drawing-room"; it is *the lady* who wields economic and cultural power, but who, ironically enough, represents at the same time that sort of culture in which poetry is but a "border of ideas." Or again, it is Mr. Nixon, not Mauberley, who brandishes all the signs of economic potency – the yacht and the clothes – and who is by the logic of patriarchy quite male in that most male of arenas. Indeed, it is this gap between Nixon's economic masculinity and the feminized culture he represents (that "old bitch gone in the teeth," as Pound puts it earlier in the poem) that generates the bitter irony of his genteel directives to the young poet. Become more of a man, Nixon tells him, by buttering up the reviewers and thereby securing economic prowess. "Don't kick against the pricks" – this is the manly, because financially sound, thing to do.

But Pound's whole point, of course – it is carried by the ribald critical undertow of his metaphors – is that Nixon's promise of economic manhood turns out to be a scene of feminization for the modern poet, and a scene of violence as well (the kind of violence recorded in section X of the poem, where "the dedicated stylist" lives in poverty beneath the "sagging roof"). Not only should the poet *not* "kick against the pricks," who take him from behind, as it were, in a kind of rape to which he must submit; but he is further degraded in that he should help his violators along by "buttering" them up. By this logic, if anyone is feminized in *Mauberley*, it is the poet of the title himself. John Espey quite aptly suggests in his detailed study of the poem that "in the person of Mauberley Pound was rejecting . . . a mask of what he feared to become as an artist by remaining in England."[26]

Along these same lines, Carolyn Burke has recently argued that Pound's well-known phallic poetics (about which more in a moment) "may be seen in part as a response to his own situation as an expatriate in literary London, where, according to Ford Madox Ford, 'a man of letters [was] regarded as something less than a man.'" "Already at a disadvantage as a 'colonial,' an exile, and a man of letters," Burke continues,

> Pound's sense of himself as a member of the more powerful sex was further challenged by the apparent threat posed by the suffragists' political and literary agitation. . . . [Thus] his recourse to theories about the passive nature of the female may have functioned to shore up some of his uncertainties about his place in the world.[27]

Pound's relationship to the rhetoric of gender is, however, considerably more complicated than this. Burke's interpretation would be plausible, perhaps, were it not for the fact that Pound was as rough on what he mockingly called "the 'school of virility,' or 'red blood,'" as he was on the culture of Aunt Hepsy. The "red-bloods" seemed – but only seemed – to offer a cultural alternative embracing all that the genteels and Aunt Hepsy feared. Poets like Bliss Carmen and Richard Hovey regularly sang the glories of what Jackson Lears has called "the martial ideal,"[28] and in doing so they spearheaded a widespread backlash against what the newspapers of the day were routinely lamenting: the enervation of a culture that had become "overcivilized." As Ernest Thompson Seton wrote in the first *Boy Scouts of America Handbook* (1910), in a passage as typical in its rhetoric as it is hilarious in its male hysteria, middle-class Americans needed to "combat the system that has turned such a large proportion of our robust, manly, self-reliant boyhood into a lot of flat-chested cigarette smokers, with shakey nerves and doubtful vitality."[29]

Hovey was downright jubilant about America's entry into the Spanish-American War, and he was more than happy to justify American militarism by linking it to a vaguely Arthurian cult of experience that might serve as an antidote to the pacific placidity of genteel America. Hovey's works were widely read, and he led the attack:

> Back to your world of books, and leave the world of men
> To them that have the habit of the real
> Nor longer with a mask of fair ideal
> Hide your indifference to the facts of pain![30]

For Pound, however, the difference between the red-bloods and the gynocracy of the genteels was no difference at all. The red-bloods, too, made poetry strictly therapeutic – and therefore strictly marginal – by turning it into a sort of self-help handbook for insecure males. As Pound put it, in hyperbole perfectly suited to the trumpeting rhetoric of Hovey and Carmen, the red-bloods seemed to believe that "man is differentiated from the lower animals by the possession of the phallus."[31]

On the other hand, Pound was not unaware of the superficial resemblance between their work and some of his early personae, and he wanted to make it clear that he stood not for red blood but for *new* blood. That difference, in fact, is the overt subject of the poem "The Condolence," published in *Lustra* (1915) but written much earlier:

> And now you hear what is said to us:
> We are compared to that sort of person
> Who wanders about announcing his sex
> As if he had just discovered it.
> Let us leave this matter, my songs,
>   and return to that which concerns us.[32]

What concerned Pound and his songs could be found no more in the work of Hovey than in the culture of Aunt Hepsy. Despite Hovey's hardihood and all his talk about "the habit of the real," his works yield not a single particularity or concrete Imagist detail. Henry James would recall later with killing kindness, in a characterization that Pound quoted approvingly, "It was a period when writers besought the deep blue sea 'to roll.'"[33]

Of course, beseeching the sea to roll was not very inventive, nor did it require the kind of self-investment Pound believed inseparable from culture's broader social function of "liberation" from set moods, conventions, and practices. The red-bloods enforced a culture not of *virtù* and invention but of anonymity, "the reflex": "They wish," Pound coolly observed, "always to be exhorted, at all times no matter how incongruous and unsuitable, to do those things which almost anyone will and does do whenever suitable opportunity is presented."[34] In open revolt against the culture of the genteels, the red-bloods nevertheless perpetuated the same kind of cultural politics. That they did so with a manly face was of no great matter, for if this literature precluded the possibility of the art of *virtù* to begin with, then what difference could it make whether this pseudoself was masculine or feminine?

From this vantage, Pound's energetic and unstinting support for women poets like Marianne Moore and Mina Loy is a good deal less "paradoxical" than it might seem at first glance.[35] And from this vantage too, it is a little easier to recognize what the gendered slant of Pound's rhetoric might obscure: that when he lambasted the culture of Aunt Hepsy he was taking on a structure and system of cultural dissemination controlled and enforced by men. Aunt Hepsy, it turns out, is no woman:

> Though males of seventy, who fear truths naked harms us,
> Must think that Truth looks as they do in wool pyjamas.
> (My country, I've said your morals and your thoughts are stale ones,
> But surely the worst of your old-women are the male ones.)[36]

If anyone produced Aunt Hepsy – that provincial moral terminator familiar from suburban lore – it was the genteel writers themselves, who, rather than rebelling against their culture's feminization of lyric, parlayed that cultural code into considerable literary power and economic profit. But Pound would help us see that they did so only at the expense of consigning poetry to those social margins that even Emerson knew were bound to be called "womanly."

But "womanly," we now know, is not exactly le mot juste. Its range and sweep might admit of some qualities that the genteels wanted to exclude from their lyric universe. Pound found those qualities throughout history in great women whom he admired: women like the matron Marozia of tenth-century Rome, whose "genius" (and shrewdness) led her to become, as Pound put it, "the most powerful person in Rome," and around whom Pound had once planned to construct an epic poem.[37] No, it was rather a specifically middle-class, antiseptic sort of world – Aunt Hepsyish, in fact – that the genteels traded upon, one of ostentatious cultivation, sanctimonious manners, and saccharine moral observance, the world of "educated churchgoing women," to use Ruthven's phrase.

For Pound, that sort of self was the enemy not only of the Whitman line but also of the kind of woman modern America promised to liberate. That sort of woman, Pound observed admiringly, was no Aunt Hepsy, but a person "of broad experience, of comprehension . . . a woman whose acquaintance with life has been first hand and various." Like any good self-reliant modernist, "she is perfectly aware that no two human beings are much alike." And consequently, she demands a culture as different from "ladies' societies" as she herself is from Aunt Hepsy and her ministers: "She is a person," Pound writes in massive understatement, "very different from the female member of a 'Society for the Discussion of Social Problems.'"[38]

But again, as James reminds us, that provincialism which stood as the enemy of any kind of selfhood whatsoever was as much a product of a specific class as it was the bane of a single country.[39] And so it is a little less surprising that most of the poems in Pound's early volume *Lustra* that mount a critique of gender are also quite class-specific. What "L'Homme Moyen Sensuel" was to the American middle class, *Lustra* would be to the English bourgeoisie. Our unsavory American, in standard modernist *épater le bourgeois* fashion, will implore his songs to "ruffle the skirts of prudes, speak of their knees and ankles."[40] In other places, *Lustra* addresses not Aunt Hepsy's English relations but rather her victims, who are "thwarted with systems, / Helpless against the control."[41] "Commission," for instance, voices both sympathy and a liberating impulse in its Whitmanian apostrophe and parallelism:

> Speak against unconscious oppression,
> Speak against the tyranny of the unimaginative,
> Speak against bonds.
> Go to the bourgeois who is dying of her ennuis,
> Go to the woman in the suburbs,
> Go to the hideously wedded,
> Go to them whose failure is concealed,
> Go to the unluckily mated,
> Go to the bought wife,
> Go to the woman entailed.[42]

In the early Pound, however, the incisive satirist is ever close at hand, and he emerges in "The Garden" to give us a rather different picture of one such woman. This figure will reappear throughout Pound's early work, and we immediately recognize that her bearing and texture are quite different from what Pound conjured up in the American name of Aunt Hepsy. America had gone provincial and preachy, but in England it was a fin de siècle world-weariness that threatened to refine an entire class out of existence in a sort of Paterian self-flagellation:

> Like a skein of loose silk blown against a wall
> >She walks by the railing of a path in
> >>Kensington Gardens,
> And she is dying piece-meal
> >of a sort of emotional anaemia.
>
> . . . .
>
> In her is the end of breeding,
> Her boredom is exquisite and excessive.
> She would like someone to speak to her,
> And is almost afraid that I
> >will commit that indiscretion.[43]

This woman lacks many things (none of them, we may conjecture, material), but what she lacks most of all is the *virtù* that opens, rather than forecloses, the possibilities of "broad experience" and "comprehension" (not to mention simple conversation!). Although she may have, for herself, nothing to look forward to, look forward she does in Pound's early career to Lady Valentine and the woman of *Mauberley*, section XI, another victim of social engineering, of whom it is recorded:

> No instinct has survived in her
> Older than her grandmother
> Told her would fit her station.[44]

But the lady of "The Garden" looks backward, too, to the early poem in which Pound would most famously memorialize her and her kind.

"PORTRAIT D'UNE FEMME"

> Your mind and you are our Sargasso Sea,
> London has swept about you this score years
> And bright ships have left you this or that in fee:
> Ideas, old gossip, oddments of all things,
> Strange spars of knowledge and dimmed wares of price.
> Great minds have sought you – lacking someone else.
> You have been second always. Tragical?
> No. You preferred it to the usual thing:
> One dull man, dulling and uxorious,
> One average mind – with one thought less, each year.
> Oh, you are patient, I have seen you sit
> Hours, where something might have floated up.
> And now you pay one. Yes, you richly pay.
> You are a person of some interest, one comes to you
> And takes strange gain away:
> Trophies fished up; some curious suggestion;
> Fact that leads nowhere; and a tale or two,
> Pregnant with mandrakes, or with something else

That might prove useful and yet never proves,
That never fits a corner or shows use,
Or finds its hour upon the loom of days:
The tarnished, gaudy, wonderful old work;
Idols and ambergris and rare inlays,
These are your riches, your great store; and yet
For all this sea-hoard of deciduous things,
Strange woods half sodden, and new brighter stuff:
In the slow float of differing light and deep,
No! there is nothing! In the whole and all,
Nothing that's quite your own.
                    Yet this is you.[45]

Like the lady of "The Garden," who is literally decentered, a diapha-
nous thing blown about by the wind, the *femme* of Pound's "Portrait"
is similarly adrift in the aimless wash of literary London. And like that
lady who is dying "piece-meal," this lady is living the death of modern
dissociation, one figured prominently in the first stroke of Pound's
"Portrait": "Your mind and you are our Sargasso Sea," as if the lady and
her "mind" were discrete things, as if mind and self were, in fact,
indistinguishable from the "oddments" they comprise. "Sargasso Sea,"
that infamous haven of weeds and flotsam, is choice: If *virtù* is "the centre of a circle which possesseth all parts of its circumference equally,"
then its antithesis is figured quite appropriately here as a slow slosh,
which literally can have no center. This lady, we might say, is all
circumference.

In a "strange" way, though, she *does* seem to possess her things, her
"ideas, old gossip," and "strange spars of knowledge," quite equally –
as equally, in fact, as the Sargasso Sea possesses its drifting cargo. So
how to distinguish, in this poem worked so thoroughly through the
language of economy, between these two kinds of possession? Is this
lady an authentic owner after all, a possessor of *virtù* in disguise?

The second and third lines will help us answer that question. Notice
first the agency: not the woman but "London" and the "bright ships"
that have navigated its social and cultural weather (some more successfully
than others). Part of what has drifted into this lady's pool is figured as
the spoils of shipwreck; she is found by "strange spars of knowledge and
dimmed wares of price." In Pound's metaphor, that knowledge once
served a crucial and in fact central function for those crafts, but it has
now been reduced to so many pieces of anonymous intellectual lumber.
It is "strange" because devoid of purpose, divorced from organic context. And those "dimmed wares," then, are not so much "of price" as
they are priceless, no longer functional in a social economy of constructive
action. This lady does not act but is acted upon. What she has has been

"left" to her. It is, in Emerson's formula, not "living" property but dead and accidental. So this woman cannot be "donative," it seems, not only because she has no *virtù* to give but also because her essential mode is not action but passion in the classical sense: "Oh, you are patient," the speaker tells her. What comes to her is not *of* her; it is not really even *for* her.

What, then, of the curious phrase that ends line three? "In fee," it appears, means payment, and payment means compensation for services rendered. So once again the poem raises this tantalizing question: Is this lady an authentic agent, a closet Poundian entrepreneur after all? And who or what is indebted here anyway? When we go to the lexicon we find these contradictions replayed in miniature. To hold "in fee," it turns out, is to hold "as one's absolute and rightful possession." But it is also to hold "on condition of homage and service to a superior lord, by whom it is granted and in whom the ownership remains." In this sense, "take a fee" is to become a vassal, a subject – to become, really, a kind of property.

It is to become, in fact, what the rest of the poem tells us is our lady's lot. For all your "riches," your "great store," the speaker tells her, there is "nothing that's quite your own." *She* is the one who "richly pay[s]," but what she pays is not really hers because she never really owned it in the first place. She is the quintessential, nonproductive middlewoman; she cannot give of herself because she has no self. This is no "permanent property," hence no "donative" transaction. And so the odd fact or tale – her payment – "that might prove useful but never proves," that "leads nowhere," can only be "strange gain" for the visitor because her "strange spars of knowledge" are strange in the etymological sense: not of one's own. "Strange" then because *es*tranged, and able to possess "in fee" because able to be possessed. "Your mind and you are our Sargasso Sea" – ours because not yours:

> No! there is nothing! In the whole and all,
> Nothing that's quite your own.
>   Yet this is you.

BORROWED LADIES AND BROKEN MIRRORS: "NEAR PERIGORD"

> Who is she coming, that the roses bend
> Their shameless heads to do her passing honour?
> Who is she coming with a light upon her
> Not born of suns that with the day's end end?
> Say is it Love who hath chosen the nobler part?
> Say is it Love, that was divinity,
> Who hath left his godhead that his home might be
> The shameless rose of her unclouded heart?[46]

Whoever she is, the woman of "Sonnet: Chi E Questa?" published in *Canzoni* (1911) is emphatically not Lady Valentine, not Aunt Hepsy, not the anemic upper-class woman of "The Garden," and not the *femme* of Pound's "Portrait." In another sense, though, the question posed by this early poem's title can only be a rhetorical one. We know who "she" is: This is the woman who always seems to show up in sonnets, whether by Spenser, Shakespeare, Petrarch, or, as here, Cavalcanti; the woman whose *harmonia* conventional form can only hint at and suggest. She is the woman who elicits the poetic mode best described by this poem's best syntactic rhyme, the mode whose purpose is to bestow "honour / upon her." "Qui e questa?" the poem asks, and we – like the speaker in a later canto – "answer in season": It is Beatrice, of course, to this not-yet-modern Dante.

This "lady of rich allure"[47] is always close at hand in the early Pound.[48] And not only in the early Pound: She makes perhaps her most unforgettable appearance in Canto XXXVI, Pound's translation of Cavalcanti's *Donna mi priegha*, where we know her through her effects, through the love she inspires, which in turn invests poetic vision:

> He is not vertu but cometh of that perfection
> Which is so postulate not by the reason
> But 'tis felt, I say.[49]

In his essay on Cavalcanti, Pound tells us, "It is only when the emotions illumine the perceptive powers that we see the reality"[50] – a contention ratified by Imagism's claim that emotion is the organizer of form. In an odd way, then, the poet of these early hymns to the Lady of Ladies is a figure not of self-reliance but of Beatrice-reliance. After all, *she* is the one who "acts as a magnet for every 'gentil virtute'"; she is the one who gives rise and focus to those "invigorating forces of life and beauty"[51] that make reality a poetic possibility: if not felt, then not known; if no *virtù*, then no "perfection."

Still, this Lady of the Sonnets seems to stand for a compensatory otherworldliness; she gives us an earthly glimpse of other-than-earthly beauty. In which case, we are forced to ask, why be concerned with modernist imperatives like precision and worldly experience? And in which case, moreover, we can admit that this lady is quite uninteresting, because she is a standard and stock male projection of frustration and fantasy. Matters become considerably more interesting, however, when we realize that perhaps the central *donna ideale* in the early Pound is figured not as a centered self but as "a shifting change, / A broken bundle of mirrors!"[52] In other words, she is figured in terms that resemble nothing so much as her apparent opposite, the lady of "Portrait d'une Femme."

In a series of poems beginning in 1908 with "Na Audiart" in *A Lume*

Spento, Pound's first volume, and ending with "Near Perigord," Pound kept returning to this strange woman and to the story of Bertran de Born's attempt to fashion an ideal image of her to replace the real lady who had rejected him. What is interesting about Pound's treatment of the story is the steady drift of focus away from the ideal image itself in "Na Audiart" and toward an interrogation in "Near Perigord" of what such a creative attempt might mean. The early poem gives voice to Bertran's effort to seek solace (and a kind of revenge) through a creation of aesthetic permanence:

> Yea tho thou wish me ill
> Audiart, Audiart
> Thy loveliness is here writ till,
> Audiart
> Oh, till thou come again.[53]

Pound reworks the story again in *Lustra*, but now the inadequacy of the fashioned "phantom" is strategically underscored at poem's end:

> I ask naught from you,
> Save that I have such hunger for
> This phantom
> As I've for you, such flame-lap,
> And yet I'd rather
> Ask of you than hold another.[54]

By the time of "Near Perigord," Bertran's attempt to create an image of his lady's perfection is fully embroiled in political intrigue and, on another level, in Pound's own attempts to construct a persona that might serve as a means of investigating the relationship between individual creation and historical material.

Coming as it does at the moment of Pound's opening struggle with the *Cantos*,[55] and emphasizing the techniques of mask and translation to treat a figure central to Pound's earliest work, "Near Perigord" stands as a crucial bridge between the poet of *A Lume Spento* and the canonized figure of the *Cantos*. But if this poem is a critical and quite overt investigation of the relations that obtain between poet and persona, translation and creation, it is also something like a litmus test for Pound's own notions of the relationship between *virtù*, property, and gender. In what sense, this poem forces us to ask, is poetry a product or expression of that potency which for Pound is sexual, productive, and creative? And in what sense does the property of self inhere, as it does in the signed column of "Patria Mia," in that production in which it should be invested? Pound's political ideal of the autonomous individual would *seem* to find its aesthetic corollary in a conception of the poem as an autonomous literary property that is authentic because expressive of self-possession ("one Catullus, one Villon"). But is this, in fact, the case with "Near Perigord," that most ambitious of Pound's early poems? The questions that the persona of Cino here asks of Bertran's creative enterprise – "Is it a love poem? Did he sing of war? / Is it an intrigue to run subtly out, . . . / Mark him a craftsman and a strategist?"[56] – are the sorts of questions Pound was asking of his own material as he prepared to write the *Cantos*, his "poem including history."[57]

What exactly was Bertran's creation anyway, the poem asks: an expression of love, a calling of *virtù* to *virtù*? Was it a calculated attempt to provoke jealousy for political gain, a pragmatic fiction that might allow his agents access to the fortresses of his rivals? And is the fate of Bertran in Dante's *Inferno* – "*that headless trunk, that bears for light / Its own head swinging*"[58] – therefore tragic, or rather just? These are questions that Pound hopes the poem will not answer with some mythological sleight of hand: "End fact. Try fiction," the poet breaks in, as if to remind himself that his modernism should tolerate no easy melding of the two.

Even if the poem cannot solve the difference between fact and fiction, this is not to say that the modern poet cannot make some sort of assessment of Bertran's creation, and by extension his own. In the poem's final section, which we must read as Bertran's own voice, the creator compares his fashioned lady with the real one, Lady Maent. And what he finds is the fact, so to speak, of his fiction. His *donna ideale* does not compensate for but rather deprives him of the lady who had rebuffed him: "She who could never live save through one person, / She who could never speak save to one person."[59] These lines describe a creation that can live only through its creator, and they therefore describe a reduction, a deprivation, and as we shall see in a moment, a kind of fetish. This image therefore displaces that which it set out somehow to capture:

> There shut up in his castle, Tairiran's,
> She who had nor ears nor tongue save in her hands,
> Gone – ah, gone – untouched, unreachable![60]

In one sense, of course, Lady Maent has ceased to exist outside the lordly terrain of Bertran's own poem. But the whole premise of Pound's poem is that the realms of fact (her actual existence) and fiction (Bertran's creation, but also Cino's and Pound's) must be kept separate. In these terms, Lady Maent remains fiercely autonomous, "untouched" by artistic creation, "unreachable" by poetic device.

Most significant of all, though, this creation is, in the poem's words, an "estrangement."[61] And well she should be, given Pound's conjugations of the relationship between property and gender. Bertran's *donna ideale* is, as the headnote to "Na Audiart" puts it, "a borrowed lady."[62] She is composed of the ideal traits or qualities of the ladies of surrounding Languedoc: of one, "her throat and her two hands," of another, "her hair golden as Iseult's."[63] Bertran does not possess Lady Maent but rather, like the woman of "Portrait d'une Femme," only "oddments," which, however bright or rich, lead nowhere. It is rather Lady Maent herself who is, it appears, in complete self-possession. If *virtù*, in Pound's formula, is the "efficient property of a substance or person,"[64] then Bertran's creation enables him to possess not the authentic property of the lady's *virtù* but only the false property, the fragments and simulacra, which he has "borrowed." His created fiction only further estranges the authentic possession he seeks. Lady Maent is "a shifting change, / A broken bundle of mirrors" not because that is what she is, but because that is what she is to Bertran. In fact, the only authentic possession in the poem, it turns out, is Lady Maent's possession of Bertran himself.

And finally, as several commentators have suggested, "a broken bundle of mirrors" aptly describes not only the lady as she escapes Bertran but also Bertran himself as he is remembered (and dismembered) by Dante, as a headless trunk carrying its visaged lamp by the hair. Section III of "Near Perigord," in fact, opens with an epigraph from the *Inferno*: "*Ed eran due in uno, ed uno in due*" ("And they were two in one and one in two"). This line does not refer to the spiritual and physical union of Bertran and his lady, as we might expect, but rather to the condemned poet and his own head as seen in the mirror of Dante's text. Bertran himself is quite literally "broken" in fragments and is in a quite explicit way, as we shall see in a moment, a figure for castration.

Pound might have made the unified, centered self of *virtù* the very emblem of masculinity, of autonomous genius and creative self-possession, but here he provides, in effect, a stunning critique of those very concepts and of the fitness of Bertran (and himself) to be a bearer of them. When we come upon the epigraph from Dante in section III, we are likely to read it as an expression of the hoped-for union between Bertran and Lady Maent. The dream of desire that opens the first stanza – "And the great wheels in heaven / Bore us together . . . surging . . . and apart"[65] – may meet our expectations. But then the poem quickly turns toward the "estrangement" that serves to rewrite the epigraph as a testament not to consummation and union but to symbolic castration and fragmentation. Bertran's final assessment of the lady is thus merged with Dante's image of Bertran himself. Appropriately enough, then, it might well be said of Bertran and his head in grisly parody of the dissociation opening "Portrait d'une Femme": "your mind and you." They are indeed "two in one" – Bertran and his Other, the woman within.

INVENTOR OR CONSERVATOR? POUND'S ESSENTIALISM

Pound's figures for feminized genteel and Victorian culture may have been materially specific and strategic, but this seems not at all the case with the theories of sexuality and creativity that he developed in conjunction with his reading and translation of Remy de Gourmont. Although Pound's principal writings on Gourmont – his piece in *Literary Essays* and his postscript to *The Natural Philosophy of Love*, which Kevin Oderman has rightly called "certainly one of the most scandalous items in the entire Pound bibliography"[66] – date from the period 1920–1922, Pound had been acquainted with his work since early 1912.[67] Gourmont was quite popular on both continents and was actively promoted by a number of other well-known modernists (D. H. Lawrence and Aldous Huxley among them), but his phallocentric notion of gender was adopted by Pound with particular zeal.

Richard Sieburth has noted in his detailed study of Pound's relationship with Gourmont that Pound saw his work as sexually liberating, as an antidote to the repressive and puritanical prohibitions of Christianity, Puritanism, and the middle class.[68] For Gourmont, Pound noted with approval, sex is natural and in fact central; only chastity, because unnatural, is evil. As Pound saw it, Gourmont's investigations confirmed that man is "really the phallus or spermatozoide charging headlong into the female chaos."[69] And artistic vision, Pound believed, again following Gourmont, was a direct result of the "superfluity of spermatozoic pressure [which] . . . up-shoots into the brain, alluvial Nile-flood, bringing new crops, new invention."[70] This quintessence of maleness is characteristic of genius, of "the strong-minded" and "the form-creator."[71] Artistic creation may therefore be seen as "an act like fecundation, like the male cast of the human seed"[72] (and like what Pound felt, for that matter, drilling Whitman into the Old World, "driving any new idea into the great passive vulva of London, a sensation analogous to the male feeling in copulation)."[73]

The female part, on the other and thoroughly predictable hand, is "the conservator, the inheritor of past gestures . . . not inventive, always the best disciple of any inventor";[74] she is "the accumulation of hereditary aptitudes"[75] – the "conservatrices des traditions milesiennes" in Gourmont's phrase.[76] The female is, in other words, a receptacle for cultural heritage and tradition, a container and transmitter of the retained past; she provides the "retentive media" for the creative male up-shoots, which create and re-create tradition. She is in herself, as in Canto XXIX, a "chaos" and needs phallic power to provide the order, form, and stability that turn shapeless "history" into shapely "tradition."

All of this would seem, perhaps, worthy of little comment were it not for the fact that this markedly phallocentric conception of sexuality and

creativity raises serious questions for the putatively phallic, manly nature of Pound's own corpus. Pound's notion of invention may now be
seen as not only the quintessentially liberating aesthetic act but also, in
light of his writings on Gourmont, as the quintessentially male one. For
Pound, the virtuous literary male would produce "the original thought,
as distinct from the imitative thought."[77] For Pound, to be avant-garde
is to be not the female inheritor of tradition but the male agent of
originality – the producer, not the reproducer, of works of difference as
unique as the particular phallic self invested in them. In these terms, the
supposed "virility" of the red-bloods was not manly – much less phallic
– at all. For the essence of a fully male literary self in Pound and
Gourmont's terms is precisely what was lacking in Carmen, Hovey, et
al.: not creativity, exactly, but *invention*, which is a politically, and now
phallically, loaded term in Pound's critical lexicon.

But what about Pound's own work? It is clear that the woman of
"Portrait d'une Femme" is the very antithesis of manly originality – but
then so is Bertran de Born and his creation. Bertran's image is not
original, it is "borrowed"; and what is more, it is but one in a long,
quite conventional line of the tradition's ideal ladies. But what of Pound's
own handling of the subject? Does *his* originality lie in his ability to bring
phallic order to what appear as only fragments to Bertran? Pound's
poem itself provides our answer: The mirrors of "fact" and "fiction" in
the whole affair cannot be soldered together by the modernist's presiding
intelligence into something whose originality might lie in detecting the
rift between the actual and the possible. In fact, the allure and power of
the poem, it seems to me, lie precisely in its failure to escape the textuality
of this little narrative, in its staging of the recognition that there is
nothing in the whole that is quite its own, except maybe that exhilarating,
and now emasculating, failure.

In one of his earliest poems, Pound conceived the poetic self in rather
uncanny anticipation of the final lines of "Near Perigord," and in doing
so he presented a figure of the poet who could not be farther from the
phallic originator praised in the writings on Gourmont. Mirrors figure
prominently here as well, but "On His Own Face in a Glass" concerns
itself not with the mirrors of poetic device but rather with what sort of
self the poet sees when he looks to the glass for its image:

> O strange face there in the glass!
>
> O ribald company, O saintly host!
> O sorrow swept, my fool,
> What answer?
>   O ye myriad

> That strive and play and pass,
> Jest, challenge, counterlie,
>
> I ? I ? I ?
>   And ye?[78]

Whatever sort of self is reflected in this factual glass – if it can be called a self at all – it is certainly not the self of *virtù*, of the inviolable party of one. This self, in fact, seems to be a guest at its own party, an object, even, of contention and prankery, as "ye myriad" ask, "Who is this guy, anyway?" and all the "self" can do is play the "fool" and say to a self already divided (*his* face, not "mine"), "What answer?" That coherent self, the "he" of "his face," who is supposedly anterior to the play of the "company," is only, the "I" now realizes, but a "sorrow swept fool." That coherent self which supposedly owns itself is, like the false possessions of the "Portrait," "strange" because *es*tranged – it belongs to others, to its "host."

Appropriately enough, then, the tone of this poem is hard to pin down because the self, of which tone is supposedly an extension, cannot be located in this triangular configuration of "he," "I," and "ye." The self, it seems, is always elsewhere – an anxious realization only underscored by the repetition of those "I"'s, dispersed amid the white space on the page, among which the self might choose. But of course he cannot choose, because there is no real self to do the choosing. Once that unified image in the mirror is unmasked as "strange," as a fool, the self is permanently decentered and under contention: Those possible selves "strive" and "challenge," the putative self is passive and empty, and "I" could be anyone except that fool, the "he," who stares back at the "I."

In these terms, Pound's repetition of "I" three times in this extremely small space is a particularly jarring way of reinforcing the dizzying sense of a self decentered and dispersed. The word "I," after all, depends upon the supposed stability of the user for its meaning. But here, it seems, the self is no such stable entity; it is not the origin of its discourse. In fact, that self is different every time it says the word "I." And if Pound's comments on his use of personae are any indication, this little poem is no fluke but rather a compressed expression of his essential early mode. "In the 'search for oneself,'" Pound wrote in the essay "Vorticism" (in what is, in light of his interest in Gourmont, a rather stunning characterization), "in the search for 'sincere self-expression,' one gropes, one finds some seeming verity. One says 'I am' this, that, or the other, and with the words scarcely uttered one ceases to be that thing."[79]

This conception of the self as an emptiness, as a lack, was in fact precisely the figure chosen by Pound himself to end his first book, *A Lume Spento*:

> For man is a skinfull of wine
> But his soul is a hole full of God
> And the song of all time blows thru him
> As winds thru a knot-holed board.[80]

Strictly speaking, this empty self is not, in a way, empty: It is "a hole full of God." To be full of God, however, is not to be masculine and original, it would appear, but quite the opposite. In fact, in the logic of patriarchy this emptiness is coded as none other than the stereotypical feminine position: desire not as an overflow or "up-surge" of presence but rather as an emptiness that is filled by it from without.

In a way, these lines locate a thoroughly American moment in Pound's early career, if only because their terms are precisely those employed by Emerson in the pivotal canonical conception of the self in American literature: the famous "transparent eyeball" passage in the essay *Nature*.[81] In his desire for a new self that might be as open and free as the new land, Emerson felt that we had to first become nothing, a perfect emptiness, because "society" meant the presence of the past, of history, of all that the old self had to purge from itself to become the new and distinctly American self. And those other selves – the Emersonian analogues to the "myriad company" that Pound saw behind the false self in the glass – these too must be gotten rid of if the self is to enjoy the "original relation" that would determine a new culture in Emerson's broad sense of the word: "I am not solitary," Emerson reminds us, "whilst I read and write, though nobody is with me."[82]

For Emerson, overcoming those other selves was one with the project of overcoming their property, the better to discover one's own self, one's own true property. In the passage that precedes that moment of transparent emptiness, Emerson writes: "Miller owns this field, Locke that. . . . [But there] is a property in the horizon which no man has but he whose eye can integrate all the parts, that is, the poet."[83] The poet, precisely because he has freed himself of society, of its titles and deeds, can possess the property of poetic vision, becoming, in Emerson's terms, the whole man, the full and "representative" self.

But Emersonian selfhood is finally a product not of one's will or power to possess but rather of one's capacity *to be possessed*.[84] Self-reliance is finally god-reliance. The moment enabling the poetic vision of the original self is a moment not of manly assertion and volition but rather of a passive surrender that is culturally coded as thoroughly feminine. To be a "whole man," the self must first assume the stereotypical feminine pose of the ravished lover: "Standing on the bare ground, – my head bathed by the blithe air and uplifted into infinite space."[85] That self, now cleansed of its possessions and its collateral social and cultural relations, now made a perfectly pure receptacle, is ready to be possessed, and so made new: "I am nothing; I see all; the currents of the Universal Being circulate through me; I am part or parcel of God."[86] The fundamental paradox of Emersonian selfhood is that only by being possessed can we come into authentic self-possession; only by becoming a prototypically feminine emptiness can the self become a new man and achieve true manly self-reliance; only by making oneself a pure repository for the up-shoot of the godhead can one be truly original and creative, and so possess the cultural terrain as only a poet can.

At age twenty-three, Pound wrote to Mary Moore that his relationship with his literary personae, like Emerson's relationship with Universal Being, was a kind of "first absolute surrender, the first utter overwhelming annihilation of self flowing in and existing thru and for another," a sensation of desire's fulfillment that was, he said, like love.[87] And in the poem "Histrion," published in *Quinzaine for This Yule* (1908), Pound further explored this intercourse with those literary others to whom the would-be original self is sacrificed:

> the souls of all men great
> At times pass through us,
> And we are melted into them, and are not
> Save reflexions of their souls.
> . . . .
> 'Tis as in midmost us there glows a sphere
> Translucent, molten gold, that is the "I"
> And into this some form projects itself:
> . . . .
> And as the clear space is not if a form's
> Imposed thereon,
> So we cease from all being for the time,
> And these, the Masters of the Soul, live on.[88]

For this poet, the "clear space" of the annihilated self was to be filled not by wonderfully impersonal Universal Being but rather by literary "masters," whose originality derived precisely from the fact that they were and remained *individual*: "Thus am I Dante for a space and am / One François Villon." Not just anybody, and not just nobody, but rather a very special somebody else: the quintessential original man, the self that Pound in so many places says he wants to be and is, but in these early texts admits he cannot be. In these terms, this early poem could well be called "Hysterion": in Greek, a coming short, a deficiency.

THE SELF THAT ONE IS NOT: POUND AND THE GENDER SYSTEM

Poems like "Near Perigord," "Histrion," and "On His Own Face in a Glass" would seem to enact a powerful and – given Pound's "phallocratic" reputation – unexpected *critique* of the centered, unified, and phallic subject of self-possession. Pound figures this critique in a whole range of images: in the dizzying dispersal of those "I"'s and the jesting "host" in "On His Own Face in a Glass," in the image borrowed from Dante in "Near Perigord" of the castrated Bertran in hell swinging his head like a lamp, and, perhaps most suggestively, in the admission that Bertran's "borrowed lady" turns out to be, for the poet, only "a broken bundle of mirrors."[89]

What we find in these moments in Pound, in other words, is an admission of an absence, a lack, but one that is curiously aligned with the poetic self, who is presumably male, given Pound's poetics of gender. What we find here, in other words, is the disclosure of a lack that is curiously (to use Kaja Silverman's phrase) a *"male* lack." To get at just what this male lack is, and how it helps us make sense of a rather uncanny set of images and displacements in the Pound poems that we have been discussing, will require a bit of a detour into psychoanalytic theory. But it will also require us, in the end, to leave psychoanalytic theory behind and return, if only by way of ending, to renewed attention to history and its crossing of gender in the Poundian project that we have been examining thus far.

As Silverman explains in her recent study *The Acoustic Mirror*, to activate the discourse of male lack is to accept Lacan's revision of Freud, which posits for the male subject a *pre-Oedipal* trauma of castration whereby the individual becomes a subject through a series of "splittings" and "removals" from the love object, the mother. Freud was at pains to maintain that the male child's fear of castration is learned only *after* he has seen the female's genitals, and thereby suddenly recognizes that he too might suffer the loss he sees in that female lack.[90] But as Silverman argues, following Lacan, this simply points up Freud's "refusal to identify castration with any of the divisions which occur prior to the registration of sexual difference." For Freud, Silverman continues,

> to admit that the loss of the object [the mother, the mother's breast, etc.] is also a castration would be to acknowledge that the male subject is already structured by absence prior to the moment at which he registers woman's anatomical difference – to concede that he, like the female subject, has already been deprived of being, and already been marked by the language and desires of the Other.[91]

What Silverman enables us to see, in other words, is that the Freud scenario masks the fact that the lack associated by Freud with the female is in fact a projection of that male lack generated by this pre-Oedipal castration and splitting away from the object that is the very condition of the subject's felt autonomy and identity – and, moreover, that this projection follows a precise trajectory "from the loss of the object, to the foreclosed site of production [of the subject through the symbolic order], to the representation of woman as lacking."[92]

As Silverman reminds us, however, this trajectory may often take a detour through fetishism as well. As Silverman puts it, in what reads like a gloss on the process of demystification (and remystification) at work in "Near Perigord,"

> Sometimes the male subject is even unable to tolerate the image of loss he has projected onto woman, and is obliged to cover it with a fetish [as happens, but is finally rejected, in the "borrowed lady" of "Perigord"]. However, whether he insists upon sexual difference through phobic avoidance or attempts to conceal that difference with a fetish, he fortifies himself less against the female subject's castration than against his own. The 'normal' male subject is constructed through the denial of his lack; he is at all points motivated by a 'not wishing to be.' In short, what he disavows is his own insufficiency, and the mechanism of that disavowal is projection.[93]

From this vantage, it is clear that Pound's "Perigord" stages the *failure* of Bertran's "borrowed lady" – a fetish composed of part-substitutes (a throat from one, hair from another, the voice of a third) – to cover over the trauma of castration and male lack, of having the love object (in this case, Lady Maent, an incarnation of the mother) removed from the poetic self.[94] In ending the poem with the admission that the lady is, not in herself but to Bertran (and, by extension, to the modern poet who writes "Near Perigord") "a shifting change, / A broken bundle of mirrors," Pound tells us that the real lady will not reflect, as fetish, the desire of the voyeuristic subject who seeks to displace his own lack by projecting it onto the feminine.[95]

In other words, the poem begins with what Silverman calls a fetishistic "imaginary sense of possession" (in this case, of Lady Maent by Bertran) but it ends by exposing that possession *as* imaginary. The fetishistic *donna ideale*, the "borrowed lady," is acknowledged for what she is, a reductive substitute for the male subject's desire: "She who could never live save through one person, / She who could never speak save to one person." And the real Lady Maent, the poem tells us, cannot be possessed but is now figured (if she can be figured at all) as a "shifting change," "Gone – ah, gone – untouched, unreachable!" Pound's poem thus stages a process of discovery: from the imaginary wholeness and self-possession of the poet to the acknowledgment of castration and male lack, which will be figured as well in poems like "Histrion" and the envoi to *A Lume Spento*;

from the construction of a fetish to cover or disavow that lack to the demystification of that fetish; and finally, to the acknowledgment of the "unreachable" autonomy and "shifting" freedom of the feminine subject itself from the voyeuristic gaze – all of which turns out to be a *remystification*, in the end, of female subjectivity (by basing it upon a male-coded autonomy) and indeed of subjectivity in general (since no subject is ever, strictly speaking, autonomous).

This is to agree with (but to complicate considerably, I think) Alan Durant's assertion in his Lacanian reading of Pound that "the ubiquitous inscription of the phallus in the *Cantos* and elsewhere in Pound's writing repeats precisely an anxiety about castration."[96] And we are forced to complicate matters even further when we remember that the manly red-blood poets are associated by Pound with a kind of lack as well – and this despite the fact that they flaunt, as Pound puts it, "the possession of the phallus." What *both* the red-bloods *and* the gynocracy lack, however, is the poetic control and authority for which a phallic relation to the order of language is, in Pound, a necessary but not sufficient condition. Indeed, the wholly unexpected feminine coding of the poetic subject in poems like "Histrion" or the envoi to *A Lume Spento* is enabled, I think, by a kind of overwhelming confidence on Pound's part in his own poetic authority. And what this projection of male lack *onto maleness itself* helps us to see is what Teresa de Lauretis has called (borrowing Fredric Jameson's term) a "political unconscious" of the rhetoric of gender as well. In other words, what is important here is not so much which side of the gender system the subject aligns itself with, but rather the acceptance of the structuring force of the gender system itself in all its rigidity. As de Lauretis characterizes it,

> With its emphasis on the sexual, "sexual difference" is in the first and last instance a difference of women from men, male from female . . . [and] ends up being in the last instance a difference (of woman) from man – or better, the very instance of difference *in* man. [This] keeps feminist thinking bound to the terms of Western patriarchy itself, contained within the frame of a conceptual opposition that is "always already" inscribed in what Fredric Jameson would call "the political unconscious" of dominant cultural discourses and their underlying "master narratives."[97]

This acceptance of the gender system, in other words, generally takes the form of an imaginary relationship of "separate but equal," and in doing so masks the real asymmetry, which allows Pound to critique *mere* maleness in the red-bloods, present his own poetic subject as a feminized one in a poem like "Histrion," and yet somehow retain a secure sense of his own relation to phallic poetic authority.[98]

In this sense, then, we must read poems like "On His Own Face in a Glass" and "Histrion" as at once critical *and* recuperative. They are critical insofar as they undermine the phallic transcendence of the poetic subject and return him to the world of textuality, the "shifting change" of historicity and the "ribald company" of the social "myriad." But they are recuperative in that they leave in place and indeed reinforce the *mechanism* of sexual difference, the gender code by which male lack may continue to be displaced onto the feminine. In this sense, then, the acceptance of the gender system – regardless of which pole one aligns oneself with – is itself the entire point. And in this respect, it is perfectly fitting that "Near Perigord" admits that the real Lady Maent is "Gone – ah, gone – untouched, unreachable!" but then qualifies that admission, as it were, by reminding us that she is unreachable *because* she is "shut up in his castle, Tairiran's." She escapes the possession and voyeuristic gaze of Bertran, which would turn her into a mirror of his own desire, but only to become the trapped subject of another male gaze of phallic possession – not of Bertran this time, but of Tairiran. In this sense, she is clearly a counter in what Eve Sedgwick has identified as the literary logic of "male homosocial desire," where male rivals bond homosocially in their shared contest for a female object of desire, and in doing so reproduce and sustain the mechanism of patriarchal power.[99]

It is important to realize, in other words, that what is at stake here is not the penis as object but rather *the phallus* as signifier, not the father but (to invoke the Lacanian distinction) "the *name* of the father," not the masculine pole of the gender system but rather *the gender system itself*, which maintains the masculine as the privileged term of the masculine/feminine dichotomy. From this perspective, Pound's accusation against the red-bloods – that they are not to be taken seriously, because they imagine that "we are separated from the lower animals by possession of the *phallus*" – is, strictly speaking, a misstatement, since that last word, we can now see, should read "*penis*." The red-bloods are endowed with everything masculine except what matters most: a privileged relation to the *phallic regime*, upon which poetic authority depends. In a poem like "Histrion," then, Pound is free to admit that he is a feminized blank space, not a centered phallic self, because he continues to affirm (on another level, as it were) the existence of the phallic poetic self, "of subjectivity as autonomous identity outside signification," as Durant puts it, a "capable and controlling source of its own meaning."[100] That is how the poetic self of "Histrion" *knows* that those "masters of the soul" are just that – "masters," and not some hallucination or fancy.

In this context, it is worth noting, as Durant does, Pound's reliance upon the blind poet/prophet figures of Homer and Tiresias in the *Cantos*,[101] both of whom may now be seen as precisely the reverse of the red-bloods, in that they are marked as figures of sexual impotence who nevertheless possess poetic authority and visionary potency. In both, the loss of the organs of sight (which, in light of Freud's essay on "The Uncanny," we must read as a symbolic loss of the male genitals) is assimilated and surpassed by the affirmation of a different order of vision – in this case, of poetic and oracular power. It is particularly significant in this regard, as Durant points out, that the various mythical accounts of Tiresias's blindness usually present it as a result of his discovery of sexual diference, the most notable version of which is Tiresias's forbidden vision of the goddess Minerva at her bath. This episode finds a strong analogue in Canto IV's telling of Actaeon's viewing of the goddess Diana bathing, which results in the voyeur being turned into a stag and then killed by his own hunting dogs.

As Durant argues, Tiresias's blindness constitutes a punishment not so much of his voyeurism and scopophilia, but rather of the inability of the gazing self to *control* and master the sexual difference that is viewed.[102] And after the foregoing discussion of male lack, we may, of course, interpret this blinding moment as a result of the castration anxiety brought on by the return of the repressed male lack projected onto the forbidden object of the male gaze. What the mythic figure of Tiresias suggests, in other words, is that the discovery of male lack must be resublimated – in what Durant calls "a restitution beyond castration"[103] – in the higher phallic authority of poetic vision. It is because Homer is "blind as a bat," as Pound puts it early in the *Cantos*, that he has such a finely tuned "ear, ear for the sea surge," in which the sound of poetic power may be heard. It is as if, in other words, the phallic eye, which, as in Emerson, sees all, is lost only to be replaced on a higher level by the phallic ear, which hears all.

Pound's description of Homer's poetry, in "I gather the Limbs of Osiris," as "a work of imagination and not of observation" is therefore not surprising.[104] In these terms, the Pound who seems to surrender phallic authority in poems like "Histrion" and the envoi to *A Lume Spento* may be seen as a kind of Tiresias figure himself. The return of the Freudian repressed – in the form of that castration anxiety which feminizes the poetic self and turns him into "a hole full of God" – masks a more primary Lacanian repression, you might say, in which what gets repressed is the whole rigid gender system, the system that allows the poet to disavow his own lack and thereby maintain a privileged relation to the phallus and the poetic authority it confers.[105]

In *The Acoustic Mirror*, Silverman argues that the projection of male lack onto woman always functions to "cover over" the "foreclosed site of production" of the subject by the symbolic apparatus.[106] But we need to conclude our discussion here by noting that this is clearly not entirely true in Pound's case, where the politics of gender and the rhetoric of feminization cannot be disentangled from the broader economic and class critique at work in Pound's cultural project. The early prose and poetry we have been discussing target class-specific constructions of gender and focus our attention upon how the production of the subject by the symbolic order is always ineluctably tied to class privilege and power. And even when Pound wants to affirm forms of accomplished individualism that (like the self of *virtù* and the "donative" author) transcend all class determinations (or so he hopes), the political unconscious of his discourse tells us that those forms of selfhood are riven by the historically specific logic and contradictions of private property under capitalism. In this regard, it is particularly suggestive that in "Near Perigord" what leads to the acknowledgment of the *failure* of phallic projection is Pound's attempt to do justice to the historical specificity of the lady and the episode he recounts, to not let "fiction" overtake "fact." Conversely, when Pound strays from historical specificity, as in the writings on Gourmont, his concept of gender becomes increasingly reified and essentialized.[107]

It is no small matter, I think, that Pound's response to the feminization of culture draws our attention to how the production of the subject is always class specific, always about property, about the means of economic and cultural production and who has power over them. As Joan Scott points out in her study *Gender and the Politics of History*, the language of psychoanalysis tends to "universalize the categories and relationship of male and female," despite protestations to the contrary. "Even though this theory takes social relationships into account by linking castration to prohibition and law," she continues, "it does not permit the introduction of a notion of historical specificity and variability. The phallus is the only signifier; the process of constructing the gendered subject is, in the end, predictable because always the same."[108] At the same time, however, class concepts have for centuries been articulated in terms of gender: "Concepts such as class are created through differentiation. Historically, gender has provided a way of articulating and naturalizing difference."[109] "There is no choice," she concludes, "between a focus on class or on gender; each is necessarily incomplete without the other."[110] The category of gender, in other words, threatens to become essentialist and transhistorical when not interwoven with the historical and economic specificities of class. And the category of class, on the other hand, threatens to dissolve too quickly the broad category of the social, in all its complexity, into that of the more strictly economic – all the while ignoring the complex relations between the economically specific social configuration and the more "enduring psychic structure" named by the term "gender."[111]

Pound himself would have done well, we can wager, to heed that sort of advice, for in seeking the leverage for his social and cultural critique by positioning the poet outside any historically specific class location, he naturalizes and essentializes the very gender distinctions that his class-specific critique handles in a strategically effective, because limited, way. Finally, we are forced to say that although Pound may not have intended his Aunt Hepsy to serve as a figure for everywoman, the poet and critic who criticizes her *is*, by Pound's logic, a man for all seasons.

In uncanny echo of Pound's self-critique in "On His Own Face in a Glass," Wyndham Lewis once wrote that "Ezra is a crowd, a little crowd," a man "without a trace of originality of any sort."[112] Lewis, with their *Blast* project decades away in a war-torn past, could now see his onetime collaborator for what he really was all along: a "parasite."[113] But, Lewis was quick to add, a parasite of a particular (and, in our terms, peculiarly Emersonian) sort, a perfectly "clean" and "sweet" emptiness, "disinterested and unspoilt."[114] Were Pound not such a perfect nonself, Lewis tells us, "I am convinced he would be unable to enter into the renowned and noble creatures whom he has passed his time in entering, so cleanly as he does."[115]

But it is finally Pound, not Lewis, whose work provides the fullest anatomy of an American poetic self familiar to us since Emerson's description of the transparent eyeball, "I am nothing; I see all" – that poetic self strangely castrated and endowed with phallic power all at once; that self who could achieve selfhood most fully only at the moment of his vanishing, who could be a self only by becoming a nothingness, who, in becoming a "hole full of God," could surrender one sort of phallic authority only to gain another, more potent kind.

Such a self-conception had been written between the lines of Pound's ideological inheritance – and of Pound's work – from the very beginning. The poet of *Homage to Sextus Propertius*, like the poet of *A Lume Spento*, told us as much, when he answered the taunts of those whom Emerson called the "so-called practical men": "Yet you ask on what account I write so many love lyrics / And whence this soft book comes into my mouth. . . . / My genius is no more than a girl."[116] And Pound would tell us again in the very first of the *Cantos*, this time in the voice of Elpenor, that victim of his own sensual desire who asks to be remembered as "*A man of no fortune and a name to come*."[117] But when that name finally came, as it did at the nadir of *The Pisan Cantos*, it told of what Pound, and Emerson before him, had been telling us all along: "noman, my name is noman."[118]

PART II

5

Visionary Capital:
Contradictions of Pound's Lyric Ideal

Looking over the Centennial Edition of Francis Palgrave's *Golden Treasury*, one is forced to say that the lyric ideal Palgrave helped make a literary fixture never dies, it just begets more anthologies. In his 1861 preface, Palgrave had promised that his collection would provide "treasures 'more golden than gold'"[1] – hence his title, but hence, too, its radical duplicity. This best-selling literary powerhouse, as it turns out, managed to have the best of both worlds: the "gold" one of monetary and financial reward and the "golden" one of lyric transcendence. A hundred years later, in his preface to the expanded, mass-circulation Centennial Edition, Oscar Williams noted in homage that the original *Treasury* had been a bit tarnished (through no fault of its own) by its "incompleteness made apparent by the passage of time" and by "changes of custom and attitude [which] have been as decided as changes brought about by invention and the upheavals of history."[2] The *Treasury*, it seems, needed replenishing, and Williams obliged with an additional three hundred pages of material from Donne to Dylan Thomas. But updating Palgrave also meant adhering to his original aesthetic principles, and it therefore meant *un*dating the new material by the later Victorians and moderns so that they too might assume their place in the golden world of lyric transcendence. And (how quickly they forget) it also meant no space for genteel figures like Van Dyke, Gilder, and Stedman – a bitter historical irony because Williams's declared standards, in solidarity with Palgrave, share more than a little with these American precursors now wiped from the face of literary history by the generation of Pound, Eliot, Frost, and Stevens.

In a gingerly worded two pages, Williams seems to realize, just beneath the surface of praise, the difficulty of his task: how to "update" that which by definition knows no time and how to "expand" that which knows no earthly boundaries? On the other hand, though, and by that same logic, what could be easier? For Williams, the only "serious flaw"

of Palgrave's original is its age, not its concept of lyric, and he is quick
to add that Palgrave's "main intention" has been "carefully kept in view."
"His own definition of the lyrical as unity of feeling or thought, as
stated in his own preface," Williams writes, "has been a determinant of
choice. And within each period the poems are grouped 'in gradations of
feeling or subject.'"[3]

Still, Williams realizes (it is 1961) that some of the selections (Eliot,
Auden, and Moore, for instance) would have proved "massively shocking to a Victorian sensibility," consisting as they do of "new techniques
... and depth of understanding in areas once considered outside the
scope of poetry":[4] areas, presumably, like Auden's indictment of imperial
injustice and everyday life in "September 1, 1939," and the forgotten
Alfred Hayes's riveting anatomy of institutionalized animal cruelty in
"The Slaughter-House."

But Palgrave is looking over Williams's shoulder, and the belated editor must demonstrate his homage by recontaining the heterogeneity
that, in truth, bears little resemblance to his neo-Palgravian dicta. Let us
speak then, Williams decides, of form, of the unity of impression and
sensation that both determines form and transcends the diverse materials
organized by it:

> All of the selections are true and complete lyrical poems, and short. No
> added poem is longer than the longest selected by Palgrave for the
> original edition. I have deviated slightly from the rule of the first edi-
> tion that all poems have rhyme and meter by including selections
> of both blank and free verse, when they were, to the modern taste,
> lyrical.[5]

So Williams not only defends but in fact expands the scope and range of
Palgrave's lyric ideal, which is now installed even more firmly in its
golden world by virtue of its ability to assimilate previously forbidden
"areas" and "techniques" to its "true and complete" self, to the Platonic
One of "unity, or truth," which Palgrave himself felt was the master of
creeping modernity's heterogeneous, material Many.

The Neoplatonism of the *Treasury*'s lyric criteria (in either edition) is
embodied, among the modern selections, nowhere better – and nowhere
more unexpectedly – than in Ezra Pound's "Envoi" to *Hugh Selwyn
Mauberley*, which Williams, grouping the poems in Palgravian fashion
by "feeling or subject," situates right in the middle of a set of poems
devoted more or less to "The Nature of Poetry." In its rather archaic
diction ("Hadst thou but song") and its rifling of the tradition's storehouse of rhyming pyrotechnics ("upon me lie / longevity"), Pound's
poem seems much closer to Palgrave than it does to nearby modernist
companions like Dylan Thomas's "In My Craft or Sullen Art" and

Marianne Moore's "Poetry." In fact, the poem in the new and improved
Treasury that most resembles Pound's own is the resolutely premodern
work upon which it was loosely modeled: Edmund Waller's "Go, lovely
Rose!" – a selection placed by Palgrave early in his original and included
by Pound in his own *Confucius to Cummings* anthology years later.[6]
Wrenched from the battle of textures and sensibilities making up
Mauberley[7] (this is not the surgical satirist of section II, nor the hell-
bound poet of modern war who calls up "laughter out of dead bellies"),
Pound's "Envoi" seems not a distinctly modernist interrogation of
Waller's lyric idealism, but quite the reverse. In fact, Pound's poem
appears, surprisingly enough, to do for Waller what Williams did for
Palgrave.

Waller's original, in apostrophe to his rose, gives voice to the carpe
diem urgency most famously captured in Marvell's "To His Coy Mis-
tress." In Waller's version:

> Small is the worth
> of beauty from the light retired;
>   Bid her come forth,
> Suffer herself to be desired,
> And not blush so to be admired.
>
>   Then die! That she
> The common fate of all things rare
>   May read in thee
> How small a part of time they share
> That are so wondrous sweet and fair![8]

Pound's "Envoi," however, rewrites Waller by singing not beauty's
earthy mutability but rather its transcendence: "Till change hath broken
down / All things save beauty alone." And Pound's poem, in apostrophe now not to the fleeting rose but to the rather more substantial book,
figures its muse in terms largely free of the devilish sexual undertow of
Waller's playful second line ("Tell her, that wastes her time and me").
In short, Pound's muse is unabashedly, and quite surprisingly, Palgravian;
her graces are "glories" and "treasure," and the poet

> [W]ould bid them live
> As roses might, in magic amber laid,
> Red overwrought with orange and all made
> One substance and one colour
> Braving time.[9]

This is not Waller's lusty rose of the here and now but the essence of all
roses, preserved against the world of history and mutability by the poet's
alchemy and "magic": a fitting abode indeed for her Palgravian treasures
more golden than gold.

Divorced from its original context and framed by the anthology's Palgravian injunctions, Pound's "Envoi" presents a picture of his poetic sensibility that is misleading (because truncated) but not exactly wrong. It is true that the extent to which the proclivities of the persona of Mauberley can be equated with Pound's own is a proverbial issue of Pound criticism. And true, Pound had argued for his own part that "Mauberley buries E. P. in the first poem."[10] That may be, but the "Envoi" is dated 1919, and by then Pound had behind him a corpus that was not only un- but quite anti-Palgravian: the Ur-Cantos (sent to *Poetry* in 1917), the satire and social critique of *Lustra*, and the first half of *Mauberley* itself. In short, even this little bit of context makes it clear that the "Envoi" points up a persistent dimension of Pound's poetic sensibility that he never outgrew but rather nurtured alongside its more famous modernist opposite.

Palgrave's "more golden than gold" would be an apt description of that lyric idealism we find in Pound's work, both early and late: the gold of poetic vision and divine light we so often find in the early poems, the *Cantos*, and (although more indirectly expressed by the "treasure" of a lady's beauty, which inspires the poet's preservative efforts) in the "Envoi." Pound made no attempt to hide the heavily Platonic cast of his early lyric idealism, and in a way he even flaunted it, quoting Coleridge in an early poem on that beauty which is "a calling to the soul,"[11] and which in turn calls forth poems that would preserve it in "finest parchment and the dearest gold" against "the changing tides" of history.[12]

Still, this attraction to the "gold" of poetic permanence cannot but be startling for practiced readers of Pound, given the well-known animus in his work after 1918 toward usury, international finance, and the fetish of the gold standard.[13] Moreover, Pound's early poems quite conventionally and quite often indulge the habit of setting the golden world of lyric against the earthly sphere of money and Mammon, and in doing so they complicate considerably Pound's relation to the Palgravian ideals he openly attacked in his early cultural project. *A Lume Spento*, for example, delivers the familiar plaint of the artist at whom the world sneers "'Cause he hath / No coin, no will to snatch the aftermath / of Mammon"[14] – an opposition, reiterated in Keatsian echo in the San Trovaso Notebook (1908), between "The truths that speak / with Beauty for a tongue" and "Mammon / his arch enemy."[15]

"Gold glories," the "gold" of "Truth," the "dearest gold" of love, "gold" of "perfection," the "gold-white" light of the Soul[16] – for Pound these, unlike *Mauberley's* "two gross of broken statues" or the poems demanded by *Harper's*, *Century*, and "the style of 1880," are not commodities to be exchanged, consumed, or used. Instead, they are the signs of an unsurpassable value that the fallen world of commerce cannot measure, the ultimate standard in an aesthetic economy defined, Pound suggests, not by exchange or production but by possession – possession, specifically, of those properties of lyric idealism that are as nonnegotiable as the lady's "treasure" in the "Envoi."

This is the sense, I think, of Pound's early and playful praise of Browning in the poem "Mesmerism": "You grabbed at the gold sure; had no need to pack cents / Into your versicles."[17] In establishing this opposition – between the rare (singular) gold that exists a priori as a universal value and the common (plural) "cents" so readily available that they can be packed into the poem like so much stuffing – Pound attempts to drive a wedge between visionary and material economy. He associates the latter with the readily available currency of poetic convention and homily, even as he declares that the former transcends all such determinations (that is why possession of it removes the compulsion to worry about "cents"). When the young apprentice accuses Browning of "Tyin' your meanin' in seventy swadelin's," he is really asking him to cast off what the poem calls the "apparel" of polysemous rhetoric, of all-too-common "cents," the better to reveal the singular "gold" at the heart of his many matters: not "gold" but "*the* gold"; not the currency of common knowledge and social convention but the poetic truth of which that currency is the debased form.

As we shall see, however, Pound's attempt to make a juridical distinction between these two realms only reinforces the specular relationship between them. Pound's gold of lyric ideals stands in the same relation to the "cents" of linguistic exchange and socially determined meaning as the gold standard of nineteenth- and early twentieth-century capitalism does to the "cents" of monetary currency. In both cases, "the value of gold," as Jean-Joseph Goux argues, "absolutely guaranteed, becomes a metaphor for the transcendental guarantee of meaning."[18] Whether we are concerned with ensuring the economic value of "cents" or the poetic value of "sense," "the multiplicity and mutability of *coins*," as Goux puts it, are "contrasted with the *gold sovereign* of the immutable One,"[19] which stands outside the realm of contingency and difference as the locus of stable and abiding value.

Even though capitalist economy in the early twentieth century was moving away from the gold standard, the practice was still alive until 1933 in the United States and 1915 in Britain, and the determination of the money supply by the supply of gold, as Tim Redman reminds us, "remained a belief in the popular mind until well after the Second World War."[20] Debates about the source and grounding of monetary and economic value, in other words, were very much in the air, had been heated and ongoing in both countries since the middle of the previous century, and reached a peak in the 1890s in the United States and in the months following the end of World War I in England.[21] In this debate, Pound stood squarely against the use of gold to back the value of currency, because precious metal could be hoarded and monopolized, thus increasing its price and creating a false increase in wealth and economic value for the few and powerful where no real economic value had in fact been created.[22] The gold standard, which was waning as the century opened, may seem, in other words, to have provided a way for capitalism to ground economic value, but Pound's whole point was that it was a *false* ground that in fact perpetuated the proliferation of ungrounded, "abstract" wealth.

It is important to note, then, that Pound's animosity toward the gold standard is motivated *not* by his belief that economic value is groundless (as we shall see in our next chapter, for Pound it is ultimately grounded in nature) but rather by his conviction that the gold standard is the wrong way to insure, circulate, and signify that value. What is of signal interest here, however, is that the gold-standard economy of value that Pound would reject in the realm of economics after 1918 survives intact in the signifying economy of his poetry, where gold continues to symbolize the source of poetic value and underwrite visionary creation. Another way to put it is to say that if both economic and poetic value for Pound are grounded in nature, the figure of gold can continue to signify that fact in the poetic realm because, as Goux's critique will help us see, only there can its ideal symbolic function be perfected.

Before we investigate that problem in more detail, however, we should note that Pound's reliance upon the gold of poetic transcendence was more than just an early, Neoplatonic attraction that he would later look back on with the colder eye of a jaded modernist. That same figure of gold, curiously enough, marks many of the central moments of vision in the *Cantos* as well. At the end of the very first canto, for example, we find the radiant Aphrodite, fitted "with golden / Girdles and breast bands" and holding "the golden bough of Argicida."[23] So at the very outset of the *Cantos*, we are faced with a fundamental problem: how to reconcile this gold and this goddess of reproductive nature with Pound's linkage, throughout the *Cantos* and the prose of the same period, of the usurious economy ruled by gold with unnatural increase and perverse propagation – all of them, as Canto XLV tells us, *Contra naturam*? What sort of gold is this, and what sort of goddess?

To address the last question first, we need to realize that this canto, as Michael André Bernstein has pointed out, sets two conjugations of female sexuality in motion.[24] The first type is bestial lust, also represented by Circe and her "ingle" and recounted in Canto XXXIX, which is the agency of the negative metamorphosis to which Elpenor has already fallen victim as the *Cantos* open.[25] The second type Aphrodite represents in Canto I is not bestial but sacred, not destructive but constructive. Her passion is contained and ordered, as it were, by the crafted golden bands, which distinguish her as a symbol of productive love and procreation.[26] What is of signal interest here, though, is that it is the gold itself and *only* the gold that marks the difference between this "good" Aphrodite and the one who, appearing without her *ceston*, is a sign of illicit and destructive passion.[27] Take away her golden bands and girdles, and all chaos, like her uncontained body, will break loose. Here, only gold itself stands between these two fundamentally opposed types of sexuality. Gold makes, literally, a world of difference.

Aphrodite's *ceston* is not the only gold in evidence at the end of Canto I. Our goddess also bears "the golden bough of Argicida," of Hermes, the slayer of Argos. The figure of Hermes, however, does not check the double movement of Aphrodite and her gold but rather sustains it: He is not only Zeus's messenger but also the patron of thieves and merchants, the god of luck and wealth. And in fact he will appear in exactly this role in Canto XII, where Pound refers to the enterprising "Baldy" Bacon under the playful epithet "miraculous Hermes" – Bacon, who arrives at a brothel by accident two minutes after being sent for (luck), who "saved his people 11,000 in four months" (merchants), and who "wanted to eat up the whole'r Wall St." (wealth).[28] Yet only a few pages later, in Canto XVII, Hermes appears in precisely the opposite role, restored, as it were, by the gold surrounding him in the famous Nerea passage, in the *paradiso terrestre* which follows the usurious hell of Cantos XIV and XV and the purgatorial landscape of Canto XVI.[29]

As we move more deeply into the *Cantos*, we can only be startled, given Pound's growing economic obsessions, by just how constant the nature and function of his visionary gold will remain. Cantos LXXIX and CVI, for example, remember the "cup of white gold" modeled upon the breast of Helen (or so legend has it) and associated with paradise and the fruitful earth.[30] But once again, the mythic figure who is accompanied by Pound's gold is an ambivalent and powerfully charged one, pregnant with all the contradictions latent in Aphrodite and Hermes. She is both the Helen of paradise, of "*Tellus feconda*," and the Helen who appears in Canto II as an incarnation of the world-destroying passion of Aphrodite without her *ceston*: "Sleek head, daughter of Lir, / eyes of Picasso," and not paradise but "doom goes with her in walking."[31] Helen too, it seems, is an overly fertile sign, and the figure of gold serves to ensure that she be understood in terms of a paradisal economy, not a lustful and avaricious one. Helen, like Aphrodite, *needs* gold to redeem her, even as she herself is its visionary agent.

These figures introduced in the first two cantos may symbolize the sacred world, but they do so only when marked by gold, which determines and circumscribes their beneficent meaning. This is less puzzling than it might otherwise seem when we remember, as Goux reminds us in his important collection *Symbolic Economies: After Marx and Freud,* that gold, as a transcendental signifier of value, organizes an essentially phallic regime. In other words, gold stands, in its function as the locus of value and the guarantor of general equivalence, in the same relation to the realm of exchangeable goods as the phallus does in relation to the objects of libidinal drive or as the father does in relation to the order of subject-positions.[32] In all three cases, Goux writes, "one element from the group is promoted to the role of exclusive and common mirror of values, arbiter of evaluations – the universal equivalent. This role is played by gold in the world of commodities; by the father in the world of others; and by the sexual organ, becoming a phallus, in the world of part objects."[33] From this vantage, we can see that the order which gold brings to Aphrodite and Helen in the *Cantos* is an essentially phallic one which submits their unruly passion and dangerous fecundity to the same strategy of containment and appropriation that we earlier saw at work in "Near Perigord" in the final imprisonment of the "unreachable" Maent and her "shifting change" in the castle of Tairiran.[34] Aphrodite and Helen thus stand in the same relation to phallic poetic order (which here appears under the sign of gold and the *ceston*) as Browning's "cents" do to the gold of lyric ideal: They are lost, unruly, and maybe dangerous without it.

But even as Pound's visionary gold limits the figural excess of these gods and goddesses, its power to so ensure the proper interpretation of them derives, of course, not from some transcendent realm but rather from the history of signifying practices (the convention of the *ceston*, for instance, which makes it a saving icon for our Aphrodite). Paradoxically, then, the timeless gold of lyric aesthesis or transcendent value must be borrowed, as it were, from history for the purposes of signifying a realm which supposedly transcends that history. And so Pound's poetic, in its attempt to reveal the truth of the permanent and transcendent value, instead reveals the very truth of historical indebtedness that all idealisms repress.

FROM THE COLOR, THE SIGN: THE POETICS OF AUTHORITY

If any figure in the *Cantos* seems to hold out some promise of bridging the abyss between the golden world and the world of gold, it is Sigismundo Malatesta, the "entire man," as Pound characterized him, who moves freely between quotidian and visionary economies. Malatesta and his Tempio seem to suggest that there might be some sort of promising dialectical relationship between a wholly unredeemable economic world and a wholly redeeming paradise.[35] Nowhere is this promise more tantalizing than in Canto XVII, in Nerea's world, where the Tempio echoes Canto XI's stunned and tragic registration of its beauty: "In the gloom the gold / Gathers the light about it."[36] This promise seems even closer to fulfillment if we accept the reading of Malatesta and the Tempio proffered by Pound and most of his critics: as an example of the "directio voluntatis"[37] that would build a *paradiso terrestre*, which might somehow transform the gold of the money changers into the gold of Nerea and in so doing redeem, through heroic action, the fallen world of economy.

After all, "Sidg," as Pound affectionately calls him, had more than his share of experience with thieves and moneygrubbers, and most readers seem to agree that the Malatesta Cantos get their torque from the tension between the romp of political, economic, and domestic intrigue of the times and the steady urgency of Malatesta's constructive efforts, which drive always toward the building of the Tempio. Peter Makin's characterization is typical: The central dynamic of these cantos, he writes, is to "present a chaos of diversions, obstructions versus *Voluntas*, will, in a perpetual struggle."[38] By design or not, Makin's interpretation is true to Pound's own: "All that a single man could," he writes in *Guide to Kulchur*, "Malatesta managed *against* the current of power."[39]

Finally, however, the forces of politics and economics with which Sigismundo must contend are not of supreme importance *for Pound* in the Malatesta Cantos – though they may be of value to the reader, and though we may well want to agree with Michael Harper's contention that the value of the sequence and its poetic lies in its antiformalism, its "denial of the conventional separation between 'poetry' and 'history.'"[40] Instead, it is Malatesta's ability to overcome and transcend those forces that serves for Pound as the centerpiece for these poems. The Tempio represents, as Peter Nicholls puts it, a "redeemed materiality"[41] because it testifies to the way in which a visionary conception may be wrested from the chaos of economics and politics and established by will *against* the currents of history and the currency of economics. If we admire the difficulty of Malatesta's progress (as Pound obviously intends us to), it is, in the end, the better to admire the Tempio. By this logic, the strategic placement of the Tempio's gold in the Nerea passage is perfectly appropriate: It suggests not the dialectical synthesis of the two worlds but rather the Tempio's capacity to transcend the realm of quotidian economy and history.

It is quite fitting, then – if a little curious – that the Malatesta Cantos provide no description of the Tempio itself. We see pieces of it – the silver, the stone, the "aliophants" – in transport and negotiation, but nothing of the final form itself, nothing to suggest its visionary power. In fact, we cannot even say, based on the information provided in these cantos, that there *is* in the Tempio any real gold that "gathers the light about it." And if we attempt to interpret Pound's famous line in any literal sense, we are forced to concoct all sorts of ingenious explanations. (Hugh Kenner, for instance, suggests that the polished limestone of the Tempio's bas-reliefs makes the light gold, but in Pound's line it is *the gold* itself that does something to the light.)[42]

In this famous line, therefore – as perhaps nowhere else in the *Cantos* – the figure of gold reveals, we might say, its true color. What this line signifies is not really the Tempio (which has no gold in it, as far as we know) but rather what the Tempio *itself* signifies: the gold standard, as it were, of visionary splendor, to which the Tempio must ultimately be referred for its lasting value.[43] After all, had there been no Tempio, it is safe to say, there would be no Malatesta Cantos, and Malatesta himself would be a maverick curiosity, not a model of aesthetic ideals put into constructive action.

To put it this way is to realize that the gold in question is also, in a sense, Malatesta's vision, or the *virtù* that separates him from his rivals and his age. Like Pound's "donative" artist, Malatesta is a "factive personality," an "entire man"[44] who is able give to culture the permanent property of the Tempio because he is able, in some sense, to transcend his age by bringing to the chaotic materials of his historical struggle the phallic order and form that should, ideally, organize them into a shapely and meaningful whole. And just as Malatesta seems the very antithesis of the self indebted to history, his Tempio appears to be the very antithesis of all commodities – even though it is in another way, like gold, the *ultimate* of all commodities, just because it is "permanent." Like the aesthetic economy of *virtù* and despite Pound's intentions, Malatesta and his Tempio constitute not so much a rejection of capitalist economy as its radical extension and imaginary double. From this vantage, the sort of transaction recorded in the frontispiece to *Guide to Kulchur* should be by now a familiar one: "There is no other single man's effort equally registered," Pound writes, and "if you consider the Malatesta and Sigismundo in particular, a failure, he was at all events a failure worth all the successes of his age."[45] What else is this but the trading of gold for "cents" that we saw in the early poem on Browning? In his willingness to trade the singular gold of Malatesta's vision for all the token successes of his age, Pound is saying, in effect, not that the latter is not property, but that it is not property *enough*.

An extraordinary passage written by Pound in 1919 ought to make that much clear. Just after reading Major C. H. Douglas's *Economic Democracy* – whose theory of Social Credit economics would shortly find an enthusiastic convert in the young poet, with enormous consequences for the rest of his career[46] – Pound speculated in a review:

It is not necessary, either in the young or in the mature artist, that all the geometry of a painting be tossed up into the consciousness and analysed by the painter before he puts brush to canvas. *The genius can pay in nugget and in lump gold; it is not necessary that he bring up his knowledge into the mint of consciousness, stamp it into either the coin of conscientiously analysed form-detail knowledge or into the paper money of words, before he transmit it.* A bit of luck for a young man, and the sudden coagulation of bits of knowledge collected here and there during years, need not for the elder artist be re-sorted and arranged into coin.[47]

We remember that "Provincialism the Enemy," written only two years earlier, had railed against the "hammering" of the student into "a piece of mechanism," and we recall as well Pound's admonition, early in "The Serious Artist," that people "do not resemble each other as do buttons cut by machine."[48] Pound's figure of minting in the passage above suggests, along the same lines, a fundamental opposition between the unique and autonomous "lumps" and "nuggets" of the artist and his artifact and the mass-produced tokens of abstract knowledge that are the cultural expressions of a repressive economic and political mechanism. The value of authentic artistic payment, on the other hand, is that it need not take the debased form of that fallen economy; it does not need those chits or vehicles that mediate value, because it already is value; it is not subject to the system of *conceptual* exchange, which would make a treatise on "form-detail knowledge" equivalent to the particular painting or poem, but rather it determines the value of those exchanges *itself.*

Still, Pound's figure tells us, the lump gold or nugget of the artist *is* "payable." But it is not at all clear what the artist pays for – for what, after all, can the individual artwork or artistic vision be exchanged? Appropriately enough, then, the passage does not answer this question but rather rewrites it. "Payment" rapidly becomes "transmission," a very different kind of transaction indeed, and one perfectly fitting for a thing that does not *receive* its value from without but instead confers the value for which no substitute exists. If this gold pays, it is a strange kind of payment indeed. In fact, it would make more sense to call this transaction not a payment, and not even a transmission, but a *gift* – precisely the kind of gift of "permanent property" (as Pound characterized it in "The Serious Artist" of 1913) left to society by the donative artist.[49]

In the *Cantos,* Pound will find this more abiding economy of value increasingly in the paradigms and authority of nature. Often, it will be focused through the lens of myth, as in his retelling in Canto IV of the story of Actaeon and his forbidden vision of the goddess Diana bathing in the sunlight, which glitters all gold. Herself a living Tempio, she seems to gather it to her, "not a lost shatter of sunlight" about "the pale hair of the goddess," the light now made even more radiant by that to which it accrues: "Gold, gold, a sheaf of hair / thick like a wheat swath."[50] But very late in the *Cantos* Pound will present the same kind of image – "the gold light of wheat surging upward"[51] – in a moment of immediacy more natural than mythic, just as he had employed similar images in his early work without the mythological trappings. In the early poem "L'Invitation," corn battered by the hail is figured as "ruined gold," and in "The Alchemist" of 1912, the "gold of the maple" and of the sun is implored to transfuse the metal with its power and precious substance.[52] It is not only the presence of the mythical, then, that is marked by the "flaked rain of the sunlight"[53] or by the "golden rain" appearing at the end of Canto IV.[54] These, and the paradisal "points of gold" and "gold-yellow saffron" of Eros in Canto V,[55] find not their origin, but rather their extension and expression, in the world of nature and myth.

Wheat, sunlight, corn, saffron – Pound borrows his gold from the things of nature to suggest a common substance, a visionary essence glimpsed in natural forms that are merely fleeting without it. His use of natural analogues to suggest the immediacy of transcendent radiance serves most of all, however, to ensure that this naturalized gold will not be mistaken for the debased gold of Pound's own economic context. For Pound, in other words, nature serves primarily to *demonetize* gold – who, after all, can possess, exchange, or monopolize sunlight? The presence of nature tells us that this is *not* the gold of the goldsmiths "not ruled by Sophia" (wisdom) in Canto XCVII; nor is it the gold of the "gold lice" that gnaw at the Crusaders' bows ("Normandy pawned"), the "coin'd gold" that "bumped off 8000 Byzantines" late in the *Cantos* in the "Notes for CIX."[56] And it is emphatically not the gold of the Wellington anecdote in Cantos L and LXXIX, which can be possessed and cornered by a handful of financiers to create mass economic chaos at the drop of a ministerial hat (in this case, Earl Grey's).[57]

But if nature serves to thus reclaim gold for a realm fundamentally without a history, that realm, for all its nature, is not really a material world. Pound's natural vehicles are of value not because of their materiality but because of the immaterial truth they express. If Pound uses natural analogues to demonetize gold, in other words, it is only the better to finally *dematerialize* it. But that dematerialization, in turn, only confirms, in a rather uncanny way, how Pound's gold standard of lyric idealism reproduces the monetary economy from which it would divorce itself. As Jean-Joseph Goux persuasively argues, following Marx, the development and perfection of the symbolic function of signifiers of universal value (of gold in relation to commodities, or the Ideal in relation to philosophical or poetic discourse) require "a constant value to be postulated in spite of difference and an ideality to be maintained throughout changes in materiality."[58] As Goux puts it, in a passage worth quoting at length:

> Just as the particular differences residing in the commodity are effaced by monetary circulation and economic value, so the concept retains only what is common to diverse representations, effacing the differences among singular images. The concept too, like the essence of the thing, becomes a metaphysical, detached quality.[59]

Thus, Pound's dematerialization of gold, which is bent toward rupture with his own economic context, may be seen to symbolically enact the full realization and perfection of the historical process of monetization at work in that very fallen and debased economy surmounted (so he hoped) by his lyric ideal. As Goux puts it – again following Marx's analysis of the money form:

> The history of the money function is marked by a progression toward abstraction and convention. In place of products with material value, increasingly abstract monetary signs are gradually substituted. . . . No longer a material value, money becomes a sign of gold, and then a simple sign of value, the sign or representative of a hypostatized abstraction.[60]

This is precisely the dynamic at work in Canto CII. Musing there on a set of famous Homeric epithets usually taken to mean "wine" – "dark-bright," and "sea-purple"[61] – Pound decides that the essence of the lot is really "russett-gold," a quality not of the concrete thing but "in the air, extant,"[62] as immaterial as light itself. This literally visionary gold is so sure, and the poet's insight so certain, that it is apparently worth trashing scholarly etymology for. And at the heart of Canto XCVII, the Homeric epithets are again forcibly read as the play of light and "not the colour."[63]

But the real ideological function of the constellation of values surrounding the "russett-gold" of Cantos XCVII and CII is not yet clear until we take into account the didactic thrust, repeated in both cantos, which suggests a whole epistemology and poetics in the aphoristic phrase "and from the nature, the sign."[64] For the full text that this fragment recalls, we must look back to the opening lines of Canto XC: " 'From the colour the nature / & by the nature the sign!' "[65] These lines refer, as Terrell tells us, to Heydon's "doctrine of signatures," which holds that the color, size, and shape of a thing reveal its true nature.[66] But what is interesting here is that Pound has fastened upon the most evanescent and immaterial of these attributes: not size and shape, but color. In Pound's rendering, "from the nature, the sign" really means "from the *color*, the sign." The one who can glimpse, through poetic vision, the *real* color is the one who can therefore deduce the true nature of the thing and therefore its "sign," its proper and fitting name. Indeed, it is this insight that authorizes Pound's departure from the accepted translations of the Homeric epithets. And this is the insight, in turn, that underwrites Canto CIX's directives to "illumine the words of procedure" – to bring the light of poetic vision to them – so that we might understand "heaven, man, earth, our law as written / not outside their natural colour."[67]

By the end of the *Cantos*, Pound's poetic gold has been worked and reworked until it is completely dematerialized – the better, first, to demonetize it in contrast to the debased economy of the marketplace; second, to remint it, as it were, in a transcendent poetic realm that might enable the full perfection of a form of universal value whose logic is essentially that of the monetary ideal; and third, to grant absolute authority over all symbolic exchanges (words, poems, readings, interpretations) to the possessor of that visionary power signified by the gold standard of poetic value. The light of visionary gold, in other words, authorizes Pound's poetic project not in spite of the fact that it is immaterial but *because* it is immaterial.

When viewed from the vantage of Pound's early politics, however, the price of such a transaction is a heavy one indeed. As we have already seen, in attempting to establish an aesthetic space free of history and economy, the later Pound establishes a domain that is free as well of difference, discord, and therefore the possibility of pluralistic and democratic forms of symbolic action. Pound's "nugget" and "lump gold" were intended to mark the active presence of a self that should be free of economic and cultural imperialism. But now, the particular sign, the particular poem – and, finally, the particular individual – must appeal to Pound's visionary gold standard for their value in exactly the same way that the currency of monetary exchange must appeal to the gold standard of capitalism for its worth. In revolt against the structure and effects of capitalist economy, Pound's idealism reproduced them – and nowhere, as we shall see, with more devastating effect than in the symbolic and political economy of his later career.

Early on, however, Pound occasionally intimated that this sort of poetic economy was a source of perpetual indebtedness rather than a source of power, because, one may suspect, early in his career he realized that his own poetic authority was ensured only insofar as he borrowed it from a host of literary masters. In "Histrion," for example, the poetic self received its power only by being given over to the inscriptions of the literary Other in a kind of ultimate dispossession of the property of the self. The surrendering of the self's "molten gold" made possible the minting of the soul into a type of currency that might keep the value of those "Masters of the Soul" in circulation.[68] And again, in the sonnet "L'Art" in *Canzoni*, Pound confronted the difficulty of originality, of owning the real poetic goods, and concluded in wincing self-critique, "'Tis Art to hide our theft exquisitely."[69]

In that same volume, "Octave"[70] presents a poet who realizes that he is writing on credit, and who attempts to make good on his debts by exchanging his poems for the *virtù* of the Other upon which they trade:

> Fine songs, fair songs, these golden usuries
> Her beauty earns as but just increment,
> And they do speak with a most ill intent
> Who say they give when they pay debtor's fees.
>
> I call him bankrupt in the courts of song
> Who hath her gold to eye and pays her not,
> Defaulter do I call the knave who hath got
> Her silver in his heart, and doth her wrong.[71]

This striking instance of "usury" in Pound's early work quite clearly undermines the intent of the poem to proffer an equal exchange. At first, the imbalance seems to tend toward these "fair songs," as if their excess of goldenness needed to be corrected, and indeed, it is corrected as the poem progresses. But no real balance is attained, because the exorbitant interest of these songs is not what they accrue but what they pay: The lady "earns" them as but "just increment." These songs are not the sort of gifts made by donative poets but rather debts the poet must pay to retain his poetic capital, to avoid being "bankrupt," a "defaulter."

Paradoxically, then, the poet must spend to preserve his gold and must meet an interest that is inextinguishable but nevertheless just. This poetic writing, it seems, is indebted, and perpetually so. The poet might possess his gold, but when he attempts to exchange it, or when he attempts to hoard it, he finds himself in the red. So it seems he is in the curious position not of "use it or lose it" (and not, as in the poetic economy of authority of the later Pound, of "use it and keep it") but of "use it *and* lose it." As in "Near Perigord" and "Portrait d'une Femme," poet and poetry are held "in fee," as an absolute possession possible only on condition of permanent indebtedness, which is very much, we are forced to say, like the structure of private property itself. This gold – because it marks the ultimate value, which *cannot* be exchanged, and because it does not belong to the self who writes – is always and only a loan.

THE POLITICS OF PATRONAGE

In a letter written to Margaret Anderson in 1917 Pound made clear his idea of a proper relation between artists and their economic contexts: "My whole position," he wrote, "and the whole backing up of my statement that the artist is 'almost' independent goes with doing the thing as nearly as possible without 'money.'"[72] It is perhaps not surprising, given his diagnosis of the conditions of literary production dominating both sides of the Atlantic, that the ideal relation Pound envisions here is in essence *no* relation. A supportive economy for the artist was not in the cards, he thought, because his experience told him that the story of this unhappy marriage was mainly one of slavish repetition of formulas being rewarded by a commodity system that found experiment and invention too risky for investment. Doing the thing as nearly as possible without "money" meant taking oneself foremost as an artist, not as a producer of commodities. You cannot, Pound says here in so many words, be a good artist and a good capitalist subject at the same time. The artist can be only half a self so long as "the lute sounds like a cash register, and a cadence is weighed down with a 'job.'"[73] Pound well knew that if the artist was "almost" independent, a whole nightmare of poverty, repetition, and economic coercion (necessity) was contained in that "almost." However, this recognition did not require, at this juncture in his career, changing the basic structure of the economic system so that this sort of schizophrenia might no longer plague those who wanted to be artists. Instead, it seemed to indicate that the economic realm *itself* was unredeemable, was a burden, in any form, to be tolerated: not a job but a "job," and not money but "money." Not work, in other words, but the abstract labor it had become in a system ruled by the commodity.

Artists have to eat, however, and the truth Pound knew about capitalist economy was not, for all its truth, edible. In 1918, Pound would discover Social Credit economics, which would "include creative art and writing in an economic scheme" by issuing a national dividend to all citizens except the wealthy[74] – and to those cultural producers, of course, whose work was not "as vendible as bath-tubs."[75] Well before the turn to Social Credit and the proposals for models of state patronage of the arts that quickly followed it,[76] however, Pound had his own ideas about how artists and writers could survive in an economy that held out little promise for invention. At the very outset of his career, Pound provided a glimpse not only of the modernist mover and shaker he would become but also of the limitations of his ideological inheritance when pushed to address problems that were economic in origin.

In surprising detail and with the kind of passion that creeping poverty inspires, Pound proposed in "Patria Mia" a system of patronage as the only means by which the artist might be free enough from the law of the commodity long enough to achieve something that might outlast its economic context. Looking back over history and its periods of artistic energy and decline, he concluded that the lesson of that history was quite clear: "Art was lifted into Alexandria by subsidy," he declared, "and by no other means will it be established in the United States."[77] The "free" market of literary enterprise had been given a fair shake, and it had summarily put the genteels and the *Atlantic* in the executive suite of American culture. (It had also returned Pound's work, from *Harper's* and the *Century*, stamped "rejected.")[78] So what now?

"Patria Mia" (1911) and "The Renaissance" (1914) both attempted to answer that question. Aware of the difficulty of his solicitous position – "I write barefacedly," he admitted, "call me an opportunist"[79] – Pound nevertheless felt that somebody had to address the would-be patron, and in "Patria Mia" he put his considerable rhetorical skills to the task. He reasoned that the current millionaire in early-twentieth-century America was not that different, in economic power, from the feudal lord, and "no more a permanent evil" either. Both are on the earth for a short period, amass great wealth and power, and then shuffle off this mortal coil more or less in infamy. "Nevertheless," he reckoned, "there seems to be no reason why he should not confer upon society, during his reign, such benefits as he is able." "The centralisation of power in his hands," he continued, "makes it very easy for him to display a virtue if he have one."[80] And just how might that virtue be displayed? How might that extraordinary concentration of economic potency be distributed so as to leave a mark that might testify to the virtue of the millionaire long after he is gone?

Pound shrewdly reasoned (foreshadowing here his later talents of negotiation and general avant-garde salesmanship) that the gifts of the patron might be thought of as really a sort of investment, but in a different kind of economy. The patron might be a big stick on Wall Street in 1910, but what about his place on the great balance sheet of the ages? The Medici, Pound reminds us, "retain honour among us not for their very able corruption of the city of Florence, but because they housed Ficino and various artists and in doing so even reaped certain credit due their forerunners, the Orsini."[81] Our advance man of modernism says to the twentieth-century millionaire, in so many words, that you will never make your mark until you can walk with the Medici, and the only way to do *that* is to find a way to make your capital continue to earn interest across the centuries, where *real* success is measured. And just for good measure he underscores the point with his punning play on the "credit" that has accrued to the name Medici, a kind of friendly takeover of the tribute due the house of Orsini made possible by the Medici's zeal in artistic investment.

Having begun, first, by flattering the modern millionaire (by calling him a lord), and having then moved subtly to force him to question his own economic potency in the world-class league of the Medici, Pound follows up with the rhetorical roundhouse of the carpe diem theme: "It is his function as it is the function of any aristocrat to die and to leave gifts. Die he must, and he may as well leave gifts, lest people spit upon his tomb and remember him solely for his iniquities." And then comes the final parry from this recreational fencer. There is still hope, Pound tells him, you may yet endure by doing the right thing – the only thing – that can save your otherwise cursed name: "Also his order must pass as all things pass from this earth, save masterwork in thought and in art. It is well, therefore" – the tone pontifical now – "that he leave behind him some record for consideration."[82]

At this point, the would-be patron – if he has a virtuous bone in his body or the least self-doubt about the commemoration of his name – is ready for the details. Sold, he now has to be presented with the bill. First, the patron must not think that all he need do now is buy some famous art and wait for the accolades. "An old thing has a fixed sort of value," Pound admonishes. "One acquires property in acquiring it." It is not retention you must be concerned with, Pound tells our millionaire, but invention. If you support the established artist whose work is behind him, you may "bolster up your own self-respect," but "you do nothing to assist awakenings or liberations."[83] What is wanted is not hero worship or a fetish for masterpieces but an age, a "Risorgimento" that will, as the young Pound put it, "make the Italian Renaissance look like a tempest in a teapot!"[84]

Doubling back now to reassure the patron, who is beginning to wonder what he has gotten himself into, Pound brings his business sense to bear: "It is most economical to do this when they are in the energetic state, to wit, at the beginning of their course, in the years when they will work for least money. Any artist who is worth powder to blow him to Sheol wants, at the start, liberty to do his work and little beyond this."[85] The patron, in other words, can get the most bang for his buck by giving a little money to a lot of struggling young artists – by enabling, as it were, the most invention per pound.

As "Patria Mia" unfolds, Pound will articulate his plans in greater detail, suggesting, for instance, that we should have a decent college of the arts in New York or San Francisco where the young artist might be housed and fed during "the impossible years."[86] And this is reasonable enough; we can subsidize so-called research, so why not what the researchers study? But these details can be taken up later (and indeed they are, here, in letters, and in "The Renaissance"). For now, Pound's bottom line – and almost the last line of this long essay – is that "there should be a class of artist-workers free from necessity."[87] Pound had done his rhetorical job. Would the millionaire now do his?

In 1915 Pound wrote a fascinating letter to John Quinn, a New York lawyer and patron of the arts whom Pound had met in 1910 while he was visiting New York and jotting down impressions for "Patria Mia."[88] In that letter, Pound describes his ideals for the patron, which Quinn himself would shortly adopt as his own, much to the later benefit of Pound and those writers and artists both thought worthy of support:

> My whole drive is that if a patron buys from an artist who needs money (needs money to buy tools, time and food), the patron then makes himself equal to the artist: he is building art into the world; he creates.
>
> If he buys even of living artists who are already famous or already making £12,000 per year, he ceases to create. He sinks back to the rank of a consumer.
>
> A great age of painting, a renaissance in the arts, comes when there are a few patrons who back their own flair and who buy from un-recognized men. In every artist's life there is, if he be poor, and they mostly are, a period when £10 is a fortune and when £100 or £200 a year without worry (without spending their time running to dealers, or editors) means a peace of mind that will let them work and not undermine them physically.[89]

Among the many significant issues raised in this passage, one of the most striking has to be Pound's equation of the patron and the artist. Pound could have perhaps put this line to good use in his sales pitch in "Patria Mia" where he had admonished the patron not to think of his involvement as a matter of acquiring property for the sake of personal enrichment but rather to look at it from the vantage of production and circulation. If money is purely instrumental (as it is here for Pound), then the real trick for the patron is to make money productive, to transform it from a thing frozen in the "fixed value" of the masterpiece hanging on the wall into a constructive agency at work in the world. By helping the struggling artist buy time, food, and tools, the patron creates not art but what makes art possible. He creates, in other words, the *conditions of invention*, which capitalist economy could not provide.

Of course, this hope was nothing new in American literary ideology. As Emerson put it, in almost identical terms, the men of capital "must drive their craft poetically." Their economy must be "inventive, alive," to be distinguished from "parsimony, which is a poor, dead, base thing."[90] For Emerson, making capital poetic meant making it fluid, a circulating power channeled by the active soul toward the cultivation of men, not toward the cultivation of more capital. Pound's distinction in the letter to Quinn between the productive and the acquisitive patron might well be drawn in Emerson's terms, which are the same terms of "Patria Mia," where Pound had set the pioneering entrepreneur, "a man of dreams in a time when dreams paid," against the modern businessman, whose fetish is "the nickel-plated cash register." "The first man," Pound wrote in an Emersonian moment, "deals with men, the latter deals with paper."[91]

The masculine "drive" that would make this sort of economy work and that would transform the patron into a kind of artist is exemplified for Pound, as Timothy Materer has pointed out, nowhere better than in John Quinn's precursor and proper model, Sigismundo Malatesta himself.[92] In him the artist and the patron are almost ideally joined. His Tempio registers a concept, as Pound put it, and at the same time he has the will and means to make the material realization of that concept possible. But of course it takes other artisans and their particular expertise to marry the material of Malatesta the patron and the concept of Malatesta the artist, and it is here that Sigismundo emerges as the ideal patron because, as Michael Harper has pointed out, he understands "the artist and the conditions under which good work is produced."[93]

In Canto VIII Malatesta writes of the *Maestro di pentore*:

> And in order that he may enter my service
> And also because you write me that he needs cash,
> I want to arrange with him to give him so much per year
> And to assure that he will get the sum agreed on.
> You may say that I will deposit security
> For him wherever he likes.
> And let me have a clear answer
> For I mean to give him good treatment
> So that he may come to live the rest
> Of his life in my land –
> Unless you put him off it –
> And for this I mean to make due provision,
> So that he can work as he likes,
> Or waste his time as he likes.[94]

The master painter, it seems, will have it considerably better than Pound's modern artist under patronage. But Malatesta is really a model, not merely an anachronism. Pound made that clear in a less public moment, when he wrote to Harriet Monroe: "A decent system would give [the writer] time to loaf in a library. Which while perhaps less important than loafing in pubs, is still a part of the complete man's loafing."[95] When we cast about for the sort of world implied here, it is perhaps not so surprising that the utopian world of art as Pound presented it in "The Serious Artist" seems to fit the bill perfectly. In that world, which art envisions and promotes, "you can admire, you can sit in the shade . . . you can do as you jolly well please."[96]

Emerson himself had had a similar idea, observing in his economically punning way, "'Tis very costly, this thinking for the market in books or lectures"[97] – costly, that is, within exactly the same economy Pound had imagined in his letter to Margaret Anderson. Musing in his journals on the ideal conditions of literary production, Emerson envisioned, with a little guilt and in terms even more radical than Pound's, just the right situation in which "whim" – that unanalyzable, undisciplined self – might be nurtured to creation:

> If I judge from my own experience I should unsay all my fine things, I fear, concerning the manual labor of literary men. They ought to be released from every species of public or private responsibility. To them the grasshopper is a burden. I guard my moods as anxiously as a miser his money. For company, business, my own household-chores untune and disqualify me for writing.[98]

In his more poetic moods, Emerson had to admit that the relation between the writer and economies of all kinds save the whimsical was mostly antagonistic, that the whole man who tills at day and writes at night might not be, after all, the poetic man. And he implied – to join the metaphors in these two passages from his journals – that it is "costly" to fritter away the capital of "moods" on those quotidian things not worthy of its expenditure. (Apparently, a little parsimony is fine if one is close in the right kind of economy.) Emerson, like a miser, loves this poetic capital of the innermost self not for what it might buy or acquire but for its own sake. Like Pound's possession of visionary gold, it is a kind of latent power kept shiny by his refusal to circulate it in any economy other than a lyric one.

Elsewhere in his journals, Emerson provides a passage that seems to anticipate Pound's modernist distinction between the "lump gold" of genius and the "coin" or "paper money" of generalized knowledge and convention:

> We all lean on England, scarce a verse, a page, a newspaper but is writ in imitation of English forms . . . & sometimes the life seems dying out of all literature & this enormous paper currency of Words is accepted instead.[99]

For Emerson, if imitation and convention are like the "paper currency" of a commodity system mired in repetition, then that sort of originality and vision which is the real thing of value in literary economy can be none other than gold, that poetic capital which we saw Emerson hoarding like a miser a moment ago. Like Pound, Emerson would have the American literary self pay in that nugget or lump gold which, because it defines itself against all earthly economies, is really not a payment at all but rather, like the patron's transaction, a gift. And like the early Pound, Emerson attempted to make that sort of cultural transaction possible by focusing our attention, as Ian Bell points out, on the *conditions* of cultural production, on the "*process* of manufacture" that "was forgotten or disguised by bourgeois modes of production."[100]

The radical individualism of Pound and his ideological ancestor Emerson may have led them both to reach many of the same conclusions about those institutions and practices that seemed an all-out assault on the first principle of their American politics, but what, exactly, did both envision as a more beneficent social and economic structure that might take that individual into just account? In his writings on patronage, Pound suggests something of what that world might look like, the kind of social and economic organization that might allow the self to get on with the business of being lyric.

In his figures of gold and in his writings on patronage, Pound tried to imagine not a realm of necessity, as Marx famously put it, but a realm of freedom. The figure of gold in Pound's poetry serves to remove lyric insight and its means of transmission from the loop of exchange, and this is precisely the case as well with the situation of patronage, which would enable the artist to do the thing without "money." If Pound's figures of gold rebel against the commodified culture of the genteel marketplace, his proposals for patronage tell us that the artist needs to be relieved of *his* status as a commodity, as a vehicle for abstract labor for sale. The artist, like the work of art, must be thought of as a bearer not of economic value but rather of another kind of value, one not negotiable but permanent.

Nowhere is this clearer than in his essay "The State," written in 1927, which shows the aesthetic economy of the early essays very much alive and well in his later career. This essay makes the same sort of distinction between "transient" and "permanent" goods that Pound had been making, in so many words, all along. In the first category, "The State" places, more than a little eclectically, "fresh vegetables," "fake art," and "pseudo-books." Though he does not really say so, what holds this rather fanciful sampling together is not only the fact that these things for immediate consumption do not survive the momentary needs they fulfill but mainly that they are produced *for the purpose* of being consumed.

"Permanent goods," however, are not economically determined by-products of the rule of the commodity. "Scientific discoveries," "works of art," and "classics" are produced with an eye toward permanent aesthetic value and intellectual law rather than transient economic value. What makes Pound's economy in "The State" of signal interest, however, is his criterion for inclusion in this latter category. These sorts of things are, as he puts it, "never consumed; or they are, in jargon, 'consumed' but not destroyed by consumption."[101] What this means, of course, is that the permanent goods of art are not really consumed at all; their value is not dissipated by use. Like gold, they still remain gold no matter what form they take or what uses to which they are put. And like "the gold thread in the pattern"[102] of the *Cantos*, these permanent goods get their special character not from their material nature, which might decay or be used up, but from the immaterial value they transmit.

"The State" provides the opportunity to explore as well the sort of social configuration this overarching economy might determine. In a passage rich in implication, Pound writes:

> The capitalist imperialist state must be judged not only in comparison with unrealised utopias, but with past forms of the state; if it will not bear comparison with the feudal order; with the small city states both republican and despotic; either as to its "social justice" or its permanent products, art, science, literature, the onus of proof goes against it.[103]

It is clear, not only in this passage but in the essay as a whole, that the efficacy of the state is now to be judged largely by the extent to which it makes possible and encourages the "permanent" products of Pound's economic hierarchy. The state is now seen, in Pound's words, as a "convenience." It is itself a kind of commodity, and when it can no longer provide the conditions of invention for the enduring goods of culture, then it too is used up and can be discarded.[104]

And when we ask, "Who will judge the convenience of the state," Pound baldly responds: "The party that follows [the artist] wins, and the speed with which they set about it, is the measure of their practical capacity and intelligence. Blessed are they who pick the right artists and makers."[105] The aesthetic economy deriving from Pound's earliest work now determines the efficacy of political structures, and the artist – and only the artist – can measure them against the gold standard of art and "permanent property" to determine their value. "The State," then, fleshes out the disturbing contradictions embedded in Pound's early ideas about patronage and the sort of social organization they imply. In the passage we just examined, Pound's examples (the feudal order, the city-state) seem offhand, but in fact they are quite symptomatic of his fatal tendency, early and late, to dissociate ethical, economic, and political concerns in order to assimilate all of them to an essentially ethical – and often strictly aesthetic – framework.

Of course, Pound did not propose in his writings on patronage a return to a feudal economic order, but that is precisely the point. The dissociation of the ethical, political, and economic dimensions that allowed Pound to hold up the energetic entrepreneur as a model of democratic self-reliance – while at the same time attacking the conditions and effects of capitalism – is the same kind of dissociation that could lead him to propose a system of patronage while simultaneously arguing, as he did in "Patria Mia," that "there need be little actual change in the existing machinery," that what was needed was "simply a more conscious and more far-calculating application of forces already present."[106] Here again, it is not a question of the structure of economic and political relations that entrepreneurship, for example, reproduces and perpetuates. Rather, it is a matter of making an essentially ethical distinction between "good" entrepreneurs and "bad," "good" uses of existing machinery and those that are more shortsighted.

This same fundamental dissociation is at work in Pound's early proposal for patronage, and now, reading by the light of "The State," we are in a better position to judge the politics of that proposal. It is not only that Pound's patronage model depends upon the perpetuation of an "aristocracy" of the capitalist rich who are as remote from the exploited mass as the feudal lord. Pound's plan is also remarkably naive.[107] In both "Patria Mia" and "The Renaissance," for instance, he proposes that the artist who does not need his annuity or who is no longer inventing can simply "pass it on to the man who, in his opinion, was most likely to use his time for the greatest benefit of the art."[108] Pound's plan for patronage, for all its seeming economic detail, is finally a purely ethical matter. It is all noblesse oblige, it stands or falls by the good graces of the patron, and it has very little to do with basic structural changes in an economic mode of production whose effects Pound quite sincerely abhorred, effects not only on artists but also, as he put it in the *Cantos*, on "folk of / ANY CONDITION."[109] As negative critique, Pound's early social vision championed the individual and the politics of difference. But what Pound's writings on patronage reveal is that when pushed to positive, pragmatic application, his early politics is dangerously regressive and undisturbed about the binding logic of political structures and the way in which cultural practices reproduce those structures.

If, as Jean-Paul Sartre (a very different sort of modernist) put it in *Search for Method*, praxis must always be viewed in terms of the future social organization it implies and suggests,[110] then Pound's patronage model appears to be a kind of cultural practice in reverse. But, of course, this sort of practice, at least in Sartre's terms, is no practice at all; it is a repetition of the past, not a transformation of it. To view Pound's proposals through the window of Sartre's concept of practice is to provide a virtual blueprint for Pound's later career, his growing attraction to ancient China and to an essentially populist vision of a precapitalist past free of plutocratic machination and Taylorized production.[111] And his model of patronage is an early sign as well of his increasing tendency (again like the Populists) to address economic problems in terms of distribution, not production.[112] For the artist, patronage may indeed be a kind of "solution," through distribution, to problems created by the mode of production that Pound never tired of attacking. But it is a solution, of course, only for those artists who receive the patron's good-will and therefore his cash.

Finally, the ultimate irony and central contradiction of Pound's patronage model is that it makes the artist dependent on that very economic structure Pound deplored, only now it is not the artist but those democratic others who must pay the price commanded by the permanent property of art. The economic fact is that the capital of the patron depends upon that very economic system and upon the exploitation of those who create its wealth – and so, therefore, does the artist and the art that was supposed to be that system's antithesis. If no abstract labor, then no exchange value; if no exchange value, then no surplus value; if no surplus value, then no capital; if no capital, then no patron; and if no patron, then no "free" artist, no "permanent" aesthetic property. So it is that Pound's gold of aesthesis is finally dependent upon the gold of capital. Under patronage, the artist is not really independent. Instead, another kind of dependence is created – in this case, dependence upon the continued existence of an aristocracy of capital.

If Pound had read much Emerson he would have found that his ideological kinsman himself had struggled to find the same kind of balance between economy and culture. What does England do with its surplus value, Emerson asked in *English Traits*; what is the "compensation" for the fragmenting and exploitive effects of its mode of production? "A part of the money earned returns to the brain to buy schools, libraries, bishops, astronomers, chemists and artists with," he wrote. "But the antidotes are frightfully inadequate, and the evil requires a deeper cure, which time and a simpler social organization must supply."[113] Unlike the later Emerson, whose early agrarian critique had long since lost (even for him) its critical force, Pound would spend a good part of his later career looking back to the times of Confucius and Jefferson for that simpler social organization which might dictate the culturally beneficial commerce of the good state. And he would find its modern avatar in Benito Mussolini, who, like "T. J." (or so Pound thought), was set against "machinery or at any rate the idea of cooping up men and making 'em all into UNITS, unit production, denting in the individual man, reducing him to a mere amalgam."[114]

But Emerson, at age fifty, recognized the difficulty of being both democratic and aesthetic, and he saw that the permanent property of art had a price that not the artist, but democracy, would have to pay if it indulged patronage. As he put it in a letter to Thomas Carlyle:

> America is incomplete. Room for us all, since it has not ended, nor given sign of ending, in bard or hero. 'Tis a wild democracy, the riot of

mediocrities, & none of your selfish Italies and Englands, where an age sublimates into a genius, and the whole population is made into paddies to feed his porcelain veins, by transfusion from their brick arteries.[115]

Porcelain veins and brick arteries; the body aesthetic and the body economic – Emerson's two types of clay to Pound's two kinds of gold. Emerson never really found a way to put them together in the body politic. And neither, despite the fearful political price, did Ezra Pound.

6

Ideologies of the Organic

> Gold and iron are good
> To buy iron and gold;
> All earth's fleece and food
> For their like are sold.
>
> . . . .
>
> Nor kind nor coinage buys
> Aught above its rate.
> Fear, Craft and Avarice
> Cannot rear a State.[1]

As we are about to see, the substance of these lines, if not their style, could easily have been written in the nineteen thirties by Ezra Pound. In fact, they were appended by Emerson in the eighteen forties to the opening of his essay "Politics" (or was the essay, we might ask of Emerson as of no other, appended to them?). Like all good epigraphs, Emerson's is mobilized in the services of compression, but what exactly is being compressed in this ambitiously simple verse? Are these lines (eight of an opening twenty-six) about the relation or the disrelation of economy, nature, and politics? And does this apparently natural economy, in which things buy only their "like," make the state necessary, or does it make political structures only redundant? Can those structures express and enforce the truth of nature's law, and if so, why does such a law need to be enforced in the first place?

To begin to answer these questions, we need to note, first, that Emerson here does not really envision some utopian economy of the future – as a shining light, say, at the nether end of capitalism's tunnel – so much as he *declares* its real existence in the here and now. The truth of this economy derives, it seems, not from any social teleology but rather from a larger coherence that is more than economic, more than historical. Does this mean then that Emerson is, willingly or unwillingly, an ideologist of capital, declaring that the economy of today is the economy of always? In the initial line, Emerson does indeed make what looks very much like an early-nineteenth-century capitalist assertion: Gold is good. But it is good, the second line tells us in counterpoint, only to buy itself. Why, though, would one want to buy gold with gold, exchange one thing for that same thing? Our answer to that question seems to answer the question we asked above about Emerson's ideological position: The only reason to exchange a thing for itself is to take advantage of a situation in which those things *are not* themselves – to take advantage, in other words, of fluctuations in that thing's exchange value, and thereby turn a profit.

But this, it turns out, is precisely the kind of transaction that Emerson's economy will not allow. In fact, it is the target of his compact poetic critique. Emerson's gold, we discover, is a limited good, particular and constrained. It is nothing special, he tells us, and the inversion of iron and gold in the second line only underscores the point by melding that most precious of metals with a cheap and common mineral. In fact, this gold is like the "fleece and food" that are sold for it. But then again, if gold "buys" and these are "sold," what unites them, what makes them "like"? The answer seems to be that nothing unites them except their difference; and this is pure unadulterated Emersonian paradox – but always, as here, with a sharp point. These things are different because they are concrete use values; if you have them, you should gain no abstract wealth from exchanging them for the only things they can bring you, namely, themselves or their "like."

In the scant space of four very short lines, then, Emerson castigates the cherished standard of his own economic moment and stages an escape, not exactly from exchange – these things are, after all, bought and sold – but rather from abstract exchange *value*. But if that is the case, we are forced to ask, then what is this "rate" that appears in the second quatrain? If exchange value does not determine the rate, then what sort of value does? Emerson's diction provides a clue: Neither "kind nor coinage buys / Aught above *its* rate." Thus, the rate is not imposed from without but rather is somehow inherent in the concrete thing itself, not dependent upon abstract equivalence. Economically, these things are, so to speak, not rate-reliant but self-reliant.

Economy is still economy, however, and here the more general movement of the passage helps us to see what sort of principle governs Emerson's strange variety. We move from an opening critique of the abstract and general in the name of the concrete and particular to a more pervasive principle of equivalence (fleece and food are somehow like iron and gold); then to the still more far-ranging coupling of "kind" and "coinage" by means of the "rate," which governs all the exchanges treated thus far. And finally – inevitably, in retrospect – we come to the

Emersonian payoff familiar from poems like "Give All to Love." Here, in capitals: "Fear, Craft and Avarice / Cannot rear a State." The subtle reversal and play on "statecraft" in this couplet, pleasurable though it is, should not obscure Emerson's critical aim of recuperating the language of economy for his own purposes – purposes, in this case, bent toward making the point that economics and politics are not autotelic but can be judged from the vantage of a more important and pervasive kind of value, one whose imperatives are so certain as to call forth the confident declaratives of these lines.

I have purposefully withheld the two lines that intervene between the two quatrains before us – two lines that clarify for us just what sort of economy this is: "Boded Merlin wise, / Proved Napoleon great." Emerson's natural economy also holds sway, apparently, over the wise or great self. What governs the authentic economy of particulars in the first quatrain is the more general ethical truth recorded in what is now the sestet. And that truth is understood by the representative man who realizes that those ethical failings (Craft, Avarice) that arise in the sort of economy Emerson has written against are the sources, not the effects, of political debacle.

Emerson stages a poetic demolition of abstract exchange and its ethical coordinates to make way not only for a new kind of economy and politics but mainly for a new kind of self. Emerson's authentic economy of use value, then, is really an economy of a particular *kind* of use – namely, as our two new lines make clear, an ethical one. The self must read the truth of the particular, of gold and iron, fleece and food, by the light of the general truth that makes the particular representative and instructive. Authentic reading of the book of things, which might determine a just economy and politics, is made possible by the light and insight of the Emersonian "I."

Emerson unpacks his epigram for us later in the circlings of his "Politics": "The less government we have the better," he writes:

> The antidote to this abuse of formal government is the influence of private character, the growth of the Individual. . . . That which all things tend to educe; which freedom, cultivation, intercourse, revolutions, go to form and deliver, is character; that is the end of Nature, to reach unto this coronation of her king.[2]

So it is not politics or economics, nor even really ethics in the strict sense, but finally nature itself that is the engine of Emerson's political economy. In this world, to be freed from abstract exchange and the politics it determines is to be freed into a self that, in realizing itself, realizes "the end of Nature" and so determines a just economy. And so – to return to the questions we raised at the outset – we can now see that for Emerson economic and political structures are merely instrumental, not constitutive. Like linguistic structures in Emerson's understanding, they are "vehicular and transitive," and when we mistake them as real, when they appear "too stark and solid," we are victimized by "an excess of the organ" of economics and politics.[3] It should come as no surprise, then, that in Emerson's rendering politics is purely negative: "The less government we have the better." Emerson's hopeful and perilous political wager was that this Jeffersonian ideal could accommodate what he knew to be the truth of a natural politics: the continual coronation of individuals of character.[4] And "character," in turn, would ameliorate the contradictions of Emerson's ideal individualist political economy, enabling us to take our place in a classless democracy of sovereigns.

NATURE AND VALUE IN POUND'S ECONOMICS

Pound's involvement in economics and politics was considerably more pragmatic and detailed than Emerson's, leading him into monetary and fiscal obsessions that Emerson, with his impatience for "the overt and practical effect," would have found beside the spiritual point. For all that, though, Pound's economics, as we shall see, never really left the topos of Emerson's "Politics." It was another "Politics," however (namely, Aristotle's), that provided an explicit source for Pound's ideas about the relationship between nature, economy, and ethics.[5] Like Emerson, Aristotle sought to distinguish between a natural economy – which is ethically just and proper and in which money serves the purely instrumental function of facilitating exchange between "like" and "like" – and the type ("chrematistic," in Aristotle's words) in which money is exchanged for itself for the purposes of making more money. For Aristotle, as for Emerson and the later Pound, chrematistics and its privileged form, usury, are "unnatural": The propagation of money out of money, in the form of interest, mocks nature's increase and procreation.[6] For Pound, who apparently took Aristotle's injunction quite literally, what makes money in the "usurocracy" of modern capitalism a "sin against nature" is that it is "a false representation in the mineral world of laws which apply only to animals and vegetables."[7] Economically because morally wrong, this sort of economy – as Pound put it in Canto XLV, in lines of which Aristotle would have approved – is "CONTRA NATURAM."[8]

Given their shared ethical coordinates, it is not surprising that Pound's reading of Aristotle's *Nicomachean Ethics* in *Guide to Kulchur* finds much to admire. Aristotle, Pound writes, has indeed "come at money from the right side, as a measure. A means of ascertaining the proportionate worth of a house and a pair of shoes."[9] But what determines this "worth" for which money is but a measure? We know it cannot be money itself, lest we be plunged back into the inferno of chrematistics and usury. Pound attempts to sort out these problems in *Guide to Kulchur* in his interpretation of Aristotle's term *Xreia*. This cornerstone of Aristotle's economics, Pound tells us, means not "value" – as it is sometimes translated[10] – but rather *demand*. "Money," Pound argues, "is not a measure of value" but only of demand, which in turn determines price.[11] Fine, but this still leaves us with the problem of the origin of value. A second reading of Aristotle's key term undertaken earlier in the *Guide*, however, further investigates the problem of value and in doing so moves us one step closer to Emerson's economy. "Yet again," Pound writes, "it makes an infinite difference whether you translate *XREIA* as *demand* or USE, its price may be distorted by its OPUS."[12] So at this juncture, then, Pound has led us through three levels of economic demystification; in answer to the question, "Wherein lies value?" he has responded, "Not in money but in demand"; and then, "Not in demand, but in use."

Marx himself had come upon this very problem in Aristotle as well and had found the ancient's concept of value at a loss to account for the commensurability that makes exchange possible. For Marx, the missing standard, which Aristotle could not see, was none other than human labor itself. "What is the homogeneous element," Marx wrote,

> i.e. the common substance, which the house represents from the point of view of the bed? Such a thing, in truth, cannot exist, says Aristotle. But why not? Towards the bed, the house represents something equal, in so far as it represents what is really equal, both in the bed and the house. And that is – human labour.[13]

As Marx goes on to point out, Aristotle could not see labor as a standard for commensurability because in his historical moment labor itself was incommensurable; Aristotle, Marx reminds us, lived in a society that accepted slavery and the inequality of labor as a natural fact.

Unlike Marx, Pound's answer to the problem of value in Aristotle is based not on the labor theory but rather on the use theory of value; for Pound, it is not the amount and type of labor that go into a thing that determine its relative worth but rather the usefulness of the thing itself, regardless of how it is produced. "All kinds of work," he writes in the *Guide*, "are no more uniform in value than are all kinds of gold ore."[14] So when we ask of Pound, what is the source of value? his answer can only be that its origin is not money, not demand, and not labor, but rather the use value, which is rooted in *nature itself.* "Work does not create wealth," Pound argues, "it *contributes to the formation of it.* Nature's productivity is the root."[15] For Marx, private property, wages, and capital are all equivalent because they all presuppose abstract and alienated labor – they presuppose, that is, the possibility of one person's

labor being owned by another. Pound's view of the relationship between labor and value is closer to Aristotle's than it is to Marx's. Where
Marx wanted to radically separate use value and exchange value and to
show how the gap between the two was the source of surplus value and
therefore of wealth and capital, Pound's ideal economy would bring the
two together by making exchange value, as Peter Nicholls puts it, "a
function of use value,"[16] and a function, therefore, of nature itself. For
Pound, the solution to the problem of exchange value and the
chrematistics and usury it breeds is not to do away with exchange value
but rather to *naturalize* it by draining it of any mediating, formative
power – to make it, in Emerson's words, "vehicular and transitive."

This seems to be precisely the sort of appeal, for Pound, of the system
of stamp scrip that the Brazilian economist Silvio Gesell formulated in
his study *The Natural Economic Order*.[17] Gesell's position was so attractive
when Pound discovered it in 1934 that it led him to seriously reframe his
commitment to Social Credit economics, to which he had been enthu-
siastically devoted since 1918.[18] In fact, recent critics of Pound have
argued that "Gesell, although a less 'loud' voice in Pound's work, appears more organically linked to Pound's economics and historical values
as a whole" because "the essential point for Pound is Gesell's recognition
of the bounty of nature as the source of true wealth."[19]

Gesell proposed a currency that would systematically devalue by 1
percent a month, and Pound liked the idea not only because it might
replace unfair systems of income taxation but mainly because stamp scrip
could not be hoarded without becoming increasingly valueless. Gesell's
system would thus prevent the accumulation of capital and would ensure active circulation and exchange. "It would be better," Pound thought,
"If money perished at the same rate as goods perish, instead of being a
lasting durability while goods get consumed and food gets eaten."[20] For
Pound, the ideal form of money is, as Lewis Hyde puts it, a kind of
"vegetable currency," one whose devaluation and decay would emulate
the natural mutability of concrete goods.[21] The genius of Gesell's stamp
scrip, in other words, is that it is a kind of money-made-nature, a
mechanism of exchange that nevertheless approaches the condition of
nature's own concrete use values.

As we might have guessed from his "Politics," the same could be said
of Emerson's view of money as well, which likewise was exercised by
the capacity of money to produce "the disruption of the 'correspondence'
between things, thoughts and symbols."[22] Emerson's position – and
indeed the entire Jacksonian critique of economic abstraction, which
implicates the banks, the stock market, and "the Paper Dynasty" of
emergent finance capital[23] – prefigure in impressive detail and with shared

ethical coordinates the critique of finance capital and the "sin against nature" of usury levied by Pound.[24] As Emerson put it, "This invasion of nature by Trade with its Money, its Credit, its Steam, its Railroad, threatens to upset the balance of man, and establish a new Universal Monarchy more tyrannical than Babylon or Rome."[25]

Like Pound, Emerson believed that the ideal kind of money would be a sort of self-annihilating currency facilitating, but not mediating, a larger natural economy. To the extent that money does have an independent, constitutive power, it is dangerous. "The system of money is a system of pledges," he writes. "You will not take my word that I have labored honestly and added to the amount of value and happiness in the world, but demand a certificate in the shape of a piece of silver or paper. By this exchange we are both degraded."[26] Emerson and Pound thought that money must paradoxically become nothing in and of itself precisely to become the only particular kind of proper currency. It must lose its social economy so that it may gain a natural one, so that it can become what Emerson might call "living money."

So for Pound and Gesell as for Emerson, the problem with money is how to keep it "natural." If its efficacy, in Pound's words, is established "not by nature but by custom,"[27] then how is its value to be ensured? If it is purely instrumental, not a source of value in itself – if it can be, as Pound puts it, *"altered or rendered useless at will"*[28] – then how do we make it an instrument of nature, that thing which *cannot* be rendered useless at will? In short, Pound's answer to this question is to base the economy upon statal money, not bank money, and to determine the value of notes in circulation by the aggregate wealth of the nation, not by the gold standard.[29] In Pound's view, no single commodity can or should serve as the basis for currency value, because that single thing (particularly if it is durable, like precious metal) can be hoarded and monopolized. Pound's aim is not that the single monetary unit should correspond to a single type of commodity but rather that the *order* of money should correspond to the order of things.[30] In the strict sense of Aristotle's storied term, the relationship between the two should be mimetic, in that the law, proportion, and balance inherent in the order of nature should determine its economic representation.[31] Pound had been hinting at this position ever since early essays like "Patria Mia" and section IV of *Hugh Selwyn Mauberley* ("usury age-old and age-thick") – well before his famous linkage of economics, nature, and artistic production in Canto XLV – but it is unmistakable in later poems like Canto XCVII. There, Pound glosses and transforms Alexander Del Mar's monetary theory to make it speak a shared harmony and order holding sway in the poetic, monetary, and natural worlds:

> If a penny of land be a perch
>   that is grammar
> nummulary moving toward prosody.[32]

In the currency of Canto XCVII, the understanding and "grammar" of money ("nummulary") and economics move toward the condition of poetry and assume the compelling precision of poetic measure insofar as they are grounded or "perched," like the poet's own self-possession, in the visionary capital of nature.

As Tim Redman argues in his study *Ezra Pound and Italian Fascism*, Pound's fierce belief in his own natural economy can be gauged by the political means he was willing to endorse to make that economy a reality.[33] It is the job of the economic enforcer, whether Douglas or Mussolini, to make sure that what is artificial behaves as if it were natural and to shear economy of its formative, mediating, and therefore appropriable power. Like Emerson, Pound wanted an economy in which the just rate of exchange would be determined not by gold or abstract value but rather by the law of nature, "like" for "like," face to face. Marx imagined that we could escape the realm of necessity called "history" only if we abolished property. Emerson and Pound, however, would make the world safe for property – but only, as we shall see, by moving to abolish history.

ONE WAY: THE SEVEN LAKES CANTO AND OTHERS

It is probably safe to assume that contemporary critics will, to some extent, view modernism and romanticism not only as antagonistic but as largely definitive and periodizing in their antagonism. What the career of Ezra Pound shows us, however, is that we may endorse this critical truism only at the expense of either declaring that Pound himself was not a modernist – a claim that few critics, I am sure, are willing to make – or denying the radical organicism that is built into the very idea of romanticism and that is unmistakable in Pound's later project. Nowhere is that supposedly unmodernist dimension of his work clearer than in his poetic and prose writings on China. T. S. Eliot wrote in his introduction to the Faber *Selected Poems* that Pound was the modernist discoverer – the inventor, in fact – of that exotic literary terrain.[34] However, as we shall see, Pound did not really discover China so much as it discovered him. In the face of those challenges posed by modern capitalism and its culture, Pound radicalized what was latent in his native ideological inheritance, and China not only enabled but compelled him to carry out a project that was, sooner or later in American literary history, waiting to happen.

In Pound's Chinese poems from *Cathay* onward, nature everywhere "wears the colors of the spirit" (to use Emerson's well-worn phrase).

Think of the wonderfully realized early poem "The River-Merchant's Wife: A Letter." "The monkeys make sorrowful noise overhead" as the young woman waits for her husband, five months gone; the mosses at the front gate are overgrown, "too deep to clear them away!"; and the "paired butterflies" communicate to her a message of loneliness and mutability that she has already read within herself. It is tempting, perhaps, to level the charge that this poem has not escaped the pathetic fallacy, which Ruskin (fed up with nature wearing the colors of the spirit) made one of the cardinal literary sins. And that charge might be justified were it not for the exquisite restraint of Pound's "translation":

> At fourteen I married My Lord you.
> I never laughed, being bashful.
> Lowering my head, I looked at the wall.
> Called to, a thousand times, I never looked back.[35]

These are the words of a young girl who knows the meaning of duty, who has married an older man and a social superior ("My Lord you") because that is what young Chinese girls do in this society.

Duty turns to love, however (whether because of the former or in spite of it is tantalizingly unclear), and by the time nature seems to speak in the poem, we listen because this young woman has earned the right to speak with nature's voice, and thus merits our attention:

> The leaves fall early this autumn in wind.
> The paired butterflies are already yellow with August
> Over the grass in the West garden;
> They hurt me. I grow older.[36]

Handled in this poem with such delicacy, nature does not teach, we might say, but rather listens to the young woman as *she* discovers herself, her longing and sadness – a process of discovery made possible by the fact that she, unlike the women of "Portrait d'une Femme" or "The Garden," confronts those emotions with honesty and ethical fortitude. This nature, it seems, has no moral agenda; it does not vaporize the individual in some overarching coherence whose truth hangs always heavy on the metaphysical bough.

In the *Cantos* and in Pound's late prose, however, nature will have plenty to teach us indeed, and its lessons will not be those of love poems but will become less and less personal and less and less debatable. It is hard to think of a word less appropriate than "totalitarian" to describe the nature of Pound's "River-Merchant's Wife." Yet that is exactly the word Pound will use to describe the power of the organic for his later cultural project.

We might never guess at such a description from these opening lines taken from a famous Chinese poem appearing at the very heart of the *Cantos*:

> For the seven lakes, and by no man these verses:
> Rain; empty river; a voyage,
> Fire from frozen cloud, heavy rain in the twilight.
> Under the cabin roof was one lantern.
> The reeds are heavy; bent;
> and the bamboos speak as if weeping.[37]

So begins one of the most celebrated moments in Pound's long poem, the so-called Seven Lakes Canto. Hugh Kenner, for instance (in a characterization now famous among Poundians), calls Canto XLIX "one of the pivots of the poem: the emotional still point of the *Cantos*."[38] And it is, moreover, part of a set of cantos that quite clearly intend to give the reader what Pound himself called "a glimpse of Paradiso."[39] Before the main block of Chinese Cantos (LII–LXXI), Pound gives us the paradisal Cantos XLVII and XLIX, strategically placed in counterpoint between Cantos XLV and LI, those famously urgent and strident condemnations of usury. The Seven Lakes Canto's power and importance are only enhanced by its placement almost at the very center of Pound's long poem. Up until Canto XLIX, the work has been mainly a record of disintegration, of history gone wrong. There are moments, flashes, of visionary brilliance – the *Donna mi priegha* of Cavalcanti and Canto XXXVI, the Confucian order of Canto XIII – but on the whole the balance of the poem has tipped far in the direction of human error and historical decline. Daniel Pearlman's characterization is standard:

> In the first phase of the poem, which persists up through Canto 46, the time-embattled human spirit struggles against overwhelming odds to achieve order in spite of surrounding chaos. . . . Western history is portrayed by and large in a state of progressive confusion and decay.[40]

The Seven Lakes Canto is indeed, it seems, some sort of structural and thematic pivot, one that points back to the "record of struggle"[41] in the previous poems and forward to the exemplary actions and order of Jefferson, Adams, Van Buren, and the world of the Chinese emperors.

The opening of Canto XLIX might remind us more than a little of those early poems in *Cathay* like "The River-Merchant's Wife." There is formal, judicious self-effacement ("and by no man these verses"); there is the measured, spartan diction that in Pound's hands helped usher in a new rigor in modernist poetry ("Rain; empty river"); and finally, there is the natural world, in which a sensibility is somehow written and read ("the bamboos speak as if weeping"). As the poem progresses, however, it becomes clear that this canto, unlike any others of Pound's Chinese idiom thus far in the poem, presents not a scene or narrative of individual discovery but really a whole moral panorama, one whose ambitious social vision matches the breadth of its landscape.

And what a landscape it is: Pound has assembled eight Chinese poems that accompany eight famous scenes from the Tung Ting Lake District of central China – all of which, poems and paintings, were collected in a manuscript book that was part of the Pound household in America.[42] We know then that Pound – as is almost always the case in his Chinese poems – is working here not from a source but rather from that more limited and demanding thing, a model. Through the first two-thirds of the poem, Pound stays close to textual home, even as the scenes gradually expand to circumscribe a world of seasonal rhythms and paradigms: "Comes then snow scur on the river / And a world is covered with jade," "geese line out with the autumn." In the space of a page, we move from the rains of what must be late summer ("Sail passed here in April; may return again in October") to the "Autumn moon," and finally to the repose of the coming winter, whose promise of solitude the snow delivers.

But then something very strange and very important begins to happen, something that will not let us mistake this poem or this nature for those, so seemingly similar, of *Cathay*. After the set of translations, we find these lines: "State by creating riches shd. Thereby get into debt? / This is infamy; this is Geryon." The sudden interlocution of the poet's voice here is all the more abrupt because it breaks an unobtrusively crafted stillness. And the mixture of Olympian judgment ("This is infamy") and economic abstraction, hard on the heels of such a determinedly unmediated landscape, only makes the voice from the pulpit doubly startling. How are we to take these lines – or why, for that matter, should we take them at all?

First, we should notice that the initial line of this poetic pronouncement is not simply a question but is, in fact, a rhetorical one: a question, in other words, that wants to be an emphatic declaration. And what it declares, in a shorthand flourish, is the economic philosophy of Jefferson, Jackson, and Van Buren – the very subject of most of the preceding eleven cantos. The second line then moves not to answer, but to extrapolate, the first: not "no" in response, but "This is infamy; this is Geryon." This last figure seems to confirm our hunch that this poem, which started as landscape, is in fact a document of moral, economic, and political exemplum. And that suspicion is clinched when we find Geryon in Dante's eighth circle of Hell as a symbol of fraud, with the head of a man, the trunk of a beast, and the tail of a serpent.[43] Geryon and his economy are, like his literal physiognomy, *contra naturam*, the very antithesis of that stately natural order that Pound has unfolded cadence by cadence throughout the poem thus far. It will come as no surprise, then, when in Canto LI Geryon speaks, with riveting candor, not Paradiso but Inferno:

> and a sour song from the folds
>   of his belly
> sang Geryon; I am the help of the aged;
> I pay men to talk peace;
> Mistress of many tongues; merchant of chalcedony
> I am Geryon twin with usura,
> You who have lived in a stage set.[44]

The land of Geryon is not the land of the Seven Lakes. It is not the land of *any* lakes.

Even before the conspicuous Geryon passage, we find, if we attend closely to Pound's translation, that this seemingly speechless nature is *already* doing its ideological work before the poet steps in to speak on its behalf. This nature, it turns out, is already an economy; in fact, it is all the economy we need. In the lines leading up to Pound's Jeffersonian reprise, we find these images:

> Rooks clatter over the fisherman's lanthorns,
> A light moves on the north sky line;
> Where the young boys prod stones for shrimp.

Curious, then, that in an authoritative translation offered by the Poundians, the lines are markedly different:

> Fisherman's light blinks
> Dawn begins, with light to the south and north
> Noise of children hawking their fish and crawfish.[45]

Notice what has happened here – conspicuous if you have the translation, inaccessible if you do not. What we find in the original is overtly economic activity, children (no less) peddling the things they have for sale, and with considerable verve and economic interest. In Pound's version, however, the fish are not peddled and (the children hope) sold. They are discovered, *found*.

Pound's recasting of the lines may seem therefore to suppress the economic dimension altogether, but in fact it substitutes one form of economy – namely, Pound's ideal, natural economy – for another. True to the Poundian form elaborated in the economic prose, these children are not creating wealth but instead are contributing to the formation of wealth that is already there, latent in nature. In Pound's hands, these lines constitute an originary scene for the sort of economy that Pound had spelled out in no uncertain terms in the years leading up to the Seven Lakes Canto.

In the *ABC of Economics* (1933), Pound's most comprehensive economic tract, we learn that "the practices of rent and interest arise out of
the natural disposition of grain and animals to multiply. The sense of
right and justice which has sustained the main practice of rent and interest through the ages . . . is inherent in the nature of animal and vegetable."[46] Or again, this time only two years before Canto XLIX, in *Social
Credit: An Impact*: "The CREDIT rests *in ultimate* on the ABUN-
DANCE OF NATURE, on the growing grass that can nourish the
living sheep."[47] Or once more, this time ten years after the Seven Lakes
Canto, in "What Is Money For?" in what reads like a gloss on Pound's
Chinese boys prodding for shrimp: "All value comes from labour and
nature. Wheat from ploughing, chestnuts from being picked up."[48]

In this last passage Pound does seem to cede some value to labor, but
as we can tell from his examples – agrarian and hunter-gatherer – it is
not a central, creative role but merely an incidental one. In fact, to return
now to the canto at hand, it is labor of a very specific sort. Having given
us his originary scene of economics, Pound now sets the stage for his
paradigmatic instance of labor by providing prominent place (and all
capitals) to a Japanese transliteration of a poem from the Fenollosa
notebooks. In English it reads:

> The auspicious clouds bright and colorful
> Twist and spread
> The sun and moon shed their rays
> Morning after morning.[49]

But again, look at what happens in Pound's translation – this one attempted in 1958, some twenty years after the Seven Lakes Canto:

> Gate, gate of gleaming,
> knotting, dispersing,
> flower of sun, flower of moon
> day's dawn after day's dawn   new fire.[50]

In Pound's hands, the organicism only faintly suggested in the authoritative translation becomes fully foregrounded ("flower of sun, flower of
moon") in what we are tempted to call a privileged figure for organicism.
Or so it seems, at least, in Pound's chosen simile for that nature which
is "one, indivisible, a nature extending to every detail as the nature of
being oak or maple" – or being flower – "extends to every part of the
oak tree or maple."[51]

But in figuring nature, of course, Pound also figures the value and
very possibility of its opposite, history. And from this vantage, it is
clear that his nature can know no time for the simple reason that it *is*
"one." Change may take place in the individual oak or maple, but not

in the nature of *being* oak or maple – that is, after all, the difference between being and becoming. Pound's "indivisible" nature is the very essence of pure recurrence, of a kind of newness that is new not by virtue of time but rather because it is timeless, immune to decay and decomposition. This, I would argue, is the newness that Pound had in mind in his famous shibboleth "MAKE IT NEW," and not the avant-gardism for which it is usually appropriated. We need to recognize that the "it" of Pound's slogan refers to something quite specific:

> Day by day make it new
> cut underbrush,
> pile the logs
> keep it growing[52]

"It" is capable of growth, but "it" is worth cultivating only because it expresses the order and harmony of nature. And if we have any doubts about what "it" is, Pound will dispel them for us in Canto CXVI: "It coheres all right," he realizes, "even if my notes do not cohere."[53] "It," in other words, is not Pound's poem but rather that timeless realm and order that the poem has attempted – and failed, in this poet's estimation – to make new by clearing the intellectual underbrush to reveal primary form.[54] "MAKE IT NEW" is a call for renovation, but it is renovation bent toward the restoration of a world in which the more things change, the more they stay the same.

Having seen how Pound has steadily closed the gap between the economic, the social, and the natural, we are now ready to see what place labor can have in this world of stasis and recurrence:

> Sun up; work
> sundown; to rest
> dig well and drink of the water
> dig field; eat of the grain

The seasonal rhythms of the land in Pound's landscapes, having been telescoped into the single, paradigmatic image of dawn's recurrence in the foregoing Japanese quatrain, determine now the rhythms of labor, of work and repose, which are themselves in harmony with all of natural existence. It is not an exaggeration to say that in this Paradiso the laborer has become simply a functionary of that nature whose value and increase he or she releases.

In Cantos XLVII and LII, Pound will flesh out the utopian vision of labor that is compressed in these lines. Working now from Hesiod's *Works and Days*, Canto XLVII provides more-detailed instructions to the natural laborer. Its imperative is almost, Pound seems to intend, the voice of nature itself:

Begin thy plowing
When the Pleiades go down to their rest,
Begin thy plowing
40 days are they under seaboard
And in valleys winding down toward the sea.
When the cranes fly high
Think of plowing.[55]

In this world, it is not the clock time of capitalist modernity that dictates the rhythms of work but rather the astrological clock, the stars, which in their movements pull the seasons, and the activities appropriate to those seasons, in their wake. And in Canto LII, Pound's transmission of nature's message is even more stately, informed as it is by the formality and composure of the *Li Ki*, the Chinese *Book of Rites*, upon which Pound's poem is based:

Virgo in mid heaven at sunset
  indigo must not be cut
No wood burnt into charcoal
  gates are all open, no tax on the booths.
Now mares go to grazing
  tie up the stallions
Post up the horsebreeding notices
  Month of the longest days
Life and death are now equal
  Strife between light and darkness.[56]

These passages, perhaps, need little commentary, and in fact from Pound's later vantage they cannot be supplemented or in any real sense interpreted. (After all, his version of *Li Ki* begins with this indisputable call to attention: "Know then.") The spirit, if not the letter, of Pound's translation is perfectly faithful to his primary text. As one critic summarizes it, the Confucian believes that "the state religion, the government of a family, and the rules of society are all founded on the true *li*, or relations of things."[57] We have, it seems, come a long way indeed from the natural world of "The River-Merchant's Wife." Or maybe the nature of *that* nature is just now, at this juncture in Pound's career, coming into view.

To attend to the end of Canto LII is to return to the final question we will need to confront in understanding what kind of paradise Pound has in mind in the Seven Lakes Canto. For the three pages leading up to the conclusion of the poem, we have had Pound's recounting of the *Li Ki* and its directives for each season. But the imperatives of nature, we now know, are imperatives for economic and political activity as well. So it is appropriate, if a little startling, that Canto LII ends with these lines:

> Begin where you are said Lord Palmerston
> > began draining swamps in Sligo
> Fought smoke nuisance in London. Dredged harbour in Sligo.[58]

Like the intercession of the poet's voice on behalf of Jefferson and Van Buren in the Seven Lakes Canto, this is vintage Pound, moving swiftly from the wisdom text to the contemporary application. Palmerston, a minor but admired example in the *Cantos* of the Poundian *directio voluntatis*,[59] is offered here as a model of the statesman whose *political* labor would make it new. But then what of the ideogram *chih*[3], the sign for "rest" (not action), which ends the canto? As Cookson puts it, *chih*[3] is "a place to stop and also a place to start from."[60] It is that state of rest which is achieved once the truth of nature, of Confucian *Li Ki*, has been communicated. Or as Pound will write later in the *Cantos*, with the flourish not of the calligrapher but of the Italian:

> in
> > discourse
> > > > what matters is
> to get it across e poi basta[61]

But *chih*[3] is a place to start from as well, as Lord Palmerston had done ("Begin where you are said"). *Chih*[3] is a kind of personal experience of timelessness that prepares the self to make it new in this world by giving that self a purchase outside history.

To return, then, to the final move in the Seven Lakes Canto:

> Sun up; work
> sundown; to rest
> dig well and drink of the water
> dig field; eat of the grain
> Imperial power is? and to us what is it?
>
> The fourth; the dimension of stillness.
> And the power over wild beasts.

The meaning of the crucial last line in the first stanza is, apparently, disputed among Poundians. Does this pivotal moment in the ancient "Clod-Beaters Song" register discontent with a lazy king or the harmonious relationship between a contented peasantry and its beneficent ruler?[62] The question of imperial power, though, is not so difficult to answer in the context of Pound's later work, or, indeed, in the context of the poems we have been discussing. If we ask these workers, these natural laborers, What is imperial power? their answer can only be that it is *natural*.

In fact, Pound himself had answered the question four years earlier, when he wrote in *Jefferson and/or Mussolini*, "in any case you can't GIVE power. . . . The extent to which you can even DELEGATE power is probably limited by laws as definite as those which govern the strength of current you can send through an electric wire of given thickness and texture."[63] The natural ruler, like Mussolini or like the Chinese emperors who will be exemplary in the cantos that follow, is one "to whom the power has not been GIVEN, but who has organized the power."[64] Political power too, then, is something latent and natural, as Pound's figures here more than suggest; it is part of that "way" which informs the *Li Ki*; it is of "the process of nature, *one*, in the sense that the chemist and biologist so find it."[65] The ruler stands in exactly the same relation to this latent, preexistent power as the laborer of the Seven Lakes stands in relation to natural increase and beneficence: He releases it, he contributes to the formation of it, and he channels it and gives it shape.

It should come as no surprise, then, that the end of the Seven Lakes Canto perfectly rhymes, as the Poundians like to say, with the end of Canto LII and its linkage of Confucian *chih*³ with exemplary political action. Imperial power, in its proper form, composes the "dimension of stillness"; it is informed by *chih*³ and puts the power and authority of nature into action. In the coherence that Pound has constructed of economy, labor, and the natural order, the final unifying component is – and must be – political power, because Confucian ethics is nothing for Pound if not volitionist: "Faith without works," he flatly declares in "Mang Tsze," "is a fake."[66] So imperial power is not only essential, it is, according to this ethic, inevitable. Indeed, if it is of nature, how could it be otherwise?

Pound would spend the next set of cantos showing us how such order was put into action in the arena of imperial China. But he would also spend the years leading up to the Seven Lakes Canto pointing not to China but to Italy as the home of a ruler who exemplified both the ethical teachings of nature and its volitionist imperatives: "I assert again," he wrote in 1933, "my own firm belief that the Duce will stand not with despots and the lovers of power but with the lovers of / ORDER."[67] But in Pound's scheme, after all, such order *was* power, part of the one way of nature itself, power's only source. And if Mussolini was not yet emperor, it made little difference, because something stronger than history connected Il Duce with a lineage of rulers of not divine, but natural, sanction, rulers who knew their politics because what drove that politics knew no time.

VISIONS OF CHINA, VERSIONS OF POPULISM

The kind of paradise we find in the Seven Lakes Canto may be Chinese in textual origin, but its core ingredients may be located surprisingly close to home in American populism's social critique and in the mythology of natural economy that underwrote it. As Reed Way Dasenbrock, Peter Brooker, and others have pointed out, a strong line of ideological succession links Pound with the populist strain of American social thought – its critique of abstract wealth and financial machination and its valorization of an ethically upright agrarian life – which runs from Jefferson through Jackson and Van Buren to William Jennings Bryan and finally, we should add, to Huey Long and Father Coughlin in Pound's own day.[68] And as Michael T. Gilmore has pointed out, Emerson himself, as we have already noted, shared much with central elements of Jeffersonian and Jacksonian thought at least through his writings of the early 1840s, vilifying the greedy elite of capital and the concentration of financial power (as the Populists would fifty years later) and praising (again in anticipation of the Populists) what Jefferson had called the "soil and industry" of the freeholding farmer.[69] It was a lineage, in other words, that Emerson often found congenial in theory and in ethical point (if not always in political practice). In *Jefferson and/or Mussolini* and in his economic prose of the thirties, Pound would situate himself squarely within that lineage as well, rarely endorsing wholesale any single figure or dimension of the tradition, but drawing freely and continually upon its main elements.

In Pound's career, those native origins are hard to see, in part because of the clear commitment to Italian fascism that had emerged unmistakably in his prose well before 1937, the year of *The Fifth Decad of Cantos* and the Seven Lakes Canto. But what is masked and poetically worked through a seductive natural ground in the central poem of that volume is unmasked in essays like the *ABC of Economics*, where Pound was already arguing that "the orders of an omniscient despot and of an intelligent democracy would be very much alike."[70] In hindsight, we can see how the natural totality of the Seven Lakes paradise (when taken on any level other than the strictly ideal) could lead Pound to believe that "when you have a perfect democracy it is pretty hard to tell it from a dictatorship." You did not need to be a modernist poet to know that; these words were spoken not by Pound but by Huey Long.[71]

Pound's relationship to fascism has been thoroughly examined and scrupulously documented, and I do not intend to rehearse those investigations here.[72] We can turn to a good deal of Pound's late work and find many or all of the qualities that are the modern fascist's stock-in-trade:

> The attacks on finance capitalism, the hatred of social democracy and socialism, the belief that representative democracy is a mask for rule by a predatory economic plutocracy, and that a strong executive is essential for the creation and preservation of a middle-class society composed of small independent landowners, suspicion of freedom of the press and

civil liberties generally as the shields and instrumentalities of the pluto-
cracy, ultra-nationalism, anti-Semitism (both latent and active), and,
finally, a peculiar interpretation of history which sees in events a working
out of a dialectic which opposes the financier and the producer.[73]

Pound's late politics is fascist, no doubt about it, but its roots run deep
in the more reactionary strains of old-fashioned American populism, an
influence foreshadowed in the uncanny subject of his very first poem,
written at age eleven, on William Jennings Bryan.[74] This is not the place
to undertake anything like a full assessment of the political character of
populism – that most ambivalent of movements which, like Pound's
own politics before his slide to the extreme right, seems to have combined elements from political Left and Right in explosive mixture. Nor
do I mean to imply that populism was the same at all times and places,
or that it was only a reactionary and nostalgic antimodernism (although
this was an important dimension of the movement, one we find very
much alive in Pound's later career).[75]

By way of China, and specifically Confucian doctrine, Pound reworked
and radicalized three fundamental aspects of American populism into
cornerstones of his later totalitarian project: a nostalgic agrarian utopian-
ism; a fiercely ethical concept of a human nature rooted in the larger
natural order; and a desire to sustain, rather than question, the institution of private property, which was seen as a central component of the
self's efficacy.

As for the first of these, the organicism of labor, economics, and
politics that Pound voices in Cantos XLVII, XLIX, and LII reads like a
page out of what Richard Hofstadter has called populism's "agrarian
myth."[76] Its motto, in fact, might well have been drawn from Canto
XCIX: "There is worship in plowing / and equity in the weeding hoe."[77]
Populism often envisioned a utopia in which the self and its productions
might be as one in nature, but it was a utopia not of the future but of
the past – a past, needless to say, that never was, a "lost agrarian Eden,"
as Hofstadter puts it, in which "prosperity should come naturally to
those who live in harmony with nature's rhythms and increase."[78] What
one critic has called populism's "modified primitivism" looked back
in longing to an unmediated existence at one with the "sacred, life-
renewing soil," to a lost world of "holy, ritual cyclical time, immune in
its revolutions from the corruptions of real historical time, change and
decay."[79]

But how could such a vision of the good and natural community be
maintained in the face of those very pressures of modernization, industrialization, and impending economic disenfranchisement that gave rise
to it? To put it another way, if such an order was the organic expression

of nature, then why was it not, in fact, the existing order? Populism's answer to this question, as Hofstadter points out, was to turn a problem of economics and politics – those dangerously historical forces – into a problem of ethics : "If the people failed to enjoy prosperity," Hofstadter writes, "it must be because of a harsh and arbitrary intrusion of human greed and error."[80] Or as one populist writer put it in 1892, seven years after Pound's birth:

> Hard times, then . . . being unnatural, not in accordance with, or the result of any natural law, must be attributed to that kind of unwise and pernicious legislation which history proves to have produced similar results in all ages of the world. It is the mission of the age to correct these errors in human legislation, to adopt and establish policies and systems in accord with, rather than in opposition to divine law.[81]

The purpose of social and political forms, then, was to express and perpetuate the harmony of the natural order, toward which society aspires. The failure of the social and the natural to converge pointed, however, not to any flaw in the natural order (a strict impossibility by this logic) but rather to the ethical failure of those who violated that order for their own self-serving purposes.

Thus, it is easy to see why Populists often "showed an unusually strong tendency," as Hofstadter puts it, "to account for relatively impersonal events in highly personal terms" (much as Pound would in his vituperative Rome Radio speeches against Sassoon and Rothschild, Roosevelt and Churchill).[82] The more politically savvy of the populists, as Lawrence Goodwyn argues, may have undertaken sustained structural analysis of the economic and political system,[83] but others focused obsessively on the obscene excesses of the plutocrats and the personal vices of the financiers. Instead of seeing their present crisis as the product of impersonal and irrepressible forces of history and economics, they fabricated "a world in which the simple virtues and unmitigated villainies of a rural melodrama [were] projected on a national and even international scale." "In Populist thought," Hofstadter writes, "the farmer is not a speculating businessman, victimized by the risk economy of which he is a part" – which is obviously what he was – "but rather a wounded yeoman, preyed upon by those who are alien to the life of folkish virtue."[84]

It is probably clear enough that this is a textbook example of scapegoating, which Kenneth Burke neatly diagnosed in the thirties as the mistaking of *agent* for *agency*.[85] And it is probably clear enough how such scapegoating could lead to the conspiratorial vision of history and the xenophobia and anti-Semitism that have been associated (rightly or wrongly) with populism and (accurately enough) with Pound and fascism. More interesting for my purposes, however, are the contradictions at the very core of conservative populist ideology, which persisted well into the modernist period and beyond, and which Pound attempted to resolve by radicalizing them.

Take, for instance, the extreme dissociation in Pound's thinking of the economic and the political, those impersonal forces that he would reassemble under the rubric of ethics. In a discussion of Gesell published in the midthirties, Pound maintained that "no monetary system can rise above the status of gadget if it be not in accord with some *order of thought*, with some system of moral criteria."[86] For all of his interest in Social Credit and economic programs, he was forced, like the Populists, to admit, "No economic system is worth a hoot without 'good will.'"[87] For Pound as for his fiery ideological ancestors, the integrity of historically determined social structures is ensured only insofar as those structures are underwritten by something that is itself transhistorical – namely, a certain kind of human nature. "You cannot," Pound writes, "make good economics out of bad ethics."[88] In which case, we must ask, who needs to worry about economic and monetary systems *at all* if they rise or fall by virtue of the ethical fortitude of the participants? The central contradiction running from Emerson's economy through the reactionary strain of populism and into the modernism of Pound is this: The kind of ethical awakening needed to build and maintain a just economy would seem to render structural economic changes unnecessary in the first place.

Pound's notion of just what constitutes *good* ethics – and therefore, in the end, good economics and good politics – is amply evident in his writings on Confucius and his inheritors. The importance of these texts for Pound is almost impossible to exaggerate. In fact, in 1934 T. S. Eliot posed in public the question: "What does Mr. Pound believe?" And Pound responded in *Make It New*, "I believe the *Ta Hio*,"[89] the Confucian *Great Learning*, which he translated in 1945. Years earlier, however, in 1938 (one year after the publication of the volume containing Cantos XLVII and XLIX, and virtually contemporaneous with Canto LII's version of the *Li Ki*), Pound had written the essay "Mang Tsze" on the Confucian ethics of Mencius. This important and totalizing work reveals just how close to populism Pound's China is, and yet how far he was willing to push that ideology to its necessary and devastating conclusions.

Aristotle's "Politics" and *Nicomachean Ethics* had pointed the way for Pound's critique of economics, but Aristotle could not serve as this modernist's Virgil in the all-important realm of ethics. Here, Kung was the only guide. "Say that Kung is superior to Aristotle by totalitarian instinct," Pound wrote. "His thought is never something scaled off the surface of facts. It is root volition branching out, the ethical weight is present in every phrase."[90] If Aristotle's failure was analytic segmentation, Kung's great virtue was his holism, his ability to deal with the particular "without cutting it from its base":[91]

> At no point does the Confucio-Mencian ethic or philosophy splinter and split away from organic nature. The man who pulled up his corn because it didn't grow fast enough, and then told his family he had assisted the grain, is Mencius' parable. The nature of things is good. . . . Any attempt to deal with it as split, is due to ignorance and a failure in the direction of the will.[92]

It is perhaps hard to see, because of Pound's exotic topos, that the themes of a reactionary populism, rooted in Jeffersonian agrarianism, are all here: the common cause of nature and the individual who works it, who realizes and releases its beneficent processes (illustrated in the negative by the Mencian parable); the suspicion of analytic, abstract forms of thought, which are divorced from organic truth; and the relegation of disagreement and difference – dealing with "it" as "split" – to ethical, personal "failure." But here we are forced to ask a variant of the question that asked a moment ago of Pound's "natural" economics: How is anything like "ignorance" or "failure of will" possible in the totalitarian world of Confucius? If the essence of being human, like being oak or maple, is to be of the total process, the good and one way, then what does *will* have to do with any of this? Why, in other words, is a self not simply a self, *e poi basta*?

Pound's answer – it is wholly anticipated by populist ideology – can only be that some selves are more "natural" than others. Which is another way of saying that some selves are also more historically determined than others – and the less historical, the better. The first of the Chinese poems to appear in the *Cantos* provides something like a précis of this dilemma in its meditation on Confucian order. After the Socratic question posed by Kung to open Canto XIII, his disciple asks, "Which has answered correctly?" And Kung replies, in what would seem to be good Emersonian fashion, "They have all answered correctly, / That is to say, each in his nature."[93] But how are we to bridge the gap between what would seem to be the two irreconcilable poles of Kung's teaching? After all, "each in his nature" might countenance not Confucian order but rather unbridled egoism and anarchy. It might, that is, were it not for the fact hammered home in "Mang Tsze": that "his nature" really is not "his" at all. "His nature" can only be a kind of oxymoron, since that natural order which makes the self "correct" is anything but personal. As with the Emersonian self, "his nature" can be "his" only if it is, paradoxically, *not* his, and he can have a nature only insofar as nature has him.

In "Mang Tsze" we find the same sort of contradiction reproduced in Pound's testament not about the nature of the self but this time about the nature of ethics in general. "It is OF the permanence of nature," Pound writes, "that honest men, even if endowed with no special brilliance, with no talents above those of straightness and honesty, come repeatedly to the same answers in ethics, without need of borrowing each others' ideas."[94] Here, the qualification that Pound goes out of his way to make does not solve the problem but only serves to rhetorically ballast it. The self must *already* be informed by the order of nature, must *already* be "straight" and "honest," to discover "for itself" – what can that now mean? – the principles of straightness and honesty, the principles, in other words, of ethics. Like Kung's teachings of Canto XIII, this wisdom text tells us that we can all possess different things – our "natures," our "ideas" – only by possessing the *same* thing.

At this juncture in our discussion, this formulation should sound familiar, for what else does it describe but the structure and allure of private property itself? What else is this except a repetition of the originary contradiction of Emersonian selfhood in its fiercest, most immediate form: that we can possess all these good and indeed foundational, inalienable things – our human properties, as it were – only if we ourselves are wholly given over to possession by something that makes our own selfhood possible by obliterating it? And finally, what does all of this mean except that Pound's appropriation of Confucius never managed, in the intellectual sphere, to escape the limitations of his own particular class in the economic and material sphere – that the conceptual construction that rebelled in his thought against one dimension of capitalism (namely, usury and international finance) was set loose only to be recontained and disarmed by a more powerful structural dimension (namely, private property) of that same economy?[95]

It is here, even more than in his agrarian myth, his ethics, and his scapegoating, that Pound's fundamental connection with the reactionary dimension of populism is most evident. Populism, like the fascism that grew out of its ruins in the United States, was no attack on the institution of private property. Instead, it was in no small part a middle-class movement of small farmers, landowners, and merchants who wanted to retain property and at the same time to avoid *becoming* it by becoming subject to the wage system through which one's labor was not self-reliant but rather, quite literally, owned.[96] Pound may have been many things, but he was nothing if not middle class. And it is the economic epicenter of his own class interest, private property, that may help to explain why this raging enemy of the bourgeoisie resisted attacking the central institution of capitalism throughout his career, and indeed defended it against critiques made by those of Marxist stripe. In Pound's words:

> The nature of property is radically (at the root, in the root) different from the nature of capital. . . . All such phrases as "capital in the form of" are misleading. Properly understood capital is liquid. The great division is between whatever is a lien on the other men's services, and what is either completely neutral or passive, or constitutes a potential responsibility, whereof the weight leans on the owner. . . . Property does not imply the enslavement of others.[97]

Of course, Pound's critique here has little to do with Marx, but it has everything to do with the propensity in Pound (and in American literary ideology generally) to view the efficacy of the self in terms that recapitulate the central contradictions of private property. Like the Populists in their nostalgic mode, Pound did not so much question the institution of property as *naturalize* it through what one critic has called "the myth of the peasant free-holder."[98] For both, it was simply (but finally not so simply) a matter of attacking the injustices of capitalism while at the same time salvaging the institution of property by tying it to a certain type of individual, to the land, or to immediate use: by making property, like the agrarian worker in Pound's utopia, an expression of nature itself.[99] In the world of Pound's China or of populism's agrarian myth, the right to property had to be transformed into the right to *use*. And once that transformation was secured, the problems of an economy based upon private property could be seen as only the result of ethical *misuse*. After all, if property was "neutral or passive," how could *it* be the problem?

But a *self* so conceived is bound to be radically unstable: as unstable, in fact, as the structure of private property itself. We remember the first line of the Seven Lakes Canto; "For the seven lakes, and by no man these verses," and we remember that the landscapes which follow are not scenes from an individual perspective. They are not limited by subjective vision. Pound would have us take these lines not as the individual voice but rather as something approaching the speech of nature itself – stately, still, no verbs until the third line. This vision is not the product of individual belief, opinion, or experience; there is no interpretation here, the poem says, only the authority of these lines, which transcend interpretation. "No man" could have written these verses, and consequently no man may challenge them.

What has happened, though, to that individual difference which was so crucial to Pound's early concept of culture? It has, with no hint of regret, been surrendered – not in the name of the individuality of the literary Other (as in early poems like "Histrion") but rather on behalf of that impersonal, natural authority to which all selves must now submit. In short, that self has indeed vanished and has been replaced by this ideologically specific self which *is* a self only to the extent that its own nature is in harmony with the law and order of nature as a whole. In that event, we are forced to say, Pound's term "totalitarian" may have been even more le mot juste than he himself knew.

This politically menacing distinction, between the self which is a self and the self which is not, becomes only more rigid and intense in Pound's later prose, which does not hesitate to condemn "the inferior individual," who "does not deem his own acts and thoughts in certain ways and degrees up and down as to their use to the state."[100] But it is also sustained (this time in the affirmative) in paradisal poetic moments like Canto XCIX, which one commentator has praised for its unsurpassed "beauty," "serenity," and "simplicity": [101]

> The plan is in nature
>   rooted
> Coming from earth, times [ch'ang²] respected
> Their power converging. . . .
> There is a must at the root of it
>   not one man's mere power.[102]

It may be that our commentator's assessment is correct, but the "serenity" and "simplicity" here is the repose, as we can now see, of absolute authority. This plan, like the verses of the Seven Lakes Canto, is "not a work of fiction / nor yet of one man."[103] This plan is one to which the self must surrender, the better to become a new kind of self – to become, in fact, the only kind of self worth having. For the later Pound, to be a natural man is to be "no man," which is to say "everyman," or at least every man worth the name.

IDEOLOGY AND INCOHERENCE IN THE PISAN CANTOS

There are several moments in the *Cantos*, however, in which this surrender of individual difference, this "no man," makes way not for the fullness and authority of nature but quite the reverse. After Pound was taken by the Allied forces and while he was held in "the Cage" at the Disciplinary Training Center in Pisa, awaiting (for months, as it turned out) trial for treason, he came face to face in *The Pisan Cantos* with the self his totalitarian politics had sought to repress. Scarcely half a page into Canto LXXIV, the poem beginning the sequence, this self seems to find its voice: "OY TIS, OY TIS? Odysseus / the name of my family."[104] *Oy tis* is Greek for "no man," but is this the same "no man" we have encountered in Pound's Chinese poems? And if so, why does he appear now, not in the paradise of the Seven Lakes, but in the inferno of the Cage?

We can begin to answer these questions by recognizing that Pound's glance at Homer here refers to Odysseus's confrontation with Poly-phemous and to the misnomer he used to trick the Cyclops and con-sequently to save himself from being, quite literally, devoured. The apparent meaning of Pound's allusion, then, is that the poet is attempting to unname himself in the face of his own Cyclops: that Gargantuan force called the Allies, but in another sense the force of history itself, which has destroyed the dream of fascist Italy. It is significant, though, that the Odysseus recalled in Pound's allusion is not the epic hero and warrior but rather the cagey trickster; when the Cyclops offers him a "noble gift" in exchange for knowing his name, Odysseus is well aware that the gift will be death. And so he proffers a false gift for a false gift; he gives the gift of his own unnaming in exchange for what would be the Cyclops's "gift" of death, a quite literal destruction of the self, for which Odysseus's own unnaming is a substitute (and a bargain).

But in Pound's own terms, this transaction can only be seen as a parody of exchange, exactly the kind of trading upon false representa-tion that Pound deplored. In this instance, however, the end apparently justifies the means; abolish the self in word to preserve the self in body and deed. But again this is strange, because the very core of Pound's later poetics, everywhere evident, is the inseparability of word and deed, their essential unity in "the root in justice."[105] As Canto XCIX conju-gates it:

> Precise terminology is the first implement,
> dish and container. . . .

> Let him analyze the trick programs
> and fake foundations.[106]

Not only words, then, and not only deeds: Words *are* deeds, and thus objects of ethical conduct and inquiry. Therefore, Pound's use of Odysseus in Canto LXXIV (his own "borrowing" of Homer's "no man") can only be seen as quite un-Poundian, and we are forced to interpret it not so much as a moment of wracking dispossession but rather as a rhetorical maneuver of cunning and cynicism. A lie is not a lie, this trickster seems to say, when it is told to those who know no truth, those whose ill will calls for a quite different kind of verbal economy and exchange – one as reprehensible for Pound as it is, in this case, useful.

One page later in the same canto, the Homeric "no man" surfaces again, this time set against the aboriginal legend of Wanjina, "whose mouth was removed by his father / because he made too many things."[107]

Wanjina, given the power to create things by speech alone, stands, in a way, as the antithesis of the Odyssean trickster. Where Odysseus/OY TIS abused the word by separating it from its object and referent, Wanjina abused their essential unity. But both – and this against Pound's apparent intention – were guilty of forgetting what was for the later Pound the central principle of verbal conduct: "sinceritas / of the word, comprehensive."[108] Thus, we are faced with two possibilities, neither of which can be reconciled with Pound's own teachings: Either his own Confucian sincerity has been abandoned, or it is now held in abeyance. In either case, Pound indulges in what he himself had condemned time and again as ethical heresy. We can only conclude that the true self, the self possessed by nature and order, has gone underground but is somehow still maintained behind the false self, behind the "no man" that Pound offers to his own Cyclops in its stead.

As *The Pisan Cantos* progress, however – and as Pound's personal ordeal in the Cage turns from weeks to months – this "no man" takes a different turn. Later in Canto LXXIV, flanked by the massive ideogram for "not" and "no," he is now "a man on whom the sun has gone down," a very different Homeric epithet indeed, one whose tone has nothing of the trickster about it. And later on the same page, as if to repeat a judgment, a sentence:

> OY TIS
> a man on whom the sun has gone down
> nor shall diamond die in the avalanche
>   be it torn from its setting
> first must destroy himself ere others destroy him.[109]

The mixture of pathos and will in this passage is entirely characteristic of this sequence and is the source, for many readers, of its appeal. It is a moment, we must feel, close to the center of this work's emotional torque. What has been lost – or all but lost – is a self, which, it is now realized, has been destroyed by its own hand. These lines, then, seem to present nothing less than a moment of tragic awareness in its high classical form, a registration of the destructive power of extraordinary but flawed character that too late realizes its flaw.

But we need to notice too that a strong countercurrent runs against the mounting tide of tragic desperation: "nor shall diamond die" in this avalanche of circumstance and consciousness, even though it is "torn from its setting." That truth, which Pound feels he has realized, will survive the poet who has provided it with a voice. But this means, of course, that the *most* central self, the self that hid behind the OY TIS of the earliest lines, really is not a self at all; it is, in fact, other than the self – that is why it will survive. And insofar as that self, its vision and its truth, are embodied by Mussolini and his Italy, it is perfectly correct to argue, as Peter Nicholls has, that Pound here does not reject, but rather intensifies, his ideological commitment to fascism.[110] Indeed, the lines that follow bear this out: "dell'Italia tradita / now in the mind indestructible."

"OY TIS," Pound repeats once more in Canto LXXX: "now there are no more days."[111] A piece of Greek follows, meaning "without time." This too, it seems, is a world without history, but one that Pound now experiences from the vantage not of the possessor but rather of the possessed, the prisoner of an ideology and its very real consequences. If the past, "temporis acti," is barely present – "God knows what else is left of our London / my London, your London"[112] – the future seems even less certain. Pound has at last achieved his world without history, but only at the heaviest price, not in Paradiso, but only in Inferno.

In this sequence of poems, Peter Brooker has argued that

> a real history, of the second world war and of the fall of fascism, overtakes and itself shapes the poem, constructing in the *Pisan Cantos* a second personal hell which significantly throws the projected Dantesque scheme of the poem out of line. . . . The *Cantos* as a whole in this respect we can then read as not only exploiting history, but as participating in a historical consciousness specific to a class and ideology whose rise and defeat is mapped in the twists and cancellations of the poem.[113]

Brooker's point is well taken, but I would argue that Pound's personal trials, regrets, and confessions, which may be found throughout the sequence, are not, finally, the surest signs by which we may read this crisis of self and ideology. Peter Nicholls's reading of *The Pisan Cantos* and the sequences that follow, in arguing that these poems constitute not a rejection of Mussolini's fascism but quite the reverse, would instead keep the self and its ideology separate.[114] If in fact Pound's commitment to fascism has not wavered, then we must ask along with Nicholls:

> How . . . does this square with the new "humility" and "compassion" for which the sequence has been praised so often? There are, to be sure, moments of contrition. . . . The context of such remarks makes it clear, however, that he is lamenting the errors of his personal life, not his intellectual life.[115]

Indeed, if Mussolini's order is rooted in nature itself – is "of the process," as Pound puts it, part of the one "way" – then how could it be otherwise? Pound himself may have erred, as he confesses many times in these poems, but that is very different from saying that the truth embodied in Mussolini's fascism is open to question.[116]

Where, then, can we locate in *The Pisan Cantos* that crisis of *both* the self and its ideology which this sequence surely records? It is revealed, I think, not so much in Pound's writing of his own personal crisis, and not in any statements made for or against Mussolini's regime, but in the breakdown of Pound's *reading* of the natural order. It is this dysfunction, I would argue, that stages in a particularly compressed and powerful way the profoundly ideological character of Pound's poem. At many points in *The Pisan Cantos*, we come upon a kind of nature that is startlingly different from the one that, in the middle and later Pound, always seems to carry a Confucian truth on its back. Consider, for instance, these lines: "And now the ants seem to stagger/ as the dawn sun has trapped their shadows."[117] How completely *other* such moments seem when nature is freed, if only for a moment, from ideological work. Or again:

> When the mind swings by a grass-blade
>   an ant's forefoot shall save you
> the clover leaf smells and tastes as its flower.[118]

At such fissures in the poem's surface, that great Book of Nature, which had performed for Pound so much ethical and political service, is no longer immediately illustrative of Confucian or fascist order, which had so relentlessly predisposed its interpretation. And the poet now looks to the natural world not for the ideological truth to which it is transparent but rather for its absolute otherness, its density of minutiae and nearly opaque difference – all of which is somehow a source of sanity and comfort, an external refuge from "the mind as Ixion, unstill, ever turning."[119]

To understand the full import of these gaps, failures, and dysfunctions, we need to remember that nature is not just any category but rather (as we know from Marx as well as from contemporary feminist criticism) the ideological category par excellence. To turn culture into nature and history into eternity is the be-all and end-all of ideology's political work. From this perspective, Pound's failure to read nature as he had read it for the decades preceding *The Pisan Cantos* is, in fact, an absolutely central and symptomatic one. When Pound's nature can no longer be deciphered, can no longer serve as immediate ideological evidence, then the ideology that once held it captive is suddenly, almost stunningly in these poems, revealed *as* ideology, its crisis enacted not by what the poet says but by what he *cannot* say.[120] This is not the truth of the confessional, we might say, but rather the truth of the epistemological. Like the broken tool of Heidegger's *Being and Time*, this epistemological and ideological machinery reveals its historicity, its real character as a product of human hands and historical purposes, in its failure.[121]

But this failure, it seems to me, is a kind of illuminating success, because it reveals the ideology of Pound's project as no mere personal confession could reveal it. It is not that the self has failed; it is that what made a certain kind of self possible has ceased to function and has exposed – movingly, from a place beyond ego and often beyond sanity – its interpretive poverty. It is no coincidence, then, that Pound's own personal crisis accompanies the breakdown of his ideology and organicism. As Paul de Man has pointed out, one of the central dynamics of organicism, in its reaction against modernity, is the tendency "for the self to borrow, so to speak, the temporal stability that it lacks from nature, and to devise strategies by means of which nature is brought down to a human level while still escaping from 'the unimaginable touch of time.'"[122]

Is Pound indulging in precisely this sort of "borrowing" when he writes: "When the mind swings by a grass-blade / an ant's forefoot shall save you"? Our answer to that question – it must also be our answer to de Man – is that all organicisms are not equal, nor are they put to the same uses. Pound borrows his stability in these lines not from nature writ large and teleological – this is not Wordsworth's "holy plan" stretched on the loom of time – but from "an ant's forefoot" and "Brother Wasp."[123] And what rescues his sanity in these moments is not the perceived unity of ideological subject and natural object in some overarching coherence (again Wordsworthian) but rather the otherness and difference which his later project had repressed under the sign of nature, and which now returns as that very thing, full of its own mystery, which Pound himself, broken and dispossessed, must borrow. Pound's new book of nature is incomplete, unfinishable; it provides no grand ideological narrative, no moral telos, but only microscapes in which each moment seems as pregnant with radical change as the volatile movements of a grass blade, as packed with difference as the many modes of life in an inch of turf. Here, at last, is a world in which *la rivoluzione continua* is not only possible but indeed imminent. Here, Pound's ideological odyssey is on the brink of chaos and inferno, but it is also on the verge of discovery.

PART III

7

Signs That Bind: Ideology and Form in Pound's Poetics

The young Ezra Pound may have seen his Emersonian respect for "the peripheries of the individual" culturally codified in Henry James – may have seen in James, that is, what James himself traced to Emerson. But Henry James was not the only go-between who enabled the literary ideology of Emerson to flourish (unbeknownst to the inheritor) in our modernist, who could not recognize his precursor's cultural politics, so much his own, through the persistent mist of transcendentalism. This other agent of ideological transmission, Ernest Fenollosa (like Emerson, a native son of Boston and its environs), would have surely fancied himself as much the opposite of his contemporary Henry James as Pound thought himself (when he thought about it at all) the antithesis of Emerson. But those differences only underscore how powerful, seductive, and flexible this ideological structure is. It can accommodate the discursions of James – "weaving an endless sentence" as Pound remembered him in Canto VII[1] – and the Chinese compression of Fenollosa alongside the modernism of Pound and the romanticism of Emerson. For reasons of temperament and training, Pound would not have taken his ideogrammic poetics from Emerson himself. But take it he did, not from the source but from the sinologist who taught Emerson in Japan when he began to explore the world of the ideogram.[2]

Throughout 1913, five years after her husband's death, Mary Fenollosa – herself a novelist of some note (a.k.a. "Sidney McCall") and an anthologized poet as well – kept watch for someone who might edit her late husband's notes on Chinese poetry and Noh drama. When she saw twelve poems in the "Contemporania" section of *Poetry* for April 1913, in what was rapidly becoming known as the Imagist mode, she became convinced that the author of "In a Station of the Metro" was just the person for the job.[3] As it turned out, Mary Fenollosa's own eye for correspondences (in this case, between Ernest's Chinese and Pound's

Imagism) would indirectly affect the entire course of modern poetry in English.

At the end of 1913, Pound was serving for three months as Yeats's "secretary," and his attention to the Fenollosa notes significantly influenced Yeats's concept of poetic drama and helped to push Yeats's poetry away from what seemed to Pound the misty aesthetic of an earlier era and toward the more spartan diction and syntax of the poems for which Yeats is famous. Pound's work with the Fenollosa notes, to put it bluntly, helped transform Yeats (as it had helped transform Pound himself) from a romantic into a modernist.[4] As for Pound's own course, the Imagist project was already under way and had taken critical shape early in the year in "A Few Don'ts by an Imagiste" in *Poetry* for March 1913. But Fenollosa's work would quickly broaden that technical base and manifesto by providing a whole epistemology and sign theory to underwrite it – a totalizing vision that Pound would not fully develop until a decade and a half later. Pound found in Fenollosa, he would later recall, "the fundamentals of all aesthetics," and he had been saying so in letters since shortly after his receipt of the Fenollosa papers.[5] As James Longenbach has pointed out, Fenollosa's work helped Pound "to see Imagism as a trans-historical tendency in poetry rather than an exclusively 'modern' technique."[6]

In this respect, Pound's investigation of Fenollosa must be read within the larger context of a sweeping reassessment of language and value then well under way on both sides of the Atlantic. For the sake of brevity, we will examine only one inaugural moment in this rich and complex movement, but it is one that throws into relief the fiercely holistic character of Pound's own appropriation of Fenollosa's notes.[7] Gottlob Frege's publication of the essay "On Sense and Reference" in 1892 marks a pivotal turn in the development of modernist thinking. It is a clear precursor, as Franco Moretti has pointed out, to what T. S. Eliot would later famously call the "dissociation of sensibility" – a modernist shibboleth if ever there was one.[8] Frege's critique announced nothing less than a fundamental epistemological crisis, one created by his discovery of an unbridgeable gap between what he called "sense" and "reference" – a discovery to be pushed, roughly twenty years later, to its modernist end and postmodernist beginnings in Saussure's "diacritical" theory of language, in which, as he wrote, "there are only differences *without positive terms.*"[9] Frege's central point was that the relationship between the reference (the object to which the sign refers) and the sense (what Frege called its linguistic "mode of presentation") was arbitrary and unmotivated. The two were unmendably separate and distinct; they constituted, really, different kinds of reality, replete with their own discrete categories and problems. In Frege's famous example, "the reference of 'evening star' would be the same as that of 'morning star,' but not the sense."[10] On the one hand, then, the word; and on the other, the thing. And never again, so the story of modernism goes, shall the twain meet.

But as Moretti reminds us, there is more to Frege's argument than this polar distinction, so chilling to those who aspired to associated sensibility. Frege was also at pains to distinguish a third term in this configuration, namely, the realm of subjective "idea," or value. Reference, the world of things, was now sundered from language, sense was fundamentally constructivist and institutional, and idea – that set of charged personal associations, values, and motives which coalesce around the word – was set wholly adrift, motivated by neither reality nor language. As Frege put it, "The same sense is not always connected, even in the same man, with the same idea. . . . [O]ne need have no scruples in speaking simply of *the* sense, whereas in the case of an idea one must, strictly speaking, add to whom it belongs and to what time."[11] As Moretti points out, the prototypically modernist consequences of Frege's critique are not far to seek. The relationship between these terms is now, Moretti writes, "no longer *sufficiently tight and univocal*, and can no longer assure any cultural cohesion and continuity."[12]

This loss of coherence is precisely what Eliot and Pound would attempt to remedy in their cultural projects of the thirties. That much would become clear in writings like Pound's "Mang Tsze," his economic prose, and *The Fifth Decad of Cantos*, and in Eliot's essays on Christianity and culture and the poetry of *Four Quartets*. Far from promoting the fragmentation and disintegration characteristic of an early "rebellious" phase of modernism (which critics often associate with modernism *tout court*), these works are fundamental consolidations of a later, "mature" (some would say too mature) phase of the modernist movement, in which we find, in the words of critic James McFarlane, "not so much that things fall *apart* but that they fall *together*" in an ambitious cultural project whose mode is not disintegration but "superintegration."[13] From this vantage, Frege's essay may be seen for our purposes to announce the onset of the modernist era, which will develop different responses over time to an initial condition in which, as Moretti characterizes it, "conceptual coherence, while considered valid in its sphere and with respect to its aims . . . can no longer *produce values*: promote an attitude toward the world, *within* the world." For the modernist, Moretti continues, "this world may well have a meaning, but not meaning *for us*."[14] As Moretti points out, Eliot's "objective correlative" and "mythical method" will attempt to suture the gap that Frege had opened with cold, surgical rigor. But the most radical response of all to this fundamental rending apart of language, reality, and value may be found not in Eliot but in

Pound's appropriation of the ideogrammic method from Fenollosa and, indirectly, from Emerson.

As several Pound critics have noted, Pound's conception of the ideogrammic method and its centrality to his poetic project changed during the course of his career. Ronald Bush, for example, has argued against seeing it as the compositional basis for the *Cantos*, and Herbert Schneidau asks us to distinguish sharply between the ideogrammic method as it is defined in the thirties by Pound and his appropriation of the ideogram proper as it is set forth in the Fenollosa essay that occupied much of Pound's attention from the end of 1913, when he received the Fenollosa drafts, until 1919, when he had the essay published in the *Little Review*.[15] Reed Way Dasenbrock argues that the ideogrammic method should not be invoked to describe the poems of *Cathay* or the early cantos, because it really "originates in a dramatic shift in Pound's thinking that takes place around 1930," when Pound became more and more interested in the capacity of the poetic sign to communicate "general statement" and "abstract law" in a way never intended in poems like "In a Station of the Metro" or "The River-Merchant's Wife: A Letter."[16] Likewise, we can amplify Bush's assertion – that after 1920 Pound recognized the incapacity of Fenollosa's syntax to represent complex and layered subjectivity – by noting that in the 1930s Pound was, for ideological reasons, no longer very *interested* in representing complex subjectivity, as he had been in *Mauberley*.[17] It is important to understand, in other words, that Pound's promulgation of the ideogrammic method as a poetics of general truth, moral law, and natural order takes place in unison with his increasingly programmatic totalitarian ambitions on all fronts – aesthetic, economic, and political. As we shall see, however, the totalizing version of the ideogrammic method that Pound gives us in the 1930s is not so much a revision of Fenollosa as it is a fearsome pursuit of the logical conclusions that Fenollosa's concept of the sign invites.

Early on, the stay against symbolism and impressionism that Pound had been struggling to formulate in the early teens, under the influence of Ford and Hulme, suddenly seemed to find an enabling ground in Fenollosa's small essay "The Chinese Written Character as a Medium for Poetry." In basing language and poetics on a whole mode of knowing and being, Fenollosa provided a purchase for a new poetics outside the literary institutions and practices that, in Pound's early assessment, had been turned not toward readerly liberation but toward reproduction and profit. We can read what Pound saw early on as the intended political thrust of the ideogrammic method in Fenollosa's diagnosis of Western modernity's mode of *linguistic* production. "Languages to-day are thin and cold," Fenollosa writes, because we think less and less into them. We are forced, for the sake of quickness and sharpness, to file down each word to its narrowest edge of meaning. Nature would seem to have become less like a paradise and more and more like a factory.[18]

If we believe Fenollosa, the Taylorization of literary production that Pound had identified in his earliest prose had invaded the very *prima materia* of literature. Consequently, the nature made accessible by language was becoming less and less available as anything other than an expression of the dominant economic context and its logic.

For Pound and Fenollosa, the problem was clear and the solution foundational. By locating first principles in nature, we might measure the fitness of linguistic representation by examining its capacity to express and adhere to those principles. "The Chinese Written Character," in other words, attempts to establish the primacy of the ideogram by confirming its natural, not social, ground: "Chinese notation is something much more than arbitrary symbols. It is based upon a vivid shorthand picture of the operations of nature. In the algebraic and in the spoken word there is no natural connection between thing and sign: all depends upon sheer convention."[19] The essay on "Vorticism" had already offered a similar critique of abstract diction – "IT MAKES NO PICTURE"[20] – but Fenollosa's essay extends the point by positing a natural basis for this newly revived *pictura loquens*: "In reading Chinese we do not seem to be juggling mental counters, but to be watching *things* work out their own fate."[21] For Fenollosa and Pound, the issue is not to make good or bad use of language's arbitrariness; the problem is rather this arbitrariness itself.

Statements such as these would no doubt prove polemically effective against the symbolists and all followers of abstract convention. But then as much could be said of Frege's critique as well, which, in prising apart word and thing – and the value thought to reside in their radiant combination – would also attack the imprecision of the symbolist aesthetic. Frege would dismantle the assumption that symbol and symbolized are, as Paul de Man puts it, different not in their being but only in their extension.[22] Pound, however, would argue exactly the reverse in attacking not the naturalist assumptions of symbolism but rather the abstract convention that made the symbol *seem* natural. For Pound, the Fregean disjunction was not the solution but the very problem. Moreover, as Fenollosa's nature-factory suggests, that disjunction was for Pound bound up with the social and economic structure of capitalism, which would cast all meaning in its own image.

From Pound's early and alienated point of view, it made perfect sense that linguistic authenticity must be located outside that social structure which Frege had made the only proper domain of language. Language and the meaning it imparts cannot be *only* social, Pound seems to say, because if that is the case, then how can we gain any leverage on the current abstract and rhetorical state of affairs? If meaning is purely social, then how can we avoid granting that the dominant language is the *right* one? Fenollosa's work would provide an answer to those questions, but only by cutting squarely against the grain of modern sign theory. Unlike Frege's "sense" or Saussure's signifier, the ideogram "*means* the thing or the action or situation" to which it gives form.[23] It means, in other words, exactly that world of "reference" which Frege had put in a bottle and banished to extralinguistic sea. It is not only other than social; it is *more* than social.

This is precisely the point of Fenollosa's critique of grammatical categories. "A true noun, an isolated thing," he writes, "does not exist in nature."[24] For Fenollosa, the absence of discrete parts of speech in the ideogram makes it not only more complex but also – a very different claim indeed – more *accurate*. The intransitive Chinese sentence, we learn, corresponds to the "universal form of action in nature";[25] its order "would be no sufficient indication, were it not the *natural order*."[26] The ideogram, in other words, is motivated by what it represents – that is the source of its power and its fidelity. Whatever meaning language generates on its own by means of linguistic or grammatical convention is, strictly speaking, a mystification: certainly wrong, maybe dangerous.

The theory of the ideogram, then, runs counter not only to the seminal investigations of Frege and Saussure but also – closer to home and virtually contemporaneous – to the semiotics of Charles Sanders Peirce. From the vantage of Peirce's sign theory, the ideogrammic model would transform all language into *icon* and *index*: icon if the sign represents objects; index if it represents actions.[27] But for Peirce, of course, linguistic signs are neither; they are unmotivated, arbitrary *symbols* that depend solely upon social convention and linguistic code. For Pound, however, the ideogram is more accurate and powerful precisely because it is *not* symbolic in Peirce's terms. In the *ABC of Reading* Pound tells us that the ideogram's fidelity is a product of its iconicity: "The Chinese still use abbreviated pictures AS pictures"; the ideogram "is still the picture of a thing."[28] From the perspective of ideogrammic method, then, the cardinal sin of semiosis is that it is *under*determined; it creates "meaning" where there is none.

This can only sound quite familiar to the student of Pound's economics.[29] Pound's critique of usury and the "unnatural" increase of abstract wealth is based upon precisely the same logic, and his conception of the relationship between exchange value and use value is nothing if not a relation of *icon* and *index*: iconic insofar as the order of coin corresponds to the order of goods, and indexical insofar as currency should decay and devalue in the same manner as concrete things. If stamp scrip would promote a kind of money made nature, Pound's ideogram would return us to a language made nature. But like the "permanent goods" of Pound's economy in "The State," the genius of the ideogram is that it does not decay. As if to underscore for us the homology between his economics and his poetics, Pound wrote in the *ABC of Reading*: "Any general statement is like a cheque drawn on a bank. Its value depends on what is there to meet it. . . . An abstract or general statement is GOOD if it be ultimately found to correspond with the facts."[30] The economic abstraction that had turned nature into a factory had issued, however, a load of bad rhetorical checks. Language, like capitalist exchange, had become self-referring; from Pound's point of view, a kind of linguistic usury was not only possible but indeed under way – hence the restorative force of Fenollosa's contribution for Pound's ideogrammic method of the 1930s.

A hundred years before, in the "Language" section of *Nature*, Emerson had made the same point, in almost exactly the same terms: "The corruption of man is followed by the corruption of language, new imagery ceases to be created, and old words are perverted to stand for things which are not; a paper currency is employed, when there is no bullion in the vaults."[31] Emerson's solution to this problem, like his diagnosis, could not be more similar to Pound's.[32] "But wise men," Emerson continued, "pierce this rotten diction and fasten words again to visible things";[33] they realize, in other words, what Emerson will call the "immediate dependence of language upon nature."[34] Thus, Emerson's *Nature* will announce, before the ideogrammic fact, "Words are signs of natural facts. . . . Every word which is used to express a moral or intellectual fact" – those types of words we would think least likely to stand in iconic or indexical relation to their referents – "if traced to its root, is found to be borrowed from some material appearance." And then Emerson gives us his famous etymological list: "*Right* means *straight*, *wrong* means *twisted*. . . ."[35] For Emerson, all language operates this way, constantly building upon nature by means of metaphor.

Like Pound in his own critique of artificial linguistic currency, Emerson is quick to remind us that our poetic language should always keep the original correspondence of words and things in view, lest our language become thin with convention, as insubstantial as paper. To make language new, we must, in a sense, make it old: "As we go back in history," Emerson writes, "language becomes more picturesque, until its infancy, when it is all poetry. . . . The same symbols are found to make the original elements of all languages."[36] If this passage seems to point toward the Chinese ideogram as the very paradigm of vital, poetic language, Emerson's essay "The Poet" signals our arrival: "The etymologist finds the deadest word to have been once a brilliant picture. Language is fossil poetry."[37]

"The Chinese Written Character" will proffer, as if in echo, exactly the same thesis:

> The whole delicate substance of speech is built upon substrata of metaphor. Abstract terms, pressed by etymology, reveal their ancient roots still imbedded in direct action. But the primitive metaphors do not spring from arbitrary subjective processes. They are possible only because they follow objective lines of relation in nature herself.[38]

It is true that, unlike Emerson, Pound and Fenollosa focus here not on objects but on actions; but object and action, by this logic, are simply two faces of the same coin, of the "bullion" of fact that nature pays. "Nature furnishes her own clues," Fenollosa writes,[39] and Emerson answers, "Nature does all things by her own hands."[40] Now Pound and Fenollosa: "The forces which produce the branch-angles of an oak lay potent in the acorn."[41] And now Emerson, in extension: "Expression or naming is not art, but a second nature, grown out of the first, as a leaf out of a tree."[42]

It would be a mistake, however, to understand from these essays that what this antimodern theory of the sign wants is some sort of one-to-one picture language, a simple matching affair of word and thing. Emerson's point is not that poetic expression of immaterial truths is forbidden because they correspond to no known object but rather that the expression of such truth depends upon signs still grounded in their natural referents but combined in new ways. Now we are ready for the next moment in Emerson's dialectic: "It is not words only that are emblematic," he writes; "it is things which are emblematic. Every natural fact is a symbol of some spiritual fact."[43] Nature itself, in other words, expresses more than the visible material items of which it is manifestly composed; it is already, in a sense, a language. Properly understood, language is not only the speech of the self or only of natural things. Rather, what really speaks in authentic language is what binds all of these together: what Emerson calls, variously, Spirit, Reason, or Oversoul. So it is that "Fact is the end or last issue of spirit. The visible creation is the terminus or the circumference of the invisible world. . . . That which was unconscious truth, becomes, when interpreted and defined in an object, a part of the domain of knowledge, – a new weapon in the magazine of power."[44]

Far from shying away from Emerson's journey into the invisible world of spirit and the power it imparts, Pound and Fenollosa are more than willing to follow. In a passage from "The Chinese Written Character" that seems straight out of Emerson right down to its phrasing, we find that "the greater part of natural truth is hidden in processes too minute for vision and in harmonies too large, in vibrations, cohesions, and in affinities."[45] These too will be handled in Emersonian fashion, as Pound and Fenollosa trace the unfolding relationship between the realms of the unseen and the seen. In a virtual replay of Emerson's famous assertion that "the near explains the far,"[46] Fenollosa writes, "The known interprets the obscure."[47] And in what reads like a précis of the Emersonian dialectic of subject and object, mind and nature, value and meaning, Pound and Fenollosa put their metaphoric cards on the table:

> Had the world not been full of homologies, sympathies, and identities, thought would have been starved and language chained to the obvious. There would have been no bridge whereby to cross from the minor truth of the seen to the major truth of the unseen.[48]

For Pound, of course, "the unseen" is not Emerson's Spirit or Oversoul – but it might as well be, because it is equally unassailable. Pound has in mind not the truth of Spirit but the truth of science, of cause and effect. By the time of the *ABC of Reading*, he will argue, in fact, that the ideogrammic method is "the method of science," the "applicability of scientific method to literary criticism."[49] The critic, taking his cue from Fenollosa, must engage in a "careful first-hand examination of the matter, and continual COMPARISON of one 'slide' or specimen with another."[50] But why would one want to do such a thing? For the same reason, presumably, that a biologist (or an Emersonian) would: to find out, through inductive method, what all those slides tell you about the general law or "universal form" expressed by each item. "All truth," we now find,

> has to be expressed in sentences because all truth is the *transference of power*. . . . No unit of natural process can be less than this. All natural processes are, in their units, as much as this. Light, heat, gravity, chemical affinity, human will have this in common, that they redistribute force.[51]

As in Emerson, knowledge of the concrete, of "fact," is power, because it is knowledge of more than just the concrete. To come into proper contact with the visible is to enter the circuit of the invisible, wherein power lies.

What does this mean, then, for the place and priority of the individual subject, which was so central to Pound's early work? "The Chinese Written Character" had complained, more than once, that it was folly to think that in language, "*we* do it all; it is a little private juggling between our right and left hands."[52] But what, we might understandably ask, is so egregious about that? Pound and Fenollosa are quick to answer: "The sentence according to this definition is not an attribute of nature but an accident of man as a conversational animal."[53] Fine, but why should we want the sentence (and indeed all linguistic forms) to be an "attribute of nature" and not an accident or invention of the human and social domain alone? Because "if it were really so," Pound and Fenollosa continue, "then there could be no possible test of the truth of a sentence. Falsehood would be as specious as verity. Speech would carry no conviction."[54]

And this, I think, is a crucial moment in the essay, because we are suddenly forced to confront these linguistic issues as fully ethical ones as well. What Frege called "idea" is now brought back into the fold of verbal conduct, because we can now measure personal motives like "conviction" and "sincerity" against something other than the purely personal – namely, against the natural law inhering in both things and words. For Pound and Fenollosa, the meaning of the concrete world *can*, it seems, be at one with the self's own values and subjective idea. But it can do so, it turns out, only if we have *already* achieved a certain kind of selfhood, only if we already possess the conviction and sincerity that language expresses: "Even if the general statement of an ignorant man is 'true,'" Pound writes in the *ABC of Reading*, "it leaves his mouth or pen without any great validity. He doesn't KNOW what he is saying."[55] The truth of a statement, in other words, depends not only on its correspondence with a set of rules and facts but mainly on the self's capacity to internalize something other than purely social or linguistic laws. You can be *right* without knowing it, we might say, but you cannot *be* right without knowing it. Verbal conduct, as Pound puts it, is not only an issue of "good guesses," "intuitions," and "logic." It is finally a matter of "the transmittability of a conviction,"[56] which has personal force because its validity is anything but personal.

What Pound and Fenollosa want is what Emerson himself had wanted: a language in which *we* do not speak, but nature does. Almost a hundred years earlier, Emerson declared that

> poetry was all written before time was, and whenever we are so finely organized that we can penetrate into that region where the air is music, we hear those primal warblings and attempt to write them down, but we lose ever and anon a word or a verse and substitute something of our own, and thus miswrite the poem.[57]

For Emerson, poets are "representative men" because, in a way, they are not men; poets should not add anything of their own to the poem that is *already* there, awaiting their transcription.[58] Poets are representative selves because they are not what we think of as selves at all – unless, of course, we think of the self as a living analogue of property. In Emerson's view, we can possess the poetic property in the horizon only if we live the truth of "Universal Soul," only if we first realize that "we are its property."[59] And once our identity is given over in transaction to that larger coherence, then our values and convictions, our words and deeds, gain an authority that is more than purely personal. Then – and only then – can we say that "the universe is the property of every individual in it."[60] Then and only then can individuals repossess the world in their own image,[61] as an expression of that self-possession which, paradoxically, they owe not to themselves but to nature. For Emerson, the self can possess its signifying properties – can make all of nature, including the nature inherent in words, its own – only by surrendering the self that might possess such natural signs in the first place.

Pound liked to recount Gaudier-Brzeska's ability to sight-read ideograms without any formal training: "You can *see* it's a horse," the young sculptor noted matter-of-factly.[62] But suppose you couldn't? Suppose you couldn't (and you can't) decipher those signs "based on something everyone KNOWS"?[63] To that reader, Pound would respond in "Mang Tsze" that "the qualities of these signs are basic and no one who does not perceive them can read ideogram save as an ape."[64] That sort of reader did not possess selfhood and its proper language, because the natural truth possessing the sign had not yet possessed that reader. In 1917, Pound had accused the modern educational factory and its abstraction of turning the self into an "ant" or a "gelding" by ignoring the individual's own value and difference. But in setting about his remedy, Pound engaged in the same sort of objectification and deformation, only this time in the name of nature, not capitalism. "We" could be at home in the world, at home in words, because "we" did not include apes and other misreaders. Language could be second nature because its potential misreaders had been banished from the first nature to ethical and therefore linguistic exile.

DIDACTICISM AND THE LOGIC OF THE IDEOGRAM

Early in his career, Pound seemed to see in the ideogram a means of bringing diverse, concrete objects and actions into a single orbit, a way of juxtaposing heterogeneous elements, the better to generate the spark of lyric immediacy through their friction. In contrast to the packaged sentiments and figures of the genteels – still the dominant (if doomed) force on the American publishing scene when Pound discovered Fenollosa – the ideogram promised to redeem poetic language by bringing it back to the dynamic world of things, by focusing and limiting it, so that *this* poem, *this* assemblage of particulars, would not be mistaken for the generic cultural products that stultified the readers and writers Pound wanted to liberate. The ideogram's power and compression were achieved not in spite of the fact that it was specific and limited but *because* it was so.[65]

This dimension of the ideogram was given prominent place in the essay "Vorticism," nine months after Pound had come into possession of the Fenollosa notes.[66] Commenting there on "In a Station of the Metro" Pound emphasized that his "*hokku*" (a tip of the hat to Fenollosa) was anything but all things to all people at all times: "I dare say [the poem] is meaningless unless one has drifted into a certain vein of thought. In a poem of this sort one is trying to record the precise instant when a thing outward and subjective transforms itself, or darts into a thing inward and subjective."[67] And when he moved to extrapolate the subject/object distinction here to aesthetics in general (as, schematically, romanticism versus realism), it was in hopes of making room for "two opposed ways of thinking": "One does not claim that one way is better than the other, one notes a diversity of the temperament."[68] This most generous of the essay's moments tells us that individual difference, the self in situation, is not an untidy fact to be mastered and resolved. Quite the reverse, it is an aesthetic reality bearing directly upon literary judgment, doctrine, and practice.

But the sort of heterogeneity and unexpectedness of meaning that the ideogram promised to make possible became in time not the liberating aim of Pound's poetics but its archnemesis. The ideogram's greatest attraction for Pound – its promise to go beyond the negative critique, the "don'ts," of Imagism by rejoining word and self with natural totality – turned out to be its greatest danger. To the individualist and pragmatist poetics of contingency in Imagism and Vorticism, the ideogrammic method wedded a totality of objective and natural law by which the value of moments, poems, and selves might be evaluated not only as different, with different social contexts and aesthetic aims, but as *better*, across *all* contexts and temperaments. And to that crucial closure in the name of natural law, the teachings of Confucius added the imperatives of volitionism: the necessary enforcement of that totality through ethically proper deeds (and words that are deeds).

What Pound's career shows us is that when you combine antinomianism (fully there in Emerson), the belief in a timeless natural law that should inform social and cultural practices (also in Emerson), and the volitionist enforcement of that law (definitely *not* in Emerson), you have the makings of a latent, if not active, authoritarian fascism. You have, in other words, *a* self which can claim that its truth is anything but personal, grounded as it is not in history (the Stalinist variant) but in nature – the better to enforce *its* truth as *the* truth for *all* selves.

By the 1930s, Pound will equate early watchwords of his poetic like "clarity" and "precision" not with provisionality and contingency but with the Confucian imperative of the rectification of names and with the limitation of any possible interpretive variance.[69] "It is a time for a clear definition of terms," he writes in "National Culture." "Immediately, of economic terms, but ultimately of all terms. It is not a revolution of the word but a castigation of the word."[70] The logic of the ideogram did not determine this conclusion, but it certainly invited it. After all, how can anything like a "revolution of the word" be possible when the essence of right language is to stand in transparent relation to an unchanging nature? By the time of "A Visiting Card" (1942), Pound's devotion to an authoritarian poetics devoid of discord and difference will be almost religious in its unquestioning faith and fervor. In what has to be one of the more chilling passages in the whole of his prose, Pound writes:

> In the beginning was the word, and the word has been betrayed. . . . We find two forces in history: one that divides and shatters and kills, and one that contemplates the unity of the mystery.
>
> "The arrow hath not two points."
>
> There is the force that falsifies, the force that destroys every clearly delineated symbol, dragging man into a maze of abstract arguments, destroying not one but every religion.[71]

And should we have any doubts about the politics authorizing this maniacal will toward clarity, Pound will neatly dispose of them, as if with relish: "We think," he admonishes, "because we do not know."[72]

In a way, the totalitarianism of Pound's Confucian philosophy and the fascism that came to be its privileged political expression were latent in the logic of the ideogram all along. Kenneth Burke's analysis of didacticism in *Attitudes toward History* (itself forged against the rising tide of fascism in the thirties) is helpful here, because it sheds considerable light on the dangers of using aesthetic forms as models for social organization in general. In what reads like a blueprint for Pound's later career, Burke emphasizes that democracy has binding *formal* qualities – an underlying logic of dispersion, mediation, and discursiveness, if you will – that run directly counter to Pound's ideogrammic designs. As Burke puts it:

> Democracies, with their attempt to put a *delegated* authority at the head of the state, and their play of factional, debunking devices whereby the chosen symbol is constantly attacked by slander, cannot permit the full expression of this integrative impulse. . . .
>
> The truncated nature of a frame lacking its culmination in an absolute may explain the disturbing willingness, on the part of so many people "trained" in democracy, to entertain favorable thoughts of some eventual apocalyptic man on horseback who will come to make "tyranny" and "good tyranny" synonymous.[73]

Of course, the "integrative impulse" (Pound's term for it in "Mang Tsze" is "totalitarian") is exactly what Pound saw in Mussolini, who provided its "culmination in an absolute" by bending the social and economic order to those principles whose authority for Pound began, but did not end, on aesthetic terrain. The bitter irony of Pound's ambitious modernism is that what Burke recognizes – that such matters are far from "purely" aesthetic – is precisely what Pound himself knew early and well. But where Burke would warn us against modeling political forms on aesthetic principles, Pound would endorse the authoritarian means that might enable us to do just that. For Pound, it is not too much to say that democracy was bad politics because it was bad culture; it made argument and revision the order of the day when there was, in Pound's Confucian view, nothing to argue about or revise. "Who," Pound wrote in "A Visiting Card," "has received honours by putting argument where before there had been faith?"[74] The irony of Pound's career, of course, is that he himself had some thirty years earlier, as modernism's most vociferous critic of the oppressions at work in genteel and Edwardian faith.

But how, exactly, did Pound's early liberationist aesthetic lead him into a desperate and despicable politics? We can begin to answer that question by following Burke again in recognizing the difference between critical and didactic culture. For Burke (and for the early Pound), the power of a radically democratic art derives from the fact that "the imaginative expression of a trend precedes its conceptual – critical counterpart."[75] The artist can engage emergent social practices, in other words, *before* they become codified and settle into institutional forms. But the didactic, Burke writes, "would attempt to reverse this process, by *coaching* the imagination in obedience to critical postulates."[76] For art to be "applied art," in other words, it must transcend what Burke calls "the limits of debunking"; it must move from negative critique – a subversive nay-saying *against* a certain set of emergent social practices and values – to positive, normative assertion of *another* set of values, which would replace that which it criticizes. To oversimplify for a moment: For the debunking, democratic aesthetic, the lines of determination run from social change to imaginative expression and critique, and then to critical formulation. For the didactic artist, however, the reverse is true. Rather than shaping itself in response to changes in society, didactic art would shape itself in accordance with first principles, the better to make society conform to the truth that art *already* knows. For a democratic art, its contingency upon social change is the source of its diagnostic power; for didactic art, however, it is that contingency itself which must be reversed.

In a factional democratic context, how is the shapely coherence of didactic art to respond to the incoherence of its social context? For Burke, since the didactic would order society according to its own principles and not the reverse, it must move to "avoid the confusions of synthesis by a schematic decision to label certain people 'friends' or 'enemies,'" a maneuver that "leads naturally to oversimplifications of character and history that can, by the opposition, be discounted as 'sentimentality.'"[77] The didactic, in other words, must move to limit interpretation and suppress contingency, because if they are acknowledged as real and binding, then the whole efficacy of the didactic project, and of the principles upon which it is based, will be called into question.

Here it becomes clear how crucial a role the ideogrammic method played in enabling Pound to push an early critical aesthetic to devastating didactic conclusions. Pound's early poetic dicta – clarity, precision, hardness, concreteness – worked to liberate critical consciousness from abstraction and imperialism by promoting subversive, ever-changing *forms* of perception and production. This new cultural practice did not point toward a fixed, overarching content but in fact worked on principle to prevent it. But when formal imperatives like clarity and precision gained, through the ideogrammic method, a basis in natural law, they became extensions of an unchanging *content* that would not only unsettle, but in fact *replace*, the logic and forms they set out to criticize. Increasingly throughout the thirties, Poundian clarity and precision, instead of being good because they enabled the sort of self that the Taylorized logic of modernity feared, became good in and of themselves because they were themselves substantial extensions of the "one way" of nature "extending to every detail."[78] We can see, then, how Pound arrived at the terms of "A Visiting Card": Words like "betrayal" and "killing" apply not to mere form but to ethical, organic content, to the body of nature in which the words are rooted. In castigating the word until it is "in accord with the root in justice,"[79] Pound would prune away language and discourse itself, the better to make social forms transparent to the natural totality, which is "one, indivisible."[80]

From this perspective, it is perfectly correct to assert, as Wendy Steiner has, that the later version of Pound's ideogrammic method aspires to something like a "universal language," one in which the sign might be *immediately evidentiary*.[81] The Poundian ideogram is not only, as Michael André Bernstein puts it, "the one form of writing free from the risk of ambiguity."[82] It is also the one mode of language that is free from the risk of *interpretation*. And if we take "interpretation" to mean precisely the exploration of discord and disagreement (as meaning in dispute, a locus of symbolic struggle), then we provide a thumbnail sketch of those democratic formal practices that Burke describes and that Pound will move in the thirties to discipline and punish. And insofar as the structure of communication is itself dialogical and polyvalent, then it is not too much to say, as Steiner has, that the ideogram – if pushed to the logical conclusion it demands – precludes the possibility of communication altogether.[83] In the world of the ideogram over which the later Pound presides, the only self who speaks – the only author whose voice is authorized – is the self whose voice is nature's own.

This conviction is not surrendered so much as it is reaffirmed in Pound's confession of his failure to be that kind of author in the very last lines of the American edition of the *Cantos*: "Do not move / Let the wind speak / that is paradise." At this juncture in our discussion, it should come as no surprise that the positioning and valuation of the social difference and historical contingency of the individual here in relation to nature and language reach back to the idealism of Emerson himself, who deeply influenced Fenollosa and, through him, Pound. As Emerson wrote in "Circles":

> Good as is discourse, silence is better, and shames it. The length of the discourse indicates the distance of thought betwixt the speaker and the hearer. If they were at a perfect understanding in any part, no words would be necessary thereon. If at one in all parts, no words would be suffered.[84]

It is precisely this desire that is figured in Pound's closing lines, where what is confessed is *not* the inadequacy or wrongheadedness of a discursive totality "at one in all parts" but only this author's inadequacy to the task – that is why we must suffer no words and let the wind speak.

Finally, then, the ideogrammic method constitutes not so much a theory as a *myth* of language; like Eliot's mythical method, the ideogram would enforce a totality of external nature, social meaning, and individual value by purging poetic discourse of its dependence upon the vagaries of social situation and individual voice. As Franco Moretti points out, as long as discourse is tied to the individual, meaning and value are products of "only one of the *many* subjects who can use language," and consequently poetic truth is still "partial and casual," not – what Eliot wants and what Pound would enforce – "*valid for all.*"[85] Pound had found a language for his totalizing desire, but now he had to find a form. And what better form to embody the mythic logic of the ideogram writ large than epic, the genre par excellence of the representative man?

THE CANTOS *AND THE POLITICS OF GENRE*

The overwhelming textual fact that must strike any reader of the *Cantos*, expert or novice, is that this long poem is (to invoke the distinction made by Mikhail Bakhtin in the 1920s) the most heteroglossious of modernist productions and yet in many ways the least dialogical. This poem goes everywhere, in over a dozen languages and even more epochs and cultures. And yet, in a sense, it goes nowhere, unified as it is (or so Pound hoped by the middle of the undertaking) by a monological world view that might make those particulars function illustratively, to didactic ends. When we come upon the *Cantos*, in other words, not only are we confronted with the fact of textual difference; we are also confronted by – and our critical approaches are interrogated by – the extent to which these differences *make a difference*. The fact of the *Cantos* ought to be enough to point up the inadequacy of recent theories that identify modernism with semiotic liberation, with the detotalizing interpretive *jouissance* generated by the differential modernist text.[86] The *Cantos* may indeed produce defamiliarization and wild textual heterogeneity, but it does so toward an end radically at odds with the flights of semiotic liberation that recent critics have associated with those textual attributes. Like Eliot's poetry and prose after *The Waste Land*, like Frost's homiletic phase and great allegorical "Directive," and like aspects as well of Yeats, Stevens, and even Williams, the *Cantos* is bent not toward the bohemian pleasures of absence but toward binding forms of cultural instruction intended to have more than a passing relationship with social and political institutions.

To return, then, to the issue with which we opened: How do we deal with this text chocked full of differences and heterogeneity, and how do we articulate the relationship between those materials and the overriding desire of the *Cantos* to "write Paradise," as Pound put it, to "establish some definition of an order possible or at any rate conceivable on earth"?[87] To judge what sort of difference a difference makes, we must ask, difference in terms of what, to what rhetorical and ideological ends? And to put these questions in this way on the terrain of literary writing is, in turn, to raise the issue of genre, of how a particular text constitutes itself in a field of other texts, how it orients itself to an audience it seeks to move by appropriating social forms and activating the conventions and institutions perpetuating them.

It is not my purpose here to survey and summarize the extensive scholarly debates over the generic status of the *Cantos*. Rather, I wish to investigate the ideological stakes in asking that generic question in the first place – in short, why it matters whether we read Pound's long poem as epic or some other genre, and how Pound's own view of the poem's genre might be symptomatic of the literary ideology we have been investigating thus far.[88] It would be something of an understatement to say that Pound's long poem is usually read as a type of epic, that is, along the lines Pound himself prescribed in the majority of his later statements about the generic form of the poem. Pound's own view seems to move from an early uncertainty to a growing conviction that he was indeed engaged in writing an epic, a conviction questioned only at the very end of his career. As early as 1908, in the poem "Scriptor Ignotus" out of *A Lume Spento*, he declared his intention to write "that great forty year epic / That you know of, yet unwrit."[89] But by 1917 his view of the poem had taken a radically different turn: "I have begun an endless poem of no known category," he wrote to James Joyce. "Phanopoeia (light- or image-making) or something or other, all about everything."[90] In that same year, he again referred to the work as simply "a new long poem (really LONG, endless, leviathanic),"[91] and by 1922, it was still not yet an epic but a Dantesque "poem in 100 or 120 cantos."[92] And even in 1924, when Pound was thirty-nine years old, he emphasized for a correspondent, with some conviction and vehemence, the provisional form of the work: "Do you recall that the title of the book is 'A DRAFT of 16 Cantos for a poem of some length.' . . . Also it ain't epic. It's part of a long poem. . . . No use selling people things on false pretenses. The collector will prefer this half-time report on the poem to a pretended complete edition."[93]

By 1927, however, we find Pound offering a much more delineated scheme, one already on the way to epic configuration.[94] As he sketched it for his father:

> 1. Rather like, or unlike subject and response and counter subject in fugue.
> A. A. Live man goes down into the world of Dead
> C. B. The "repeat in history"
> B. C. The "magic moment" or moment of metamorphosis, bust thru from quotidien [*sic*] into "divine or permanent world." Gods, etc.[95]

Pound would reiterate his fugal design more than once in the coming years,[96] but often with the kind of qualification ("Rather like, or unlike") that he offered to his father. What is less uncertain, however, are the conspicuously epic qualities of Pound's tripartite structure. Items one and three, in particular, point toward conventional themes of the epic in its classic form. As Northrop Frye explains the relation between these two elements: "In the traditional epic the gods affect the action from a continuous present" (Pound's "divine or permanent world"). "To gain information about the future, or what is 'ahead' in terms of the lower cycle of life, it is normally necessary to descend to a lower world of the dead, as is done in the nekyia, or katabasis, in the eleventh book of the *Odyssey* and the sixth of the *Aeneid*"[97] (and, we should add, in the very first of Pound's cantos, where our Odysseus confronts the "Souls out of Erebus").[98]

Canto I links the poem to the episodic structure of epic as well, which typically begins in medias res, at what Frye calls the "nadir of the total cyclical action," which is visible, in its totality, only to divinity.[99] From the vantage of that "permanent world" of the gods, the opening of Pound's poem in medias res thereby "ties a knot in time," as Frye puts it, by connecting the linear and disjunctive lower cycle of life with a larger stable and cyclical process that leads us to realize, as Eliot famously wrote in *Four Quartets*, that "in my beginning is my end."[100] In fact, what Frye writes of *Four Quartets*-as-epic applies equally well to the third item in the scheme Pound sketched for his father: "Time in this world is a horizontal line, and God's timeless presence is a vertical one crossing it at right angles, the crossing point being the Incarnation."[101] If we remove the Christian theology here, we have what is clearly an apt description of Pound's "magic moment" of metamorphosis, the "bust thru" from the lower to the higher world.

By 1935, Pound will be describing the *Cantos* as "an epic," "a poem including history,"[102] and in the same year he will reiterate his plan for an organizing fugal structure, but only to undercut it ("*Not* that I mean to make an exact analogy of structure") in favor of his growing epic intention:

> The Cantos are in a way fugal. There *is* a start, descent to the shades, metamorphoses, parallel (Vidal–Actaeon). All of which is mere matter for little ——rs and Harvud instructors *unless* I pull it off as reading matter, singing matter, shouting matter, the tale of the tribe.[103]

In this scheme, we seem to have an overlapping or friction between fugal and epic structures. But what has really happened, it seems, is that the fugal has become absorbed by, and indeed dependent upon, Pound's growing epic design. Again, Frye's definition will help make the point: The epic attempts "to preserve the convention of recitation and a listening audience" (Pound's "singing matter, shouting matter"), the better to realize its desire to be "the poetry of the social spokesman."[104] As if to ratify Frye, Pound says in so many words that the sinews and skeleton of the fugal structure matter little – are "academic" in the worst sense – unless the *Cantos* can somehow activate and sustain the epic relation between poet, poem, and public in the services of its overriding social function, its mission to tell "the tale of the tribe."

With a couple of notable exceptions, this will continue to be the frame within which Pound apparently sees the poem. There are the occasional reservations, as in 1939: "As to the *form* of The Cantos: All I can say or pray is: *wait* till it's there."[105] On the whole, however, Pound seems to have settled upon the epic (with fugal and Dantesque structures added to the mix) as the proper generic description of the project. Nowhere is this clearer than in an essay of 1944, where nothing short of conviction undergirds his explanation of the poem, which is now approaching, from its uncertain origins, forty years of age:[106] "For forty years, I have schooled myself, not to write an economic history of the U.S. or any country, but to write an epic poem which begins 'In the Dark Forest,' crosses the Purgatory of human error, and ends in the light, and 'fra i maestri di color che sanno'" (among the masters of those who know).[107] Only in the early 1960s, ten years before his death, did Pound's epic certainty seem to waver again and show the open-ended hesitation that marked his earliest assessments of the poem.[108]

As this brief overview suggests, we seem to have, on the face of it, a fairly good case for arguing that Pound's intention, as it became clear to him, was to write an epic poem. One notable Poundian has contended, however, that Pound's earlier uncertainties carry more weight: "I think that statements made by a poet just before or while embarking on a new work," Max Nänny argues, "tell us more about his true intentions than later pronouncements that often sound like justifications after the fact."[109] Nänny's point is well taken, but what it raises, of course, is what the record seems to bear out: the possibility that Pound's intention, over nearly five decades, had changed. As we will see, this is indeed the case, and there are, moreover, very good reasons why Pound's conviction grew toward epic, away from the "long poem," and not the reverse.

That aside, it seems for the moment that we have solid structural and thematic reasons as well for reading the *Cantos* as a kind of epic. Michael André Bernstein, in his study *The Tale of the Tribe: Ezra Pound and the Modern Verse Epic*, has presented the most ambitious contemporary attempt to sustain this very case. Bernstein offers four main criteria for the epic and locates them with varying degrees of success in the *Cantos*. First of all, the epic provides a narrative frame for the "cultural, historical, or mythic heritage, providing models of exemplary conduct."[110] "The writer of epos," as Pound puts it in *The Spirit of Romance*, "must voice the general heart."[111] And as for models of conduct, the *Cantos* is full of them (Adams, Van Buren, and Mussolini himself, to name only a few).

Bernstein's second criterion is essentially an extension of the first, one more than hinted at in Frye's description: The source of epic narrative is not so much the individual poet as it is the audience's shared heritage and store of values and experience. Again, Pound's own view of epic seems to ratify Bernstein's description: The epic, for Pound, is "the speech of a nation through the mouth of one man."[112] Third in Bernstein's scheme, the epic's address is predicated upon a unified and homogeneous audience, a "tribe," as Bernstein notes in approving echo; it assumes that its audience will recognize the poem's "psychological, ethical, emotional, or aesthetic imperatives." And finally – again an extension – the epic contains a strong didactic component; it "offers its audience lessons presumed necessary to their individual and social survival."[113] Here again, it is scarcely necessary to point out that this criterion applies, in spades, to the *Cantos*, with its welter of instructive figures and exemplary historical details.

No doubt Bernstein's criteria are exemplified in aspects of the *Cantos*, but there is much in this poem that violates these dicta as well, as Bernstein himself recognizes. In fact, he is forced to conclude toward the end of his study that the *Cantos* "clearly violate" a number of the characteristics he outlines at the beginning of his argument. Still, he clings to the assertion that the *Cantos* "did really resurrect the epic as a genre that modern poets could again attempt."[114] This is precisely the claim we will want to investigate: "attempt," sure, but for what reasons, in the services of what kind of social vision and at what ideological price?

We will pursue these issues in a moment, but for now we should note that there is another way to read the genre of the *Cantos*, one promoted by the Poundian Max Nänny. Sensing hesitation and gaps in Bernstein's argument, Nänny has moved to argue that we read the *Cantos* not as epic but as a poem that has more in common with the tradition of Menippean satire.[115] In contrast to epic, this beguiling and seemingly shapeless genre contains, according to Bakhtin, "the specific weight of a comic element"; it has, to varying degrees, "a specifically *carneval* nature."[116] Now this would seem to be, from the outset, the most serious impediment to viewing the *Cantos* as Menippean satire. But in fact (and Nänny concedes this point too readily, I think), the *Cantos* contains a good deal of carnivalizing, if not exactly comedy. In many, many places (particularly later in the poem), we hear the poet in pseudo-Continental speech ("Haff you gno bolidigal basshunts?"), mixed with burlesque ("crack a flea on eider wan / of her breasts"), and in many other ribald tongues and playful moods as well.[117] This is particularly true of *The Pisan Cantos*, the very sequence most readers find most fertile and rewarding. To take only one example, Canto LXXX: There is the famous parody of Browning's "Home Thoughts from Abroad" ("Oh to be in England now that Winston's out / Now that there's room for doubt");[118] there is the genuinely irreverent and hilarious verse of the prankster:

> When a butt is $^1/_2$ as tall as a whole butt
> That butt is a small butt
>   Let backe and side go bare
> and the old kitchen left as the monks had left it
> and the rest as time has cleft it.[119]

There is the mixture of hayseed and blackface that opens the poem ("Ain' committed no federal crime, / jes a slaight misdemeanor");[120] and there is even some play with the name of the revered Il Duce ("It will not take uth twenty yearth / to cwuth Mutholini").[121]

This carnivalization of tongues and literatures, both "high" and "low," is, as Leslie Fiedler reminds us, a hallmark not only of this poem but of Pound's career as a whole. From his early slap at the genteels in "L'Homme Moyen Sensuel," through *Mauberley*, to the publication of *The Poems of Alfred Venison*, a volume of all-out parody, in 1935, the carnivalizer (and cannibalizer) walked hand in hand with the would-be Odysseus. Fiedler is right on target when he notes that "if all of Pound's work in this intentionally burlesque mode were gathered together, it would make a substantial and not unimpressive volume."[122] This could be said as well of Pound's long poem itself, from which we could make a very different *Selected Cantos* of irrepressible and irreverent wit. In fact, Fiedler sees the *Cantos* as not a "failed Epic" but rather "a mock epic, an anti-epic, a comic travesty of the genre."[123] For Fiedler, the model for the *Cantos* is not Homer, not Virgil, not Dante, not even *Leaves of Grass*, but Flaubert's unfinished *Bouvard et Pecuchet*, which "bears the same parodic relationship to the bourgeois novel as [Pound's] unfinished, unfinishable poem does to the classic Epic"[124] – and which Pound saw as a crucial link between two writers (Rabelais and the Joyce of *Ulysses* and *Finnegan's Wake*) who are very arguably indeed practitioners of the Menippean mode.[125]

Even if we are unwilling to endorse Fiedler's broad claims (which are calculated, after all, to outrage the "Poundolators," as he puts it), it is clear that the *Cantos* includes carnivalization in much the same way that it "includes" history: not as the only dimension but as a crucial one, in the manner of those Menippean satires in which the comic element "disappears," as Bakhtin puts it, "or rather is reduced."[126] It makes a little more sense to read the *Cantos* (or Bakhtin's Dostoevsky!) as Menippean satire if we understand that the radical sense of "carnivalization," as a formal innovation, is not so much comedy pure and simple as it is *dialogism*, the "destruction of all barriers between genres, between self-enclosed systems of thought, between various styles."[127]

This dimension of Menippean satire is a little easier to see in the *Cantos* – and, in fact, impossible to miss. Pound underscored it himself in the passage from the Ur-Cantos that he used in his foreword to the *Selected Cantos*:

> say I take your whole bag of tricks,
> Let in your quirks and tweeks, and say the thing's
>   an art-form,
> . . . and that the modern world
> Needs such a rag-bag to stuff all its thought in[128]

But we need not depend only on Pound's assessment. Max Nänny's brief sampling of the *Cantos* makes it clear just what a ragbag this supposed epic is:

Brief narratives or "miniature epics" (the *nekyia* in Canto 1, the Ovidian story of the Tyrrhenian sailors in Canto 2); letters, ambassadors' reports, recorded conversation (e.g. in the Malatesta Cantos); expository prose from history books, economic and legal treatises and even from a fly-tying manual (Canto 51); a canzone (Canto 36); short lyrics and a folk song from the Chinese (Canto 49); chronology (Chinese History Cantos); lists (e.g. 100/720); inscriptions (on a placard at 22/103, on a pyramid at 34/171, on a bathtub at 53/265); diatribes (e.g. Hell Cantos); an epitaph (37/186); a charter (42/212); an emblem (42/214); a litany (Canto 45); accounts (e.g. 41/205); a prayer (59/327); an electioneering slogan (71/418) and Confucian sayings (e.g. 55/290); a libretto (81/519–20) and two kinds of musical notation (Canto 75 and Canto 91); notes (e.g. pp. 254 and 256; 96/659); a table of contents (pp. 255–256) and an explication of ideograms (77/476).[129]

And then Nänny adds, with no hint of humor, "etc."

An exhaustive inventory of Pound's poem would surely reveal other Menippean qualities as well: its wildly polyglot texture (perhaps the *Cantos*' best-known feature); its topicality; its forays into what Bakhtin calls "slum naturalism" (particularly in *The Pisan Cantos*); and the vision of social utopia often given prominent place in the Menippea.[130] Finally, the *Cantos* conspicuously shares what Bakhtin identifies as a key feature of the Menippea: its "three-planed construction" of nether world, earth, and the realm of the divine.[131]

This structural feature of Menippea, however, leads us to the very critical impasse we now want to investigate. As we have seen, the three-tiered structural scheme of the *Cantos* can be associated with either epic or Menippean satire. And the arguments I have just surveyed (far from exhaustively, to be sure) suggest that we can make a persuasive case for reading the *Cantos* as a modern variant of either of these genres. So how are we to decide and, more urgently, what is at stake in our interpretive decision? Again, we are back to the question with which we began: There are differences here, but what kind of difference do these differences make?

What I want to suggest now is that the debate between Bernstein and Nänny, between reading the *Cantos* as epic and reading it as Menippean satire, cannot, in fact, be decided within the terms and assumptions that frame their arguments, because those terms are purely literary – "academic" in exactly the sense that Pound himself had in mind when he wrote that his fugal structure was mere matter for "Harvud instructors" unless the poem could reignite the social relations between the poem and its public. Both critics believe that the question of genre is a pressing one because only after we have settled it can we know what questions we may appropriately address to the work.[132] Here is Bernstein: "Questions of genre need to be clarified before specific issues of interpretation can be resolved."[133] And here is Nänny: "Once we detach this poem from such genre models as *The Odyssey* or *The Divine Comedy*, we begin to see its true literary affiliations more adequately."[134] Clearly, both arguments are perfectly circular: You make a schematic decision to read the particulars of the text a certain way so that those particulars might be properly read. But of course, you have no basis for that a priori decision unless you have already confronted the particulars of the text in the first place. Sooner or later, you are asking the right questions and reading the work correctly because you have already asked the right questions and read the work correctly.

Bernstein, I think, senses this dilemma and he is quick to add, by way of recuperation, that "such a decision [to read the text as a given genre] tells us nothing about the success of any individual work."[135] Bernstein would enable us, through a sort of critical escape valve, to displace the possible inadequacy or inappropriateness of our choice of genre onto the individual work itself. But if that is the case, instead of acknowledging "the limits of their [the *Cantos'*] success as epic,"[136] why not own up to the limits of our own a priori generic decision? In fact, if our generic decisions tell us nothing about the success of a given work, then why make them at all?

Nänny's position gives us no respite. He would view the *Cantos* in terms of Menippean satire because then we need "no longer demand that *The Cantos* have a major form, thematic and formal continuity, a narrative plot, a consistent logic of discourse or a limited cast of characters." In short, we should read the *Cantos* as Menippea because we would "accept with less grumbling the rag-bag quality – and all its implications – of Pound's poem."[137] Again, we find the same problem we found with Bernstein's argument, only this time in reverse. Finding the poem to be a failure as an epic, we fit our generic category to the poem. We no longer ask the poem to be the genre, we ask the genre to be the poem.

Expert as they are in their knowledge of Pound's texts and career (and they are very expert indeed), Bernstein and Nänny cannot answer the sort of question which Franco Moretti has posed about formalist theories of genre in a different context:

> In what sense does Shakespeare "violate" the conventions of Eliza-
> bethan tragedy? Why not say the opposite: that he was the only writer
> to realize them fully, establishing as it were the "ideal type" of an entire
> genre? Does *Wilhelm Meister's Apprenticeship* "defamiliarize" the con-
> ventions of the *Bildungsroman*? Is not the opposite the case: that with
> this novel Goethe founds them and makes them reproducible?[138]

Why not say, in other words, that the *Cantos* itself reveals the true form and structure of epic? Instead of letting Homer determine the way we read the *Cantos*, why not the reverse?

The critical point that both Bernstein and Nänny want to acknowledge and yet politically disarm is that genre, as Frye puts it, "in any case is rhetorical, in the sense that the genre is determined by the conditions established between the poet and his public."[139] Bernstein and Nänny want to exploit the power of the generic contract without being bound by its broadly social function. What they refuse to admit, in other words, is that genre not only binds the text to other texts but also binds it to its social and ideological ground and, in doing so, also binds *us*. To make any headway with the question of genre in the *Cantos* – and to escape the circularity of the purely literary argument – we need to recognize what Lukács proposed in his "Observations on the Theory of Literary History": "Every form is an evaluation of life, a judgment on life, and it draws this strength and power from the fact that in its deepest foundations form is always an ideology. . . . The world view is the formal postulate of every form."[140]

With that in mind, we can now return to our Bakhtin, whose critique of epic is anything but politically antiseptic. For Pound as well as Frye, we remember, the essence of epic lay in the rhetorical relationship between poet and public; notwithstanding all its structures, schemes, and devices, epic for Pound is successful only if it is "the tale of the tribe." However, this fundamental feature of epic, Bakhtin reminds us, is predicated not so much upon the abilities of the poet as it is upon certain kinds of social relations that make possible the literary forms expressing and reproducing them. All genres, in other words, are based upon what Fredric Jameson calls a social "logic of content,"[141] upon specific social materials that come to the poet *already* structured and configured, materials that empower the poet because they are already invested with social significance. For the epic, Bakhtin tells us, these include

> an impersonal and sacrosanct tradition, . . . a commonly held evaluation and point of view – which excludes any possibility of another approach. . . . The epic world is an utterly finished thing, not only as an authentic event of the distant past but also on its own terms and by its own standards; it is impossible to change, to re-think, to re-evaluate anything in it. It is completed, conclusive and immutable, as a fact, an idea and a value.[142]

Pound himself, in fact, well realized that epic had to be based upon exactly this kind of social structure: "The past epos has succeeded," he argued, "when all or a great many of the answers were assumed, at least between author and audience, or a great mass of audience."[143] It is this sort of holism and consensus to which Pound's versions of Hesiod's *Works and Days* and the Confucian *Li Ki* (to name only two) aspire – a "sacrosanct tradition" whose force derives not from the individual but from an objective and natural coherence that has aesthetic authority because it *is* "finished," because it is, as Pound put it, a "permanent world."

The epic universe, then, is fundamentally a realm without history. It is a world, in Jameson's words, in which

> each generation repeats the same experiences, reinvents the same basic human situations as though for the first time. . . . The works of art characteristic of such societies may be called concrete in that their elements are all meaningful from the outset. The writer uses them, but he does not need to demonstrate their meaning beforehand: in the language of Hegel, this raw material needs no *mediation*.[144]

The point here is not that it is impossible to write an epic (or to rewrite the *Odyssey*, for that matter) in twentieth-century Western society. Of course it is possible. But were we to come upon the *Odyssey* in our day and read it as a contemporary offering, we would no doubt find it psychologically thin, woodenly conventional, naive and opaque in its rituals and repetitions. That newly discovered *Odyssey* might indeed be a meaningful symbolic act to us, but it would only be meaningful *as epic* (and not as some ironic or parodic text) within the social structure presupposed by the epic form, and that social structure, just as clearly, is no longer available to us.[145]

But the odd thing about the *Cantos* is that its formal logic presupposes those very social conditions within which epic might be meaningful *as* epic, organic with its social context. And it does so with such certitude that its formal procedure has been described as everything from "authoritarian" to "fascistic" in its refusal to explain, justify, or otherwise mediate those signs (the massive ideograms of *Thrones*, for instance) that Pound presents with the certainty of the epic spokesman but that appear quite opaque to readers who are not enfolded in the coherence they presuppose. In its epic assumptions and the signifying practices they underwrite, the *Cantos* creates, as M. L. Rosenthal and Sally M. Gall put it, an "increasing reliance on the arbitrary, ultimately personal sensibility of the poet," leading Pound into the "rhetorical self-indulgence" that blocks readers from the vision the poem would communicate.[146] In fact, for the objectivist poet Charles Olson that is the very methodology of the *Cantos*, which relies upon an "ego-system" that "destroys historical time," the better to collapse social and historical materials into its "space-field."[147]

We should not assume from Olson's critique (or Rosenthal and Gall's) that the merely personal vicissitudes of the poet can be so easily separated from the ideological and formal problems in which the poem is embroiled. In fact, the case is quite the reverse. As Bakhtin makes clear, nothing could be farther from the truth. He argues that for the monological writer, "the affirmation of the unity of *existence* [is] . . . transformed into the unity of the *consciousness*," which is, in turn, "inevitably transformed into the unity of a *single* consciousness." It is this movement that is "characteristic of ideology in general,"[148] and what it maps is nothing less than the process through which concrete individuals are made ideological subjects insofar as they see themselves reflected whole in a larger order that makes possible their own sense of self and coherence.

The ideological movement that Bakhtin describes here finds unmistakable and extreme expression in Pound's *Cantos*. The opaque signs and dogmatic assertions that litter the poem are self-evident to Pound within his own monologic context – a context in which the *directio voluntatis* in Dante, say, is immediately recognizable in certain passages of the correspondence of Thomas Jefferson and John Adams – but they are often bizarre to readers precisely because that context is not ours. Indeed, as Pound himself finally admitted, the unmediated coherence of meaning and value that epic requires is no longer possible in the modern world.[149]

The central contradiction of the *Cantos*, however, is that Pound's explicitly didactic project not only presupposes that larger coherence but also attempts to bring it into being through its own instructive agency. When read as epic, Pound's poem is a paradox: It both assumes and attempts to create the social conditions – and the forms of knowledge and the shared meanings based on those conditions – whereby it would be possible to read the poem *as* epic, whereby its formal procedure might be not cryptic and opaque but immediately meaningful. From this perspective, to call the *Cantos* an epic is not the solution to the question of major form in the poem, it is precisely the *problem*.

In the context of Bakhtin's critique, though, it makes a good deal of sense that Pound's certitude about the fact that he was writing an epic poem increased and solidified in the late twenties and early thirties. First of all, during this period his ideological commitment to authoritarian fascism was increasing as he became more and more convinced that Mussolini would implement the economic policies that had moved more and more to center stage in Pound's concerns.[150] Pound's work during this period moved more and more toward a poetic of general statement and abstract law,[151] in large part because Pound himself ranged more and more beyond the usual purview of poetry into investigations of the economic and social totality that would sustain a healthy culture – and reveal the authority of his own epic endeavors.[152] Mussolini promised to make a political reality of the social and economic truth that Pound's aesthetics already knew. And once that was accomplished, what looked like Pound's own cryptic "ego system" would be revealed for what it was: the inscriptions of the order of existence.

Pound's epic conviction was ratified in an even more specific way by a fundamental component of the economic philosophy he had long since ceased to question: that distribution, not production, was the primary problem for the man of proper economic principles.[153] This same distributive logic, as Richard Sieburth points out, drives the didactic dimension of the *Cantos* (and, I would argue, of epic in general). The poet is no longer a producer of new meanings but rather a dispenser of those truths that, like economic wealth, are already there, latent in nature. The didactic poet's task, like that of the economically sound statesman, is, as Sieburth puts it, "to distribute or to place into circulation what has been entrusted to his care, to apportion the sustenance that has been deposited in his keeping."[154] The epic poet, in other words, is not a producer but a *reproducer* of a changeless totality that should not be altered or transformed by individual invention. And from this vantage, we can see that Pound's work increasingly invites the critique Bakhtin makes of the monological writer: "From the point of view of truth, there are no individual consciousnesses. Idealism recognizes only one principle of cognitive individualization: *error*. True judgments are not attached to a personality, but correspond to some unified, systemically monologic context."[155] But of course, such individuals are not individuals at all; they are cardboard cutouts, *types* whose "individuality" (if we can put it that way) emerges insofar as they stray from the ideal coherence that gives the monological writer his authority and voice.

In *Time and Western Man*, Wyndham Lewis made a similar point, not about the monological writer in general, but about Pound himself in particular. As Lewis wrote, with delicious composure: "There is no direct contact between Ezra and an individual person or thing. Ezra is a crowd; a little crowd. People are seen by him only as types. There is the 'museum official,' there is the 'norman cocotte,' and so on."[156] And T. S. Eliot, another ideological bedfellow who knew Pound early and well, prefigured Lewis's sentiments (and Bakhtin's pointed conclusions) in *After Strange Gods* in 1934. In Pound's Hell, Eliot writes, we find

> politicians, profiteers, financiers, newspaper proprietors and their hired men, *agents provocateurs*, Calvin, St. Clement of Alexandria, the English, vice-crusaders, liars, the stupid, pedants, preachers, those who do not believe in Social Credit, bishops, lady golfers, Fabians, conservatives and imperialists; and all "those who have put money lust before the pleasures of the senses."

For Eliot, as for Lewis and Bakhtin, "these are types, and not individuals." "Mr. Pound's Hell," Eliot continues, "for all its horrors . . . is a Hell for the *other people*, the people we read about in the newspapers, not for one's self and one's friends." But what, we must ask, separates "one's self" from "the other people"? And what could those others, like lady golfers and Calvin, possibly have in common in their essential infamy? Eliot provides our answer:

> [If you] maintain that by tolerance, benevolence, inoffensiveness and a redistribution or increase of purchasing power, combined with a devotion, on the part of an elite, to Art, the world will be as good as anyone could require, then you must expect human beings to become more and more vaporous. This is exactly what we find of the society which Mr. Pound puts in Hell.[157]

And it is here that we may now return to the genre of Menippean satire, as a tool for reading the *Cantos*, with more conviction. As Frye reminds us,

> The Menippean satire deals less with people as such than with mental attitudes. Pedants, bigots, cranks, parvenus, virtuosi, enthusiasts, rapacious and incompetent professional men of all kinds, are handled in terms of their occupational approach to life as distinct from their social behaviour. The Menippean satire . . . differs from the novel in its charcacterization, which is stylized rather than naturalistic, and presents people as mouthpieces of the ideas they represent. . . . The novelist sees evil and folly as social diseases, but the Menippean satirist sees them as diseases of the intellect.[158]

How increasingly true this is of the *Cantos*, which will systematically praise or vilify historical figures (famous or obscure) solely on the basis of their real or perceived commitment to Pound's economic and political ideals. As the didactic program of the *Cantos* develops, historical and contemporary figures will be whittled down more and more to what Frye calls their "mental attitudes." In Wendy Flory's words, "Pound's villains, even when they have proper names, are not individuals, but types and often caricatured types at that."[159] These are not individuals – or, in terms of literary genre, characters – who change and develop, who are products of a matrix of social conditions, but rather *vehicles* into whose mouths the words of truth or blasphemy may be inserted.[160] And if we recognize *that*, then we must also recognize that the coherence of the *Cantos* is not organic and substantial – as Pound would have us believe – but rather discrete, conceptual, and abstract. It is a poem unified not by the essence and order of existence but by the logic of the Menippea, by what Frye calls "a serious vision of society as a single intellectual pattern."[161]

In a way, Pound's poem itself finally forces this reading upon us by providing its own devastating self-critique. In that epic world envisioned by the poem, change in any real sense is impossible and so, therefore, is character. Finally, however, we *do* find one character in the *Cantos*, one who changes and in so doing destroys any epic wholeness that the poem might have had. That character, of course, is Pound himself. Suddenly, in *The Pisan Cantos*, we are confronted at the very center of the work not with a type or "mental attitude" but with a flesh-and-blood character, one whose future is uncertain because his end has not been, and indeed cannot be, foretold. With Pound's arrest and detention, what could not happen in the epic world *has* happened, and that is simply history itself – specifically, in these poems, the history of the Second World War and the fall of Italian fascism. Here, something foreign to epic but wholly of a piece with the Menippea now takes place. In Bakhtin's words, "the epic and tragic wholeness of a person and his fate" is destroyed; "the possibilities of another person and another life are revealed to him, he loses his finalized quality and ceases to mean only one thing; he ceases to coincide with himself."[162]

This is indeed an apt description of Pound in "the Cage," a poet who is suddenly, vividly human because fractured and unfinished – open, for better or worse, to social and historical change and to the power of other readings of his work, other interpretations, which he can no longer control or authorize. Awaiting trial for treason and the death sentence it promised, Pound confronts the stark otherness of history and writes what an earlier epic self could never write:

> end of   Dungeon
> Jan.   Domenica
> mental torture
> constitution a religion
> a world lost
> grey mist barrier impassible
>   ignorance absolute
>   anonyme
> futility of "might have been"
> coherent areas
>   constantly invaded
>   aiuto [help]
>   Pound[163]

Up until its ideological unmasking and transformation in *The Pisan Cantos*, Pound's poem had managed to maintain a dialectic of Menippean satire and epic, of critical anatomy and paradisal vision. But now, caught in the historical maelstrom, in the "grey mist barrier" that enveloped the natural transparency of his ideology as surely as the Allies enveloped fascist Italy, Pound could no longer situate himself outside the Menippean dimension of the *Cantos*, outside the vice and failure of which the *Cantos* had been the forty-year castigation and anatomy. With that epic world now in ruins, its carefully crafted frame broken in a flash by the history it had so long repressed, there *was* no outside.[164] Pound was suddenly alone with his poem, awash in the gulf between the terrible fact of his ideology and its fictions, which now receded from him, one by one, into a lost past.

Afterword

He has clapped copyright on the world. . . . But the mouthful proves too large. *Boa constrictor* has good will to eat it, but he is foiled. He falls abroad in the attempt; and biting, gets strangled: the bitten world holds the biter fast by his own teeth. There he perishes: unconquered nature lives on and forgets him.[1]

Late in his career, Emerson used this little story to size up what he called "the ambition of individualism," a subject he could claim, mutatis mutandis, to know a little something about. But so could Ezra Pound, of course, who in the *Cantos* seems to take the possibility of clapping copyright on the world more seriously than even Emerson himself could have imagined. And Emerson's image of the bitten world holding the biter fast by the teeth is, in an almost uncanny way, an accurate image for the death struggle in which Pound found himself at the Disciplinary Training Center outside Pisa, when the bitten world of history – not Pound's ideal history of a fascist "city of Dioce" built upon the timeless principles of a Confucian order, but the real history of the Second World War and the lunar rubble of liberal democracy's triumph over fascism – would not let Pound disengage himself from the ideological commitments he had latched onto in his poetry, prose, and radio speeches.

Emerson's little parable, however, is not, finally, about the price one pays for one's ideological positions; it is not even an admonition about the dangers of politicizing one's cultural practice. Emerson's story is at once more and less ambitious than that, because it is mainly a parable (as the bestial imagery and the biblical echoes of the fall from Eden suggest) about an essential condition, about desire, lack, and appetite. Emerson's parable is about what happens whenever *any* kind of self – Republican or Whig, Fascist or Communist – desires to eat *everything*, to swallow the world entire like a ball or an egg. What is repressed by that desire – what Heidegger would have called the historicity or "world-ness" of the "earth," and what the later Sartre called the "practico-inert" nature of the object world, which is the "congealed" practice of others[2] – returns in Emerson's parable to ironically inscribe the would-be devourer in his own voracious equation. The self is thus doomed to starvation, and that in direct proportion to the enormity of his appetite.

More important than that, though, is to understand that Emerson's parable is also a story about property, about confusing one's imaginary ability to own the world as property, to clap copyright on it, with one's real ability (or inability) to do with it as one wishes. And most important of all, for the genealogy I have been tracing, is the fact that Emerson's story is finally about the uncontrollable instability and reversibility of ownership and alienation that ensue when "individualism" is conceived in terms of property; here, the self asserts its ownership over the property of the world only to have that relation immediately reversed. This is the sense, too, in which "the bitten world holds the biter fast by his own teeth." Once in the loop of property relations, the individualist cannot get out; once bitten by the desire to express one's self-possession as possession of the world outside the self – once the individual claims his copyright – he is immediately in peril of becoming property himself. The world he would own (by copyright) in his own image-as-property turns out to be the real owner; it adds the would-be Lockean owner to its collection of sundry things in a drawer and, bored with ownership of all these overly ambitious selves, it "lives on and forgets him."

This is a parable, in other words, not only about individualism but about individualism in its specifically liberal form. And from this vantage, we can put an even finer point on Emerson's parable about the boa constrictor and its mise en scene of the political unconscious (to borrow Fredric Jameson's phrase) of the liberal subject. When we look in Emerson's story for a mediating third term between the mutually devouring autonomous self and the "unconquered" object world – when we look, in other words, for the site of *the social* – we find that that site is configured by a property relation (here, a "copyright"). All of which would be of little moment were it not for the fact that we have known at least since Marx's early critique that the property relation cannot constitute a social space in which self and other might do something other than devour each other, because the property relation is always already *antisocial*. As we have seen, Marx's critique of classical political economy makes it clear that if my freedom consists of my ability to freely dispose of my self-possessed capacities and potentialities (including, of course, my labor power) as I wish, then other selves who are trying to do the same will *always* constitute an alienation of my freedom, because our projects of self-realization will always mutually limit and constrain each other (a fact most readily apparent when self and other compete for the same job in which to freely dispose of their labor power, with the result of falling wages).[3] Thus, the liberal subject, constituted as it is by the structure and logic of private property, is not pluralist but antisocial to its very core – and this despite whatever attempts have been made to mask, attenuate, or recontain this fact by the familiar strategies of political amelioration and democratic cultural "consensus."

As recent studies in Americanist criticism have shown, those strategies were busily at work in the canonization of Emerson's oeuvre and the simultaneous constitution of American studies as a legitimate field of scholarly inquiry in the 1950s.[4] In the cold war context in which the traditional canon of American literature was codified under the imprimatur of liberal intellectuals like Lionel Trilling, the sort of radical individualism we find in Emerson could be put to good use in the construction of a cultural consensus against Stalinist communism and, more broadly, against politicized notions of culture in general, for which Stalinism served as a kind of handy metonymy. But to do *that* was seemingly to threaten precisely what made Emerson, from the liberal intellectual's point of view, exemplary and useful for that very project: namely, his transcendence, as "culture," of historical, economic, and political determinations.

In putting American writers to use in the construction of an anti-Stalinist cultural consensus, in other words, liberal intellectuals flirted with reproducing the very Stalinist view of culture they wished to oppose, because they themselves made culture – that supposedly autonomous realm of individual freedom – subservient to a political and ideological project. Liberal consensus intellectuals like Lionel Trilling attempted to solve this dilemma not by denying the claims of politics and materialism (or, more immediately, of the progressive critiques by Beard and Parrington) but rather by resituating them so that they might be heroically transcended by the work of authentic culture, which staked out the only true space of the individual's freedom. By doing so, one could, for example, admire the heroism of Emerson's critique of the division of labor, Jacksonian democracy, and the debasements of the marketplace without tethering the *value* of Emerson's work to those constitutive social forces.

As Donald Pease points out, Richard Chase's *The American Novel and Its Tradition* (published in 1957, seven years after Trilling's *The Liberal Imagination*) is in this regard an exemplary project. Accepting Trilling's assertion that "American writers of genius have not turned their minds to society,"[5] Chase attempted to accommodate the antinomian, antisocial experience of Emersonian individualism by providing for it a valorized generic topos. Chase declared that, in contrast to the novel, which foregrounded the self's determination by class, church, and the structuring force of history, the romance cleared a space for the self's unruly freedom by its willingness "to ignore the spectacle of man in society,"[6] and so could serve as the very hallmark of a distinctly American literature. Chase, then, allows us to accommodate the radical implications of an Emersonian individualism, but only because the romance contains it within a privileged sphere of culture that is cordoned off from the social and political realms.

The work of Quentin Anderson provides an even more sophisticated critical mechanism for maintaining the separation between culture and politics while simultaneously enlisting culture in the services of a liberal consensus political vision. I say "sophisticated" here because Anderson's work *seems* to recognize full well the alienating logic of the property paradigm for American liberal individualism.[7] Following the classic Tocquevillean critique, Anderson reminds us that "possession, no matter how spiritualized, does not free you since the freedom of those who live in society lies in the character of their relation to other persons and nowhere else."[8] At the same time, however, Anderson extends and refines the liberal consensus separation of culture and politics into the post–cold war era in his important study *The Imperial Self*. As Pease articulates it, the demise of the Stalinist specter in the 1960s robbed the liberal consensus of the ideological enemy that had unified and sustained its claims against politicized culture. With the disintegration of that cold war rationale, Americans – and particularly American students who had been reared on the freedom, fantasy, and self-exploration definitively at work for Richard Chase in the American romance – felt less and less compulsion to respect the separation of the cultural and political realms. And so they were ready, as Pease puts it, to "desublimate" the disruptive and destabilizing energies of the American self imagined by Emerson and Whitman and bring them fully into the *political* realm as well.[9]

Many Americans (Anderson's Columbia students foremost among them) enacted that desublimation by taking the imperatives of Emersonian freedom seriously and putting them into practice in the form of protests and demonstrations against imperialism and the war in Vietnam. And *The Imperial Self*, when viewed in this context, may be seen as an effort to reintroduce the culture/politics division so essential to consensus liberalism by insisting that any attempt to extend the imperial ego of American literary imagination outside the realm of culture is *itself* an instance of imperialism. As Pease explains it, "Anderson as a representative of the liberal consensus rediscovers within [counterconsensus movements] the symptoms of absolutist drives, which, when acted upon in the public world, turned counterimperialism [in the form of student anti-war protests] into imperialism."[10] For Anderson, forms of dissent that take the liberal imagination at its word without respecting the consensus intellectual's attendant separation of culture and politics are rewritten as instances of imperial selfhood. Thus, Anderson's project works not so much to resublimate or repress the disruptive energies of the liberal imagination as to recontain them once again within the realm of culture alone.

And thus, too, Anderson produces, in his important essay "Property and Vision in Nineteenth-Century America," what looks like a compelling critique of property-based individualism in Emerson, while at the same time holding to an unabashedly liberal vision himself. The problem with the structuring force of property in Emerson's individualism turns out to be no problem at all for Anderson, because the *real* Emerson, the cultural Emerson, transcends it. From Anderson's point of view, the real danger is not so much that Emerson's putatively liberating individualism reproduces the alienating logic of private property but rather the failure of critical imagination (itself an exercise of imperial intellectual selfhood) that acknowledges the logic of property as real and binding in its overdetermination of Emerson's cultural production.

This means, of course, that Anderson's liberal *consensus* self – the self who engages in the cultural recontainment of the desublimated individualist imagination – *knows better* than the liberal *antinomian* self of Emersonian imagination and American romance. But to insist that you really know better is to be not only un- but even *anti-Emersonian*. It is to abandon, for better or worse, the radical implications and political power of Emersonian individualism, which is nothing if not a no-compromise affair. From Emerson's point of view, the very power and promise of his individualism would reside in its lack of patience with *either* the "vital center" position of liberal consensus intellectuals *or* the hard-left entrenchment of Stalinist communism.[11] Emerson's individualism is so radical, so true to its founding promise, that it could never be contingent, as consensus liberalism was, upon its opposition to any *specific form* of politics.

The fact that Emerson's individualism outstrips any liberal consensus attempts to stabilize or contain it is most clear in what we might call the "heretical" strain in Emerson's work, the Emerson who tells us in "Circles" that "we must cast away our virtues."[12] Nowhere is that essential anarchic wildness of Emerson's vision more in evidence than five pages into the text of "Self-Reliance," where he begins one of the more remarkable passages in American literature by declaring, "If I am the Devil's child, I will live then from the Devil," only to follow *that* pronouncement with the assertion, "The doctrine of hatred must be preached, as the counteraction of the doctrine of love, when that pules and whines." *Then* we are given the famous transvaluation of *whim*, where the self shuns father and mother and wife to follow its own god, a passage that is itself bracketed by angry denunciations of knee-jerk abolitionism and charity. "I am ashamed to think," Emerson laments, "how easily we capitulate to badges and names, to large societies and dead institutions. Every decent and well-spoken individual affects and sways me more than is right."[13]

Emerson's animus toward anything resembling the ameliorating management strategies of liberal consensus pluralism[14] is unmistakable at these moments, and even when he attempts to accommodate those demands, he finds time and again that he cannot do so in good conscience. Toward the end of "Self-Reliance," Emerson moves to meet the charge of "mere antinomianism" and address the suggestion that his "rejection of popular standard is a rejection of all standard." This supposed refutation, however, quickly turns into a somewhat devilish embrace of the charge itself; Emerson does not deny his antinomianism but rather reconfirms it in an act of radical transvaluation: "But the law of consciousness abides," he concludes; "I have my own stern claims and perfect circle. It denies the name of duty to many offices that are called duties. But if I can discharge its debts it enables me to dispense with the popular code. If any one imagines that this law is lax, let him keep its commandment one day."[15]

It is important to note that these moments of feigned reasonableness masking an untamable individualism are not limited to "Self-Reliance." In "Circles," for example, we find a reprise of this "failed" refutation, only this time the charge is radical relativism. "And thus, O circular philosopher, I hear some reader exclaim," Emerson writes, "you have arrived at a fine Pyrrhonism, at an equivalence and indifferency of all actions, and would fain teach us that *if we are true*, forsooth, our crimes may be lively stones out of which we shall construct the temple of the true God!" Here as before, Emerson does not deny his radicalism but rather turns it into a virtue. After offering an essentially Augustinian response – he is pleased, he tells us, to note "that unrestrained inundation of the principle of good into every chink and hole that selfishness has left open, yea into selfishness and sin itself" – he reminds us that "I am only an experimenter": "Do not set the least value on what I do, or the least discredit on what I do not, as if I pretended to settle any thing as true or false. I unsettle all things. No facts are to me sacred; none are profane; I simply experiment, an endless seeker, with no Past at my back."[16]

The Emersonian self's ceaseless guerrilla war on consensus pluralism, centrist stability, and all manner of "facts" and "settled" things is recorded with particular power in a remarkable passage in "Circles," which, to my mind, rivals anything Emerson ever wrote in the sheer hyperbolic accuracy (to indulge my own Emersonian oxymoron) with which it characterizes the negative and critical power of his fierce individualism:

In common hours, society sits cold and statuesque. We all stand waiting, empty, – knowing, possibly, that we can be full, surrounded by
mighty symbols which are not symbols to us, but prose and trivial
toys. Then cometh the god and converts the statues into fiery men, and
by a flash of his eye burns up the veil which shrouded all things, and
the meaning of the very furniture, of cup and saucer, of chair and clock
and tester, is manifest. The facts which loomed so large in the fogs of
yesterday, – property, climate, breeding, personal beauty and the like,
have strangely changed their proportions. All that we reckoned settled
shakes and rattles; and literatures, cities, climates, religions, leave their
foundations and dance before our eyes.[17]

This vision of Emersonian selfhood (in the figure of the poet-god) is
exhilarating, dynamic, and charismatic, but it is also something else –
it is *terrifying*. This fully realized self creates a kind of perceptual and
cognitive earthquake that casts us into a whirling, almost hallucinogenic
landscape of weird proportions and strange sights that makes the
"defamiliarization" theorized by the Russian formalists sound relatively
cozy by comparison. In its fury to break up our "chain of old habits"
and admit us to "a new scene,"[18] Emersonian self-reliance calls the very
fixity and *there-ness* of the world into question.

   "Circles," like "The Poet," thus forms a kind of bridge between the
exultant individualism of "Self-Reliance" and the more troubled, mel-
ancholy reflections on the price of autonomous selfhood we find later in
Emerson's "Experience."[19] In that essay, Emerson confronts in a very
different tone indeed the same structure of individualism celebrated in
"Self-Reliance," where he announced triumphantly, "When good is near
you . . . you shall not discern the footprints of any other; you shall not
see the face of man; you shall not hear any name."[20] In "Experience,"
however, that same phenomenon is rendered less as heroic independence
and more as isolation and loss: "There will be the same gulf between
every me and thee as between the original and the picture. . . . The soul
is not twin-born but the only begotten, and though revealing itself as a
child in time, child in appearance, is of a fatal and universal power,
admitting no co-life."[21]

   This acknowledgment of the poverty and alienation of atomistic individualism is anticipated, if not wholly so, in "Circles," where we learn
at the very beginning of the essay that "every action admits of being
outdone. Our life is an apprenticeship to the truth that around every
circle another can be drawn."[22] But even as this essay reaches back to the
central figure of the transparent eyeball in *Nature*, it looks forward to the
troubled consciousness of "Experience" by situating that circling activity
of "the active soul" in a world where every action and circle not only
can but *must* be immediately outdone, where that outdoing constitutes

one's social – or antisocial – relations with others. The world of "Circles," in other words, is a world not simply of individualism but of *competitive* individualism. Early on in the essay, Emerson dramatizes this fact in a brief but potent scene of instruction:

> The man finishes his story, – how good! how final! how it puts a new face on all things! He fills the sky. Lo! on the other side rises also a man and draws a circle around the circle we had just pronounced the outline of the sphere. Then already is our first speaker not man, but only a first speaker. His only redress is forthwith to draw a circle outside of his antagonist.[23]

All of which would be of less moment, perhaps, were it not for the fact that Emerson two pages later unpacks the alienating consequences of this good-natured contest in a passage of rather stunning egotism. "How often must we learn this lesson?" he asks with some impatience.

> Men cease to interest us when we find their limitations. The only sin is limitation. As soon as you once come up with a man's limitations, it is all over with him. Has he talents? has he enterprise? has he knowledge? It boots not. Infinitely alluring and attractive was he to you yesterday, a great hope, a sea to swim in; now, you have found his shores, found it a pond, and you care not if you never see it again.[24]

But finding the limitations of others and their circles – just as with ourselves and our own – is precisely what we *should* and *must* do; to draw "new and larger circles" is the very "way of life" for the Emersonian self.[25] To do anything else is to surrender the very promise of the active soul to that ossified world of social convention and material reality which is, we already know from *Nature*, a kind of "*scoriae*" or detritus.[26] In this essay, Emerson tells us about the circling self precisely what Marx will tell us later about the Lockean individual: that insofar as that self realizes its own selfhood, it will alienate the selfhood of the social Other.[27]

Undermining the consensus strategies of liberal intellectuals in the cold war period, Emerson everywhere tells us that in the end there can be, strictly speaking, no liberal individualist praxis, because when you begin to tinker with the autonomy of the self-reliant individual by enlisting him in the services of specific political and cultural ideologies, you have killed the very rationale for such visions in the first place. This is most clear in Emerson's concept of action, which underscores the irreconcilable relationship between a praxis taken seriously and a liberal individualism taken to heart. That difference is unmistakable in essays like "Politics" or "The American Scholar," where Emerson tells us that "the world of any moment is the merest appearance. Some great decorum, some fetish of a government, some ephemeral trade, or war, or man, is cried up by half mankind and cried down by the other half, as if all depended on this particular up or down."[28] It is not that material forms and institutions like books, laws, and governments are for Emerson completely worthless or impotent; it is rather that their capacity to carry the truth of Reason or the power of Spirit finally has nothing to do with concrete specificity of the particular action or the particular form practice takes.

Emerson articulates this crucial distinction in many, many places, but nowhere with more precision than in the first series of essays, where he develops two fundamental variations of his theory of action. On the one hand, he tells us, the self can never really know the meaning of an action at the time it is undertaken – a position elaborated in some detail in the single most important essay for Emerson's concept of action, "The American Scholar." There, Emerson insists that action is "essential" to the scholar, that without it he "is not yet man." "The new deed is yet a part of life," Emerson writes,

> – remains for a time immersed in our unconscious life. In some contemplative hour it detaches itself from the life like a ripe fruit, to become a thought of the mind. Instantly it is raised, transfigured; the corruptible has put on incorruption. Henceforth it is an object of beauty, however base its origin and neighborhood. . . . In its grub state, it cannot fly, it cannot shine, it is a dull grub. But suddenly, without observation, the selfsame thing unfurls beautiful wings, and is an angel of wisdom.[29]

In this remarkable passage, Emerson makes it clear that you may be able to know what you are doing when you are doing it, but you cannot know the true meaning and *value* of what you are doing until the action-in-the-world has been disengaged from its original material context and transformed into something *other than* action – into an *object of contemplation*. And this is so because "the final value of action" is that "it is a resource" to "make me acquainted with myself," to extend "my being, my dominion."[30] The value of action, in other words, is to acquaint you with the principles of self-reliance and self-trust upon which right action might be undertaken in the first place. But the necessity and possibility of praxis are undercut in a stroke by that same logic, because once you have understood those principles, you no longer have any reason for acting at all.

From this vantage, the second variant in Emerson's concept of action makes a little more sense. Emerson tells us in other places that the self *can* know, immediately, the meaning and value of its action. But the self who is equipped to know *that* (through the self-reliance made possible by a prior ethical renovation) is *also* Emersonian enough to know that "all things preach the indifference of circumstances,"[31] that "my wilful actions and acquisitions are but roving," that "it is profane to seek to interpose helps."[32] This is precisely the logic driving Emerson's strategic rants against falsely held abolitionism and charity in "Self-Reliance," where the self being castigated is the self who thinks that circumstances are *not* "indifferent," that action in and on the world *can* result in the right sort of selfhood for the actor. Here again, as in our earlier examples, the fundamental contradiction of Emerson's concept of action is that to be qualified to act at all is to remove the rationale and necessity for doing so.[33]

It is important to understand that Emerson's debilitating concept of action is not a betrayal of the logic of self-reliance but, in fact, a quite consistent and indeed rigorous application of it. What gives Emersonian individualism its real force as negative critique of social convention, political authority, and cultural ossification is precisely what makes it completely unthinkable as a praxis. The critical "active soul" of the Emersonian self is fluid and ductile, ever original and new, constantly revealing the inability of collective structures and undertakings to be adequate to it. It cannot be constituted by practice because it always, in strictest principle, outstrips it; it cannot be realized in practice because, in a fundamental sense, it is the very *antithesis* of practice.

This is even clearer when we remember that for Emerson the attempt to *will* self-reliance into being through practice constitutes a kind of massive hubris. "We lie in the lap of immense intelligence," he tells us in "Self-Reliance," "which makes us receivers of its truth and organs of its activity. When we discern justice, when we discern truth, we do nothing of ourselves, but allow a passage to its beams. If we ask whence this comes, if we seek to pry into the soul that causes, all philosophy is at fault." So it is that to "involuntary perceptions a perfect faith is due."[34] But volitionism in all its forms is not only mistaken for Emerson, it is also *dangerous*. As Frank Lentricchia has pointed out, "Any act of will attached to the organic action of antinomian selfhood is pure overlay, neither necessary nor appropriate: any act of would-be anti-imperialist will might become (ironically) a trace of the will of the imperialist."[35]

It is at this juncture that the relation – and disrelation – of the politics and ideology of Emerson and Pound come most fully into view, enabling us to explain how the political careers of these two writers could be so different when they are genealogically bound, as I have argued, by the same literary ideology. Pound's acceptance of a startlingly direct relationship between the ethical ideals infusing the subject of *virtù* and the material forms – cultural, economic, and political – that might institute and enforce those ideals is already nascent, as we have seen, from the very beginning of his career in essays like "Patria Mia" (with its proposals for patronage) and "Provincialism the Enemy" (with its critique of economic and educational regimentation). That belief in the direct relationship between ethical ideals and economic and political practice is even more pronounced after Pound's "discovery" of Major C. H. Douglas's Social Credit theory of economics in 1918; "a better economic system," Pound wrote, would help materialize Pound's ethical and aesthetic values by releasing "more energy for invention and design."[36]

The quintessentially Poundian interest in translating principles of ethical individualism into economic and political practice is most unmistakable in his economic prose of the thirties and in *Jefferson and/or Mussolini*, which labels the author as a kind of spokesman for "Volitionist Economics."[37] For Pound, the truth of *virtù* that the artist or poet knows *can and should* be legislated and embodied in specific economic and political forms. Nowhere is this clearer than in his admiration of Mussolini – an "artifex," Pound writes, who rivals Brancusi and Picabia in his grasp of the basic formal principles necessary to organize both the work of art *and* the work of state.[38] Mussolini knows what the artist knows, but, more important, he possesses *directio voluntatis*, which gives him "the moral force to translate knowledge into action"[39] – hence Pound's admiration of his "passion for construction," which manifests itself in the draining of swamps to create farmland (commemorated by Pound in Canto XLI).[40] Pound's premium upon *directio voluntatis* even led him across political lines to praise, of all people, Lenin: "This is Lenin's calm estimate of all other Russian parties," Pound writes approvingly. "They are very clever, yes, they can do EVERYTHING except act."[41] Lenin, like Jefferson and Mussolini, is a man of "essential dynamism," a "man who did *get things* DONE."[42]

So although Pound, like Emerson, believed that the efficacy of any political or economic system depended upon the virtue of the individuals who participated in it, unlike Emerson he usually equated the exercise of virtue with the exercise of *will*. And – most un-Emersonian of all – he believed that the necessary extension of virtue was practice, that material and social forms *could* objectify the "active soul," the *directio voluntatis*, without alienating it.

By focusing upon the very different relationships between ideology and praxis in these two writers, we can begin to see how Pound and Emerson, *precisely because they take their liberal individualism seriously*, unmask the political unconscious of liberal individualism. In these two writers as in few others, we find spectacular testimony to what is often sublimated in the milder, pluralist forms of liberalism: the fact that liberal individualism is all at once exhilarating and alienating, totalizing and atomistic, powerful and impoverished – in short, that what makes it seductive and promising is also what makes it disenchanting and dangerous.

Pound and Emerson, by virtue of the very intensity of their individualism, disrupt and expose those "strategies of containment"[43] at work in the liberal consensus cultural politics of the founding generation of Americanist critics. And they do so, moreover, in two fundamentally different ways. Emerson, as we have seen, finally *does* respect the separation of culture and politics at work in critics like Trilling and Anderson, if only because he radically subsumes the latter under the former. But he just as surely subverts the liberal consensus position in other ways, because he insists upon the terrifying, bewildering, and essentially anarchic nature of the self, which would never have tolerated the meliorative, centrist strategies of the liberal consensus view. Emerson's vision of self-reliance would never have put up with being saddled with that sort of *content*. Instead of aligning his individualism with the liberal consensus against Stalinism, Emerson would have set self-reliance against *both*.

Because of the purity and rigor of his individualism, Emerson was willing to admit, finally, what is masked by liberal consensus cultural politics: that for the liberal self, the world is an "unhandsome," alienating, and terrifying place, because "we believe in ourselves as we do not believe in others. We permit all things to ourselves, and that which we call sin in others is experiment for us." Thus, through Emerson liberal individualism reveals what liberal pluralism attempts to repress: "God delights to isolate us every day."[44]

But one way for the radically atomistic individual not to be so isolated and alienated is to enforce *its* truth as the truth for all selves, to build, through material practice, a world adequate to itself. That was Pound's "volitionist" strategy, of course, and it bodies forth the disturbing political consequences of liberal individualism that are forestalled and held in check by Emerson's idealism. Pound remained faithful to the structure of liberal individualism but refused – as we surely must – to indulge the idealism (in Emerson) and the separation of culture and politics (in cold war consensus intellectuals) that so often accompany it, smoothing its bristling contradictions. More than almost any other writer, Pound meant to make good on the promise of individualism, and the bitter irony of his career is that in doing so he transformed the ideological symptom of Emersonian individualism into the full-blown condition of authoritarian egoism and fascism that, like Emerson's boa constrictor, wanted to eat the world whole. My point, however, is that we should be critical not of Pound's commitment to praxis but rather of the very ideal of individualism that drove that praxis to such terrible consequences. Only by doing so can we confront with renewed vigilance the elitism harbored in every pluralism, the alienation shadowing every freedom, the fascism hiving in every liberalism. And only by doing so can we identify not only the Pound in Emerson but also the Pound in us.

Notes

INTRODUCTION

1. The recent exchange between Reed Way Dasenbrock, "Pound's Demonology," and Robert Casillo, "Damage Control in the Pound Industry: Response to Dasenbrock," in *American Literary History* 1: 1 (Spring 1989): 231–243, provides a taste of the current climate. This is not to suggest, of course, that such is the case with all studies of Pound. See, e.g., Peter Nicholls's politically measured *Ezra Pound: Politics, Economics, and Writing* (Atlantic Highlands, N.J.: Humanities Press, 1984), and Peter Brooker, "The Lesson of Ezra Pound: An Essay in Poetry, Literary Ideology, and Politics," in *Ezra Pound: Tactics for Reading*, ed. Ian F. A. Bell (London: Vision Press, 1982), pp. 8–49.

2. Contradiction *between* what and what continues to be a disputed question. Ideology may be seen as either internally contradictory or as a seamless and internally consistent whole that is in contradiction not with itself but with the social and economic conditions it seeks to resolve or master. After deconstruction, it is increasingly difficult to maintain the latter position and almost impossible, as I suggest, not to ratify the former. For an overview of the problem of ideology, see Terry Eagleton, *Ideology: An Introduction* (London: New Left Books, 1991), and Göran Therborn, *The Power of Ideology and the Ideology of Power* (London: New Left Books, 1980). For a brief survey, the reader may consult Myra Jehlen's introduction to *Ideology and Classic American Literature*, ed. Sacvan Bercovitch and Myra Jehlen, Cambridge Studies in American Literature and Culture (Cambridge: Cambridge University Press, 1987), pp. 1–18. For useful contrasting discussions of conflicting tendencies within contemporary Marxist critiques of the concept, see James H. Kavanagh, "Marxism's Althusser: Toward a Politics of Literary Theory," *diacritics* 12 (1982): 25–45, and John Higgins, "Raymond Williams and the Problem of Ideology," in *Postmodernism and Politics*, ed. Jonathan Arac, Theory and History of Literature, Vol. 28 (Minneapolis: University of Minnesota Press, 1986), pp. 112–122.

3. Quite the reverse, Pound mentions Emerson only a few times in his entire career – usually in passing, occasionally (as we see in Chapter 1) in more detail – but always with light regard.

229

4. Reed Way Dasenbrock, "Jefferson and/or Adams: A Shifting Mirror for Mussolini in the Middle Cantos," *ELH* 55: 2 (summer 1988): 505–526.

5. Ibid., 512–513. It should be noted that Dasenbrock's essay draws heavily upon (and indeed is, in essence, an application of) J. G. A. Pocock's *The Machiavellian Moment: Florentine Political Thought and the Atlantic Republican Tradition* (Princeton: Princeton University Press, 1975). It should be noted, too, that Pocock's thesis argues that the driving force of Anglo-American political thought during the revolutionary period was not what Pocock calls the "Lockean paradigm" but was instead the concern with *virtù*, inherited from the Italian Renaissance, as the means by which republics may combat corruption and so avoid their demise. As will become clear later in this study, my reading of *virtù* (at least, Pound's version of it) argues that it is indeed Lockean in its structure and phenomenology – that is to say, it is a figure of identity-as-possession.

6. Dasenbrock, "Jefferson and/or Adams," pp. 518–519.

7. It is worth noting in this connection that the concept of *virtù* is firmly installed in Pound's work well before the appearance of either Malatesta or Jefferson in the *Cantos*; in fact, it is fully there from the beginning of his career, in the very early essay "I gather the Limbs of Osiris" (1911–1912) and again (as we shall see in Chapter 3) in "Patria Mia" (1912–1913). Dasenbrock points out that the original meaning of *virtù* in English is "fairly close to Pound's usage" but then argues that the "Osiris" essay employs "a rather different earlier Poundian use" (ibid., pp. 525–526, n. 22). In fact, the reverse seems true; if, according to the *OED* reference cited by Dasenbrock, the earliest definition is "the power or operative influence inherent in supernatural or divine being," then the sense of Poundian *virtù* closest to this is clearly the "Osiris" definition. See Pound, *Selected Prose, 1909–1965*, ed. William Cookson (New York: New Directions, 1973), pp. 28–29.

   Later in Pound's career, economic programs and political theories of whatever kind continue to be dependent upon a more fundamental ethical individualism, whether in the will toward "order/ *Tò Kalón*" of Jefferson and Mussolini or in the Confucian belief, so crucial to the later Pound, that one must first achieve order within one's self before setting out to instill order in one's family, community, and finally in one's lands.

8. *Emerson in His Journals*, ed. Joel Porte (Cambridge, Mass.: Belknap Press of Harvard University Press, 1982), p. 125.

9. The characterization belongs to Marvin Meyers in his classic study *The Jacksonian Persuasion: Politics and Belief* (Stanford: Stanford University Press, 1957), p. vii; quoted in Michael T. Gilmore, *American Romanticism and the Marketplace* (Chicago: University of Chicago Press, 1985), p. 30. For a revisionist reading of the "Jacksonian paradox" and its relation to "Emerson's America," see Carolyn Porter's *Seeing and Being: The Plight of the Participant Observer in Emerson, James, Adams, and Faulkner* (Middletown, Conn.: Wesleyan University Press, 1981), pp. 67ff. Porter's analysis draws on the critique of Meyers's reading of Jacksonianism undertaken by the political historian Michael Lebowitz in "The Jacksonians: Paradox Lost?" in *Towards*

a New Past: Dissenting Essays in American History, ed. Barton J. Bernstein (New York: Vintage, 1968), pp. 65–89.

10. See Houston A. Baker, Jr.'s important exploration of this problem in "Figurations for a New Literary History," in Bercovitch and Jehlen's *Ideology and Classic American Literature*, pp. 145–171 (esp. pp. 167–169).

11. As Louis Hartz demonstrated years ago in his influential study, the "tyrannical force of Lockean sentiment" is most fully realized in American culture, where the self – uncompromised, as Tocqueville told us, by Continental encumbrances of class, church, and crown, and free to "make it new," as Pound put it, without the burden of a crushing feudal past – could now finally realize a proper cultural politics of, by, and for the individual. See Hartz, *The Liberal Tradition in America* (New York: Harcourt Brace, 1955), p. 6.

12. Larzer Ziff, *Literary Democracy: The Declaration of Cultural Independence in America* (New York: Penguin, 1982), pp. 257, 244.

13. Donald E. Pease, *Visionary Compacts: American Renaissance Writings in Cultural Context*, Wisconsin Project on American Writers (Madison: University of Wisconsin Press, 1987), p. 126. See also pp. 149ff.

14. Pound, *Selected Prose*, p. 145.

15. The phrase belongs to Fredric Jameson in his *The Political Unconscious: Narrative as a Socially Symbolic Act* (Ithaca: Cornell University Press, 1981). See pp. 10, 53–54, 210–219, 266–270.

16. For a more fully theorized and articulated discussion of the imperfect closure and lack of seamlessness of ideological structures, see my "Antinomies of Liberalism: The Politics of 'Belief' and the Project of Americanist Criticism," in *Discovering Difference: New Essays on American Culture*, ed. C. K. Lohmann (Bloomington: Indiana University Press, 1993).

17. This process of dissent and recontainment has been read by Sacvan Bercovitch, in one of the more famous critiques in Americanist criticism, as the essential structure of the American Jeremiad. See his *The American Jeremiad* (Madison: University of Wisconsin Press, 1978). Donald Pease has recently argued, however, that for Bercovitch this process constitutes a *ritual* of dissent, which cannot effect social or political change but "only reveals the incomparable cooptative power of American ideology." See Pease, "New Americanists: Revisionist Interventions into the Canon," *boundary 2* 17: 1 (Spring 1990): 1–37, esp. pp. 19–23, 28–29.

18. Frank Lentricchia, *Ariel and the Police: Michel Foucault, William James, Wallace Stevens* (Madison: University of Wisconsin Press, 1988), p. 121.

19. Kenneth Burke, *Permanence and Change*, 3d ed. (Berkeley and Los Angeles: University of California Press, 1984), p. 282. For a related discussion of what Burke calls the "Bureaucratization of the Imaginative," see his *Attitudes toward History*, 3d ed. (Berkeley and Los Angeles: University of California Press, 1984), pp. 225–226.

20. See Dasenbrock, "Jefferson and/or Adams," p. 516.

21. Howard Horwitz, "The Standard Oil Trust as Emersonian Hero," *Raritan* 6: 4 (Spring 1987): 97–119, esp. pp. 117–118.

22. Kaja Silverman, *The Acoustic Mirror: The Female Voice in Psychoanalysis and Cinema* (Bloomington: Indiana University Press, 1988), p. 1.

23. The Emersonianism of "The Chinese Written Character" was, to my knowledge, first noted by Hugh Kenner in *The Pound Era* (Berkeley and Los Angeles: University of California Press, 1971), pp. 105, 157–158, 230–231. Kenner's interpretation of this fact, however, differs in many significant ways from my own.

1. A POLITICS OF DIFFERENCE

1. See Régis Debray, "A Modest Contribution to the Rites and Ceremonies of the Tenth Anniversary," *New Left Review* 115 (May–June 1979): 45–65; Jean Baudrillard, *America*, trans. Chris Turner (London: New Left Books, 1988).

2. Fredric Jameson, "On *Habits of the Heart*," *South Atlantic Quarterly* 86: 4 (Fall 1987): 545–565, esp. pp. 549–550.

3. Stuart Hall, "On Postmodernism and Articulation: An Interview," *Journal of Communication Inquiry* 10: 2 (Summer 1986): 46. This point is made by a host of other commentators on postmodernism. Andreas Huyssen, for example, like Jameson finds poststructural discourse to be primarily a phenomenon of European intellectuals thinking about the United States and its curious ahistoricity. See Huyssen's *After the Great Divide: Modernism, Mass Culture, Postmodernism* (Bloomington: Indiana University Press, 1986), p. 190.

4. Alexandre Kojève, *Introduction to the Reading of Hegel* (New York: Basic Books, 1969), p. 160. Quoted in Jean-Philippe Mathy, "Out of History: French Readings of Postmodern America," *American Literary History* 2: 2 (Summer 1990): 267–298, esp. p. 271. Mathy's article provides an excellent overview of the "end of history" tradition in critical views of America and is doubly useful in mapping how different ideological positions interpret the fact of American exceptionalism (an intellectual terrain we might describe as having Sartre at one horizon, Jean-François Revel at the other, and Baudrillard – ideologically if not methodologically – somewhere in between).

5. Kojève, *Introduction to the Reading of Hegel*, p. 161. Quoted in Mathy, "Out of History," p. 271.

6. Kojève, *Introduction to the Reading of Hegel*, p. 158. Quoted in Mathy, "Out of History," p. 270.

7. For an incisive review of Baudrillard's text, which underscores how Baudrillard's vision shares with Tocqueville's study many of the same blind spots in its reading of American society, see Paul Buhle, "America: Post-Modernity?" *New Left Review* 180 (March–April 1990): 165–175. See also Mathy, "Out of History," pp. 284ff.

8. Warren Susman's essay "Socialism and Americanism" is an informative speculation on the political convertibility of the American Dream. As Susman points out, in the thirties the *Daily Worker* framed communism as a "twentieth-century Americanism" (with pictures of George Washington and Lenin side by side). "Americanism ordered a Labor Day," Susman writes, "while the Popular Front proposed an Americanism Day." See Susman,

Culture as History: The Transformation of American Society in the Twentieth Century (New York: Pantheon, 1984), pp. 75–85.

9. Ralph Waldo Emerson, *Nature*, in *The Complete Works of Ralph Waldo Emerson*, Centenary Edition, 12 vols., ed. Edward Waldo Emerson (Boston: Houghton Mifflin, 1903–1904), Vol. I, p. 3. Subsequent references to this edition will be abbreviated *W*.

10. Donald Pease sees this simultaneity of promise and fulfillment at work in the American "Revolutionary Mythos" itself (but also in the liberal cultural criticism of the cold war). See his *Visionary Compacts: American Renaissance Writings in Cultural Context*, Wisconsin Project on American Writers (Madison: University of Wisconsin Press, 1987), esp. pp. 32, 36, 44.

11. Emerson, "The American Scholar," *W*, Vol. I, pp. 81–82.

12. See, e.g., Maurice Gonnaud, *An Uneasy Solitude: Individual and Society in the Work of Ralph Waldo Emerson*, trans. Lawrence Rosenwald, foreword by Eric Cheyfitz (French ed., 1964; Princeton: Princeton University Press, 1987), p. 189.

13. For a detailed exploration of what Jean-Paul Sartre calls the "counterfinality" of the "practico-inert," see the *Critique of Dialectical Reason*, trans. Alan Sheridan-Smith (London: New Left Books, 1976), esp. Chap. 3, "Matter as Totalized Totality – A First Encounter with Necessity."

14. Emerson, "The American Scholar," *W*, Vol. I, pp. 89–90.

15. Michel Foucault, *The Archaeology of Knowledge and the Discourse on Language*, trans. A. M. Sheridan-Smith (New York: Pantheon, 1972), p. 21.

16. Emerson, "The American Scholar," *W*, Vol. I, p. 88.

17. Emerson, "Self-Reliance," *W*, Vol. II, p. 87.

18. The point here is that all social forms project or imply a stance toward temporality and the possibility of history. For important investigations of the question of genre in precisely these terms, see the line of criticism running from Sartre's *What Is Literature?* trans. Bernard Frechtman, introduction by Wallace Fowlie (New York: Harper and Row, 1965), through his *Saint Genet: Actor and Martyr*, trans. Bernard Frechtman (New York: Pantheon Books, 1983), to Roland Barthes's *Writing Degree Zero*, trans. Annette Lavers and Colin Smith, preface by Susan Sontag (New York: Hill and Wang, 1984).

19. Emerson, *Nature*, *W*, Vol. I, pp. 25–26.

20. Myra Jehlen points our in her reading of *Nature* that in Emerson's view, Nature is *already* a language – in fact, in its freedom from the mediation of social man and his institutions, it is all the language we need. Which is another way of saying, for my purposes, that for Emerson language is inauthentic insofar as it *is* a social and historical construct. We will investigate these matters in more detail in Chapter 7. See Jehlen's *American Incarnation: The Individual, the Nation, and the Continent* (Cambridge, Mass.: Harvard University Press, 1986), pp. 102ff.

21. Emerson, "The Poet," *W*, Vol. III, pp. 20, 12.

22. See Daniel Bell, *The End of Ideology: On the Exhaustion of Political Ideas in the Fifties* (New York: Free Press, 1960); idem, *The Coming of Post-industrial Society*

(New York: Basic Books, 1973); and idem, *The Cultural Contradictions of Capitalism* (New York: Basic Books, 1976).

23. Gerald Graff, "American Criticism Left and Right," in *Ideology and Classic American Literature*, ed. Sacvan Bercovitch and Myra Jehlen, Cambridge Studies in American Literature and Culture (Cambridge: Cambridge University Press, 1986), p. 95.

24. Emerson, "Experience," *W*, Vol. III, p. 84.

25. Emerson, "Circles," *W*, Vol. II, p. 302.

26. Emerson, *Nature*, *W*, Vol. I, p. 10. As with most things in Emerson, this moment is one of extreme political ambivalence. On the one hand, he suggests that individual difference should likewise be "uncontained." On the other, Emerson would thus seem to countenance an expansionist if not protoimperialist self, one for whom Nature, as he famously put it, "wears the colors of the spirit."

27. Emerson, "Circles," *W*, Vol. II, p. 319.

28. Emerson, "The American Scholar," *W*, Vol. I, p. 114.

29. The phrase belongs to Donald Pease in his *Visionary Compacts*, p. 207. Pease's discussion of Emerson's *Nature*, though different in emphasis from my own, provides an excellent analysis of the "double bind" of Emerson's relation to the problem of history. See esp. pp. 213–234.

30. Frank Lentricchia, *Criticism and Social Change* (Chicago: University of Chicago Press, 1983), p. 30.

31. Emerson, "Circles," *W*, Vol. II, p. 320; idem, "The Poet," *W*, Vol. III, p. 33.

32. This technique, incidentally, was also being used at this moment by the rock star Prince (as in "I Would Die 4 U" on the album *Purple Rain*) in his own project of self-fashioning.

33. Strictly speaking, Reebok inverts Emerson by promising to produce originality with a wonderful object, rather than the reverse, as Emerson would have it. It is also true, however, that Emerson's logic invites such an appropriation by making matter and Spirit immediately convertible, by telling us that materiality does not contain and shape the self but is rather immediately subject to the self's appropriation for its own expression.

34. This is not to suggest a blanket condemnation of Emerson's postmodern aspect. We should remember that postmodern culture and theory are themselves politically ambivalent, insofar as they also imagine the possibility of new and potentially radical forms of global, collective experience. This too, if we believe Daniel T. O'Hara, is anticipated by Emerson's imagination of "every soul as a revolutionary principle without restraint," which itself provides a basis for some new "collective revisionary self." As O'Hara puts it, however – with apparently little faith in the political potential of postmodernism – "the celebrants of the postmodern subject are, perhaps, celebrating an unwitting parody of this essentially Emersonian, oppositional critical vision" (pp. 701–702). See his "Socializing the Sublime in American Renaissance Writers," *South Atlantic Quarterly* 88: 3 (Summer 1989): 691–703. The best speculation on the decentered subject and the potential of

postmodern collective experience is Fredric Jameson's "Postmodernism, or the Cultural Logic of Late Capitalism," *New Left Review* 146 (July–August 1984): 53–93, esp. pp. 75ff., and his extensive study incorporating that essay, *Postmodernism, or The Cultural Logic of Late Capitalism* (Durham: Duke University Press, 1991).

35. Emerson, *Nature*, *W*, Vol. I, p. 71.
36. Emerson, "Self-Reliance," *W*, Vol. II, pp. 68–69.
37. Ezra Pound, *Selected Prose, 1909–1965*, ed. William Cookson (New York: New Directions, 1973), p. 146.
38. Ibid., p. 145.
39. *The Selected Letters of Ezra Pound, 1907–1941*, ed. D. D. Paige, preface by Mark Van Doren (New York: New Directions, 1971), pp. 123–124.
40. Ezra Pound, "Indiscretions," in *Pavannes and Divagations* (New York: New Directions, 1974), p. 6.
41. See Kathryne V. Lindberg, *Reading Pound Reading: Modernism after Nietzsche* (New York: Oxford University Press, 1987). Lindberg's discussion of Pound and Whitman in her "Postscript" is particularly worth consulting in this context.
42. Pound, *Selected Prose*, p. 119.
43. Quoted in Wendy Stallard Flory, *The American Ezra Pound* (New Haven: Yale University Press, 1989), pp. 27–28.
44. *Literary Essays of Ezra Pound*, ed. T. S. Eliot (New York: New Directions, 1968), p. 154.
45. Ibid.
46. Ibid., p. 296.
47. Ibid.
48. Emerson, "Politics," *W*, Vol. III, pp. 214–215.
49. Pound, *Literary Essays*, p. 296, n. 2.
50. Ibid. Lentricchia – accurately, I think – calls this the "definitive metaphor of [Pound's] politics." See his discussion of the relationship between Pound and the James line in his forthcoming contribution to the new *Cambridge History of American Literature*.
51. Pound, *Selected Prose*, p. 115.
52. Ibid., p. 189.
53. This passage is from F. O. Matthiessen, *The James Family: A Group Biography* (Cambridge, Mass.: Harvard University Press, 1975), p. 429, quoted in Frank Lentricchia, "On the Ideologies of Poetic Modernism, 1890–1913: The Example of William James," in *Reconstructing American Literary History*, ed. Sacvan Bercovitch (Cambridge, Mass.: Harvard University Press, 1986), p. 233.
54. We should remember, as Warren Susman reminds us, that "character" (James) and "personality" (Pound) are historically distinct concepts. The former, essentially a nineteenth-century construct, connotes what Emerson called "Moral Order through the medium of individual nature." The latter, predominant in twentieth-century America's culture of abundance, was geared not toward self-control and moral integrity but rather toward self-expression

and self-gratification. As Susman points out, Emerson is an important source for *both* of these concepts, and the same sort of doubleness may be found in Pound's concept of "personality." See Susman's "'Personality' and the Making of Twentieth-Century Culture," in his *Culture as History*, esp. pp. 274–281.

55. Quoted in Lentricchia, "On the Ideologies of Poetic Modernism," p. 232.
56. Ibid., p. 238.
57. Patricia Rae, "From Mystical Gaze to Pragmatic Game: Representations of Truth in Vorticist Art," *ELH* 56: 3 (Fall 1989): 689–720, esp. p. 699.
58. See Walter Sutton, "Coherence in Pound's *Cantos* and William James's Pluralistic Universe," *Paideuma* 15: 1 (Spring 1986): 7–21.
59. Lentricchia's reconsideration of James may be found in his essay "On the Ideologies of Poetic Modernism" and in the chapter devoted to James in his *Ariel and the Police: Michel Foucault, William James, Wallace Stevens* (Madison: University of Wisconsin Press, 1988). For the place of James in the broader context of American philosophy and modernism, see Lentricchia's "Philosophers of Modernism at Harvard, circa 1900," *South Atlantic Quarterly* 89: 4 (Fall 1990): 787–834.
60. Kenneth Burke, *Attitudes toward History*, 3d ed. (Berkeley and Los Angeles: University of California Press, 1984), p. 374.
61. On academic philosophy and antiimperialism in James, see Lentricchia's *Ariel and the Police*, esp. pp. 112–113ff. and pp. 20–21.
62. William James, *Pragmatism and the Meaning of Truth*, introduction by A. J. Ayer (Cambridge, Mass.: Harvard University Press, 1975), pp. 17–18.
63. See Lentricchia, *Ariel and the Police*, pp. 113, 125.
64. Ibid., p. 113.
65. "What Pragmatism Means," in William James, *Essays in Pragmatism*, ed. Alburey Castell (New York: Haffner Publishing Co., 1948), p. 152.
66. James, *Essays in Pragmatism*, p. 144.
67. James, *Pragmatism and the Meaning of Truth*, p. 126; see Lentricchia, *Ariel and the Police*, p. 110.
68. Rae, "From Mystical Gaze to Pragmatic Game," p. 705.
69. See Lentricchia, *Ariel and the Police*, p. 119. As Jehlen puts it, for Emerson "willful intervention can only distort the perfect order that already exists implicitly. . . . Not only are deeds and revolutions not needed, they are forbidden." See her *American Incarnation*, p. 85.
70. For a brief account, see Noel Stock, *The Life of Ezra Pound* (New York: Pantheon Books, 1970), pp. 133–134.
71. For the relevant correspondence, see Pound, *Selected Letters*, pp. 16–17, 19; for the quotation from the letter to Homer Pound, see p. 20.
72. See e.g., Pound, *Selected Letters*, p. 19, where he writes to Harriet Monroe, "I don't doubt that the things Frost sent you were very bad."
73. These are reprinted as "Robert Frost (Two Reviews)," in Pound, *Literary Essays*, pp. 382–386. Further references are to this reprint.
74. Ibid., p. 382.
75. Pound, *Selected Prose*, pp. 461–462.

76. Ibid., pp. 191–192.
77. Pound, *Literary Essays*, p. 11.
78. *Selected Letters of Robert Frost*, ed. Lawrance Thompson (New York: Holt, Rinehart, and Winston, 1964), p. 102.
79. Ibid., p. 141.
80. Pound, *Literary Essays*, p. 373.
81. Ibid., p. 377.
82. Pound, *Selected Letters*, p. 49.
83. Pound, *Literary Essays*, p. 383.
84. Pound, *Selected Prose*, p. 41.
85. Pound, *Literary Essays*, p. 384.
86. Ibid., p. 385.
87. Ibid., p. 298.
88. Ibid.
89. Emerson, "Self-Reliance," *W*, Vol. II, p. 49.
90. Pound, *Literary Essays*, p. 42, emphasis mine.
91. Emerson, "Self-Reliance," *W*, Vol. II, pp. 51–52.
92. Pound, *Literary Essays*, p. 46.
93. Karl Marx and Friedrich Engels, *The German Ideology*, ed. C. J. Arthur (New York: International Publishers, 1970), p. 105. For other relevant passages see pp. 108–109, 118.
94. Ibid., p. 52. For a helpful discussion of the relationship between Marxism and liberal individualism, see D. F. B. Tucker, *Marxism and Individualism* (New York: St. Martin's Press, 1980), esp. pp. 59–84.
95. Marx and Engels, *The German Ideology*, p. 105.
96. Ibid., p. 53.
97. Pound, *Literary Essays*, p. 46.

2. CRITIQUES OF CAPITALIST (LITERARY) PRODUCTION

1. Emerson, "The American Scholar," in *The Complete Works of Ralph Waldo Emerson,* Centenary Edition, 12 vols., ed. Edward Waldo Emerson (Boston: Houghton Mifflin, 1903–1904), Vol. I, pp. 82–84. Subsequent references to this edition will be abbreviated *W*.
2. *The Early Lectures of Ralph Waldo Emerson*, Vol. 3, *1838–1842*, ed. Stephen E. Whicher, Robert E. Spiller, and Wallace E. Williams (Cambridge, Mass.: Harvard University Press, 1959–1972), p. 190.
3. Michael T. Gilmore, *American Romanticism and the Marketplace* (Chicago: University of Chicago Press, 1985), p. 6.
4. Emerson, *English Traits*, *W*, Vol. V, p. 212.
5. Emerson, *Nature*, *W*, Vol. I, p. 3.
6. *Emerson in His Journals*, ed. Joel Porte (Cambridge, Mass.: Belknap Press of Harvard University Press, 1982), p. 221.
7. Ezra Pound, *Selected Prose, 1909–1965*, ed. William Cookson (New York: New Directions, 1973), pp. 191–192.
8. Emerson, "The American Scholar," *W*, Vol. I, p. 84.
9. Emerson, "The Poet," *W*, Vol. III, p. 9.

10. Carolyn Porter, *Seeing and Being: The Plight of the Participant Observer in Emerson, James, Adams, and Faulkner* (Middletown, Conn.: Wesleyan University Press, 1981), p. 19.

11. See Douglass C. North, *The Economic Growth of the United States, 1790–1860* (New York: Norton, 1966), p. 210, and George R. Taylor, *The Transportation Revolution, 1815–1860* (1915; rpt., New York: Harper and Row, 1968), pp. 388, 325. See as well Gilmore's overview in his introduction to *American Romanticism and the Marketplace,* and Michael Paul Rogin, *Fathers and Children: Andrew Jackson and the Subjugation of the American Indian* (New York: Alfred A. Knopf, 1975).

12. Robert L. Heilbroner, *The Economic Transformation of America* (New York: Harcourt Brace Jovanovich, 1977), p. 49.

13. Ibid., pp. 44–45. See also Richard D. Brown, *Modernization: The Transformation of American Life, 1600–1865* (New York: Hill and Wang, 1976), pp. 134–135, 104–105, 112. For a brief overview of these sources, see Porter, *Seeing and Being,* pp. 64–65.

14. Heilbroner, *Economic Transformation of America,* p. 42.

15. Ibid., p. 49; Porter, *Seeing and Being,* p. 62.

16. *The Journals and Miscellaneous Notebooks of Ralph Waldo Emerson,* 16 vols., ed. William H. Gilman et al. (Cambridge, Mass. : Belknap Press of Harvard University Press, 1960–1982), Vol. XVI, p. 304.

17. Heilbroner, *Economic Transformation of America,* p. 38. For further discussion of the Lowell System, see Porter, *Seeing and Being,* p. 63, and W. Elliot Brownlee, *Dynamics of Ascent: A History of the American Economy* (New York: Knopf, 1974), p. 108.

18. Heilbroner, *Economic Transformation of America,* p. 38.

19. Ibid., p. 40.

20. See Porter, *Seeing and Being,* p. 63, and Norman Ware, *The Industrial Worker: 1840–1860* (1924; rpt., New York: Quadrangle, 1964), p. 121.

21. Emerson, *Journals and Miscellaneous Notebooks,* Vol. IV, pp. 334–335.

22. Maurice Gonnaud reminds us that in the Concord of the second quarter of the nineteenth century, "the difficult days of settlement and clearing were past; those of intensive industrialization, with its brutal migrations and class conflicts, were still in the future." See his *An Uneasy Solitude: Individual and Society in the Work of Ralph Waldo Emerson,* trans. Lawrence Rosenwald, foreword by Eric Cheyfitz (French ed., 1964; Princeton: Princeton University Press, 1987), p. 143. In leaving Boston for Concord, in other words, Emerson was in part recoiling from impending modernity, which had not yet impinged upon the rather more pastoral confines of his new home.

23. These figures are quoted in Larzer Ziff, *Literary Democracy: The Declaration of Cultural Independence in America* (New York: Penguin Books, 1982), p. 18. On the panic of 1837, a more detailed treatment is available in Samuel Rezneck, "The Social History of an American Depression: 1837–1843," *American Historical Review* 40 (July 1935): 662–687.

24. *Emerson in His Journals,* p. 161.

25. See Gonnaud, *An Uneasy Solitude,* p. 225. For a fuller discussion of the

uneven regional effects of the panic, see William Charvat, "American Romanticism and the Depression of 1837," *Science and Society* 2 (Winter 1937): 67–82.

26. *Emerson in His Journals*, p. 164.
27. Ziff, *Literary Democracy*, p. 18.
28. The paradigm for the articulation of this socioeconomic construct in the previous epoch remains the Benjamin Franklin of the *Autobiography* as diagnosed by Max Weber in 1905 in his study *The Protestant Ethic and the Spirit of Capitalism*, trans. Talcott Parsons (London: George Allen and Unwin, 1930), pp. 48ff.
29. Quoted in Ziff, *Literary Democracy*, p. 13.
30. For a brief summary of the technology of the Second Industrial Revolution and its effects, see T. J. Jackson Lears, *No Place of Grace: Anti-modernism and the Transformation of American Culture, 1880–1920* (New York: Pantheon Books, 1981), pp. 8ff.
31. A fine discussion of Taylorization in historical context is available in Harry Braverman's important *Labor and Monopoly Capital: The Degradation of Work in the Twentieth Century* (New York: Monthly Review Press, 1974). See esp. Chap. 4. For a discussion of Braverman versus Foucault on labor and discipline, see Frank Lentricchia's discussion in *Ariel and the Police: Michel Foucault, William James, Wallace Stevens* (Madison: University of Wisconsin Press, 1988), pp. 29–102.
32. Heilbroner, *Economic Transformation of America*, p. 146.
33. Gabriel Kolko, *Main Currents in Modern American History* (New York: Harper and Row, 1976), pp. 72–73.
34. James F. Knapp, *Literary Modernism and the Transformation of Work* (Evanston: Northwestern University Press, 1988), p. 4. My discussion of the relationship between Taylorization and Pound's social critique would be deeply indebted to Knapp's study had I not written it before I discovered his book. In Chapters 2 and 3, Knapp discusses Pound, along with other writers, in light of these sweeping changes in production and the labor process.
35. See Braverman, *Labor and Monopoly Capital*, esp. Chaps. 3, 5, 6, 8, 10, and 20.
36. Pound, *Selected Prose*, pp. 193, 190.
37. Knapp makes a similar point in *Literary Modernism,* pp. 30ff. For his discussion of the relationship between Taylorization and Foucault, see pp. 11ff.
38. Pound, *Selected Prose*, p. 195.
39. Michel Foucault, *Discipline and Punish,* trans. Alan Sheridan (New York: Vintage Books, 1979), p. 187.
40. Pound, *Selected Prose*, p. 193.
41. Foucault, *Discipline and Punish*, p. 194.
42. Peter Nicholls, *Ezra Pound: Politics, Economics, and Writing* (Atlantic Highlands, N.J.: Humanities Press, 1984). See esp. the section "The Quarrel With Marxism," pp. 47ff.
43. Karl Marx, *Economic and Philosophical Manuscripts,* in *Early Writings*, trans.

Rodney Livingstone and Gregor Benton, introduction by Lucio Colletti (New York: Vintage Books, 1975), p. 326.

44. Ibid., p. 324.

45. Ibid.

46. Georg Lukács, *History and Class Consciousness,* trans. Rodney Livingstone (Cambridge: MIT Press, 1971), pp. 88–89; quoted in Knapp, *Literary Modernism,* pp. 13–14.

47. Pound, *Selected Prose,* p. 191.

48. The Osiris of his early essay refers to the ancient "male productive principle in nature," the "source of renewed life," according to Hugh Kenner, *The Pound Era* (Berkeley and Los Angeles: University of California Press, 1971), p. 150. Pound's "Postscript to *The Natural Philosophy of Love* by Remy de Gourmont" is in Pound, *Pavannes and Divagations* (New York: New Directions, 1974), pp. 203–214. See also his even more remarkable essay "The New Therapy" in *New Age* (March 16, 1922): 259–260. The definitive study of Pound's relationship to Remy de Gourmont is Richard Sieburth, *Instigations: Ezra Pound and Remy de Gourmont* (Cambridge, Mass.: Harvard University Press, 1978). For a useful general discussion of the Eleusinian cult, see Peter Makin, *Pound's Cantos* (London: George Allen and Unwin, 1985), pp. 89–98. For Pound's views on the relationship between the cult of Eleusis and the troubadours, see his essay "Terra Italica" in Pound, *Selected Prose,* pp. 54–60.

49. Gramsci was arrested in 1926 and tried and imprisoned in 1928, by the later Pound's beloved Benito Mussolini.

50. *Selections from the Prison Notebooks of Antonio Gramsci,* ed. and trans. Quintin Hoare and Geoffrey Nowell Smith (New York: International Publishers, 1971), p. 302.

51. Quoted in Alan Trachtenberg, *The Incorporation of America: Culture and Society in the Gilded Age* (New York: Hill and Wang, 1982), p. 148.

52. Gramsci, *Prison Notebooks,* p. 303.

53. Ibid., p. 297. As Gramsci points out, Ford showed a keen interest in the sexual conduct and family affairs of his workers. In fact, he devoted a whole department of Ford Motors to keeping track of these matters.

54. These, of course, are critiques of a specific moment in the development of modern capitalism. For a seminal critique of the more recent phenomenon of the "liberated" workplace, which shares, however, an emphasis on the psychosocial "nexus" of work, see Herbert Marcuse's chapter "Repressive Desublimation," in his *One-Dimensional Man* (Boston: Beacon Press, 1964), pp. 56–83.

55. Ziff, *Literary Democracy,* p. 27.

56. Emerson, *English Traits, W,* Vol. V, pp. 166–167.

57. Ibid., pp. 167–168.

58. In this, Emerson seems to challenge rather than reproduce what Carolyn Porter calls "the hegemonic function of the 'technological sublime' in Emerson's day: the reduction of the capitalist mode of production to industrialization, and industrialization, in turn, to the labor-saving machinery technology which made it possible" (*Seeing and Being,* p. 79).

59. Pound, *Selected Prose*, p. 199.
60. Ibid.
61. Ibid.
62. Or having attended to these extremes of what Sacvan Bercovitch calls the American Jeremiadic mode, in *The American Jeremiad* (Madison: University of Wisconsin Press, 1978). See also Wendy Stallard Flory, *The American Ezra Pound* (New Haven: Yale University Press, 1989), who views moments such as these in Pound in terms of the Jeremiadic tradition (pp. 6–12).
63. Emerson, "The American Scholar," *W*, Vol. I, p. 114.
64. Ibid., pp. 114–115.
65. Quoted in Ziff, *Literary Democracy*, p. 22.
66. See Michel Foucault, *The Archaeology of Knowledge and the Discourse on Language*, trans. A. M. Sheridan-Smith (New York: Pantheon, 1972), p. 224. See also Foucault's "What Is an Author?" in *Textual Strategies*, ed. Josue V. Harari (Ithaca: Cornell University Press, 1979), pp. 141–160.
67. See, e.g., Pound, *Selected Letters*, pp. 11, 19, 78, 108.
68. Foucault, *Archaeology of Knowledge*, p. 27.
69. For a similar critique of Foucault's *Archaeology of Knowledge*, see Herbert L. Dreyfus and Paul Rabinow, *Michel Foucault: Beyond Structuralism and Hermeneutics*, 2d ed. (Chicago: University of Chicago Press, 1983), pp. xxiv–xxv.
70. *Golden Treasury of the Best Songs and Lyrical Poems in the English Language*, Selected and Arranged with Notes by Francis Turner Palgrave (London: Macmillan and Co., 1861), preface (no page numbers). I am indebted to Lentricchia's acute discussion of Pound's reaction to Palgravean lyricism in "Lyric in the Culture of Capitalism," *American Literary History* 1: 1 (Spring 1989): 63–88.
71. Palgrave, *Golden Treasury*, preface.
72. For a critique that is very much to the point, see Adorno's attack on Sartre's call for literary "relevance" in "Commitment," trans. Francis McDonagh, in *Aesthetics and Politics*, ed. Ronald Taylor, afterword by Fredric Jameson (London: New Left Books, 1977), pp. 177–195.
73. Lears, *No Place of Grace*, p. 17. See also pp. 52–57, 303–307.
74. Pound, *Literary Essays*, p. 18. For an account of the episode, see Noel Stock, *The Life of Ezra Pound* (New York: Pantheon, 1970), p. 201.
75. Pound, *Literary Essays*, p. 18.
76. Pound, *Selected Letters*, p. 44
77. Ibid.
78. As he wrote in 1914, giving voice to the populist inheritance, which had not, as yet, drawn him to the extreme ideological Right, "The artist is one of the few producers. He, the farmer and the artisan create wealth; the rest shift and consume it" (*Literary Essays*, p. 222). As we shall see, however, for the later Pound, the poet is more of a *reproducer*, a vehicle for a stable natural order, which he should not – and, strictly speaking, cannot – alter.
79. Pound, *Selected Letters*, p. 78.
80. "L'Homme Moyen Sensuel," in *Personae: The Collected Shorter Poems of Ezra Pound* (New York: New Directions, 1971), p. 239.

81. Ibid., p. 244.
82. Pound had a personal motivation here as well. In 1908, from both Venice and London, he had sent poems to *Harper's, Century*, and *Scribner's* and had been rejected. See John Tytell's biography, *Ezra Pound: The Solitary Volcano* (New York: Anchor Press, Doubleday, 1987), pp. 35, 39.
83. Pound, *Selected Prose*, p. 111. Knapp highlights this passage as well in *Literary Modernism*, though his central claim about it ("The true object of his wrath was the practice of writing mechanically – without thought – to patterns already determined by those who manage the production of culture" [p. 31]) does not do justice to the full range and challenge of Pound's critique.
84. Pound, *Selected Prose*, p. 107.
85. Ibid., p. 110.
86. Ibid.
87. Karl Mannheim, "On the Nature of Economic Ambition and Its Significance for the Social Education of Man," in *Essays on the Sociology of Knowledge*, ed. Paul Kecskemeti (New York: Oxford University Press, 1952), p. 246.
88. Pound, *Selected Prose*, p. 110.
89. Fredric Jameson, "Reification and Utopia in Mass Culture," *Social Text* 1 (Winter 1979): 130–148, esp. p. 136.
90. The large-circulation magazines as Pound views them perfectly exemplify commodity fetishism as Marx defines it: "The commodity reflects the social characteristics of men's own labour as objective characteristics of the products of labour themselves, as socio-natural properties of these things." And the reverse is true as well: Social relations between human beings become reified, thinglike, endowed with the static fixity of objects and matter. See Marx, *Capital*, trans. Ben Fowkes, introduction by Ernest Mandel (New York: Vintage Books, 1977), Vol. I, pp. 164–165.
91. Roland Barthes, "Myth Today," in *A Barthes Reader*, ed. Susan Sontag (New York: Hill and Wang, 1982), p. 129.
92. Ibid., p. 130.
93. Pound, *Selected Prose*, p. 112.
94. Ibid., p. 198.
95. Ibid., p. 231.
96. See, for a brief history, William Pratt's introduction to his anthology *The Imagist Poem* (New York: Dutton, 1963), pp. 11–39. For more extensive histories see Glenn Hughes, *Imagism and the Imagists: A Study in Modern Poetry* (Stanford: Stanford University Press, 1931), and Stanley K. Coffman, Jr., *Imagism: A Chapter in the History of Modern Poetry* (Norman: University of Oklahoma Press, 1951). Though I disagree rather sharply with his interpretation of the politics of Imagism, K. K. Ruthven's *Ezra Pound as Literary Critic*, Critics of the Twentieth Century (London: Routledge, 1991), provides a useful discussion of how and why Hughes's study came to privilege the Amy Lowell line of Imagism over Pound's (see pp. 157–159).
97. Quoted in Kenner, *The Pound Era*, p. 177.
98. Pound, *Selected Prose*, p. 21.

99. Pound, *Literary Essays*, p. 4.
100. Pound, *Selected Prose*, p. 22.
101. Ibid., p. 23.
102. Ibid., p. 33.
103. But see James Longenbach's discussion of Pound's interest, under the influence of Yeats, in esoteric and occult symbolism, in *Stone Cottage: Pound, Yeats, and Modernism* (New York: Oxford University Press, 1988), pp. 78ff.
104. W. B. Yeats, "The Symbolism of Poetry," in *Critical Theory since Plato*, ed. Hazard Adams (New York: Harcourt Brace Jovanovich, 1971), p. 725.
105. Longenbach, *Stone Cottage*, pp. 78–80.
106. Yeats, "The Symbolism of Poetry," in Adams, *Critical Theory since Plato*, p. 722.
107. Pound, *Literary Essays*, p. 3.
108. Ibid., p. 9.
109. Pound, *Selected Prose*, pp. 23, 376, 115. For a further investigation of the poetry/science connection in Pound, see the collection *Critic as Scientist: The Modernist Poetics of Ezra Pound*, ed. Ian F. A. Bell (London: Methuen, 1981).
110. Patricia Rae, "From Mystical Gaze to Pragmatic Game: Representations of Truth in Vorticist Art," *ELH* 56: 3 (Fall 1989): 689–720, esp. p. 699. Rae's view of the relationship between Imagism and symbolism may be read in direct contrast to Longenbach's in *Stone Cottage*.
111. This is not surprising, because, as Longenbach points out in *Stone Cottage*, Pound changed the title from "Imagism" to "Vorticism" only at the last minute before publication (p. 78).
112. Pound, "Vorticism," in idem, *Gaudier-Brzeska: A Memoir* (New York: New Directions, 1960), p. 84.
113. Pound, *Literary Essays*, p. 4.
114. Our fears are partly confirmed by Pound's interpretation of Dante's *Paradiso* – that supposed allegory to end all allegories – as "the most wonderful image": "The permanent part is Imagisme, the rest, the discourses with the calendar of saints and the discussions about the nature of the moon, are philology." See "Vorticism," in *Gaudier-Brzeska*, p. 86.
115. Theodor Adorno, *Negative Dialectics*, trans. E. B. Ashton (New York: Seabury Press, 1973), p. 183.
116. In Martin Jay's reading, Adorno's concept of reification contrasts with Lukács's, which for Adorno would too readily assimilate the heterogeneity of the object world to an imperial subject at the center of Lukács's "expressive" totality. What is at stake, in other words, is the status and recalcitrance of the object world itself. See Martin Jay, *Adorno* (Cambridge, Mass.: Harvard University Press, 1984), pp. 64ff.
117. Ibid., p. 68. For Adorno's refusal "to place the object on the orphaned royal throne once occupied by the subject" (his refusal, roughly, to replace idealism with positivism), see Adorno, *Negative Dialectics,* p. 181. For a more detailed explanation of Adorno's "negative dialectics" as the philosophical imperative of such a refusal, see Jay, *Adorno*, pp. 14–15, 74ff.
118. Pound, *Literary Essays*, p. 298.

119. Ezra Pound, "The New Sculpture," *Egoist*, February 16, 1914, 68.
120. Ezra Pound, "The Approach to Paris," *New Age* 13 (October 2, 1913): 662.
121. Quoted in Michael H. Levenson, *A Genealogy of Modernism: A Study of English Literary Doctrine, 1908–1922* (Cambridge: Cambridge University Press, 1984), p. 56. In what follows I am indebted to Levenson's perceptive discussion of Ford's aesthetic.
122. Pound, *Selected Prose*, p. 461.
123. Pound, *Literary Essays*, p. 377.
124. As Levenson indicates, there has been some dispute as to whether the primary influence on Imagism was Ford or T. E. Hulme. I am persuaded, in part by Levenson's argument, that Ford's impact was the more significant; see Levenson, *Genealogy of Modernism*, pp. 104ff. For further corroboration from Pound's own corpus, see "This Hulme Business," Appendix I in Hugh Kenner, *The Poetry of Ezra Pound* (1951; rpt., Lincoln: University of Nebraska Press, 1985), pp. 307–309.
125. Once those principles were reworked by Pound, Ford himself was not immune to being taught a lesson from his own book: Pound's favorite example of anti-Imagist technique – "dim lands of peace" – is taken, in fact, from a poem by Ford written in 1904 (pointed out by Kenner in *The Pound Era*, p. 181).
126. Pound, *Literary Essays*, p. 376.
127. Noted by Levenson, *Genealogy of Modernism*, p. 106.
128. Quoted in ibid., p. 108.
129. Quoted in ibid., p. 116.
130. Ibid.
131. Ibid., p. 119.
132. See Rae, "From Mystical Gaze to Pragmatic Game," esp. pp. 696–705.
133. Pound, *Literary Essays*, p. 3.
134. Pound, *Selected Prose*, p. 375, emphasis mine.
135. Ibid., pp. 374–375.
136. Ibid., p. 375.
137. Ibid.
138. Ibid., p. 376.
139. See Kenner, *The Pound Era*, p. 238.
140. Pound, *Selected Prose*, p. 360.
141. Pound, *Literary Essays*, p. 9.
142. Pound, "Vorticism," in *Gaudier-Brzeska*, p. 85.
143. Ibid., p. 88.
144. Ibid.

3. ECONOMIES OF INDIVIDUALISM

1. Jean-Paul Sartre, *Search for a Method*, trans. Hazel E. Barnes (New York: Vintage Books, 1963), p. 56. Sartre's attempt to join an understanding of the total life of the individual with the historical conditions that create and are created by him or her – Sartre's figure for it is what he calls the "universal singular" – was a project only partly (and still not wholly) fulfilled. Sartre explored various dimensions of this problem in *Saint Genet*, in

Mallarmé, and in the massive work on Flaubert. But in his failure to complete the second volume of the *Critique of Dialectical Reason*, Sartre also failed to join these investigations of the individual subject to a promised explanation of the larger structures of class and history. For an insightful account of Sartre's failure and the subsequent rise of structuralism, see Perry Anderson's chapter "Structure and Subject," in his *In the Tracks of Historical Materialism* (London: New Left Books 1983), pp. 32–55.

2. In this regard, see Sebastiano Timpanaro's incisive critique of Althusser in his study *On Materialism* (London: New Left Books, 1975), pp. 64ff.

3. Emerson, "Self-Reliance," in *The Complete Works of Ralph Waldo Emerson*, Centenary Edition, 12 vols., ed. Edward Waldo Emerson (Boston: Houghton Mifflin, 1903–1904), Vol. II, p. 64. Subsequent references to this edition will be abbreviated *W*.

4. Emerson, "Politics," *W*, Vol. III, pp. 215–216; idem, "Self-Reliance," *W*, Vol. II, p. 70.

5. Myra Jehlen, *American Incarnation: The Individual, the Nation, and the Continent* (Cambridge, Mass.: Harvard University Press, 1986), p. 85.

6. For a detailed but problematic discussion of these matters in contemporary Emerson criticism, the reader can consult Richard Grusin's review article, "Revisionism and the Structure of Emersonian Action," *American Literary History* 1: 2 (Summer 1989): 404–431. Grusin's critique seems to me finally unconvincing, in part because the category of "action" he uses is so broad and general that it becomes difficult to distinguish it from, say, thought or intellection. Hence, it indulges in the same sort of idealism as Emerson's own concept of action, which we will investigate more fully in the Afterword.

7. Emerson, "The Divinity School Address," *W*, Vol. I, p. 144.

8. Michael H. Levenson, *A Genealogy of Modernism: A Study of English Literary Doctrine, 1908–1922* (Cambridge: Cambridge University Press, 1984), pp. 68ff.

9. Quoted in ibid., p. 76.

10. The review is reprinted in Pound, *Selected Prose, 1909–1965*, ed. William Cookson (New York: New Directions, 1973), pp. 407–412; for the quotation, see p. 411. We should note that Pound had reviewed Upward six months earlier in the *New Freewoman* (reprinted in *Selected Prose*, pp. 403–406). For more on Upward's influence on Pound, see Donald Davie, *Ezra Pound: Poet as Sculptor* (New York: Viking Press, 1975).

11. Quoted in Levenson, *Genealogy of Modernism*, p. 75. In Pound's letters, we find not a break so much as a vacillation between these positions. In 1908, for example, he writes to William Carlos Williams: "As for the 'eyes of the too ruthless public': damn their eyes." But in 1913, to Harriet Monroe: "I'm the kind of ass that believes in the public intelligence." See *The Selected Letters of Ezra Pound, 1907–1941*, ed. D. D. Paige, preface by Mark Van Doren (New York: New Directions, 1971), pp. 4, 12.

12. *Emerson in His Journals*, ed. Joel Porte (Cambridge, Mass.: Belknap Press of Harvard University Press, 1982), p. 40.

13. For further examination of this aspect of Pound, see the discussion of the

Nietzschean, aristocratic side of Pound's individualism offered by Kathryne V. Lindberg in her *Reading Pound Reading: Modernism after Nietzsche* (New York: Oxford University Press, 1987). Though we cannot take up the matter in these pages, Nietzsche's well-known enthusiasm and admiration for Emerson is worth mentioning here.

14. Pound, *Selected Prose*, p. 230.
15. Ezra Pound, interview with Donald Hall, in *Writers at Work: The Paris Review Interviews*, Second Series, introduction by Van Wyck Brooks (New York: Viking Press, 1963), pp. 57, 53.
16. See J. G. A. Pocock, *The Machiavellian Moment: Florentine Political Thought and the Atlantic Republican Tradition* (Princeton: Princeton University Press, 1975). For a useful discussion of Pocock's thesis and its relevance to Poundian *virtù*, see Reed Way Dasenbrock, "Jefferson and/or Adams: A Shifting Mirror for Mussolini in the Middle Cantos," *ELH* 55: 2 (Summer 1988): 505–526. Dasenbrock argues for the relevance of the concept of *virtù* in establishing the point that for Pocock, and for Pound, "there is a parallel between the Italian Renaissance and the American Revolution as well as a line of influence from the former to the latter" (p. 511).
17. See Marianne Korn, *Ezra Pound: Purpose/Form/Meaning* (London: Middlesex Polytechnic Press, 1983), pp. 20–28, and James Longenbach, *Modernist Poetics of History: Pound, Eliot, and the Sense of the Past* (Princeton: Princeton University Press, 1987), pp. 55ff.
18. Walter Pater, *The Renaissance: Studies in Art and Poetry*, ed. Donald L. Hill (1893; rpt., Berkeley and Los Angeles: University of California Press, 1980), pp. xx–xxi. Quoted in Longenbach, *Modernist Poetics of History*, pp. 55–56. See also Korn, *Ezra Pound*, p. 21.
19. Korn is right in this respect to assert that Pound's early conjugation of *virtù* is "the basis for Pound's mature poetic. It is the basis for understanding Pound's version of Imagism" (*Ezra Pound*, p. 23).
20. Longenbach, *Modernist Poetics of History*, p. 57.
21. Pound, *Selected Prose*, p. 28.
22. Ibid.
23. Ibid., p. 29.
24. As Longenbach puts it, Pound may have believed in "a spiritual presence that enveloped all individuals," but he was "not so concerned with this abstract world of spirit as with its individual concrete manifestations" (*Modernist Poetics of History*, p. 58).
25. Pound, *Selected Prose*, p. 29.
26. In "Patria Mia," in fact, *virtù* will name the principle not only of literary difference but of human difference in general, the individuality that no abstraction should master – and that, Pound would add, no abstraction can express. In that essay, Pound laments the fact that most Americans "have wrapped themselves about a formula of words instead of about their own centres" (ibid., p. 102).
27. I borrow this application of Dilthey's phrase to Poundian *virtù* from Longenbach, *Modernist Poetics of History*, p. 58.

28. Ezra Pound, *ABC of Reading* (New York: New Directions, 1960), p. 36.
29. Pound, *Selected Prose*, p. 31. Pound's figure here helps to distinguish again his sense of objectification from that of Emerson and Hegel. As this figure suggests, for Pound the self's difference *can* persist, is not automatically alienated, in its objects of practice.
30. Ibid., p. 25.
31. Ibid.
32. Ibid.
33. Ibid., p. 229.
34. Ibid.
35. Korn, *Ezra Pound*, p. 27.
36. Longenbach, *Modernist Poetics of History*, p. 57.
37. Korn, *Ezra Pound*, p. 27.
38. Pound, *Selected Prose*, p. 114.
39. Alan Durant's discussion of the Poundian self-as-Vortex in light of the Derridian critique of the Cartesian subject is pertinent here as well. As Durant puts it, the Poundian self amounts to "a claim that the opposing energies of human beings are reconciled in a still centre," that "the homogeneous subject is endowed with power to control contradiction, such that its discourses can be what are called in *Gaudier-Brzeska* 'lords over fact.'" See his *Ezra Pound, Identity in Crisis* (Sussex: Harvester Press, 1981), p. 31.
40. *Literary Essays of Ezra Pound*, ed. T. S. Eliot (New York: New Directions, 1968), p. 47. In the essay "The State" (1927) Pound sets up a hierarchy of "transient," "durable," and "permanent" goods, and puts "works of art" and "scientific discoveries" in the last category. This will be discussed in the context of Pound's writings on economics and patronage in Chapter 5.
41. Pound, *Selected Prose*, p. 130.
42. Pound, *Literary Essays*, p. 409.
43. Ibid., pp. 223, 222.
44. See Barbara Herrnstein Smith, *Contingencies of Value* (Cambridge, Mass.: Harvard University Press, 1988), esp. Chap. 6.
45. As in the "god-given" right to property, the "natural price" of Adam Smith, and many another familiar example derived from nineteenth-century political economy and its ideology.
46. Michael T. Gilmore, *American Romanticism and the Marketplace* (Chicago: University of Chicago Press, 1985), p. 12.
47. This point was made by Warren Susman in his essay "History and the American Intellectual," in his *Culture as History: The Transformation of American Society in the Twentieth Century* (New York: Pantheon, 1984), pp. 7–26.
48. On this point, see Maurice Gonnaud's reading of a fascinating letter written in 1822, where Emerson maps the tripartite class structure of Boston, all the while ironically aware that schoolteachers (his vocation at the time) are at the very bottom of the structure, along with n'er-do-wells and day laborers. See Gonnaud's *An Uneasy Solitude: Individual and Society in the Work of Ralph Waldo Emerson*, trans. Lawrence Rosenwald, foreword by

Eric Cheyfitz (French ed., 1964; Princeton: Princeton University Press, 1987), pp. 40–41.

49. Quentin Anderson, "Property and Vision in Nineteenth-Century America," *Virginia Quarterly Review* 54: 3 (Summer 1978): 385–410, esp. p. 394. As we shall see below in the Afterword, Donald Pease's critique of Anderson's *The Imperial Self* is helpful in situating the politics of Anderson's understanding of the relationship between property and individualism. See Pease's editorial introduction, "New Americanists: Revisionist Interventions into the Canon," *boundary 2* 17: 1 (Spring 1990): 1–37, esp. pp. 27ff.

50. Emerson, "Compensation," *W*, Vol. II, p. 95.

51. Emerson, *Nature*, *W*, Vol. I, p. 32. See Jehlen, *American Incarnation*, pp. 3–5, 8–13.

52. Wai-chee Dimock, "Scarcity, Subjectivity, and Emerson," *boundary 2* 17: 1 (Spring 1990): 83–99, esp. pp. 90–91. It should be pointed out that Dimock's paradigm is based largely on Emerson's "Experience" and the economy she finds there, in which scarcity and overabundance are unstable and convertible terms. Dimock's more recent study of Melville should also be consulted for its critique of the economy of selfhood in the Jacksonian context. See her *Empire for Liberty: Melville and the Poetics of Individualism* (Princeton: Princeton University Press, 1989).

53. Emerson, "Experience," *W*, Vol. II, p. 81.

54. See Jehlen, *American Incarnation*, p. 94, and Howard Horwitz, "The Standard Oil Trust as Emersonian Hero," *Raritan* 4: 6 (Spring 1987): 97–119, esp. p. 101.

55. Quoted in Horwitz, "The Standard Oil Trust," p. 101.

56. Emerson, *Nature*, *W*, Vol. I, p. 8. Contrast Horwitz's reading of this moment in Emerson ("The Standard Oil Trust," p. 103) with Frank Lentricchia's in "On the Ideologies of Poetic Modernism, 1890–1913: The Example of William James," in *Reconstructing American Literary History*, ed. Sacvan Bercovitch (Cambridge, Mass.: Harvard University Press, 1986), p. 235.

57. Emerson, *Nature*, *W*, Vol. I, p. 76.

58. Gilmore, *American Romanticism and the Marketplace*, p. 30.

59. Ibid., p. 31.

60. Emerson, "Self-Reliance," *W*, Vol. II, p. 87.

61. Emerson, *Nature*, *W*, Vol. I, pp. 37–38.

62. William James, *The Principles of Psychology* (New York: Dover Publications, 1950), Vol. 1, pp. 297–298, 299–305. Quoted in Frank Lentricchia, *Ariel and the Police: Michel Foucault, William James, Wallace Stevens* (Madison: University of Wisconsin Press, 1988), pp. 118, 119.

63. Lentricchia, *Ariel and the Police*, p. 118.

64. James, *Principles of Psychology*, p. 226. Quoted in ibid.

65. Walter Benn Michaels, *The Gold Standard and the Logic of Naturalism: American Literature at the Turn of the Century*, The New Historicism: Studies in Cultural Poetics, Vol. 2 (Berkeley and Los Angeles: University of California Press, 1987), p. 22. See also pp. 8–9. I have elsewhere examined in

greater detail the important differences between Michaels's and Lentricchia's
reading of this problem in James. See my "Antinomies of Liberalism: The
Politics of 'Belief' and the Project of Americanist Criticism," in *Discovering
Difference: New Essays on American Culture*, ed. C. K. Lohmann (Bloomington: Indiana University Press, 1993).

66. Quoted in Lentricchia, *Ariel and the Police*, p. 118.
67. Ibid., p. 121.
68. C. B. McPherson, *The Political Theory of Possessive Individualism: Hobbes to
Locke* (Oxford: Oxford University Press, 1962), p. 3.
69. Ibid., p. 142.
70. Karl Marx, "On the Jewish Question," in *Early Writings*, trans. Rodney
Livingstone and Gregor Benton, introduction by Lucio Colletti (New York:
Vintage Books, 1975), pp. 229–230.
71. Pound, *Selected Prose*, p. 165.
72. Dimock, "Scarcity, Subjectivity, and Emerson," p. 97.
73. *The Journals and Miscellaneous Notebooks of Ralph Waldo Emerson*, 16 vols.,
ed. William H. Gilman et al. (Cambridge, Mass.: Belknap Press of Harvard
University Press, 1960–1982), Vol. XIII, pp. 114–115.
74. Sacvan Bercovitch, "Emerson, Individualism, and the Ambiguities of Dissent," *South Atlantic Quarterly* 89: 3 (Summer 1990): 623–662, esp. p. 641.
75. Quoted in ibid., p. 641.
76. Ibid., p. 645.
77. The definitive discussion of Jacksonianism remains Marvin Meyers's *The
Jacksonian Persuasion: Politics and Belief* (Stanford: Stanford University Press,
1957). An important revision of Meyers may be found in Michael Lebowitz,
"The Jacksonians: Paradox Lost?" in *Towards a New Past: Dissenting Essays
in American History*, ed. Barton J. Bernstein (New York: Vintage Books,
1968), pp. 65–89.
78. Emerson, "The American Scholar," *W*, Vol. I, p. 107.
79. *Emerson in His Journals*, p. 384.
80. Ibid., p. 125.
81. Ibid., p. 131.
82. See Gonnaud, *Uneasy Solitude*, p. 429.
83. *Emerson in His Journals*, p. 320.
84. Ibid., p. 250. See also "Plato; or, the Philosopher," in Emerson, *W*, Vol.
IV, pp. 64ff.
85. *Emerson in His Journals*, p. 125.
86. Emerson, *Journals and Miscellaneous Notebooks*, Vol. V, p. 100.
87. *Emerson in His Journals*, p. 439.
88. See, for a related reading of this moment in Emerson, Larzer Ziff, *Literary
Democracy: The Declaration of Cultural Independence in America* (New York:
Penguin, 1982), p. 27.
89. Emerson, "Self-Reliance," *W*, Vol. II, p. 52.
90. Ibid.
91. For a detailed theoretical articulation of these issues, see Jean-Joseph Goux's
important collection *Symbolic Economies: After Marx and Freud*, trans. Jennifer

Curtiss Gage (Ithaca: Cornell University Press, 1990). As Goux argues, following Marx's analysis in Vol. 1 of *Capital*, "Use-value is the physical, incarnated, perceptible aspect of the commodity, while exchange-value is a supernatural abstraction, invisible and supersensible" (p. 19).

92. *Emerson in His Journals*, p. 297.

93. See Ziff, *Literary Democracy*, pp. 21–22.

94. As Gilmore points out, there was a fivefold increase in the number of banks and the value of notes in circulation between 1820 and 1860 – an astronomical escalation that Jacksonianism would, in a definitive gesture, challenge (*American Romanticism and the Marketplace*, p. 2).

95. Emerson, "Human Culture," in *Emerson, Essays and Lectures*, ed. Joel Porte (New York: 1983), Vol. II, p. 242. Quoted in Gonnaud, *Uneasy Solitude*, p. 230.

96. On Emerson's complex relationship to socialism, see Bercovitch, "Emerson, Individualism, and the Ambiguities of Dissent."

97. *Emerson in His Journals*, pp. 383–384.

98. A contributing factor here as well, as Maurice Gonnaud has argued, is that Emerson was born, raised, and to some extent remained a Federalist in politics and social attitudes throughout his career; he was, on balance, dedicated to the proposition that civilization depends largely on the security of property and the political leadership of those who have it. See Gonnaud, *Uneasy Solitude*, pp. 65, 86, 107.

99. As Horwitz puts it, for Emerson "commerce and property are not in themselves lapses from virtue; virtue or sin lies in one's relation (mastery or dependence) to property" ("The Standard Oil Trust," p. 101).

100. Emerson, "Self-Reliance," *W*, Vol. II, pp. 87–88.

101. Emerson, "Wealth," *W*, Vol. VI, p. 106.

102. Emerson's "living property" is a strange, though virtually contemporaneous, refraction of what Marx would call, a few years after "Self-Reliance," the "necromancy" of the commodity: that process whereby active human powers and relations are transformed into relations between things. Marx's materialism, however, knew what Emerson's idealism refused to recognize: that property cannot, strictly speaking, be created – only concrete objects and goods can. Unlike Emerson, Marx knew, in other words, that all property is dead. See *Capital*, trans. Ben Fowkes, introduction by Ernest Mandel (New York: Vintage, 1977), Vol. 1, pp. 168–169.

103. Emerson, "Politics," *W*, Vol. III, pp. 202–203.

104. Emerson, "Wealth," *W*, Vol. VI, p. 100.

105. Emerson, *Journals and Miscellaneous Notebooks*, Vol. V, p. 100; quoted in Ziff, *Literary Democracy*, p. 22.

106. Emerson, *Nature*, *W*, Vol. I, pp. 37–38.

107. *Emerson in His Journals*, p. 234.

108. For an incisive interpretation of this episode in Pound, which differs somewhat in emphasis from my own, see Frank Lentricchia, "Reimagining the Lyric," in the new *Cambridge History of American Literature* (forthcoming).

109. Pound, *Selected Prose*, p. 108.
110. Emerson, "Compensation," *W*, Vol. II, p. 114.
111. As both Horwitz and Susman remind us, however, at the end of his career Emerson also anticipated the modern managerial (as opposed to the waning entrepreneurial) ideal of agency. As Susman puts it, we find in Emerson's "The Progress of Culture" (1860) "one of the first great testaments in praise of the new middle class of managers and technicians, organizers and engineers, what [Emerson] calls the 'rapid addition to our society of a class of true nobles'" (*Culture as History*, p. 240).
112. Any number of sources may be consulted on Pound's relationship with Thaddeus. See, e.g., Wendy Stallard Flory, *The American Ezra Pound* (New Haven: Yale University Press, 1989), pp. 15–23.
113. Pound, *Selected Prose*, p. 123.
114. Pound, *Selected Letters*, p. 13.
115. Pound, *Selected Prose*, p. 109.
116. Ibid., p. 123.
117. Ibid.
118. As Daniel Joseph Singal points out, modernism in general is marked not only by the desire to "perfect one's ability to experience experience" but also by the premium on "fusing together disparate elements of that experience into new and original 'wholes.'" See his "Towards a Definition of American Modernism," *American Quarterly* 39: 1 (Spring 1987): 7–26, esp. pp. 11–12.
119. Pound, *Selected Prose*, pp. 108–109.
120. Ibid., p. 123.
121. Ibid.
122. Pound, *Literary Essays*, p. 149.
123. Pound, *Selected Letters*, p. 10.
124. Fredric Jameson, "Periodizing the 60s," in *The Ideologies of Theory: Essays, 1971–1986*, Vol. 2, *The Syntax of History*, Theory and History of Literature, Vol. 49 (Minneapolis: University of Minnesota Press, 1988), p. 199.
125. Fredric Jameson, *The Political Unconscious: Narrative as a Socially Symbolic Act* (Ithaca: Cornell University Press, 1981), p. 59. See also pp. 116, 234.
126. Pound, *Selected Prose*, p. 33.
127. Peter Nicholls, *Ezra Pound: Politics, Economics, and Writing* (Atlantic Highlands, N.J.: Humanities Press, 1984), p. 30.
128. *The Cantos of Ezra Pound* (New York: New Directions, 1986), p. 54.
129. Pound, *Selected Prose*, pp. 145–146.
130. *Cantos of Ezra Pound*, p. 549.
131. Emerson, "The American Scholar," *W*, Vol. I, p. 86.
132. *Emerson in His Journals*, p. 372. For a quite different account of what she calls the "rhizomatic" or "weedlike" self-conception of American culture, see Kathryne V. Lindberg, *Reading Pound Reading: Modernism after Nietzsche* (New York: Oxford University Press, 1987), pp. 211–231.
133. "A Pact," in *Personae: The Collected Shorter Poems of Ezra Pound* (New York: New Directions, 1971), p. 89, emphasis mine.

4. "GYNOCRACY" AND "RED BLOOD": POUND AND THE POLITICS OF FEMINIZATION

1. "L'Homme Moyen Sensuel," in *Personae: The Collected Shorter Poems of Ezra Pound* (New York: New Directions, 1971), p. 239. Stedman was a powerful genteel poet, editor, and critic, best known for his *An American Anthology* (1900). Gilder, another genteel guru, edited the *Century* from 1881 to 1909, where he was succeeded as editor by Johnson. John Tomisch provides the definitive study of the genteel writers and intellectuals in his *A Genteel Endeavor: American Culture and Politics in the Gilded Age* (Stanford: Stanford University Press, 1971).

2. On the so-called feminization of American culture in the nineteenth century, see Ann Douglas, *The Feminization of American Culture* (New York: Alfred A. Knopf, 1977). Jane Tompkins's critique of Douglas in "The Other American Renaissance" should also be consulted, in her *Sensational Designs: The Cultural Work of American Fiction, 1790–1860* (New York: Oxford University Press, 1985), pp. 147–185.

3. The tag belongs to K. K. Ruthven in his study *Ezra Pound as Literary Critic*, Critics of the Twentieth Century (London: Routledge, 1990), p. 78. Ruthven's study rightly draws our attention to the "masculinist practices" and "sexist fantasies" at work in Pound's conception of gender and its relation to artistic creation and cultural power. According to Ruthven, not only was Pound apt to engage in "an *ad feminam* style of criticism" that responded to the "strong-mindedness" of woman writers like Amy Lowell and Gertrude Stein by "ridiculing their bodies"; he was also driven, in his relations with male writers like T. S. Eliot, to always construct himself as the most "aggressively masculine" writer on the block (see pp. 105, 65, 99–108, 75–80). For a fascinating, if sometimes overread, account of misogyny and the homosocial (and in some ways homosexual) economy at work in Pound's relations with Eliot, see Wayne Koestenbaum, "*The Waste Land*: T. S. Eliot's and Ezra Pound's Collaboration on Hysteria," *Twentieth Century Literature* 34: 2 (1988): 113–139.

4. See Toril Moi, *Sexual/Textual Politics: Feminist Literary Theory*, New Accents (London: Methuen, 1985), pp. 65, 113–119, 137–149. See also, for other powerful critiques of essentialism, Teresa de Lauretis, *Technologies of Gender: Essays on Theory, Film, and Fiction* (Bloomington: Indiana University Press, 1987); Joan Wallach Scott, *Gender and the Politics of History* (New York: Columbia University Press, 1988); and Donna Haraway, *Simians, Cyborgs, and Women: The Reinvention of Nature* (New York: Routledge, 1991).

5. I borrow this formulation – the "political unconscious of gender" – from Teresa de Lauretis's revision of Fredric Jameson's well-known term. See my discussion of de Lauretis later in this chapter in the section "The Self That One Is Not."

6. Frank Lentricchia, *Ariel and the Police: Michel Foucault, William James, Wallace Stevens* (Madison: University of Wisconsin Press, 1988), p. 146. See also the opening of Alan Trachtenberg's chapter "The Politics of Culture" in

his study *The Incorporation of America: Culture and Society in the Gilded Age* (New York: Hill and Wang, 1982). As Trachtenberg puts it, "As culture came to seem the repository of elevating thoughts and cleansing emotions, it seemed all the more as if the rough world of masculine enterprise had called into being its redemptive opposite" (p. 145).

7. Quoted in Lentricchia, *Ariel and the Police*, p. 138.
8. Ezra Pound, *Selected Prose, 1909–1965*, ed. William Cookson (New York: New Directions, 1973), p. 109.
9. Ibid.
10. Ibid., p. 41.
11. Quoted in Fred Lewis Pattee, *The Feminine Fifties* (New York: Appleton-Century Co., 1940), p. 110.
12. Hjalmar Hjorth Boyesen, "The American Novelist and His Public," quoted in Alfred Kazin, *On Native Grounds: An Interpretation of Modern American Prose Literature*, Fortieth Anniversary Edition (New York: Harcourt Brace Jovanovich, 1982), p. 26.
13. See Douglas, *The Feminization of American Culture*, pp. 19–20, 96. For numerous other examples of this phenomenon, see T. J. Jackson Lears, *No Place of Grace: Anti-modernism and the Transformation of American Culture, 1880–1920* (New York: Pantheon, 1981), pp. 15–17, 74–75, 98–124, 145–146, and 218–225. See also Tompkins, *Sensational Designs*, pp. 122–185.
14. Eric Cheyfitz, *The Trans-Parent: Sexual Politics in the Language of Emerson* (Baltimore: Johns Hopkins University Press, 1981), p. 180, n. 63. Any detailed discussion of the sexual and gender dimensions of Emerson's work must be indebted to Cheyfitz's study, which takes issue with the traditional view of Emerson as "a prophet of manliness, a father figure who is either divorced from the mother or in whom the mother is so strongly repressed that she is of no visible account" (p. 96). As Cheyfitz points out, manliness is more a desire than an accomplishment in Emerson, and his relation to it is "ironic," "volatile," and "ambivalent" – in a word, troubled.
15. Emerson, "Self-Reliance," in *The Complete Works of Ralph Waldo Emerson*, Centenary Edition, 12 vols., ed. Edward Waldo Emerson (Boston: Houghton Mifflin, 1903–1904), Vol. II, p. 56. Subsequent references to this edition will be abbreviated *W*.
16. Emerson, "The American Scholar," *W*, Vol. I, p. 94.
17. *Emerson in His Journals*, ed. Joel Porte (Cambridge, Mass.: Belknap Press of Harvard University Press, 1982), p. 306.
18. William James, "What Makes a Life Significant," in *The Writings of William James*, ed. John J. McDermott (New York: Random House, 1967), p. 647. Trachtenberg's discussion of this essay differs in emphasis from my own and should be consulted as well (*The Incorporation of America*, pp. 140ff.).
19. James, "What Makes a Life Significant," p. 648.
20. Ibid., p. 647.
21. Ibid., p. 648.
22. Ibid., p. 657.
23. Ibid., pp. 657, 659. Emerson writes in "Compensation": "An inevitable

dualism bisects nature, so that each thing is a half, and suggests another things to make it whole; as, spirit, matter; man, woman; odd, even; subjective, objective; in, out; upper, under; motion, rest; yea, nay" (*W*, Vol. II, p. 97).

24. *Literary Essays of Ezra Pound*, ed. T. S. Eliot (New York: New Directions, 1968), p. 17.

25. Quoted in John Espey, *Ezra Pound's Mauberley: A Study in Composition* (Berkeley and Los Angeles: University of California Press, 1955), p. 87.

26. Ibid., p. 83.

27. Carolyn Burke, "Getting Spliced: Modernism and Sexual Difference," *American Quarterly* 39: 1 (Spring 1987): 98–121, esp. pp. 104–105.

28. See Lears, *No Place of Grace*, pp. 97ff.

29. Quoted in Mark Seltzer, "The Love-Master," in *Engendering Men: The Question of Male Feminist Criticism*, ed. Joseph A. Boone and Michael Cadden (New York: Routledge, 1990), p. 140. See also, in a different register, Daniel Joseph Singal, "Towards a Definition of American Modernism," *American Quarterly* 39: 1 (Spring 1987): 7–26, esp. pp. 10ff.

30. Richard Hovey, "Call of the Bugles," quoted in Lears, *No Place of Grace*, p. 119.

31. Pound, *Selected Prose*, pp. 109–110.

32. Pound, "The Condolence," in *Personae*, p. 82.

33. Pound, *Literary Essays*, p. 281.

34. Ibid.

35. The characterization belongs to Carolyn Burke ("Getting Spliced," p. 106). Burke's explanation of this fact – that Pound "championed them for the wrong reasons" (p. 104), not as *women* poets but as "honorary men, 'geniuses above all'" (p. 106) – is apt, I think, but in a more complicated and mediated sense than she imagines, as I attempt to show below in my discussion of Pound and "male lack."

36. Pound, "L'Homme Moyen Sensuel," in *Personae*, p. 243.

37. This information comes from an exchange that took place between Pound and Gaudier-Brzeska in 1914, as recorded in the diary of Sophia Brzeska. The exchange is recounted in Timothy Materer's *Vortex: Pound, Eliot, and Lewis* (Ithaca: Cornell University Press, 1978), pp. 70–73, and in the source from which I have taken it, Burke, "Getting Spliced," p. 105.

38. Ezra Pound, "Through Alien Eyes," *New Age*, February 6, 1913; 324; quoted in Wendy Stallard Flory, *The American Ezra Pound* (New Haven: Yale University Press, 1989), p. 29.

39. "The conjunction of culture with wealth and property on the one hand, with surrender, self-denial, and subordination to something larger on the other, gave it a cardinal place among instruments of social control and reform" (Trachtenberg, *The Incorporation of America*, p. 147).

40. Pound, "Salutation the Second," in *Personae*, p. 86.

41. Pound, "The Rest," in ibid., p. 92.

42. Pound, "Commission," in ibid., p. 88.

43. Pound, "The Garden," in ibid., p. 83.

44. Pound, *Hugh Selwyn Mauberley*, section XI, in ibid., p. 195.
45. Pound, "Portrait d'une Femme," in ibid., p. 61.
46. Pound, "Sonnet: Chi E Questa?" in *Collected Early Poems of Ezra Pound*, ed. Michael John King, introduction by Louis L. Martz (New York: New Directions, 1976), p. 143.
47. Pound, "La Regina Avrillouse," in ibid., p. 46.
48. See, for numerous examples, ibid., pp. 13, 24–26, 46, 51, 79–80, 93, 114, 115, 117, 141, 143, 146, 147, 151, 154.
49. *The Cantos of Ezra Pound* (New York: New Directions, 1986), p. 177.
50. *The Translations of Ezra Pound* (New York: New Directions, 1963), p. 24.
51. Ezra Pound, *Make It New* (New Haven: Yale University Press, 1935); quoted in Donald Davie, *Ezra Pound: Poet as Sculptor* (New York: Oxford University Press, 1964), p. 108. See in general Davie's helpful discussion of Pound's revisions of Cavalcanti on pp. 102ff.
52. Pound, "Near Perigord," in *Personae*, p. 157.
53. Pound, "Na Audiart," in *Collected Early Poems*, p. 14.
54. Pound, "Dompna Pois de Me No'us Cal," in *Personae*, pp. 105–107.
55. The appearance of "Near Perigord" in *Poetry* for December 1915 is contemporaneous with the composition of the Ur-Cantos. See Peter Makin, *Pound's Cantos* (London: Allen and Unwin, 1985), pp. 49–54, for a brief discussion of the composition of the Ur-Cantos. And see, for an extensive treatment, Ronald Bush, *The Genesis of Ezra Pound's Cantos* (Princeton: Princeton University Press, 1976).
56. Pound, "Near Perigord," in *Personae*, p. 153.
57. For a brief "anthology" of statements made by Pound about the *Cantos*, see William Cookson, *A Guide to the Cantos of Ezra Pound*, foreword by M. L. Rosenthal (New York: Persea Books, 1985), pp. xvii–xxiii.
58. Pound, "Near Perigord," in *Personae*, p. 156.
59. Ibid., p. 157.
60. Ibid.
61. Ibid.
62. Pound, "Na Audiart," in *Collected Early Poems*, p. 13.
63. Ibid.
64. Pound, *Translations*, p. 18.
65. Pound, "Near Perigord," in *Personae*, p. 157.
66. Kevin Oderman, *Ezra Pound and the Erotic Medium* (Durham: Duke University Press, 1986), p. 25.
67. See Noel Stock, *The Life of Ezra Pound* (New York: Pantheon, 1970), p. 112; and for the definitive study, Richard Sieburth, *Instigations: Ezra Pound and Remy de Gourmont* (Cambridge, Mass.: Harvard University Press, 1978). Detailed discussion of Pound and Gourmont is also available in Oderman, *Ezra Pound and the Erotic Medium*.
68. See Sieburth, *Instigations*, pp. 24ff.
69. Pound, "Postscript to *The Natural Philosophy of Love* by Remy de Gourmont," in *Pavannes and Divagations* (New York: New Directions, 1974), p. 204.

70. Ibid., p. 213.
71. Ibid., pp. 203, 206.
72. Ibid., p. 207.
73. Ibid., p. 204.
74. Ibid., p. 213.
75. Ibid., p. 204.
76. Pound employs this phrase in *Hugh Selwyn Mauberley*, section XI (*Personae*, p. 195).
77. Ezra Pound, "The New Therapy," *New Age*, March 16, 1922, 260.
78. Pound, "On His Own Face in a Glass," in *Collected Early Poems*, pp. 34-35.
79. Pound, "Vorticism," in idem, *Gaudier-Brzeska: A Memoir* (New York: New Directions, 1960), p. 85.
80. Pound, envoi to *A Lume Spento*, in *Collected Early Poems*, p. 52.
81. In what follows I am indebted to Lentricchia's reading of this and related passages in Emerson; see his "On the Ideologies of Poetic Modernism, 1890-1914: The Example of William James," in *Reconstructing American Literary History*, ed. Sacvan Bercovitch (Cambridge, Mass.: Harvard University Press, 1986), pp. 220-249, esp. pp. 235-239; and idem, *Ariel and the Police*, pp. 117ff.
82. Emerson, *Nature*, W, Vol. I, P. 7. Richard Sieburth has suggested in his study *Instigations* (p. 153) that Emerson's transparent eyeball finds analogues in Pound's important figures of the "great acorn of light" and "great ball of crystal" late in the *Cantos*.
83. Emerson, *Nature*, W, Vol. I, p. 8.
84. Lentricchia, *Ariel and the Police*, p. 117.
85. Emerson, *Nature*, W, Vol. I, p. 10.
86. Ibid.
87. Quoted in John Tytell, *Ezra Pound: The Solitary Volcano* (New York: Doubleday, 1987), p. 40.
88. Pound, "Histrion," in *Collected Early Poems*, p. 71.
89. The last image is most suggestive, I think, for my discussion here because, as Kaja Silverman points out, in Freud "vision provides the agency whereby the female subject is established as being both different and inferior" and whereby the male's own castration or lack "seems to confront him from without, in the guise of the 'mutilated' female body" – which is, of course, precisely how the "borrowed" Maent appears to the castrated poet Bertran. Given Pound's image, it is suggestive, too, that the emotional "content," if there can be said to be any, of the Lacanian Mirror Phase – that stage of infancy when the child first perceives itself as a separate, whole identity – is what Lacan, Jane Gallop, and Silverman call the "jubilation" at the "anticipation of self-mastery and a unified identity," jubilations that will be fulfilled, as it were, by the Freudian male subject. See Kaja Silverman, *The Acoustic Mirror: The Female Voice in Psychoanalysis and Cinema* (Bloomington: Indiana University Press, 1988), pp. 7, 17.
90. See ibid., p. 15, for a more detailed discussion of Freud's reading of this

structure of desire. As Silverman points out, it is important to note, for Lacan, that the removal of "part objects" from the infant self – the mother's breast and voice, the blanket – is experienced as castration only later, with the child's entry into language and the symbolic order (p. 7).

91. Ibid., p. 15.
92. Ibid., p. 10.
93. Ibid., p. 18.
94. See ibid, p. 4. See also, for a reading of Pound in terms of Lacan, the Mirror Phase, the fetish, and Lacan's revision of Freud's castration complex, Alan Durant's *Ezra Pound, Identity in Crisis* (Sussex: Harvester Press, 1981), esp. pp. 6–15, 74–78, 90–95, 109–113, 129ff.
95. As Silverman points out, Freud's account of the male castration crisis confirms that "vision provides the agency whereby the female subject is established as being both different and inferior, the mechanism through which the male subject assures himself that it is not he but another who is castrated" (*The Acoustic Mirror*, p. 17). The relevance and importance of vision in this dynamic will become clearer below.
96. Durant, *Ezra Pound, Identity in Crisis*, p. 91. Durant provides an excellent catalog of examples of this phallic presence in the *Cantos* (pp. 96–106). As he points out, the female principle in the later *Cantos* is almost always "a reflection of phallic light," " a virtual mirror reflection of that male consistency" – "her deep waters," as Pound writes in Canto CVI, "reflecting all fire" (Durant, p. 102).
97. De Lauretis, *Technologies of Gender*, p. 1.
98. De Lauretis provides a good working definition of the "gender system": "The cultural conceptions of male and female as two complementary yet mutually exclusive categories into which all human beings are placed constitute within each culture a gender system, a symbolic system or system of meanings, that correlates sex to cultural contents according to social values and hierarchies. . . . In this light, the cultural construction of sex into gender and the asymmetry that characterizes all gender systems cross-culturally (though each in its particular ways) are understood as 'systematically linked to the organization of social inequality'" (ibid., p. 5).
99. See Eve Sedgwick's *Between Men: English Literature and Male Homosocial Desire* (New York: Columbia University Press, 1985), pp. 3–4, 21–25.
100. Durant, *Ezra Pound, Identity in Crisis*, p. 133. My reading of Imagism in Chapter 2, however, disagrees pointedly with Durant's assessment of it as a "fundamental exclusion of the subject from the field of language" (p. 18).
101. Ibid., pp. 173–175. Tiresias figures centrally in Cantos I, XLVII, and LXXX.
102. Kevin Oderman (in *Ezra Pound and the Erotic Medium*) notes that Pound lampoons "simple copulation" "as an inferior approach to sexuality" – as "stupefaction by excess" in Oderman's words (p. 29) – and that in his review essay "The New Therapy," Pound makes it clear that "*orderliness*" of vision is his primary value (p. 45). (Oderman also points out that this is one place where Pound diverges from the position of Gourmont, because for Gourmont, "nothing is 'CONTRA NATURAM'" [p. 38].) For

these reasons, Pound "is drawn to what he calls visionary experiences but abhors experiences he deems to be hallucinatory" (p. 46).

103. Durant, *Ezra Pound, Identity in Crisis*, p. 176.

104. This passage is quoted in ibid., p. 175. In these terms, it is worth noting Richard Sieburth's discussion of Pound's important category of *phanopoeia* and Pound's interest in Gourmont's "focus on the visual dimension of style." Pertinent here too is Pound's review "The New Therapy," which praised not vision purely and simply but "orderly visualization," vision subjected to the order of what Pound called the "phallic heart." See Sieburth, *Instigations*, pp. 62-63, 145ff.

105. In these terms, it is important to note that Pound found in Gourmont an anti-Freudian, anti-Oedipal vision of sexuality that provided, as Pound put it, "a comforting relief from Freudian excess." See Sieburth, *Instigations*, pp. 25, 129ff., 146.

106. Silverman, *The Acoustic Mirror*, p. 2. It should be noted that Silverman is addressing here the "viewer's exclusion from the site of cinematic production" (p. 13), which is also, however, itself but a metonymy in her Lacanian reading for the production of the subject by the symbolic order generally.

107. This is to second Durant's call for the need to always historicize psychoanalytic (and, more specifically, Lacanian) interpretations (*Ezra Pound, Identity in Crisis*, pp. 12-13).

108. Joan Wallach Scott, *Gender and the Politics of History* (New York: Columbia University Press, 1988), p. 39.

109. Ibid., p. 60. "Since all institutions employ some division of labor, since the structures of many institutions are premised on sexual divisions of labor (even if such divisions exclude one sex or the other), since references to the body often legitimize the forms institutions take, gender is, in fact, an aspect of social organization generally" (ibid., p. 6).

110. Ibid., p. 66.

111. The phrase belongs to Ellen Ross and Rayna Rapp, "Sex and Society: A Research Note from Social History and Anthropology," in *Powers of Desire: The Politics of Sexuality* (New York: Monthly Review Press, 1983), p. 53; quoted in Scott, *Gender and the Politics of History*, p. 36.

112. Wyndham Lewis, *Time and Western Man* (Boston: Beacon Press, 1957), pp. 70, 69.

113. Ibid., p. 69.

114. Ibid.

115. Ibid., p. 70.

116. Pound, *Homage to Sextus Propertius*, section V, in *Personae*, p. 217.

117. *The Cantos of Ezra Pound*, p. 4.

118. Ibid., p. 426. Burke argues that "Pound later abandoned the attempt to 'drive' his own intelligence into the world, perhaps because of his reduction to a more 'feminine' position during his cruel incarceration near Pisa" ("Getting Spliced," p. 116). That conclusion, it seems to me (as my critique here and my discussion of *The Pisan Cantos* in Chapter 6 suggest), is only half right.

5. VISIONARY CAPITAL: CONTRADICTIONS OF POUND'S LYRIC IDEAL

1. F. T. Palgrave, *The Golden Treasury of the Best Lyric Songs and Lyrical Poems*, Centennial Edition, Revised, Greatly Enlarged, and Brought Up to Date by Oscar Williams (New York: New American Library, 1961), p. x.
2. Ibid.
3. Ibid.
4. Ibid., p. xi.
5. Ibid., p. xii.
6. See Peter Brooker, *A Student's Guide to the Selected Poems of Ezra Pound* (London: Faber and Faber, 1979), pp. 212ff.
7. See John Espey's excellent and exhaustive study *Ezra Pound's Mauberley: A Study in Composition* (Berkeley and Los Angeles: University of California Press, 1955).
8. Palgrave, *Golden Treasury*, rev. ed., p. 63. Interestingly enough, Pound had parodied the concluding sentiment here eight years before his "Envoi" in a slap at A. E. Houseman: "O woe, woe / People are born and die, / We also shall be dead pretty soon / Therefore let us act as if we were / dead already." See Pound, "Song in the Manner of Houseman," in *Collected Early Poems of Ezra Pound*, ed. Michael John King, introduction by Louis L. Martz (New York: New Directions, 1976), p. 163.
9. Pound, *Hugh Selwyn Mauberley*, "Envoi," in *Personae: The Collected Shorter Poems of Ezra Pound* (New York: New Directions, 1971), p. 197.
10. Quoted in Brooker, *Guide*, p. 188; see also pp. 186, 222. On this point and its relation to the "Envoi" of *Hugh Selwyn Mauberley*, see Espey, *Ezra Pound's Mauberley*, esp. pp. 76–83.
11. Pound, "In Durance," in *Collected Early Poems*, p. 86. See also John Espey's discussion in "The Inheritance of Tò Kalón," in *New Approaches to Ezra Pound*, ed. Eva Hesse (London: Faber and Faber), pp. 319–330.
12. Pound, [Additional Poems in the San Trovaso Notebook], in *Collected Early Poems*, p. 256.
13. See, e.g., Pound's "Gold and Work," in which he rejects the gold standard because gold can be hoarded and monopolized (Ezra Pound, *Selected Prose, 1909–1965*, ed. William Cookson [New York: New Directions, 1973], p. 345). For a detailed and lucid discussion of these concerns in Pound's work, see Tim Redman, *Ezra Pound and Italian Fascism*, Cambridge Studies in American Literature and Culture (Cambridge: Cambridge University Press, 1991), and Peter Nicholls, *Ezra Pound: Politics, Economics, and Writing* (Atlantic Highlands, N.J.: Humanities Press, 1984).
14. Pound, "Famam Librosque Cano," in *Collected Early Poems*, p. 23.
15. Pound, "For the Triumph of the Arts," in ibid., p. 244.
16. See ibid., pp. 151, 244, 256, 268, 27.
17. Pound, "Mesmerism," in ibid., p. 18.
18. Jean-Joseph Goux, *Symbolic Economies: After Marx and Freud*, trans. Jennifer Curtiss Gage (Ithaca: Cornell University Press, 1990), p. 103.
19. Ibid., p. 100.

20. See ibid., pp. 112ff, and Redman, *Ezra Pound and Italian Fascism*, p. 38.

21. See Redman, *Ezra Pound and Italian Fascism*, pp. 52–53.

22. In any case, Pound thought that money should be neutral in value and purely instrumental in function, and hence, he promoted a kind of currency – statal money – whose value was insured not by the value of gold but by the state. Redman's discussion is lucid and helpful here (ibid., pp. 130–131, 134–135, 138–139, and 148–149).

23. *The Cantos of Ezra Pound* (New York: New Directions, 1986), p. 5.

24. Michael André Bernstein, "Image, Word, and Sign: The Visual Arts as Evidence in Ezra Pound's *Cantos*," *Critical Inquiry* 12: 2 (Winter 1986): 147–164, esp. pp. 359–360. Here as elsewhere in my reading of the *Cantos*, I am indebted to Carroll F. Terrell's *A Companion to the Cantos of Ezra Pound*, 2 vols. (Berkeley and Los Angeles: University of California Press, 1980–1984).

25. *The Cantos of Ezra Pound*, pp. 4, 193.

26. Bernstein, "Image, Word, and Sign," pp. 359–360.

27. A point made by Robert Hollander and noted in ibid., p. 360.

28. *The Cantos of Ezra Pound*, p. 54.

29. Ibid., pp. 78–79. This is not the Hermes of Bacon's copper *centavos*, as is more than suggested by the waters "bronze-gold" reflecting the "splendour" of his sacred attire, which is itself doubled by the "gold loin-cloth" of an unknown goddess.

30. Ibid., p. 487. Helen's cup of gold appears as well in Canto CVI (ibid., p. 752). See also Tellus-Helena in Canto LXXVI (p. 473), and Terrell, *Companion*, Vol. II, pp. 426, 690.

31. *The Cantos of Ezra Pound*, p. 6.

32. See Goux, *Symbolic Economies*, pp. 3–4, 27ff.

33. Ibid., p. 23.

34. See my discussion of "Near Perigord" in Chapter 4.

35. As Michael Harper writes, "Malatesta's great achievement, the Tempio, is possible only on the basis of the first kind of relationship, in which patron and protégé cooperate in mutual respect to produce something lasting and beautiful. . . . Malatesta's downfall takes place in a situation in which individuals are fighting to increase their own wealth and power through the acquisition of property. . . . His drama is that he exists in both worlds at the same time." See Harper's "Truth and Calliope: Ezra Pound's Malatesta," *PMLA* 96: 1 (January 1981): 94. For the authoritative discussion of the significance of Malatesta for Pound, see Lawrence S. Rainey, *Ezra Pound and the Monument of Culture: Text, History, and the Malatesta Cantos* (Chicago: University of Chicago Press, 1991).

36. *The Cantos of Ezra Pound*, pp. 78–79.

37. Ezra Pound, *Jefferson and/or Mussolini* (New York: Liveright, 1970), p. 17.

38. Peter Makin, *Pound's Cantos* (London: Allen and Unwin, 1985), pp. 141–142.

39. Ezra Pound, *Guide to Kulchur* (New York: New Directions, 1970), p. 159.

40. Harper, "Truth and Calliope," p. 100.

41. Nicholls, *Ezra Pound*, p. 42.

42. See Hugh Kenner, *The Pound Era* (Berkeley and Los Angeles: University of California Press, 1971), pp. 331–332.

43. My formulation here perhaps invokes Walter Benn Michaels's important study *The Gold Standard and the Logic of Naturalism: American Literature at the Turn of the Century*, The New Historicism, Vol. 2 (Berkeley and Los Angeles: University of California Press, 1987). This is not the place to mount an extended critique of Michaels's work. Suffice it for now to point out that Michaels rejects the concept of "ideology," which is central to my study here. As I have argued elsewhere, however, Michaels's understanding of ideology is a reductive one (a perspective largely abandoned even *within* Marxist criticism), and he substitutes for it an equally reductive concept of exchange value or "the market" and its constitution of subjectivity under capital. I have taken up these matters in detail in "Antinomies of Liberalism: The Politics of 'Belief' and the Project of Americanist Criticism," in *Discovering Difference: New Essays on American Culture*, ed. C. K. Lohmann (Bloomington: Indiana University Press, 1993). See also, for other helpful discussions of Michaels that are close to my own, Christopher Wilson, "Containing Multitudes: Realism, Historicism, American Studies," *American Quarterly* 41: 3 (September 1989): 466–497, and Fredric Jameson's critique in Chap. 7 of his *Postmodernism, or The Cultural Logic of Late Capitalism* (Durham: Duke University Press, 1990).

44. Pound, *Guide to Kulchur*, p. 194. As Lawrence S. Rainey convincingly demonstrates in his recent study of the Malatesta Cantos (*Ezra Pound and the Monument of Culture*), Sigismundo is for Pound the great example of the individual who, in possession of *virtù*, "discovers true being insofar as he sheds his historical traits" (p. 220). The paradox of Pound's Malatesta – and, as I am arguing, of Pound's project as a whole – is that he is, as Rainey puts it, "the historical exemplar of an ahistorical form of life" (p. 220).

45. Pound, *Guide to Kulchur*, frontispiece, no page number.

46. For a helpful overview of the major features of Social Credit, see Redman, *Ezra Pound and Italian Fascism*, pp. 51–75. For a briefer account, see Wendy Stallard Flory, *The American Ezra Pound* (New Haven: Yale University Press, 1989), esp. pp. 68–70.

47. Pound, "Art Notes by B. H. Dias," *New Age* 26: 4 (November 27, 1919): 60; quoted in Nicholls, *Ezra Pound*, p. 28.

48. *Literary Essays of Ezra Pound*, ed. T. S. Eliot (New York: New Directions, 1968), p. 42.

49. For an influential but very problematic discussion of literature-as-gift, one that pursues a very different line of inquiry from my own, see Lewis Hyde, *The Gift: Imagination and the Erotic Life of Property* (New York: Random House, 1983).

50. *The Cantos of Ezra Pound*, p. 14.

51. Ibid., p. 753.

52. Pound, "L'Invitation," in *Collected Early Poems*, p. 208; idem, "The Alchemist" (Version 1), in ibid., p. 225.

53. Pound, "The Alchemist" (Version 2), in ibid., p. 227.
54. *The Cantos of Ezra Pound*, p. 16.
55. Ibid., p. 17; see also Terrell, *Companion*, Vol. I, p. 18.
56. *The Cantos of Ezra Pound*, pp. 674, 699, 783.
57. Ibid., pp. 486, 248; see also Terrell, *Companion*, Vol. II, p. 195.
58. Goux, *Symbolic Economies*, p. 5.
59. Ibid., p. 99.
60. Ibid., p. 49.
61. See Terrell, *Companion*, Vol. II, p. 661.
62. *The Cantos of Ezra Pound*, p. 730.
63. Ibid., p. 675.
64. Ibid., p. 730.
65. Ibid., p. 605.
66. Terrell, *Companion*, Vol. II, p. 540.
67. *The Cantos of Ezra Pound*, p. 698.
68. In a recent article, Richard Sieburth discusses "Histrion" in the context of Pound's figures of minting as well, though his conclusions are different from – and sometimes opposed to – my own. See his "In Pound We Trust: The Economy of Poetry/The Poetry of Economics," *Critical Inquiry* 14 (Autumn 1987): 142–172.
69. Pound, "L'Art," in *Collected Early Poems*, p. 163.
70. Sieburth's treatment of this poem (in "In Pound We Trust") should be consulted for an interesting counterpoint to my own.
71. Pound, "Octave," in *Collected Early Poems*, p. 146.
72. *Selected Letters of Ezra Pound, 1907–1941*, ed. D. D. Paige, preface by Mark Van Doren (New York: New Directions, 1971), p. 111.
73. Ibid., p. 99.
74. Pound, *Selected Prose*, p. 232. For an excellent discussion of the major features of Social Credit, see Redman, *Ezra Pound and Italian Fascism*, pp. 51–75, and, for a briefer account, Flory, *The American Ezra Pound*, pp. 68–70.
75. Pound, *Literary Essays*, p. 221.
76. For a useful discussion of Pound and patronage in the context of Pound's important relationship with John Quinn, see Timothy Materer, "From Henry James to Ezra Pound: John Quinn and the Art of Patronage," *Paideuma* 17: 2/3 (Fall/Winter 1988): 47–68. I would be especially indebted to Materer's discussion had I not drafted my own before I discovered his.
77. Pound, *Selected Prose*, p. 128.
78. Reported by Noel Stock in *The Life of Ezra Pound* (New York: Pantheon, 1970), pp. 45, 47.
79. Pound, *Selected Prose*, p. 126.
80. Ibid.
81. Ibid.
82. Ibid.
83. Ibid., p. 127.
84. Pound, *Selected Letters*, p. 10.

85. Pound, *Selected Prose*, p. 127.
86. Ibid.
87. Ibid., p. 141.
88. See Materer's informative discussion of Pound and Quinn's developing relationship in "From Henry James to Ezra Pound," pp. 47–49.
89. Pound, *Selected Letters*, p. 54.
90. *Emerson in His Journals*, ed. Joel Porte (Cambridge, Mass.: Belknap Press of Harvard University Press, 1982), p. 234.
91. Pound, *Selected Prose*, p. 108.
92. See Materer, "From Henry James to Ezra Pound," pp. 49–56.
93. As Harper rightly points out, Malatesta's understanding of "conditions" in the broadest sense here (military and economic as well as artistic) is very much to the point of Pound's admiration of him. See Harper, "Truth and Calliope," pp. 93–94.
94. *The Cantos of Ezra Pound*, p. 29.
95. Pound, *Selected Letters*, p. 115.
96. Pound, *Literary Essays*, p. 46.
97. *Emerson in His Journals*, p. 446.
98. Ibid., p. 251.
99. Ibid., p. 125.
100. Ian F. A. Bell, "The Hard Currency of Words: Emerson's Fiscal Metaphor in *Nature*," *ELH* 52: 3 (Fall 1985): 733–753, esp. pp. 736.
101. Pound, *Selected Prose*, p. 215.
102. *The Cantos of Ezra Pound*, p. 797.
103. Pound, *Selected Prose*, p. 214.
104. Ibid., p. 214.
105. Ibid., p. 215.
106. Ibid., p. 131.
107. The naivete of Pound's plan was perhaps driven by the extremely idealistic faith in human goodness that, as Flory has pointed out, was a strong component of Pound's character (*The American Ezra Pound*, pp. 49ff.).
108. Pound, *Selected Prose*, p. 140. See also Pound, *Literary Essays*, p. 224.
109. *The Cantos of Ezra Pound*, p. 211.
110. See Jean-Paul Sartre, *Search for a Method*, trans. Hazel E. Barnes (New York: Vintage, 1963), pp. 92–97.
111. I will discuss Pound's relationship to populism in more detail in the following chapter.
112. Significantly, Italian fascism, as any overview will show, was in fact productionist, not distributionist, in its economic policies. See, e.g., S. William Halperin, *Mussolini and Italian Fascism* (New York: Van Nostrand Reinhold, 1964), pp. 54–64, esp. p. 62. In contrast, Social Credit aimed to change not the mode of *production* but the mode of *distribution* by (1) establishing a "Just Price" based on the balance of production and consumption, (2) regulating the money supply in accord with the nation's "Real Capital Assets," and (3) issuing a National Dividend to all whose income was less than four times the dividend (see Flory, *The American Ezra Pound*, p. 68). For the

central text by the "inventor" of Social Credit, consult C. H. Douglas, *Social Credit* (New York: Norton, ca. 1933).

113. Emerson, *English Traits*, in *The Complete Works of Ralph Waldo Emerson*, Centenary Edition, 12 vols., ed. Edward Waldo Emerson (Boston: Houghton Mifflin, 1903–1904), Vol. V, pp. 169–170.

114. Pound, *Jefferson and/or Mussolini*, p. 63.

115. *The Correspondence of Emerson and Carlyle*, ed. Joseph Slater (New York: Columbia University Press, 1964), p. 486.

6. IDEOLOGIES OF THE ORGANIC

1. Emerson, "Politics," *The Complete Works of Ralph Waldo Emerson*, Centenary Edition, 12 vols., ed. Edward Waldo Emerson (Boston: Houghton Mifflin, 1903–1904), Vol. III, p. 197. Subsequent references to this edition will be abbreviated *W*.

2. Ibid., pp. 215–216.

3. Emerson, "The Poet," *W*, Vol. III, pp. 34–35. For an instructive discussion of the homology between language and economics in Emerson, see Ian F. A. Bell, "The Hard Currency of Words: Emerson's Fiscal Metaphor in *Nature*," *ELH* 52: 3 (Fall 1985): 733–753.

4. As Maurice Gonnaud points out, Jefferson, in fact, exerted no direct influence on Emerson. See his *An Uneasy Solitude: Individual and Society in the Work of Ralph Waldo Emerson*, trans. Lawrence Rosenwald, foreword by Eric Cheyfitz (French ed., 1964; Princeton: Princeton University Press, 1987), p. 207. In any case, Emerson's somewhat federalist attitudes made his Jeffersonian ideal of self-sufficiency and minimal government just that – an ideal. For a detailed discussion of Emerson and the Jeffersonian line, see D. C. Stenerson, "Emerson and the Agrarian Tradition," *Journal of the History of Ideas* 14 (January 1953): 95–115.

5. See the following discussions of Pound's relationship to Aristotle: Richard Sieburth, "In Pound We Trust: The Economy of Poetry/The Poetry of Economics," *Critical Inquiry* 14 (Autumn 1987): 142–172, esp. pp. 162, 170; David Murray, "Pound-Signs: Money and Representation in Ezra Pound," in *Ezra Pound and History*, ed. Marianne Korn (Orono, Maine: National Poetry Foundation and the University of Maine, 1985), pp. 173–197; and Andrew Parker, "Ezra Pound and the 'Economy' of Anti-Semitism," in *Postmodernism and Politics*, ed. Jonathan Arac, Theory and History of Literature, Vol. 28 (Minneapolis: University of Minnesota Press, 1986), pp. 70–90.

6. Sieburth, "In Pound We Trust," p. 170; Parker, "Ezra Pound and the 'Economy' of Anti-Semitism," p. 71.

7. Ezra Pound, *Selected Prose, 1909–1965*, ed. William Cookson (New York: New Directions, 1973), p. 346.

8. See also Canto LI, in *The Cantos of Ezra Pound* (New Directions, 1986), p. 250.

9. Ezra Pound, *Guide to Kulchur* (New York: New Directions, 1970), p. 323.

10. See Murray, "Pound-Signs," p. 183.

11. Pound, *Guide to Kulchur*, p. 357.
12. Ibid., p. 324.
13. Karl Marx, *Capital*, trans. Ben Fowkes, introduction by Ernest Mandel (New York: Vintage, 1977), Vol. I, p. 151; See also Murray's reading of this moment in Marx ("Pound-Signs," p. 183).
14. Pound, *Guide to Kulchur*, p. 359.
15. Ibid., p. 357.
16. Peter Nicholls, *Ezra Pound: Politics, Economics, and Writing* (Atlantic Highlands, N.J.: Humanities Press, 1984), p. 57.
17. For a useful summary, see Wendy Stallard Flory, *The American Ezra Pound* (New Haven: Yale University Press, 1989), pp. 70–72.
18. See, e.g., Tyrus Miller, "Pound's Economic Ideal: Silvio Gesell and *The Cantos*," *Paideuma* 19: 1/2 (Spring/Fall 1990): 168–180; and esp. Chap. 5 of Tim Redman's *Ezra Pound and Italian Fascism*, Cambridge Studies in American Literature and Culture (Cambridge: Cambridge University Press, 1991). Redman argues that Pound saw in Gesell's stamp scrip "an easily understandable mechanism to put Social Credit into action" (p. 129), whereas Miller argues that Pound's interest in Gesell's stamp scrip eventually resulted in a break with C. H. Douglas, the founder of Social Credit economics (p. 171). It should be noted in any case (as Redman points out) that Gesell was a dedicated Social Darwinist in economics and a fierce free-marketeer who felt that the "untrammeled self-interest and competition" that makes for healthy capitalism was not free *enough* because of the existing monetary system, which he hoped to reform (Redman, *Ezra Pound and Italian Fascism*, p. 129).
19. Miller, "Pound's Economic Ideal," pp. 171, 172.
20. Pound, *Selected Prose*, p. 330.
21. Lewis Hyde, *The Gift: Imagination and the Erotic Life of Property* (New York: Random House, 1983), p. 259.
22. Bell, "The Hard Currency of Words," p. 734.
23. See William Leggett's essay "Equality" in the *New York Evening Post* for December 6, 1834. Quoted in Bell, "The Hard Currency of Words," p. 737.
24. A central difference here, of course, is that the Jacksonians and Emerson himself were deeply suspicious of paper currency and tended to favor gold and specie, whereas Pound and Gesell favored paper money – and specifically statal money – while they vociferously attacked gold. More important, though, both views share largely the same position on the relationship between nature and economic value. For Emerson and the Jacksonians, paper money contributes to unhealthy practices; for Pound and Gesell, gold is the culprit. But in both cases those practices are attacked according to the same set of idealist ethical coordinates.
25. Quoted in Carolyn Porter, *Seeing and Being: The Plight of the Participant Observer in Emerson, James, Adams, and Faulkner* (Middletown, Conn.: Wesleyan University Press, 1981), p. 59.
26. Emerson, "Reforms," in *Emerson, Essays and Lectures*, ed. Joel Porte (New

York: Library of America, 1983), vol. III, p. 486. Quoted in Gonnaud, *Uneasy Solitude*, p. 251.

27. Pound, *Selected Prose*, p. 329.
28. Pound, *Guide to Kulchur*, p. 278.
29. For a representative tract, see "What Is Money For?" in Pound, *Selected Prose*, pp. 290–302.
30. See Parker's discussion, "Ezra Pound and the 'Economy' of Anti-Semitism," p. 73.
31. See Gerald R. Else, *Aristotle's Poetics: The Argument* (Cambridge, Mass.: Harvard University Press, 1963), pp. 12–13, 305–306. Else points out that the essence of Aristotle's sense of mimesis is not "imitation" but rather the *"drafting of the plot."*
32. *The Cantos of Ezra Pound*, p. 671. See the readings of this passage in Sieburth, "In Pound We Trust," pp. 143–144, and Nicholls, *Ezra Pound*, pp. 217–218.
33. See, e.g., Redman, *Ezra Pound and Italian Fascism*, p. 7.
34. T. S. Eliot, Introduction to *Selected Poems of Ezra Pound* (London: Faber and Faber, 1928).
35. Pound, "The River-Merchant's Wife: A Letter," in *Personae: The Collected Shorter Poems of Ezra Pound* (New York: New Directions, 1971), p. 130.
36. Ibid.
37. *The Cantos of Ezra Pound*, p. 244.
38. Hugh Kenner, *The Poetry of Ezra Pound* (1951; rpt., Lincoln: University of Nebraska Press, 1985), p. 326.
39. Quoted in Angela Jung Palandri, "The 'Seven Lakes Canto' Revisited," *Paideuma* 3: 1 (Spring 1974): 51.
40. Daniel Pearlman, *The Barb of Time: On the Unity of Ezra Pound's Cantos* (New York: Oxford University Press, 1969), pp. 27–28.
41. Pound, *Guide to Kulchur*, p. 135.
42. See John J. Nolde's essay "Ezra Pound and Chinese History," in Korn, ed., *Ezra Pound and History*, p. 105.
43. See Peter Brooker, *A Student's Guide to the Selected Poems of Ezra Pound* (London: Faber and Faber, 1979), p. 295.
44. *The Cantos of Ezra Pound*, pp. 251–252.
45. See Brooker, *Guide*, p. 295.
46. Pound, *Selected Prose*, p. 256.
47. Ibid., p. 270.
48. Ibid., p. 294.
49. Sanehide Kodama, "The Eight Scenes of Sho-Sho," *Paideuma*, 6: 2 (Fall 1977): 131–145. Quoted in Carroll F. Terrell, *A Companion to the Cantos of Ezra Pound* (Berkeley and Los Angeles: University of California Press, 1980), Vol. I, p. 191.
50. Quoted in Hugh Kenner, "More on the Seven Lakes Canto," *Paideuma* 2: 1 (Spring 1973): 45–46.
51. Pound, *Selected Prose*, p. 82.
52. *The Cantos of Ezra Pound*, p. 265.

53. Ibid., p. 797.

54. The contradictions of Pound's concept of nature are evident even in these few lines. If nature is ordered by those laws that govern its growth, then why does any "underbrush" need to be cleared? For a persuasive critique of Pound's concept of nature, see Robert Casillo, "Nature, History, and Anti-Nature in Ezra Pound's Fascism," *Papers on Language and Literature* 22: 3 (Summer 1986): 284–311.

55. *The Cantos of Ezra Pound*, p. 237.

56. Ibid., p. 259.

57. This characterization of *li* belongs to S. Wells Williams, quoted in Terrell, *Companion*, Vol. I, p. 201.

58. *The Cantos of Ezra Pound*, p. 261.

59. And, as my colleague Patrick Brantlinger has reminded me, Palmerston's gunboat diplomacy (as foreign secretary he presided over the Opium Wars of 1839–42 and therefore over Britain's imperial incursions against China) is clearly a precursor to similar practices of modern fascism.

60. William Cookson, *A Guide to the Cantos of Ezra Pound*, foreword by M. L. Rosenthal (New York: Persea Books, 1985), p. 57.

61. *The Cantos of Ezra Pound*, p. 486.

62. See Terrell, *Companion*, Vol. I, p. 191.

63. Pound, *Jefferson and/or Mussolini* (New York: Liveright, 1970), p. 109.

64. Ibid., p. 108.

65. Pound, *Selected Prose*, p. 87.

66. Ibid., p. 96.

67. Pound, *Jefferson and/or Mussolini*, p. 128.

68. See, e.g., Reed Way Dasenbrock, "Jefferson and/or Adams: A Shifting Mirror for Mussolini in the Middle Cantos," *ELH* 55: 2 (Summer 1988): 505–526, esp. pp. 515–516; and Tyrus Miller, "Pound's Economic Ideal: Silvio Gesell and *The Cantos*," *Paideuma* 19: 1/2 (Spring/Fall 1990): 169–180, esp. p. 177. I will discuss Brooker's critique in more detail in the next section.

69. Quoted in Michael T. Gilmore, *American Romanticism and the Marketplace* (Chicago: University of Chicago Press, 1985), p. 20. For a discussion highlighting Emerson's differences with the Jacksonian lineage, see Gonnaud, *Uneasy Solitude*, pp. 132, 294.

70. Pound, *Selected Prose*, p. 248.

71. Quoted in Arthur Schlesinger, *The Age of Roosevelt*, Vol. III, *The Politics of Upheaval* (Boston: Houghton Mifflin, 1960), pp. 66–67.

72. See, among many others, Redman's *Ezra Pound and Italian Fascism*; C. David Heymann, *Ezra Pound: The Last Rower, A Political Profile* (New York: Viking, 1976); John R. Harrison, *The Reactionaries: A Study of the Anti-Democratic Intelligentsia* (New York: Schocken Books, 1967); Victor Ferkiss, "Ezra Pound and American Fascism," *Journal of Politics* 17: 2 (May 1955): 173–197; John Lauber, "Pound's *Cantos*: A Fascist Epic," *Journal of American Studies* 12: 1 (April 1978): 3–21; Peter Brooker, "The Lesson of Ezra Pound: An Essay in Poetry, Literary Ideology, and Politics," in *Ezra*

Pound: Tactics for Reading, ed. Ian F. A. Bell (London: Vision Press, 1982), pp. 8–49; William H. Chace, *The Political Identities of Ezra Pound and T. S. Eliot* (Stanford: Stanford University Press, 1973).

73. Ferkiss, "Ezra Pound and American Fascism," p. 174.

74. John Tytell notes this in his biography *Ezra Pound: The Solitary Volcano* (New York: Doubleday, 1987), p. 17.

75. For a helpful overview of the range of opinions on the political character of populism, see Alan Brinkley, "Richard Hofstadter's *The Age of Reform*: A Reconsideration," *Reviews in American History* 13: 3 (September 1985): 462–480.

76. Hofstadter's influential interpretation of the political character of populism as a whole should be balanced by the very different views of Norman Pollack in *The Populist Response to Industrial America* (Cambridge, Mass.: Harvard University Press, 1962) and of Lawrence Goodwyn in his encyclopedic *Democratic Promise: The Populist Moment in America* (New York: Oxford University Press, 1976). Both of these works see populism as politically more coherent, sophisticated, and promising than Hofstadter's reading does. It should be noted, too, that part of what is at issue here is Hofstadter's *own* liberal consensus politics during the cold war era, when *The Age of Reform* (New York: Vintage Books, 1955) was written and published. As Hofstadter put it in his introduction, he was drawn to accentuate that dimension of populism "which seems very strongly to foreshadow some aspects of the cranky pseudo-conservatism of our time. Somewhere along the way a large part of the Populist–Progressive tradition has turned sour, become illiberal and ill-tempered" (p. 20). As his brief glance at Pound (p. 80) makes clear, Hofstadter probably found the negative fulfillment of populism in modernists like Pound himself, who were anything but defenders of the political center to which Hofstadter himself clung. So in a curious way, Hofstadter's cold war liberalism leads him to accentuate the reactionary strain of populism by reading the ultraconservatism (or fascism) of modernists *back into* the populist moment. Here again, Brinkley's overview is helpful. For a critique of Hofstadter as a sort of latter-day Arnoldian, see Warren Susman, *Culture as History: The Transformation of American Society in the Twentieth Century* (New York: Pantheon, 1984), pp. 61–62. I will discuss in my Afterword the broader issues that frame my reservations here about Hofstadter.

77. *The Cantos of Ezra Pound*, p. 711.

78. Hofstadter, *Age of Reform*, pp. 62–63,

79. The characterization belongs to Donald McRae, quoted in Brooker, "The Lesson of Ezra Pound," p. 27.

80. Hofstadter, *Age of Reform*, p. 63.

81. B. S. Heath, *Labor and Finance Revolution* (1892), quoted in ibid.

82. Hofstadter, *Age of Reform*, p. 73. Pollack's attempted refutation of this aspect of Hofstadter's interpretation seems rather to ratify it. See Pollack, *The Populist Response to Industrial America*, pp. 21–22, 80. Pound's Rome Radio speeches are collected in *Ezra Pound Speaking: Radio Speeches of World War II*, ed. Leonard W. Doob (Westport, Conn.: Greenwood Press, 1978).

83. Goodwyn, *Democratic Promise*, p. 386.
84. Hofstadter, *Age of Reform*, p. 73.
85. See Burke's "The Scapegoat as an Error in Interpretation," in *Permanence and Change*, 3d ed. (Berkeley and Los Angeles.: University of California Press, 1984), pp. 14–17.
86. Pound, *Selected Prose*, p. 274.
87. Ibid., p. 238.
88. Ibid., p. 282.
89. In *Literary Essays of Ezra Pound*, ed. T. S. Eliot (New York: New Directions, 1968), p. 86.
90. Pound, *Guide to Kulchur*, p. 279.
91. Pound, *Selected Prose*, p. 86.
92. Ibid., p. 87.
93. *The Cantos of Ezra Pound*, p. 58.
94. Pound, *Selected Prose*, p. 89.
95. This is a paraphrase, of course, of Marx's famous formulation of the concept of ideology in *The Eighteenth Brumaire of Louis Bonaparte*, trans. C. P. Dutt (New York: International Publishers, 1963), p. 51.
96. For a useful overview, see Victor C. Ferkiss, "Populist Influences on American Fascism," *Western Political Quarterly* 10: 2 (June 1957): 350–373.
97. Quoted in Murray "Pound-Signs," p. 186.
98. Burton Hatlen, "Ezra Pound and Fascism," in Korn, ed., *Ezra Pound and History*, p. 168.
99. In this regard, see Marx's observation in "On the Jewish Question" that the supreme concept and value of a society based upon private property is *security*. In Marx, *Early Writings*, trans. Rodney Livingstone and Gregor Benton, introduction by Lucio Colletti (New York: Vintage Books, 1975), p. 230. See also Marx, *The Eighteenth Brumaire*, p. 66.
100. Pound, *Guide to Kulchur*, p. 190.
101. See Cookson, *A Guide to the Cantos of Ezra Pound*, p. 122.
102. *The Cantos of Ezra Pound*, p. 709.
103. Ibid., p. 708.
104. Ibid., p. 425.
105. *The Selected Letters of Ezra Pound, 1907–1941*, ed. D. D. Paige, preface by Mark Van Doren (New York: New Directions, 1971), p. 277.
106. *The Cantos of Ezra Pound*, pp. 711–712.
107. Ibid., pp. 426–427.
108. Ibid., p. 695.
109. Ibid., p. 430.
110. See Nicholls, *Ezra Pound*, pp. 161ff.; and, for a diametrically opposed reading, see Flory's interpretation of Pound during the period of *The Pisan Cantos* and later in *The American Ezra Pound*.
111. *The Cantos of Ezra Pound*, p. 499.
112. Ibid., p. 516.
113. Brooker, "The Lesson of Ezra Pound," p. 32.
114. Nicholls, *Ezra Pound*, pp. 161ff.
115. Ibid., p. 170.

116. As Alan Durant points out, this problem persists into the very last cantos, where similar moments of contrition punctuate the text: "That I lost my center / fighting the world," Pound writes in one famous passage. Durant argues, however, "Even in this admission that subjectivity is put into question . . . the 'I' escapes, since the 'I' whose centre has been lost is a different 'I' from the reconstituted 'I' who recognizes that loss. Rather than examining what causes this loss of the self in language, the impetus of these last *Drafts and Fragments* is towards the possibility of a transcendent force which might alter that condition." See Durant's *Ezra Pound, Identity in Crisis* (Sussex: Harvester Press, 1981), p. 65.

117. *The Cantos of Ezra Pound*, p. 531.

118. Ibid., p. 533.

119. Ibid., p. 790. For related interpretations, see Nicholls, *Ezra Pound*, p. 179; Donald Davie, *Ezra Pound: Poet as Sculptor* (New York: Oxford University Press, 1964), pp. 176–177; and esp. Richard Sieburth, *Instigations: Ezra Pound and Remy de Gourmont* (Cambridge, Mass.: Harvard University Press, 1978), pp. 149ff., who pays particular attention to insect imagery in *The Pisan Cantos* and notes perceptively that "one of the central motifs of the *Pisan Cantos* is quite simply the question of scale, the ratios and proportions between animal, man, landscape, elements, gods, history" (p. 149).

120. For an exemplary and influential work of critical theory that stresses the text's gaps, absences, and silences, see Pierre Macherey, *A Theory of Literary Production*, trans. Geoffrey Wall (London: Routledge and Kegan Paul, 1978), esp. pp. 3–105. For a useful overview and discussion of related works in critical theory, see Tony Bennett, *Formalism and Marxism*, New Accents (London: Methuen, 1979).

121. The relevant passage in Heidegger is in *Being and Time*, trans. John Macquarrie and Edward Robinson (New York: Harper and Row, 1962), p. 104. For a helpful brief discussion of this concept in Heidegger's work, see Frank Lentricchia, *After the New Criticism* (Chicago: University of Chicago Press, 1980), pp. 86–88.

122. Paul de Man, "The Rhetoric of Temporality," in *Blindness and Insight*, 2d ed., Theory and History of Literature, Vol. 7 (MInneapolis: University of Minnesota Press, 1983), p. 197. De Man's quarry here is finally an ontological, not political, point. But as Frank Lentricchia has shown in *Criticism and Social Change* (Chicago: University of Chicago Press, 1983), that point is nevertheless political through and through.

123. *The Cantos of Ezra Pound*, p. 532.

7. SIGNS THAT BIND: IDEOLOGY AND FORM IN POUND'S POETICS

1. One of the most informative discussions of Pound's relationship with James remains John Espey's chapter "The Major James" in his *Ezra Pound's Mauberley: A Study in Composition* (Berkeley and Los Angeles: University of California Press, 1955).

2. Fenollosa's teaching of Emerson is recorded in L. W. Chisholm's *Fenollosa: The Far East and American Culture* and is noted in Hugh Kenner, *The Pound Era* (Berkeley and Los Angeles: University of California Press, 1971), p. 230.

3. For an account, see Kenner, *The Pound Era*, pp. 197–198.

4. For an exhaustive history of the relationship during this period, see James Longenbach, *Stone Cottage: Pound, Yeats, and Modernism* (New York: Oxford University Press, 1988). I say "helped" here quite deliberately because, as Longenbach points out, the usual accounts of this dramatic transformation are "largely apocryphal" (p. xii), since Yeats had already begun moving in this direction before he met Pound. Still, after their first winter together, Longenbach reports, "Yeats had told an audience in Chicago that 'a young man' had gone over all his work with him 'to eliminate the abstract'" (p. 204). That "young man," of course, was Pound.

5. Editorial headnote to Ernest Fenollosa, "The Chinese Written Character as a Medium for Poetry," in Ezra Pound, *Instigations* (New York: Boni and Liveright, 1920), p. 357. Pound told Felix Schelling in 1915 that Fenollosa offered "a whole basis of aesthetic"; and in a letter to John Quinn in 1917, he put the study of Chinese above even his beloved Provencal: "China," he declared, "is fundamental." See *The Selected Letters of Ezra Pound, 1907–1941*, ed. D. D. Paige, preface by Mark Van Doren (New York: New Directions, 1971), pp. 61, 102. See also Pound's *ABC of Reading* (New York: New Directions, 1960), p. 19.

6. Longenbach, *Stone Cottage*, p. 142. It should be noted that the central thesis of Longenbach's account – that at Stone Cottage Yeats and Pound were driven by their imaginings of a "secret society" of "an artistic and social elite" (p. xi) – is largely at odds with my own.

7. For an extensive discussion of these developments, see Gerald L. Bruns, *Modern Poetry and the Idea of Language* (New Haven: Yale University Press, 1974).

8. For the Frege text, see *Translations from the Philosophical Writings of Gottlob Frege*, ed. Peter Geach and Max Black (Oxford: Oxford University Press, 1952); Franco Moretti, "From *The Waste Land* to Artificial Paradise," in *Signs Taken for Wonders*, trans. Susan Fischer et al. (London: New Left Books, 1983), pp. 209–239. Eliot's formulation is in "The Metaphysical Poets" (1921), in T. S. Eliot, *Selected Essays, 1917–1932* (New York: Harcourt, Brace, and Co., 1932), pp. 241–250.

9. Ferdinand de Saussure, *Course in General Linguistics*, ed. Charles Bally et al., trans. and introduction by Wade Baskin (New York: McGraw-Hill, 1966), p. 120.

10. *Translations from Frege*, p. 57.

11. Ibid., pp. 59–60; Moretti, "From *The Waste Land* to Artificial Paradise," pp. 214ff.

12. Moretti, "From *The Waste Land* to Artificial Paradise," p. 215.

13. James McFarlane, "The Mind of Modernism," in *Modernism, 1890–1930*, ed. Malcolm Bradbury and James McFarlane (Atlantic Highlands, N.J.:

Humanities Press, 1978), as quoted in Daniel Joseph Singal, "Towards a Definition of American Modernism," *American Quarterly* 39: 1 (Spring 1987): 13. McFarlane's thesis is that modernism moves from an initial bohemian, rebellious phase, in which the conventions and structures of Victorian and genteel culture are broken down and disintegrated; into a second, or middle, phase, in which these cultural fragments are recombined in new and unexpected ways; and finally to a stage of ambitious, synthetic, and eclectic totalizations of the sort we find in the later work of Pound and Eliot.

14. Moretti, "From *The Waste Land* to Artificial Paradise," p. 217.
15. See Ronald Bush, *The Genesis of Ezra Pound's Cantos* (Princeton: Princeton University Press, 1976), pp. 10–14, 21, 178–179; and Herbert N. Schneidau, *Ezra Pound: The Image and the Real* (Baton Rouge: Louisiana State University Press, 1969), pp. 58–73.
16. Reed Way Dasenbrock, *The Literary Vorticism of Ezra Pound and Wyndham Lewis: Towards the Condition of Painting* (Baltimore: Johns Hopkins University Press, 1985), p. 205.
17. See Bush, *The Genesis of Ezra Pound's Cantos*, p. 204.
18. Fenollosa, in Pound, *Instigations*, p. 379.
19. Ibid., p. 362.
20. Pound, "Vorticism," in idem, *Gaudier-Brzeska: A Memoir* (New York: New Directions, 1960), p. 91.
21. Fenollosa, in Pound, *Instigations*, p. 363.
22. Paul de Man, "The Rhetoric of Temporality," in *Blindness and Insight*, 2d ed., Theory and History of Literature, Vol. 7 (Minneapolis: University of Minnesota Press, 1983), p. 207.
23. Pound, *ABC of Reading* (New York: New Directions, 1960), p. 21.
24. Fenollosa, in Pound, *Instigations*, p. 364.
25. Ibid., p. 367.
26. Ibid., pp. 367–368.
27. Terence Hawkes explains the Peircean triad nicely in his *Structuralism and Semiotics* (Berkeley and Los Angeles: University of California Press, 1977). In the *icon*, the operative quality is resemblance, as a portrait is motivated by the appearance of its object. In *index*, the relationship is "concrete, actual and usually of a sequential, causal kind. . . . Smoke is an *index* of fire." And in the *symbol*, the relation between word and thing is purely arbitrary and code-dependent (p. 129).
28. Pound, *ABC of Reading*, p. 21.
29. This is not at all surprising. For Pound, language too is a means of exchange. As early as 1912, he was arguing that "language, the medium of thought's preservation, is constantly wearing out. It has been the function of the poets to new-mint the speech, to supply the vigorous terms for prose." See Pound, *Selected Prose, 1909–1965*, ed. William Cookson (New York: New Directions, 1973), p. 361. For an instructive discussion of homologies between Pound's theories of language and economics, whose emphasis is often different from – and sometimes opposed to – my own, see Richard Sieburth, "In Pound We Trust: The Economy of Poetry/The Poetry of Economy," *Critical Inquiry* 14 (Autumn 1987): 142–172.

30. Pound, *ABC of Reading*, p. 25.
31. Emerson, *Nature*, in *The Complete Works of Ralph Waldo Emerson*, Centenary Edition, 12 vols., ed. Edward Waldo Emerson (Boston: Houghton Mifflin, 1903–1904), Vol. I, pp. 29–30. Subsequent references to this edition will be abbreviated *W*. For a useful discussion of this and related passages from Emerson in the context of Jacksonian Monetary debates, see Ian F. A. Bell, "The Hard Currency of Words: Emerson's Fiscal Metaphor in *Nature*," *ELH* 52: 3 (Fall 1985): 733–753.
32. Kenner in *The Pound Era* examines some of the similarities between Fenollosa's poetics and that of Emerson, though his interpretation is different in spirit and intent from my own (see pp. 105, 157–158, 230–231). See as well the discussion of Emerson, Fenollosa, and the ideogram in Hwa Yol Jung, "Misreading the Ideogram: From Fenollosa to Derrida and McLuhan," *Paideuma* 13: 2 (Fall 1984): 211–227. Michael F. Harper also speculates upon lines of relation between Emerson and Pound (though not specifically with regard to the ideogram) in "Truth and Calliope: Ezra Pound's Malatesta," *PMLA* 96: 1 (January 1981): 86–103.
33. Emerson, *Nature*, *W*, Vol. I, p. 30.
34. Ibid., p. 29.
35. Ibid., p. 25.
36. Ibid., p. 29.
37. Emerson, "The Poet," *W*, Vol. III, p. 22.
38. Fenollosa, in Pound, *Instigations*, p. 377.
39. Ibid.
40. Emerson, "The Poet," *W*, Vol. III, p. 22.
41. Fenollosa, in Pound, *Instigations*, p. 377.
42. Emerson, "The Poet," *W*, Vol. III, p. 22.
43. Emerson, *Nature*, *W*, Vol. I, p. 26.
44. Ibid., pp. 34–35. Barbara Packer perceptively argues that the famous doctrine of "re-attachment" of words to things in *Nature* and in "The Poet" is accompanied in the later essay by a second strategy, which is concerned not with language's iconic dimension but rather with its indexical one, its capacity to create what Emerson characterizes as a kind of ecstasy brought on by the poet's production of new tropes and figures, and which therefore allows us to participate in the "metamorphic" power of the imagination. See Packer's *Emerson's Fall: A New Interpretation of the Major Essays* (New York: Continuum, 1982).
45. Fenollosa, in Pound, *Instigations*, p. 376.
46. Emerson, "The American Scholar," *W*, Vol. I, p. 112.
47. Fenollosa, in Pound, *Instigations*, p. 377.
48. Ibid.
49. Pound, *ABC of Reading*, pp. 20, 18.
50. Ibid., p. 17.
51. Fenollosa, in Pound, *Instigations*, p. 366.
52. Ibid., p. 365.
53. Ibid., p. 366.
54. Ibid.

55. Pound, *ABC of Reading*, p. 26.

56. Ibid., p. 27.

57. Emerson, "The Poet," *W*, Vol. III, p. 8.

58. I would be indebted to a similar point in Myra Jehlen's reading of *Nature* had I not come upon it after my own was written. As she puts it, Emerson's concept of language as an attribute of nature *"forbids the creation of new worlds."* See her *American Incarnation: The Individual, the Nation, and the Continent* (Cambridge, Mass.: Harvard University Press, 1986), p. 103.

59. Emerson, *Nature*, *W*, Vol. I, p. 27.

60. Ibid., p. 20.

61. A formulation I borrow from Jehlen, *American Incarnation*, p. 77.

62. Pound, *ABC of Reading*, p. 21.

63. Ibid., p. 22.

64. Pound, *Selected Prose*, p. 94.

65. As Dasenbrock points out, Pound's early attraction to the ideogram was based in large part on how Fenollosa's poetic encouraged an "exploratory stance towards the world" and had a "reorienting effect on the reader" (*Literary Vorticism*, p. 111).

66. On the relationship between the ideogram and Vorticism, see ibid., esp. Chap. 3.

67. Pound, "Vorticism," in *Gaudier-Brzeska*, p. 89.

68. Ibid.

69. See Dasenbrock, *Literary Vorticism*, p. 206.

70. Pound, *Selected Prose*, p. 162.

71. Ibid., p. 306.

72. Ibid., p. 334.

73. Kenneth Burke, *Attitudes toward History*, 3d ed. (Berkeley and Los Angeles: University of California Press, 1984), pp. 77–78.

74. Pound, *Selected Prose*, p. 317.

75. Burke, *Attitudes toward History*, p. 75.

76. Ibid.

77. Ibid., p. 79.

78. Pound, *Selected Prose*, p. 82.

79. Pound, *Selected Letters*, p. 277. See also Wendy Stallard Flory's discussion of this tendency in the later Pound in *The American Ezra Pound* (New Haven: Yale University Press, 1989), pp. 88–89. And see Peter Nicholls, *Ezra Pound: Politics, Economics, and Writing* (Atlantic Highlands, N.J.: Humanities Press, 1984), for an analysis of Pound's obsession with "right reason" and "right naming" (pp. 92–94, 102).

80. Pound, *Selected Prose*, p. 82.

81. Wendy Steiner, *The Colors of Rhetoric: Problems in the Relation between Modern Literature and Painting* (Chicago: University of Chicago Press, 1982), pp. 100, 120.

82. Michael André Bernstein, "Image, Word, and Sign: The Visual Arts as Evidence in Ezra Pound's *Cantos*," *Critical Inquiry* 12: 2 (Winter 1986): 347–364, esp. p. 358.

83. Steiner, *The Colors of Rhetoric*, p. 100.

84. Emerson, "Circles," *W*, Vol. II, p. 311.
85. Moretti, "From *The Waste Land* to Artificial Paradise," p. 218.
86. I have in mind, for example, some of the work on modernism by Julia Kristeva. For convincing critiques of her work along these lines, see Toril Moi, *Sexual/Textual Politics: Feminist Literary Theory* (London: Methuen, 1985), pp. 170ff., and Franco Moretti, "The Spell of Indecision," *New Left Review* 164 (August 1987): 27–31.
87. Ezra Pound, interview with Donald Hall, *Writers at Work: The Paris Review Interviews*, Second Series, introduction by Van Wyck Brooks (New York: Viking Press, 1963), p. 58.
88. For these reasons, I will focus largely upon two representative critiques – those of Max Nänny and Michael André Bernstein – which approach the genre of the *Cantos* from diametrically opposed positions. Scholars interested in pursuing these exhaustive debates over the genre of the *Cantos* may consult the following authoritative discussions: Kenner, *The Pound Era*; Daniel D. Pearlman, *The Barb of Time: On the Unity of Ezra Pound's Cantos* (New York: Oxford University Press, 1969); Wendy Stallard Flory, *Ezra Pound and the Cantos: A Record of Struggle* (New Haven: Yale University Press, 1980); Jean–Michel Rabaté, *Language, Sexuality, and Ideology in Ezra Pound's Cantos* (London: Macmillan and Co., 1986); M. L. Rosenthal, *A Primer of Ezra Pound* (New York: Macmillan, 1960); Peter Makin, *Pound's Cantos* (London: Allen and Unwin, 1985).
89. Pound, "Scriptor Ignotus," in *Collected Early Poems of Ezra Pound*, ed. Michael John King, introduction by Louis L. Martz (New York: New Directions, 1976), pp. 24–25.
90. Forrest Read, Jr., ed., *Pound/Joyce* (New York: New Directions, 1970), p. 102. See also William Cookson, *A Guide to the Cantos of Ezra Pound*, foreword by M. L. Rosenthal (New York: Persea Books, 1985), which contains a useful compendium, "An Anthology of Statements by Ezra Pound on the *Cantos*," on pp. xvii–xxiii.
91. Pound, *Selected Letters*, p. 104.
92. Ibid., p. 180.
93. Ibid., p. 189.
94. Poundians who promote the epic reading have insisted that Pound, after the Ur-Cantos, "ceased having any doubts whatsoever about the fact that he was engaged in writing an epic poem" (Michael André Bernstein, "Distenguendum Est Inter Et Inter: A Defense of Calliope," *Paideuma* 13: 2 [Fall 1984]: 269–274, esp. p. 272). Ronald Bush argues that, through the 1920s, "Pound out of deference to certain intellectual fashions of his youth at first preferred to call the *Cantos* a 'long poem' rather than an epic" (*The Genesis of Ezra Pound's Cantos* [Princeton: Princeton University Press, 1976], pp. 73–74). But as Max Nänny responds, against the epic reading, when the above letter to William Bird was written, Pound was thirty-nine years old and was no longer, we can safely assume, the plaything of "intellectual fashions of his youth" (Nänny, "More Menippus than Calliope: A Reply," *Paideuma* 13: 2 [Fall 1984]: 263–268, esp. p. 264). We will investigate the exchange between Bernstein and Nänny in more detail below.

95. Pound, *Selected Letters*, p. 210.
96. See, e.g., ibid., pp. 293–294.
97. Northrop Frye, *Anatomy of Criticism* (Princeton: Princeton University Press, 1957), p. 321.
98. *The Cantos of Ezra Pound*, p. 3.
99. Frye, *Anatomy of Criticism*, p. 318.
100. Ibid., pp. 318–319.
101. Ibid., p. 321.
102. Quoted in Cookson, *A Guide to the Cantos of Ezra Pound*, p. xviii.
103. Pound, *Selected Letters*, p. 294.
104. Frye, *Anatomy of Criticism*, pp. 248, 54.
105. Pound, *Selected Letters*, p. 323.
106. In the *Paris Review* interview in *Writers at Work*, Pound said, "I began the *Cantos* about 1904, I suppose. I had various schemes, starting in 1904 or 1905" (p. 38).
107. Pound, *Selected Prose*, p. 167; see also Cookson, *A Guide to the Cantos of Ezra Pound*, pp. xix–xx.
108. See Pound, interview in *Writers at Work*, p. 57.
109. Nänny, "More Menippus than Calliope," p. 264.
110. Michael André Bernstein, *The Tale of the Tribe: Ezra Pound and the Modern Verse Epic* (Princeton: Princeton University Press, 1980), p. 18.
111. Ezra Pound, *The Spirit of Romance* (New York: New Directions, 1968), p. 216.
112. Quoted in Bernstein, *The Tale of the Tribe*, p. 18.
113. Ibid., p. 14.
114. Ibid., p. 182.
115. Nänny has argued elsewhere for the many formal similarities between *The Waste Land*, *Ulysses*, and the Menippean tradition. See Nänny, "Ezra Pound and the Menippean Tradition," *Paideuma* 11: 3 (Winter 1982): 395–405, esp. p. 397, n. 10. Nänny's conclusions have been accepted by scholars of diverse critical stripe. See, e.g., Richard Sieburth, "The Design of the *Cantos*: An Introduction," *Iowa Review* 15: 2 (Spring/ Summer 1985): 12–33, esp. pp. 15–16; and Bernard Duffey, "The Experimental Lyric in Modern Poetry: Eliot, Pound, Williams," *Journal of Modern Literature* 3: 5 (July 1974): 1085–1103.
116. Mikhail Bakhtin, *Problems of Dostoevsky's Poetics*, ed. and trans. Caryl Emerson, introduction by Wayne C. Booth, Theory and History of Literature, Vol. 6 (Minneapolis: University of Minnesota Press, 1984), p. 114.
117. *The Cantos of Ezra Pound*, p. 469.
118. Ibid., p. 514.
119. Ibid., p. 515.
120. Ibid., p. 493.
121. Ibid., p. 497.
122. Leslie Fiedler, "Pound as Parodist," in *Ezra Pound: The Legacy of Kulchur*, ed. Marcel Smith and William A. Ulmer (Tuscaloosa: University of Alabama Press, 1988), p. 141.
123. In a provocative insight, Fiedler interprets Pound's account of his meeting

with Mussolini in Canto XLI as a disguised attempt to reveal "his not-so-secret parodic intent." "Catching the point / before the aesthetes got there" is how Pound assessed Il Duce's impacted critique of the long poem. But Mussolini's single comment about the work was "'MA QVESTO,' . . . 'è divertente'" ("But this, this is amusing"), anything but grave and serious in the high epic mode (ibid., pp. 142–143).

124. Ibid., p. 144.
125. Nänny, "Pound and the Menippean Tradition," p. 399; see also, for Pound's pertinent comments, *Literary Essays*, pp. 403, 405, 416.
126. Bakhtin, *Problems of Dostoevsky's Poetics*, p. 114.
127. For Bakhtin, the power of carnivalization is not simply that it is funny but that it surmounts "any attempt on the part of genres and styles to isolate themselves and ignore one another" (ibid., pp. 134–135).
128. *Selected Cantos of Ezra Pound* (New York: New Directions, 1970), p. 1.
129. Nänny, "Pound and the Menippean Tradition," p. 401.
130. Bakhtin, *Problems of Dostoevsky's Poetics*, pp. 115, 118. As for the utopian dimension, Pound's poem provides many vehicles: the agrarian worlds of the Chinese emperors and early America, the repeated motif of "the city of Dioce" and its many utopian associations, to name only a few. In classic Menippea, the utopian element is usually expressed in a dream motif, which, as Bakhtin puts it, introduces "the *possibility* of a completely different life, a life organized according to laws different from those governing ordinary life (sometimes directly as an 'inside-out world')" (p. 147). Although there are, strictly speaking, very few dreams in the *Cantos*, there is indeed the unmistakable juxtaposition of two completely different kinds of life, namely, life under usury and life beyond it. Moreover, the economy, ethics, aesthetics, and sexuality of the usurious world constitute a symmetrical, negative inversion of the utopian vision promoted by Pound. The sort of world we find in the Hell Cantos, for example, is precisely what Bakhtin calls an "inside-out world."
131. Ibid., pp. 133, 116.
132. See Bernstein, "A Defense of Calliope," pp. 269–270; Nänny, "Pound and the Menippean Tradition," p. 405.
133. Bernstein, "A Defense of Calliope," p. 269.
134. Nänny, "Pound and the Menippean Tradition," p. 405. Both critiques are essentially based upon the schema/correction model of genre and text made famous by Gombrich and Jauss, and both are open to essentially the same criticisms. See, for a persuasive critique of such models, Adena Rosmarin, *The Power of Genre* (Minneapolis: University of Minnesota Press, 1984), pp. 34ff.
135. Bernstein, "A Defense of Calliope," p. 270.
136. Bernstein, *The Tale of the Tribe*, p. 182.
137. Nänny, "Pound and the Menippean Tradition," p. 405.
138. Moretti, "The Soul and the Harpy: Reflections on the Aims and Methods of Literary Historiography," in idem, *Signs Taken for Wonders*, p. 13.
139. Frye, *Anatomy of Criticism*, p. 247.
140. Quoted in Moretti, "The Soul and the Harpy," p. 10.

141. Fredric Jameson, *Marxism and Form* (Princeton: Princeton University Press, 1971), pp. 327ff.

142. Mikhail Bakhtin, *The Dialogic Imagination*, ed. and trans. Michael Holquist and Caryl Emerson, University of Texas Press Slavic Series, No. 1 (Austin: University of Texas Press, 1981), pp. 16–17.

143. Pound, interview in *Writers at Work*, p. 57.

144. Jameson, *Marxism and Form*, p. 165.

145. An amusing and insightful contemporary reflection on this process can be found in Jorge Luis Borges's short story "Pierre Menard, Author of the *Quixote.*"

146. M. L. Rosenthal and Sally M. Gall, *The Modern Poetic Sequence: The Genius of Modern Poetry* (New York: Oxford University Press, 1983), p. 229.

147. Charles Olson, *Selected Writings*, ed. Robert Creeley (New York: New Directions, 1966), pp. 81–82.

148. Bakhtin, *Problems of Dostoevsky's Poetics*, p. 80.

149. Pound, interview in *Writers at Work*, p. 57.

150. See Tim Redman's excellent discussion in the chapter "The Turn to Fascism" in his *Ezra Pound and Italian Fascism*, Cambridge Studies in American Literature and Culture (Cambridge: Cambridge University Press, 1991), pp. 93–121.

151. See Dasenbrock, *Literary Vorticism*, pp. 207–208.

152. See Redman, *Ezra Pound and Italian Fascism*, Chap. 4.

153. See, e.g., Pound's preface to *Jefferson and/or Mussolini*.

154. Sieburth, "In Pound We Trust," p. 168.

155. Bakhtin, *Problems of Dostoevsky's Poetics*, p. 81.

156. Wyndham Lewis, *Time and Western Man* (Boston: Beacon Press, 1957), p. 70.

157. T. S. Eliot, *After Strange Gods* (New York: Harcourt Brace and Co., 1934), pp. 46–47.

158. Frye, *Anatomy of Criticism*, p. 309.

159. Flory, *The American Ezra Pound*, p. 12.

160. For an instructive discussion of the political ramifications of literary "character" vs. "type" or "role" in Eliot's *The Waste Land*, see Moretti, "From *The Waste Land* to Artificial Paradise," p. 226.

161. Frye, *Anatomy of Criticism*, p. 310.

162. Bakhtin, *Problems of Dostoevsky's Poetics*, p. 117.

163. This passage is taken from a letter Pound wrote to his lawyer three months after leaving the Disciplinary Training Center at Pisa. Quoted in Cookson, *A Guide to the Cantos of Ezra Pound*, p. 89.

164. On the dilemma of the modern satirist, see Fredric Jameson's discussion of Robert C. Elliott's *The Power of Satire,* in *Fables of Aggression: Wyndham Lewis, the Modernist as Fascist* (Berkeley and Los Angeles: University of California Press, 1981), pp. 137–138.

AFTERWORD

1. Emerson, "Plato; or, The Philosopher," in *The Complete Works of Ralph Waldo Emerson*, Centenary Edition, 12 vols., ed. Edward Waldo Emerson (Boston:

Houghton Mifflin, 1903–1904), Vol. IV, p. 77. Subsequent references to this edition will be abbreviated *W*.

2. Heidegger's distinction is developed in *Being and Time*; Sartre's, in Vol. 1 of *Critique of Dialectical Reason*. A useful brief description of the former may be found in Frank Lentricchia, *After the New Criticism* (Chicago: University of Chicago Press, 1980), and of the latter in Fredric Jameson, *Marxism and Form* (Princeton: Princeton University Press, 1971).

3. As I have noted earlier, this critique of liberal subjectivity is particularly accessible in Marx's "On the Jewish Question," and in C. B. McPherson, *The Political Theory of Possessive Individualism: Hobbes to Locke* (Oxford: Oxford University Press, 1962). See also in this connection the collection of essays in *Socialism and the Limits of Liberalism*, ed. Peter Osborne (London: New Lefe Books, 1991), esp. Michael Rustin's "Life beyond Liberalism? Individuals, Citizens, and Society" and Peter Osborne's "Radicalism without Limit? Discourse, Democracy, and the Politics of Identity." In recent years, the very concept of "the social" itself has been subjected to considerable critique, most notably be Ernesto LaClau and Chantal Mouffe in *Hegemony and Socialist Strategy: Towards a Radical Democratic Politics* (London: New Left Books, 1985). Osborne's essay provides a useful overview of these discussions and offers a response to them.

4. See e.g., Geraldine Murphey, "Romancing the Center: Cold War Politics and Classic American Literature," *Poetics Today* 9: 4 (1988): 737–747; Russell Reising, *The Unusable Past: Theory and the Study of American Literature*, New Accents (New York: Methuen, 1986); Chap. 8 of Gregory S. Jay, *America the Scrivener: Deconstruction and the Subject of Literary History* (Ithaca: Cornell University Press, 1990); Donald Pease, "New Americanists: Revisionist Interventions into the Canon," *boundary 2*, 17: 1 (Spring 1990): 1–37; and idem, "The Cultural Office of Quentin Anderson," *South Atlantic Quarterly* 89: 3 (Summer 1990): 583–622.

5. Lionel Trilling, *The Liberal Imagination: Essays on Literature and Society* (New York: Viking, 1950), p. 212; quoted in Pease, "New Americanists," 24.

6. Richard Chase, *The American Novel and Its Tradition* (Garden City: Doubleday, 1957), pp. ix, xi. Quoted in Pease, "New Americanists," p. 24.

7. See, e.g., Quentin Anderson, "Property and Vision in Nineteenth-Century America," *Virginia Quarterly Review* 54: 3 (Summer 1978): 121–410; and idem, *The Imperial Self: An Essay in American Literary and Cultural History* (New York: Random House, 1971).

8. Anderson, "Property and Vision," p. 396.

9. Pease, "New Americanists," p. 26.

10. Ibid., p. 28.

11. I borrow the phrase "the vital center" from Arthur Schlesinger's book of the same title published in 1949 and, more immediately, form Geraldine Murphey's critique of it in "Romancing the Center," pp. 742–743.

12. Emerson, "Circles," *W*, Vol. II, p. 317.

13. Emerson, "Self-Reliance," in ibid., pp. 50–51.

14. As Geraldine Murphey points out, "as a force field of dialectical oppositions, the romance resembles nothing so much as a microcosm of pluralist

society, abuzz with tensions and thereby inoculated against radical change" ("Romancing the Center," p. 746).

15. Emerson, "Self-Reliance," *W*, Vol. II, p. 74.
16. Emerson, "Circles," in ibid., pp. 317–318. This sort of Emersonian selfhood is also the generative center of "The Poet," where Emerson praises the "flowing or metamorphosis," the *"ascension"* or ecstasy, of which the poet is supreme agent (*W*, Vol. III, pp. 20, 24). The poet thus makes good on the desire that ends "Circles": "The one thing which we seek with insatiable desire is to forget ourselves, to be surprised out of our propriety, to lose our sempiternal memory and to do something without knowing how or why" (*W*, Vol. II, p. 321).
17. Emerson, "Circles," *W*, Vol. II, p. 311.
18. Ibid., p. 312; "The Poet," *W*, Vol. III, p. 33.
19. As Barbara Packer suggests in her discussion of "The Poet," the economy of poetic production set forth in that essay – which insists that the poet ceaselessly produce new tropes and thereby allow the fluid workings of imagination to do their metamorphic work – turns out to be a rather exhausting one for the poet. And it is therefore no coincidence, she argues, that we move in *Essays: Second Series* from the end of that essay immediately into the exhausted and perplexed opening of "Experience." See her *Emerson's Fall: A New Interpretation of the Major Essays* (New York: Continuum, 1982).
20. Emerson, "Self-Reliance," *W*, Vol. II, p. 68.
21. Emerson, "Experience," *W*, Vol. III, pp. 77–78.
22. Emerson, "Circles," *W*, Vol. II, p. 301.
23. Ibid., pp. 304–305.
24. Ibid., pp. 307–308.
25. Ibid., pp. 304, 321.
26. See Emerson, *Nature*, *W*, Vol. I, p. 35.
27. As Murphey points out, liberal consensus intellectuals of the cold war era did, in a way, own up to the alienation built into the liberalism of the Emersonian legacy, simply because they so clearly reproduced it. As she puts it, "the freedom of the romance form exacted as high a price, aesthetically speaking, as political freedom did in the age of anxiety. 'Against totalitarian certitude,' Schlesinger had said, 'free society can only offer modern man devoured by alienation and fallibility.' . . . The formal freedom of romance led not only to the distinctive American masterpiece but also to fragmentation and instability" ("Romancing the Center," p. 745).
28. Emerson, "The American Scholar," *W*, Vol. I, p. 102.
29. Ibid., p. 96.
30. Ibid., pp. 98, 95.
31. Emerson, "Compensation," *W*, Vol. II, p. 120.
32. Emerson, "Self-Reliance," in ibid., p. 65.
33. This is to agree, in essence, with Myra Jehlen's critique of what she calls the "paradox" of "the necessary actor" in Emerson's work. See her *American Incarnation: The Individual, the Nation, and the Continent* (Cambridge, Mass.: Harvard University Press, 1986), pp. 76ff. And it is to disagree with Richard

Grusin's discussion of these matters in "Revisionism and the Structure of Emersonian Action," *American Literary History* 1: 2 (Summer 1989): 404–431.

34. Emerson, "Self-Reliance," *W*, Vol. II, pp. 64–65.

35. Frank Lentricchia, "On the Ideologies of Poetic Modernism, 1890–1914: The Example of William James," in *Reconstructing American Literary History*, ed. Sacvan Bercovitch (Cambridge, Mass.: Harvard University Press, 1986), p. 241.

36. Pound, *Selected Prose, 1909–1965*, ed. William Cookson (New York: New Directions, 1973), p. 232.

37. A point noted by Tim Redman in *Ezra Pound and Italian Fascism*, Cambridge Studies in American Literature and Culture (Cambridge: Cambridge University Press, 1991), p. 102.

38. Pound, *Jefferson and/or Mussolini* (New York: Liveright, 1970), p. 34.

39. Ibid., pp. 16, 95.

40. Ibid., p. 34. As Pound writes, "No one denies the material and immediate effect [of Mussolini's rule]: *grano, bonifica, retauri*, grain, swamp-drainage, restorations, new buildings. . . ." (p. 73).

41. Ibid., p. 34. See also Redman's chapter "The Turn to Fascism," esp. pp. 108–114, in his *Ezra Pound and Italian Fascism.*

42. Pound, *Jefferson and/or Mussolini*, p. 89.

43. I borrow this phrase from Fredric Jameson, who makes use of it in his study *The Political Unconscious: Narrative as a Socially Symbolic Act* (Ithaca: Cornell University Press, 1981).

44. Emerson, "Experience," *W*, Vol. III, pp. 49, 78, 67.

Index

Continued from the front of the book

ACQ-3509

6/1/94
55 –

PS
169
I53
W65
1993